MAINSTREAMING PORN

MAINSTREAMING PORN

Sexual Integrity and the Law Online

ELAINE CRAIG

McGill-Queen's University Press
Montreal & Kingston • London • Chicago

ISBN 978-0-2280-2239-8 (cloth)
ISBN 978-0-2280-2240-4 (ePDF)
ISBN 978-0-2280-2241-1 (ePUB)

Legal deposit third quarter 2024
Bibliothèque nationale du Québec

Printed in Canada on acid-free paper that is 100% ancient forest free
(100% post-consumer recycled), processed chlorine free

This book has been published with the help of a grant from the Canadian Federation for the Humanities and Social Sciences, through the Awards to Scholarly Publications Program, using funds provided by the Social Sciences and Humanities Research Council of Canada.

We acknowledge the support of the Canada Council for the Arts.
Nous remercions le Conseil des arts du Canada de son soutien.

McGill-Queen's University Press in Montreal is on land which long served as a site of meeting and exchange amongst Indigenous Peoples, including the Haudenosaunee and Anishinabeg nations. In Kingston it is situated on the territory of the Haudenosaunee and Anishinaabek. We acknowledge and thank the diverse Indigenous Peoples whose footsteps have marked these territories on which peoples of the world now gather.

Library and Archives Canada Cataloguing in Publication

Title: Mainstreaming porn : sexual integrity and the law online / Elaine
   Craig.
Names: Craig, Elaine, author.
Description: Includes bibliographical references and index.
Identifiers: Canadiana (print) 20240360443 | Canadiana (ebook)
   20240360494 | ISBN 9780228022398 (hardcover) | ISBN 9780228022404
   (ePDF) | ISBN 9780228022411 (ePUB)
Subjects: LCSH: Internet pornography—Law and legislation. | LCSH:
   Internet pornography—Social aspects.
Classification: LCC K5293 .C73 2024 | DDC 344.05/4702854678—dc23

This book was designed and typeset by studio oneonone in
Minion 11/14

For Steve, Richard, Jocelyn, and Ronalda

Contents

Acknowledgments

As with any project, this one benefited enormously from the generosity of friends and colleagues. I would like to thank Allison Christians, Selene Etches, Rob Currie, Alicia Kennedy, Sonia Lawrence, Matt Hebb, Camille Cameron, Debra Parkes, Catherine Bryan, Jon Penney, Constance Backhouse, Janine Benedet, Cheryl Schurman, Constance MacIsaac, and Joanna Birenbaum for their insights and support. I am particularly indebted to Matthew Herder for his friendship and the numerous conversations we had about navigating aspects of this project.

The financial support of an Insight Grant from the Social Sciences and Humanities Research Council advanced the research for this book. I also received support from the Schulich School of Law. Thank you to Dean Sarah Harding. Thank you to my research assistant, Kiran Sharma, who worked on this project throughout her time at law school, to Roisin Boyle, and to David Cruz, Ashley Hilton, and Grace Longmire for assistance with citations.

This is my second book published by McGill-Queen's University Press and second project working with Jonathan Crago, who has once again been wonderfully supportive. Thank you to Kathleen Fraser, Correy Baldwin, Alexandra Peace, and everyone at MQUP for working so hard to transform this manuscript into a book.

I am extraordinarily grateful to Ummni Khan, Lise Gotell, Jane Bailey, Suzie Dunn, Teresa Donnelly, Constance MacIntosh, and Sheila Wildeman, who read a draft of the manuscript and then spent a weekend workshopping it together with me. A truly special thank you to Jocelyn Downie, who not only participated in but also organized this workshop.

I must acknowledge my deep gratitude for the support, insight, and patience of my family. My sons, Coltrane and Beckett, countenanced, with grace and maturity, numerous dinner discussions on the topic of porn-streaming platforms over the course of their adolescence. My brilliant partner, Kim, was the first person to read every word I have written in this book; she spent weekends and holidays reviewing and commenting on drafts of my manuscript. She is inextricably woven into everything I do and am in the most enriching and wondrous manner.

And finally, I would like to acknowledge my four friends, colleagues, and former teachers for getting me started and keeping me going. Thank you to Steve Coughlan for decades of conversation and willingness to work out an analysis with me on any topic about which I happen to be thinking; thank you to Richard Devlin who has steadfastly, almost doggedly, championed my career, since before it even began; thank you to Jocelyn Downie, whose Freudenfreude is as genuine as her support is expansive; and thank you to Ronalda Murphy for, in addition to so many other generosities at a critical time in my life, encouraging me to think about hard things.

Parts of chapter 6 originally appeared in an article published in the *Windsor Yearbook of Access to Justice*: Elaine Craig, "The Legal Regulation of Sadomasochism and the So-Called 'Rough Sex Defence,'" vol. 37, no. 2 (2021): 402–27.

MAINSTREAMING PORN

CHAPTER 1

Introducing Porn on the Platform

Porn has changed. And if we do not pay attention to what this means for our relationships, our social and legal systems, and our sexual norms and practices, it will change us. In fact, this has already happened, and continues to happen.

I do not mean that the content of porn has changed. Rather, the technologies and modalities of porn – its production, commodification, dissemination, and consumption – have changed. To be clear, these transformations *have* changed the content of mainstream porn. However, the statement "porn has changed" is not intended to focus your attention on the empirical claim that the content of porn is different today, such as, for instance, the assertion that it keeps getting more graphic, or "harder and harder," or that today's porn is "Not Your Father's Playboy."[1] I leave those debates for others to continue.[2] I am referring primarily to the ways in which porn is produced, distributed, marketed, and consumed.

Most mainstream porn today is distributed and consumed on free streaming platforms in which revenue generation occurs not through commodifying the product, like in the "golden era"[3] of Hugh Hefner and the San Fernando Valley, but through advertising, and to a lesser extent subscription and download fees. It is a business model that arose because of the inadequacy of intellectual property law to deal with content piracy.[4] It relies for its success on the mass popularity and consumption of free (often pirated) online porn, and, from the perspective of those who own these platform businesses, it has worked. There has been a staggering explosion in the number of people consuming porn on a regular basis.[5] But the paradigm shift in the porn industry is about much more than just this massive increase in consumption.

These changes have also introduced a networked, quasi-participatory, quasi-interactive, and communal element to the consumption of porn. In addition, porn has become data driven. When you visit Pornhub, the world's largest free porn-streaming platform, it records what you watch, what time of day it is, what device you are on, how long you view, whether and how you rate what you watch, whether you share it with others, what you search for, and your geographic location. The platform keeps track of what you watched the last time you visited, how many videos you click on in a given visit, whether that differs depending on the time of day, what you do on Pornhub during the Super Bowl, when it snows, and when the power goes out but you still have a cellular data connection.[6] This data is used to inform not only what you are shown next but also what other users watch and what type of porn is produced and platformed in the future.[7]

In short, mainstream porn today is consumed on data-driven platforms with affordances and algorithms designed to engage, attract, and maintain the attention of users through mechanisms similar to those used on other social media sites. While porn has always had a social role, its social media character makes it markedly different today. This matters enormously in terms of pornography's relationship to our sexual integrity.

Media studies and platform governance scholars agree on the constitutive impact of platforms on our social and cultural norms.[8] Platforms, they tell us, are shaping society.[9] But these scholars tend to focus on platforms like Google, Facebook, Airbnb, Instagram, and YouTube. If platforms are constitutive of social, cultural, and behavioural norms – if indeed our engagements with one another, our cultural norms, and the nature of our social arrangements are being shaped by and through our practices on, and experiences with digital platforms – there is no reason to think that our sexual norms are somehow exceptional or immune. If, as Professors van Dijck, Poell, and de Waal compellingly argue, we are living in a "platform society," one in which public values are shaped and re-shaped in digitally connected communities,[10] then porn-streaming sites and the networked communities that they create are unquestionably a part of our social landscape – and in particular, a contributive part of the socially acquired aspects of our sexualities.

Not only is this conclusion supported by the research of platform governance and media studies scholars, but also by the work of cultural criminologists and those who study sexual script theory.[11] Put simply, the changes to the business model of mainstream porn have amplified the social impact and role of mainstream pornography. This has implications for the promotion and protection of everyone's sexual integrity, and in particular, implications for the sexual integrity of women and girls.

A Brief Outline of the Book

Assessing the social role played by mainstream porn today, and its relationship to sexual integrity, requires close consideration of how porn platforms have changed the way that porn is produced, marketed, distributed, and consumed. This is the aim of chapters 2 and 3.

Mainstream porn is ubiquitous, quasi-communal, quasi-interactive, quasi-participatory, and data-driven *because* of its "platformization." Chapter 2 focuses on the implications of this transformation for mainstream porn, and in particular the implications for the social role of porn today. Technological advances allow porn users today to connect and interact, form community, and participate in the production and distribution of porn in ways which shape, and shift the resonance of, the content they consume. For instance, as noted, companies like Pornhub use the data they collect about users' activities to govern content creation. This data-driven approach, as philosopher Amia Srinivasan observes, results in an increasingly homogenized representation of sexuality; rather than an explosion of diversity, the same bodies, acts, and perspectives are replicated over and over again in mainstream porn.[12]

Chapter 3 examines in greater detail the ways in which the activities of users on porn-streaming platforms – in these networked porn communities – contribute to the social meaning ascribed to the content on porn platforms and the relationship between this process and the shaping of sexual norms. Chapter 3 also considers how porn-streaming platforms, through their affordances and platform infrastructure, but also through the way they position themselves publicly, their user agreements, and their community standards policies, contribute to social understandings of sexuality and consent, and the nature of our sexual scripts.

Consider the following illustration, which involves porn videos with titles that frame the content to be depicted as non-consensual anal penetration. Videos with titles such as "It's Not a Pussy Its My Asshole,"[13] "Skinny Bitch Asks for Slower but the Man Fucks Her Ass Even Harder,"[14] and "WRONG HOLE! She Tries to Escape While I Fuck Her Ass!"[15] are readily available on platforms like Pornhub and xHamster (another of the world's largest mainstream porn-streaming platforms). Indeed, "wrong hole" and "surprise anal" are search terms on Pornhub and xHamster that yield entire catalogues of porn videos. In some of the videos the sexual activity itself is consensual; in others the depictions in the videos are of non-consensual sexual acts.

There are some common themes in how many of these videos are framed. One theme reflected in the titles of some videos in this type of porn involves the surreptitious removal of condoms, followed by anal penetration that is (mis)represented to the women being penetrated as accidental. Titles such as "Snuck Condom Off and Accidently Rammed It up Her Ass"[16] and "Oops I Take Off the Condom and Fuck Her Ass"[17] exemplify this type of framing.

Titles that invite the user to interpret the unprotected anal penetration that they are about to view as occurring without the woman being penetrated knowing that it is unprotected frame the content as a depiction of sexual assault, at least in jurisdictions like Canada.

A second theme in this "wrong hole" category of mainstream porn involves the suggestion that anal penetration, often following consensual vaginal penetration, was initiated without consent – as a "surprise." Videos such as "Real Surprise Painful Anal with Anal Cream Pie for Amateur Teen"[18] and "*** Sneak ***"[19] exemplify this theme. In both of these videos women were being penetrated vaginally when the men in the video switched to anal penetration, surprising the women or causing them pain, without first obtaining consent.

Several of these types of titles suggest that the video will depict anal penetration as painful, or at least initially painful, for the woman being penetrated, such as "WTF. That's the Wrong Hole. Stop Fucking My Ass It Hurts!"[20] or "Wrong Hole Compilation. Painal – Not for the Faint Hearted."[21]

When the former top executives of MindGeek, which was re-branded as Aylo in 2023 and is the company that owns Pornhub, were called before the Canadian House of Commons Standing Committee on Access to Information, Privacy and Ethics on 5 February 2021, they offered the following comments as part of their testimony:

- "[E]ven a single unlawful or non-consensual image on MindGeek's platforms is one too many, full stop."[22]
- "Every single piece of content is viewed by our human moderators."[23]
- "We always instruct all of our agents to err on the caution side. Basically, if you have any doubt at all, just don't let it up, versus just letting it up."[24]
- "Even one video ... could create irreparable harm to us."[25]

Pornhub maintains that human moderators review all content uploaded to its platform.[26] Do platform executives, or the human moderators they employ, see sexual assault in titles that frame anal intercourse as a surprise for the women being penetrated? What do platform users who have consumed porn that is framed as sexual violence – such as "surprise anal" or "stealthing" – by its titles and/or tags, or that depicts these types of sexual assaults, think when platform executives repeatedly assert that their companies do not tolerate any non-consensual images?

Pornhub's Non-consensual Content Policy prohibits any content that promotes non-consensual acts, real or simulated, and prohibits any content that features or *depicts* non-consensual sexual activity (including fictional, simulated, or animated depictions).[27] As Professors Vera-Gray et al. observe, user agreements that prohibit depictions of non-consensual content represent to the user that the content on the platform is limited to depictions of consensual sex.[28] What meaning do users make of the marked disjuncture between what is purportedly prohibited on a platform and the titles and/or content on that platform? Do users identify the contradiction between a platform's terms of service that prohibit the depiction of non-consensual sexual acts and the presence of, for example, "surprise anal porn" and "stealthing porn" on these sites? Do they even read these terms of service? These questions inform the focus of chapter 3.

At risk of reigniting the feminist porn battles of an earlier era, chapter 4 highlights aspects of the platformization of porn which force us to recognize the fallibility of efforts to distinguish it as fantasy rather than fact, as merely or *Only Words*.[29] Aspects of porn on the platform make it impossible to deny that what porn does, it does in the real world.[30] Such qualities include the quasi-participatory and quasi-interactive features afforded by Web 2.0, which in this context include "camming" (performing via webcam), the creation of (micro)porn, user-generated porn, the sharing of porn on sites like

Twitter/X and Reddit, and virtual reality porn. It also includes the data-driven nature of porn-streaming platforms.

Our understandings of what counts as sexual, of how sexual interactions should proceed, and of what is desirable, are informed by and in turn inform pornography – and the digital dialogue enabled or created by the data-driven nature of porn on the platform, including its social media character, further facilitates porn's role in this process. In other words, the constant circulation of data between users, and between users and porn-streaming platforms, echoes and amplifies the iterative and complex set of interactions and interpretations that shape our sexual scripts. Using examples of videos on xHamster and Pornhub, chapter 4 excavates and exposes the types of platform mechanisms that drive mainstream porn's contributions to our sexual culture.

If mainstream porn is one of the resources in our social environment drawn upon to iteratively shape and re-shape sexual meaning, what *are* some of its contributions and what might this mean for law? Chapters 5 and 6 take up these questions.

Chapter 5 interrogates the incredible rise in popularity of incest-themed porn on mainstream porn-streaming platforms, and in particular the subset of this genre of porn that replicates the sexual scripts that appear in intra-family sexualized violence cases involving the sexual assault of children, adolescent girls, and women by their (step)fathers, (step)brothers, and other family members. Neither academia nor mainstream media has been forthcoming about the fact that a subset of this very popular genre of mainstream porn eroticizes not simply incestuous sexual activity, but incestuous sexual violence. Chapter 5 compares videos on Pornhub and xHamster that feature (step)fathers sneaking into the childlike bedrooms of female performers dressed in pigtails and baby doll pyjamas, or (step)-brothers imposing sexual acts upon adolescent girls while they are depicted as being asleep or unconscious, with comments from users responding to this type of content (including users who purport to have engaged in this type of sexual violence themselves), with the fact patterns in reported sexual assault cases, and with interviews that other researchers have conducted with both survivors and perpetrators of intra-family child sexual abuse. These comparisons demonstrate how this subset of incest-themed porn on mainstream platforms frequently replicates the sexual scripts and family dynamics reflected in the grooming and offending patterns of sexually abusive fathers and brothers.

Relying on trial transcripts from two recent sexual assault proceedings, and comparing the erroneous definition of consent relied upon by the trial judges in these two cases to a well-scripted articulation of consent in a sado-masochism video on Pornhub, and a paltry and inadequate representation of consent in a "rough sex" video on Pornhub, chapter 6 asks rhetorically: "do judges watch porn?" Motivating this question is the need to assesses the relationship between the sexual scripts that dominate mainstream pornography and the legal "rough sex" scripts that appear to increasingly inform contemporary sexual assault prosecutions: the so-called consensual rough sex defence to allegations of sexual assault. As explained in chapter 6, there has been an immense rise in reported cases involving allegations of non-consensual anal penetration, spitting, choking, strangulation, and hitting. While it is not possible to determine whether this means more incidents of these harmful acts are occurring, it does suggest that judges in sexual assault cases are increasingly being called upon to adjudicate cases that involve these types of factual allegations – allegations which parallel the depictions of rough sex readily found in mainstream pornography. Chapter 6 explains why, if this is true, the already critically important affirmative, subjective, contemporaneous, and communicative legal definition of consent becomes even more critical to the protection of women's sexual integrity. Put simply, some judges already struggle with applying the law of sexual assault in a stereotype-free manner. The contributions that mainstream porn-streaming platforms make to both our legal and sexual scripts are likely to aggravate this legal circumstance.

What, then, is to be done about the problematic aspects of porn on the platform, such as those highlighted in chapters 5 and 6? How should law respond? There are obviously differing views and a multiplicity of answers to the question: what to do about porn on the platform? This question is the focus of the last two chapters of this book, which divides the topic into two areas: what to do about unlawful porn, in chapter 7, and what to do about lawful but nevertheless potentially harmful porn, in chapter 8.

Chapter 7 examines the strengths and failings of Canada's criminal law regime as it pertains to child pornography laws and obscenity laws. Chapter 7 concludes that, with the exception of non-consensually produced porn (including child sexual abuse material), criminal law is unlikely to serve as an effective tool for holding mainstream porn-streaming platforms accountable. Hate speech prohibitions, under a human rights law framing, may provide a more viable option. Platforms like Pornhub permit users to tag and title videos using phrases such as "Stupid Cunt," "Dumb Bitch," "Cum Dumpster," and "Stupid Sluts."[31] Platforms then rely on this metadata for the purposes of classifying, curating, and promoting the platform's content. As explained in chapter 7, the taxonomy of hatred created by these platforms, through their use of this type of metadata, meets the definition of hate speech under Canadian law – hate speech on the part of platforms. This is a discriminatory practice for which these companies should be held liable under human rights law. Chapter 7 recommends that the federal government re-enact a version of section 13 of the *Canadian Human Rights Act* to address this discriminatory practice, but make its primary target platforms rather than individual users. Chapter 7 also considers and makes recommendations regarding civil liability for platforms under provincial statutes enacted to address the non-consensual distribution of intimate images.

The final chapter focuses on what to do about lawful porn on the platform. Chapter 8 considers porn as pedagogy, but also pedagogy on porn, as part of an assessment of porn literacy education in juxtaposition to the feasibility, legitimacy, and desirability of age-verification legislation. Several jurisdictions, Canada among them, have considered or adopted legislation targeted at limiting the access of people under the age of eighteen to porn-streaming platforms. Chapter 8 concludes that relying on (age verification) technology, rather than pedagogy, is likely to leave children and adolescents with less skill, knowledge, and competency to mitigate the harms, or access any benefits, arising from the porn they produce, seek out, or are confronted by online. Age-verification laws are also very unlikely to work. Trying to lock down the Internet, or lock out determined and curious adolescents, is like chasing rainbows.

An approach more likely to benefit young people would be to offer them genuine, age-appropriate educational interventions, which to be certain, does not mean reductionist and pedantic public health warnings disguised as porn literacy. Chapter 8 draws on the insights of experts who have identified some of the principles that might guide such educational interventions. Among those experts are youths themselves, media and porn studies scholars, and porn performers. Indeed, chapter 8 highlights the importance of including the knowledge and expertise of those most likely to be impacted by legislative efforts aimed at mitigating the harmful aspects of porn on the platform. In this case, that includes porn performers, sex workers, and youth.

Chapter 8 also offers recommendations for legislators, specific to the regulation of porn-streaming platforms, as Canada develops a broader administrative legal regime to regulate platforms in pursuit of online safety more generally. To state it most plainly, the administrative regime currently being designed in Canada to reduce online harm, if it is to have any impact in this context, must take into account the particular harms posed by mainstream porn platforms, not only to children but to women. In doing so, legislators must take seriously the need to (1) incentivize these platforms to comply with and uphold their own terms of service and community standards (which often does not occur), and (2) hold these platforms truly accountable when they continue to fail in this regard.

A Word about Words and Methods

This book is not about gay porn and for the most part it is not about child sexual abuse material or child pornography, as it is often called, although both are discussed. It is not about whatever one might find browsing anonymously in the depths of the dark web. This book is not about feminist, indie, kink, or queer porn, nor for the most part about porn that you pay for (which is less common, given that companies like MindGeek have made so much content widely available for free). *Mainstreaming Porn* is about free, online, heterosexual (as in, almost always designed to appeal to heterosexual men)[32] videos, or what is often referred to as "mainstream porn."[33] Certainly some of these other forms of porn appear on mainstream porn-streaming platforms, but they are neither representative of the orientation of most of the content distributed on sites like Pornhub and xHamster, nor the focus of this book. The examples of videos, advertising, and metadata (the titles, tags, and categories used to classify and curate content on porn-streaming platforms) that I rely upon are all drawn from free, publicly available content on Pornhub and xHamster. Pornhub and xHamster were chosen because they are among the largest free porn-streaming platforms in the world, Pornhub being the largest. My focus is on free, mainstream porn because my concern is with sexual integrity, including the impact of sexualized violence on our sexual integrity. I suspect that given the scale of social participation on free mainstream porn-streaming platforms, and the contributions this form of social media is making to our sexual landscapes, this form of pornography is most pertinent to the topic of my concern.

I use both the terms "gender-based violence" and "violence against women" in this book; I use the former to clearly denote that the harms referenced include, and my scope of consideration includes, those harms done to trans women, trans men, and non-binary folks. I also unapologetically use gendered language and focus on sexualized violence against women and girls in particular, because of the gendered nature of mainstream porn, and more importantly the gendered nature of misogyny, patriarchy, and harmful sexual behaviour – the latter being an activity which is overwhelming perpetrated against women and girls (which to be very clear includes *all* women and girls, whatever their chromosomes) by men.

As will already be evident to those who have read this far, I do not sanitize the titles, tags, and classifications that users choose, and that platforms approve, for the videos uploaded and distributed on these sites. This is the content users are uploading and consuming. It is the content platforms are producing, permitting, and promoting. Throughout the book I confined my use of examples to the first two pages of search results for the searches I conducted on these platforms, and to content linked to videos or metadata produced on the first two pages of search results, on the publicly available sections of these two platforms.

Accepting that the more time one spends on these platforms, the more their algorithms learn about you, I obviously do not rely on the examples drawn from my own searches to make quantitative claims about the prevalence of particular types of content in mainstream porn. That said, the examples in this book are examples of what some members of our community – our kids, coworkers, service providers, clients, patients, neighbours, friends, and family – also see when they visit free, publicly available mainstream porn-streaming platforms. None of the examples included in this book represent a deep reach into the underbelly of Pornhub or xHamster's catalogues of content.

In providing their justification for including the titles for some of the videos in their sample in a recent study of the titles of videos in mainstream porn, Vera-Gray et al. explained that "we provide uncensored examples of the titles in our data set in order to ground our discussion in the realities of pornography."[34] I agree with their approach. To understand what shape this aspect of our "platform society"[35] takes and how it might be shaping us requires grounding ourselves in the reality of the content on porn-streaming platforms. I have tried to do that, which means that some of the language and descriptions in this book may be disturbing for some readers. Some might find it exhausting or overwhelming to be repeatedly confronted with examples of some of this content. Like other forms of social media, the platformization of porn is unrelenting. I have not obscured that reality in this book. But to be clear, I am not intending to re-create the feminist "anti-porn roadshows" that porn studies scholars have critiqued as an anti-intellectual effort to use shock value, horror, and outrage rather than scrutiny, contextualization, and consideration of diverse perspectives to address the contentious issue of pornography.[36] Indeed, I have aimed for the latter approach. You will decide whether I have hit my mark.

With a few exceptions, the examples of videos relied on are *not* repeated throughout the book. I note this because readers might think they are reading the same titles again and again. They are not; however, the incredibly homogenizing impact of platformization extends not only to the content of mainstream porn – the sexual acts depicted – but to the titles and tags users choose to attach to their videos.

All of the content on Pornhub (and xHamster) that I relied on was viewed between December 2021 and December 2023. That is to say, it is all content that remained on Pornhub *after* the December 2020 *New York Times* exposé, the resulting Mastercard/Visa sanction, and the platform's corresponding purge of millions of videos, as described next.

While chapters 5 and 6 converge on sexual assault law, my method shifts somewhat between the two. Chapter 5 focuses on the social matrix in which intra-family sexualized violence occurs and the parallels between this context and the narrative device used in a prominent subset of incest-themed mainstream porn. Thus, I relied on empirical research that gathered the voices and experiences of survivors of intra-family sexual abuse – on their narratives. Conversely, the focus of chapter 6 is on the potential impact of mainstream porn on how Canadian courts apply the legal doctrine of consent – on legal narratives. As such, I use a close reading of two sexual assault trial transcripts as the empirical foundation in this chapter.

The trial transcripts drawn on in chapter 6 provide a level of texture and detail not available in reported cases. Trial transcripts represent a rich source of data. However, at least in sexual assault cases, they are also recordings of people speaking about their own or someone else's painful, horrifying experiences, and when studied and relied upon in research, are typically being used without that person's consent. The transcripts examined in chapter 6 are no exception, and while they are public documents and I believe the value of, and purpose for, using them justifies the creation of this ethical dilemma it does not resolve the dilemma.

Real Talk about Corporate Porn and the Media

One of the barriers to designing effective law and policy-based responses to the harmful aspects of porn is that mainstream porn-streaming platforms are not always transparent, accurate, or forthright with the public about the historical foundations of their companies, the nature of their operations, some of the content on their sites, and the implications and efficacy of their user agreements, terms of service, and content moderation practices. Indeed, one of the most difficult challenges, in terms of mainstream porn, is the disjuncture between what these companies say about the safety and responsibility of their operations – about what they prohibit and prevent – and what is actually happening on their platforms.

In March 2023, a newly formed private equity firm, with an all-Canadian executive suite, called Ethical Capital Partners (ECP) bought MindGeek. Sarah Bain is one of the founding partners and vice-president of public engagement at ECP. Bain is a communications and public affairs professional who has advised federal cabinet ministers and local and provincial governments, as well as worked as a registered lobbyist for the cannabis industry in Canada.[37] Between 2010 and 2013, Bain was the director of communications and official spokesperson for the Liberal Party of Canada.[38]

Shortly after ECP bought MindGeek, Bain issued a statement asserting that MindGeek platforms operate with "trust and safety at the forefront of everything they do" and that the challenge for MindGeek is actually a "misalignment between how MindGeek operates and what the public perceives about this industry and these platforms."[39] She reportedly told the media that she is "confident" that MindGeek operates "legally"; but more than that, Bain said she is "confident" that MindGeek operates "responsibly."[40] Consider Bain's assertions that MindGeek operates not just legally but *responsibly*, and that the company's real challenge is public perception, not aspects of its operations, in light of some of the company's conduct after it was purchased by ECP.

MindGeek's revenue in 2018, the most recent year available, was a reported US$460 million with a profit of $22 million.[41] A significant portion of its revenue, by some accounts 50 per cent,[42] is derived from advertising. In 2023, after ECP purchased MindGeek, Pornhub was running (and MindGeek was presumably generating revenue from) a set of animated advertisements at the start of many of its publicly available videos – including its incest-themed videos. The advertisements were for free, incest-themed "family simulator

porn games."[43] The advertisements included close-up, very graphic, animated point-of-view porn, and an audio statement promising users that the
game would allow them to design their own scene in a way that allowed
users to immerse themselves and "feel the real experience" of "fuck[ing their]
step family members."[44] For example, one of the advertisements, which was
playing before a video entitled "Teen (18+) Stepsis Tricked into Sex. She Just
Wanted a Massage," offered the following:

> Fuck your stepfamily members in the newest sex simulator games.
> Control the actions, scenes, and positions, immerse yourself and feel
> the real sex experience rather than just watching normal porn. Pause,
> scroll, or watch from above as you experience your immersive sexual
> experience. Your erotic adventure starts with your imagination.[45]

Another advertisement, in April 2023, played before a video which begins
with a depiction of a teenage girl in pigtails, wearing little girl pyjamas, asleep
in her bed, clutching a teddy bear.[46] The video then fades to a scene of a man
penetrating her vagina with his penis. The video is entitled "Fuck My Teen
Stepsis Pussy While Her Mom Is Not Home"; the ad which played before
this video encouraged users to:

> Create your sex experience using your imagination. In this game the
> girls are there for your pleasure. A quickie with your stepsister. Deep-
> throat by your stepmother. Or would you fuck her big tits? In this game
> all scenarios are possible![47]

This advertisement played before numerous incest-themed videos during
this time period on Pornhub, including ones with titles such as "The Stepdaughter Was Tired of the Dick, but the Stepfather Did Not Stop Fucking
Her."[48]

A third animated advertisement playing on Pornhub in the spring of
2023, after ECP had purchased the platform, depicted a large, muscular man
penetrating a significantly smaller, naked, young woman forcefully from
behind, while holding her head and body in place with a sword across her
throat. This ad played before a video depicting the sexual assault of a sleeping teenage girl or young woman. The video was entitled "Step Sister with
a Perfect Ass Woke Up When I Fucked Her."[49] The advertisement encouraged users to "try this family-simulator porn game" in which you "lock your

door and fuck your stepsister."[50] Another video that played after this "Warning! lock your door and fuck your step-sister" advertisement was entitled "Waking Up Step-Daughter with a Cock inside Her."[51] This video opens with a man penetrating the vagina of a woman who is depicted as asleep or unconscious. After a period of time, she awakens and begins to participate in the sexual activity.

The porn videos just described, following these "family sex-simulator porn game" advertisements, depict sexual assault or in some manner imply or reference non-consensual sexual acts.[52] The video "The Stepdaughter Was Tired of the Dick, but the Stepfather Did Not Stop Fucking Her" does not depict sexual assault but frames the content as a sexual assault in its title.[53] Despite including the word "teen" in its title, the video entitled "Fuck My Teen Stepsis Pussy While Her Mom Is Not Home" implies that the female performer, who is clutching a teddy bear and wearing braided pigtails and pyjamas, is under the age of consent, framing the depiction as a sexual assault.[54] It also fades directly from a depiction of her asleep to a scene in which she is being penetrated, making it unclear whether she awoke before the sexual acts commenced. As explained in chapter 5, the factual narrative underpinning this type of video – the perpetration of this type of sexual abuse while a child's mother is not at home – is a common factual context reflected in reported sexual assault cases involving intra-family sexual violence.

The title of the video "Teen (18+) Stepsis Tricked into Sex. She Just Wanted a Massage" implies that the adolescent girl or young woman depicted was tricked or coerced into sexual activity that she did not want.[55] Her face is not shown in the video.

The last two examples, "Step Sister with a Perfect Ass Woke Up When I Fucked Her"[56] and "Waking Up Step-Daughter with a Cock inside Her,"[57] show men initiating sexual acts on young women who are depicted as initially asleep. People cannot consent to sexual acts while they are asleep or unconscious;[58] a video which depicts a man penetrating a sleeping teenager or woman is a depiction of sexual assault – regardless of whether it is his (step)sister or (step)daughter, how long it takes her to wake up, or how she responds when she does regain consciousness. In other words, the titles of these two videos frame the acts as sexual assault and the content of these videos depicts sexual assault.

Pornhub's terms of service prohibit not only videos of non-consensual sex but videos that *depict* non-consensual sexual activity.[59] With the possible exception of the video "The Stepdaughter Was Tired of the Dick, but the

Stepfather Did Not Stop Fucking Her"[60] – which promotes itself by using a
title that suggests the sexual assault of a (step)daughter by her (step)father
– all of these videos violate the platform's policy on non-consensual content.
Although arguably, even this video, "The Stepdaughter Was Tired of the
Dick, but the Stepfather Did Not Stop Fucking Her," violates the part of the
platform's policy that prohibits content that *promotes* non-consensual sexual activity.

MindGeek appears to generate revenue from advertising, perhaps falsely,[61]
the opportunity to create a computer-simulated animation in which the
user can "immerse" himself in the experience of what it really feels like to
"fuck [his] stepfamily members" from "exactly the position and angle he desires."[62] That is to say, MindGeek (and thus ECP, presumably) generates revenue from advertising an activity – to users who are consuming porn, about
to consume porn, and in some cases seeking out and about to consume porn
– that promotes and depicts not simply sexual activity between (step)family
members, but porn that eroticizes/borrows from narratives that closely parallel the factual context in which intra-family sexual violence frequently occurs. As explained in detail in chapter 5, a subset of the incest-themed porn
on platforms like Pornhub depicts (step)brothers and (step)fathers, creeping
into their (step)sisters' and (step)daughters' bedrooms and initiating sexual
acts while they sleep. A subset of this content parallels the grooming patterns
and fact patterns commonly seen in intra-family sexualized violence. These
videos are widely viewed, commented on, "liked," and rated very highly by
the platform's community of users. And most importantly, this subset of
content on Pornhub – from which ECP seemingly generates revenue in part
through advertisements encouraging those who consume these videos to
try out videogames in which they can feel what it is really like to, for instance,
"lock the door and fuck [their] stepsisters"[63] – operates in a social context
in which the sexual assault of girls, teenagers, and women by their family
members is tragically, horribly common.[64]

Whatever might be at the "forefront" of a business that earns its revenue
from running "fuck your family member" ads in front of videos that promote through their titles, or actually depict, (step)brothers sexually assaulting their (step)sisters, it is not "trust and safety."[65] Despite Bain's claim, it is
hard to imagine that anyone would describe this as a responsible way to operate a porn business.

Upon ECP's purchase of MindGeek, Fady Mansour, a criminal defence
lawyer and ECP's managing partner, spoke publicly of the need to "educate

the public about MindGeek's *absolute* commitment to safe, responsible sex-positive free expression."[66] As noted, chapter 7 examines the ways in which platforms curate and classify, or maintain classifications of, videos on the basis of misogynistic, racist, classist, and ableist metadata. Examples of such metadata from Pornhub include videos with the following titles: "this stupid whores only good for one thing,"[67] "Slutty Step-Daughter Is a Cum Dumpster,"[68] and "Dumb Black Bitch Squirts."[69] In addition to its family sex-simulator advertisements, in the spring of 2023 Pornhub also ran advertisements that explicitly degraded women at the beginning of videos with these types of titles, such as an ad that ran before the video "Dumb Girl Begs to Suck Your Dick and Get Fucked."[70] The video shows a woman crawling on her hands and knees, begging to suck the male performer's "dick" as he spits in her face and then eventually penetrates her orally with his penis. The advertisement that ran before this video showed an animated close-up of a woman's genitals with the audio caption, "this hole has only one task: to make you cum."[71] Another advertisement tells users that "in these games you will fuck more bitches than you ever saw in porn."[72]

Mansour is right: the public does need to be educated about MindGeek. But to suggest that the lesson the public needs to learn about MindGeek is that it has an "*absolute* commitment to safe, responsible sex-positive free expression"[73] is incorrect. As explained in chapter 7, the taxonomy of hatred created by Pornhub through its use of metadata, and the risk that this discriminatory practice could cause its audiences to view women, or Black women, or women living in poverty, as less worthy of dignity, humanity, and equality,[74] is very far from "safe, responsible sex-positive free expression."[75]

Solomon Friedman, another ECP founding partner, promises that the new owners of MindGeek will be "public and transparent."[76] This demands that its spokespeople and executives not make untenable assertions, such as Bain's suggestion that MindGeek operates responsibly, or that it was "built on a foundation of trust and safety," as Mansour has asserted.[77] Indeed, for over a decade MindGeek allegedly did not properly comply with mandatory Canadian laws requiring that online intermediaries report child sexual abuse material on their sites to the Canadian Centre for Child Protection.[78] In February 2024, and following a three-year investigation that culminated in a scathing report that MindGeek sought to prevent from being released publicly, Canada's federal privacy commissioner concluded that in 2015, MindGeek's processes for ensuring against the non-consensual distribution of intimate images were "wholly ineffective," "completely inadequate," and "clearly insufficient."[79] This consent model, the commissioner concluded, "could only result in devastating consequences for thousands of individuals whose [intimate] images were shared online without their knowledge and consent."[80] According to the commissioner, these issues are not a thing of the past. The commissioner also found that MindGeek still lacks an effective mechanism for people to have sexually explicit content that they did not consent to have uploaded removed from Pornhub, and that the company still does not have adequate mechanisms in place to obtain meaningful consent directly from all of those appearing in all of the content on its platforms. Moreover, according to the privacy commissioner, MindGeek "did not accept responsibility" for these findings and has "yet to offer any commitments" on how it might respond to the commissioner's recommendations on fixing these harmful problems.[81] This is hardly a company built on a *foundation* of trust and safety, as ECP executives assert.

Being public and transparent, as Friedman promises, also requires that those who own and run these large multinational porn companies admit that indeed, despite their statements to the contrary, and despite their terms of service and user agreements, their platforms host a plethora of porn that depicts non-consensual sexual activity, and that violates their own community standards, terms of service, and hate speech policies (as explored in chapters 5, 7, and 8). We need mainstream porn-streaming platforms to get real about porn.

Mainstream media is not always helpful in this regard. Following initial journalistic reports of ECP's purchase of MindGeek, there was a flurry of media coverage about the new company and its acquisition – much of it involving well-placed human-interest articles relying on varying degrees of titillation or frivolity, with very little analysis. For instance, a Canadian Broadcast Company (CBC) article reporting on ECP's new advisory board included seemingly irrelevant details about those who sat on the board, such as that one of the advisory board members could crush three watermelons between her thighs in under eight seconds.[82]

While the article's author, Mark Gollom, did touch on the controversies surrounding Pornhub, including the allegation that it monetizes child rape, the focus of the piece was the advisory board. Yet there was no serious, critical examination of its legitimacy. This is a striking omission given that the advisory board has no decision-making power, and that some of its members are graduate students or relatively junior in their academic careers.

One might be concerned that this large, multinational corporation with major public image problems as a result of lawsuits, and negative press coverage related to widespread allegations of monopolistic business practices and intellectual property theft, might be leveraging the academic, feminist, sex work, and/or queer credentials and reputations of these new board members for the profit of the major shareholders of the company, or as a public relations stunt to reduce public scrutiny. The CBC piece did not examine this issue with any degree of rigour.

A human-interest story in the *Ottawa Citizen* by Andrew Duffy, published around the same time and entitled "Solomon Friedman Is on a Mission to Save Pornhub," offers a similar example.[83] Friedman is an Ottawa criminal defence lawyer, and as noted, one of ECP's other founders and its vice-president of compliance. The piece delves into significant detail on Friedman's background, sharing with the reader that he is an ordained rabbi, firearms advocate, and organ donor to his ailing brother, and that he became a licenced pilot during the COVID-19 pandemic. Duffy goes to great lengths to reinforce Friedman's attempt to portray himself as a saviour whose aim, in purchasing the world's largest mainstream porn conglomerate, is a mainly selfless effort to make the world a better place: "Friedman views the taming of Pornhub as a personal challenge, as the culmination of his professional experience, and as an extension of his often-difficult work for the greater good."[84]

The article does provide some background on the troubled history of MindGeek, but it is an unbalanced presentation of the issues. For example, the piece paints MindGeek as a responsible company "rocked to its foundation" following the 2020 *New York Times* exposé alleging that Pornhub was monetizing child sexual abuse material and rape videos. Duffy reports that MindGeek removed "10 million pieces of user-generated content from Pornhub following the *New York Times* story and introduced a program … to verify the age and personal identity of anyone uploading content to the site. Now, only verified users can post material to Pornhub."[85] While this is true, it is only part of the story. As explained in chapter 3, victims who had had videos of themselves uploaded to Pornhub without their consent had been trying unsuccessfully, for years in some cases, to have them removed.[86] Yet, the company eliminated these ten million videos virtually overnight directly following the decision by Visa and Mastercard to suspend their payment services on the platform seemingly in response to the *New York Times* exposé and ensuing public outcry.[87]

The efforts of sex workers, content producers, and performers who had been struggling for years to convince Pornhub not to permit unverified users to upload content to the platform, and to prevent user downloads (which significantly aggravated the problem of non-consensual content being distributed on the platform and compromised the intellectual property rights of performers), had reportedly met with a similar lack of success.[88] But public censure, lawsuits, and the economic threat posed by estrangement from credit card companies appears to have had an immediate impact on Mind-Geek, which appears to have responded in a lightning-quick manner.

Likewise, multiple adolescent girls and women have come forward alleging that even when they were successful in getting Pornhub to remove videos of themselves that had been created or uploaded without their consent, someone would almost immediately upload them again on the platform. They allege being told by Pornhub to track down all copies of these videos and submit takedown requests, or being told that there was nothing that could be done to help them.[89] Some girls and women report having had their lives consumed by the burden of constantly searching for, and making repeated takedown requests regarding, copies of their rape videos, only to have them re-uploaded onto Pornhub again and again.[90] Yet, according to the testimony that MindGeek executives provided to the Canadian House of Commons Standing Committee on Ethics in 2020, the company has always had the technical ability to prevent this from happening by digitally fingerprinting content once it has been taken down. According to MindGeek executives, all these victims had to do was ask.[91]

To make matters worse, it is not clear that this supposedly "world leading"[92] photo ID technology that the company touts, and the use of which it placed the onus on victims to request, even works. According to some, as recently as 2020, MindGeek's photo fingerprint technology could be "easily and quickly circumvented with minor editing," allowing users to re-upload unlawful content, such as videos of someone being sexually assaulted or that were made or distributed without the consent of those appearing in them.[93]

The story of MindGeek's response to the public exposure and censure following the *New York Times* article exposing these problems is not remotely a story of corporate responsibility, and it ought not to be told as one. Yet, the narrative spun by Duffy and the *Ottawa Citizen* presents MindGeek as a responsive and responsible corporate actor, rather than a reactive and self-interested company that took none of the "insanely reasonable" steps available to them, as porn performer Siri Dahl described them,[94] until forced to do so because of public censure, impending lawsuits, and economic sanction by financial institutions. As the lawyer of one of the women victimized by MindGeek's business practices stated in describing her client's efforts to have non-consensual content removed from Pornhub: "We had reached out to MindGeek many times over the years … It's not really 'believing victims' when it takes a team of lawyers and years of litigation before you lift a finger. It's not really 'doing the right thing' when you only act when it is in your self-interest."[95]

Despite Duffy's spin, MindGeek appears to be a company that ignored the pleas and requests of women and girls for years, and that only, *finally*, responded when credit card companies imposed sanctions and lawyers became involved – but then seemed able to do so on a dime, suggesting the barrier to action had been a lack of will, not capacity.

Friedman's status as a lawyer is repeatedly emphasised and drawn upon in the *Ottawa Citizen* article. Duffy describes him as a "high-profile criminal defence lawyer," "an acclaimed officer of the court," and a "leading member" of "Ottawa's tight-knit legal community."[96] Oddly, most of the article's focus on Friedman's legal practice discusses his work related to firearms advocacy.[97] But if Friedman's status and experience as a lawyer is such a vital part of the story of ECP's acquisition of MindGeek, then surely it is worth examining the aspect of his legal background most relevant to the controversies, challenges, and potential harms related to sexualized violence presented by MindGeek's porn platforms. It is not guns.

The focus ought to have been on what Friedman has said not as a firearms advocate, but as a sexual assault lawyer. Since acquiring MindGeek, Friedman has made public assertions about porn, "consensual and sex-positive adult entertainment," and the "[enormous] scale for change and positive effect" he sees in MindGeek.[98] As is almost always the case when it comes to public discourse about the harms of porn, Duffy's article limits itself in this regard to the type of content that almost everyone agrees is harmful and ought to be unlawful: child sexual abuse material and content that captures non-consensual sexual acts or is distributed without the consent of all those appearing in it. Beyond the issues presented by such content, Friedman appears not to have said much of anything publicly about the complex relationship between porn, the business activities of ECP's newly acquired company, and the social and legal problems arising from sexualized violence. But as a sexual assault lawyer he has made several public comments about issues related to the criminal prosecution of sexualized violence.

For instance, Friedman has publicly criticized as unnecessary government programs that offer sexual assault survivors a modest two to four hours of legal advice.[99] He accused the sexual assault complainants in the prosecution of former broadcaster Jian Ghomeshi of being "uniformly *incapable* of simply telling the truth."[100] He insisted that it is a "lie" to suggest that "sexual assaults are notoriously difficult to prosecute" and he has claimed that "almost half of all sexual assault charges result in convictions," an assertion which is wildly inaccurate.[101]

Drawing a connection between Friedman's contributions to public discourse surrounding legal responses to sexualized violence and ECP's acquisition of the world's largest mainstream porn streaming platform is not intended to take a position on the *Ottawa Citizen*'s claims about Freidman's stature in the Ottawa legal community. Again, the point is this: if Freidman's public reputation as a lawyer was of such central significance to this article about ECP's ownership of MindGeek and his new role as an altruistic "porn magnate,"[102] then why not talk about what he has said as a lawyer regarding rape, not guns?

Focusing on advisory board members who can crush watermelons between their thighs, and organ-donating pilots on a mission to "save Pornhub" is reminiscent of media coverage on the popularity of incest-themed porn that likens it to *Game of Thrones* and ignores the reality that a subset of it eroticizes the sexual assault of sisters and daughters by their (step)-brothers and (step)fathers as discussed in chapter 5. Journalism of this sort does not contribute to a thoughtful and informed public discourse on how to respond to the difficult issues presented by the platformization of porn.

Porn Polemics Are a Problem

If the platformization of porn has demonstrated one thing definitively, it is that a significant proportion of human folk, when given the opportunity and low barriers to access, seems interested in watching other people have sex. Porn is not an unwanted corner of the Internet. It would seem, based on the volume of traffic received by porn-streaming platforms, as highlighted in chapter 2, that it is very much a wanted part of the online lives of many people, in many countries. Instead of denying or mischaracterizing the demand for porn, social and legal practices and systems must be adapted in light of this reality. An example of this type of adaptation can be found in the discussion in chapter 6 regarding the need to ensure that legal actors rigorously apply an affirmative, subjective, and contemporaneous definition of consent in light of the rise of the so-called rough sex defence and the potential impacts of the platformization of porn on our legal system. But accepting porn means more than just adaptation and acclimatization.

Accepting porn means refusing absolutist positions that reject all pornography, and that do so in highly alarmist, judgmental, and prejudicial terms, like the following one offered by an *Ottawa Citizen* reader:

> Porn is never good, brings nothing good, and will always be bad and sinful. I don't speak about this from a self-righteous position. I've seen porn, and have to be careful not to view it as it's extremely addicting to me.
>
> Whether a viewer looks at it occasionally, or all the time, it's still sinful. Sex is reserved for a husband and wife in marriage.
>
> Porn, unfortunately is a button click away. It demeans, dehumanizes and objectifies body parts, accentuating sensuality without commitment, relationship, trust, as a foundation. When we lust after someone, it's adultery of the heart. Porn wrecks relationships, causes divorces, fuels all kinds of addictions, and can act as catalysts to further sins or crimes of a sexual nature.[103]

These comments articulate some of the moral and religious objections underpinning abolitionist and absolutist positions regarding porn, and sex work generally. The connection between anti-porn views and homophobia also lurks barely below the surface; it is discernible in this reader's comments about heterosexual marriage, and perhaps even in his ominous if somewhat oblique reference to "crimes of a sexual nature."[104]

History suggests that making sex exceptional relative to other social practices, and disciplining and regulating it on the basis of religion or morality, has not been good for women.[105] It has certainly not been to the advantage of sexual minorities and sex workers. Think for example of the manner in which first-wave feminists marshalled religion and morality to campaign for the criminalization of sex workers in the first half of the twentieth century.[106] In its most vicious manifestation, sister suffragettes advocated for eugenic responses to women, particularly racialized and disabled women, including those deemed to be involved in activities such as sex work.[107] As Clarissa Smith and Feona Attwood observe, the voices of those motivated by these types of religious – and family morality–based objections to porn "take their place among the many and various worries about family breakdown, infidelity, rising STI (sexually transmitted infections) rates, AIDS, teenage pregnancies, abortion, promiscuous sex, gay marriage and more generalized fears of homosexuality."[108]

Researchers and journalists have documented the homophobic and religious underpinnings of prominent anti-porn/abolitionist organizations like Exodus Cry and the National Centre on Sexual Exploitation (formerly known as Morality in Media).[109] Similarly, sex workers have been clear about the harms caused to them by anti-trafficking organizations that take an abolitionist approach to pornography and conflate sex work with trafficking.[110] Instead of advocating that porn-streaming platforms improve their working conditions and protect the intellectual property rights of the performers who are producing content on these platforms, some high-profile campaigns waged against platforms like Pornhub have been couched in the language of abolition of porn or sex work, or both – presumably trading on the emotion and history of the anti-slavery movement, as Robert Heynen and Emily van der Meulen observe in their research on the anti-trafficking movement.[111]

Responding with nuance, and humanity, to the social complexities raised by the platformization of porn requires those engaged in public and academic discourse on all sides of the issues to take reasonable positions. Academic and public discourse and the policy terrain surrounding porn has become so deeply politicized that the "feminist porn wars"[112] have morphed into a war on porn, "whorephobia," and the discriminatory "deplatforming" of sex workers.[113]

Rejecting moralistic and absolutist accounts of porn involves recognizing that there is nothing inherently harmful about the creation and consumption of sexually explicit material. Consider porn that is not radically imbalanced towards male sexual pleasure and a patriarchal conception of sexuality;[114] not infused with sexism, racism, and misogyny;[115] and instead more likely to reflect the depictions of sex, sexuality, and gender associated with feminist or queer pornography.[116] Niki Fritz and Bryant Paul characterize feminist pornography, or queer feminist pornography, as work that "depicts genuine pleasure, agency, and desire for all performers, especially women and traditionally marginalized people."[117] The editors of *The Feminist Porn Book* understand feminist porn as favouring "fair, ethical working conditions for sex workers and the inclusion of underrepresented identities and practices.

Feminist porn vigorously challenges the hegemonic depictions of gender, sex roles and the pleasure and power of mainstream porn."[118]

What *Mainstreaming Porn* reveals, however, is that our sexual integrity – understood not only as an individual interest in the emotional, psychological, and physical circumstances of and conditions necessary for sexual autonomy, but also as a shared good, as a set of norms, practices, and values consistent with human flourishing – is being shaped by corporate porn platforms in the same way that companies like Google and Facebook have commodified the individual and impacted the shape of our societies more broadly. Law and policymakers, and the public generally, have begun to recognize that the contributions that platforms like Instagram, Facebook, and YouTube make to our relationships, norms, and social institutions are often deeply harmful, and that this harm is embedded in the very structure of these businesses. We need the same type of recognition regarding the contributions that monopolistic, corporate porn platforms are making to the contours, degree of, and respect for sexual integrity in our communities.

• • •

Some of the videos in mainstream porn are downright silly: women bent into positions that seem physically impossible, upside-down sex presented as over-the-top orgasmic rather than totally exhausting, or preposterously campy narratives without any real-world analogue. Videos of this sort seem almost as much about spectacle as they are aimed at arousing the audience. Other mainstream porn videos strike me as banal: unrelentingly heterosexual and almost always explicitly male-oriented in their perspective, but innocuous albeit tedious and repetitive.

Some of the content in mainstream porn, while clearly consensual, must be body punishing for the women performers. And while I do not make claims in this book about the specific proportion of mainstream porn that is violent or aggressive – an epic and unremittingly contested issue among content analysis scholars who do not seem to agree even on the terms of the debate[119] – content-based analysis and research on mainstream porn does demonstrate clearly that a significant proportion of mainstream pornography depicts consensual acts of slapping, hair pulling, hitting, facial ejaculation, gagging, and forceful penetration – executed, almost always, on and against women by men.[120]

There is also the content that eroticizes intra-family sexual violence, the videos that depict men sexually assaulting unconscious or sleeping girls, and the non-consensual distribution of content on mainstream porn-streaming platforms. And finally, there is the hate porn and the ways in which some platforms write algorithms and marshal metadata into a taxonomy of misogyny and racism that envelops users who demonstrate an interest in this type of hateful content.

Our approach to mainstream porn-streaming platforms must be underpinned by an acceptance of the reality that lots of people – youth and adults – want to, and do, consume porn. But equally, to accept porn in its modern manifestation – its platformization – surely must mean accepting that it is constitutive of cultural norms, that it informs sexual scripts. It is true that we will likely never be able to account for and measure, or even identify, every variable that informs the evolution and ongoing development of sexual norms and behaviour in a community, such that simplistic causal claims about porn can be made. But this does not mean we should assume that an activity that is so widely engaged in has no impact on our social landscape. To add to this, as Tarleton Gillespie observes, we know that algorithms and platforms govern us.[121] Platforms are constitutive of our cultural and social norms – they help to shape not only the content of *what* we interact about, but *how* we interact with one another.[122] Porn-streaming platforms are no exception.

If we are to improve our engagements with pornography, mitigate its harmful contributions to the social problem of sexualized violence, and accentuate its potential benefits, we have to respond to its platformization. This must start with addressing the platforms themselves. Given the constitutive role that mainstream porn-streaming platforms, like other social media, play in shaping our cultural landscape, our sexual scripts, and how we understand our sexual selves, the need to force these platforms to take responsibility is pressing. A failure to use whatever civil, criminal, human rights, and administrative law instruments available to hold these companies responsible, where possible, and to encourage and if feasible compel them to comply with and enforce their own content moderation policies, is one that we will deeply regret. It is a failure the burden of which will be disproportionately borne by women and girls – particularly women and girls marginalized on the basis of race, ableism, ethnicity, gender identity, Indigeneity, and poverty.

CHAPTER 2

Porn Has Changed

Online-porn users don't necessarily realize that their porn-use patterns
are largely molded by a corporation.
– Shira Tarrant, 2016 interview in the *Atlantic*

Pornography and technology have always had an intimate and symbiotic
relationship. Technology shapes the ways in which pornography is con-
ceived, produced, distributed, and consumed. In return, demand for porn
has historically propelled technological evolution, with consumers and
producers demanding ever more accessible and massified mechanisms for
its dispensation. The consequences of this relationship between technology
and pornography pervade our experiences of the world and each other,
often in ways we overlook or fail to appreciate. Indeed, porn was at the
forefront of many of the significant digital advances of the twentieth century.[1] This chapter compels attention to that relationship: demonstrating
how the intimate and symbiotic relationship between porn and technology
has resulted in significant changes to the representation of activity designed
to sexually arouse.

Technological advances in the latter part of the twentieth century shifted
pornography consumption from public spaces, such as adult theatres and
sex shops, to private ones – substantially expanding the market for pornography (and technology).[2] While porn may no longer be the primary driver

of innovation in the tech world,[3] tech developments in the last ten to fifteen years continue to impact the nature of porn today. These developments include a change in the business model relied upon to generate revenue through pornography – resulting in a massive increase in consumption; the creation of networked porn communities – making pornography interactive and participatory in new ways, including through the production and dissemination of so-called user-generated content; the ability to harness big data – opening up a data-driven approach to both the creation and marketing of mainstream porn; the widespread adoption of mobile devices – allowing participants to consume pornography anywhere, anytime; and a reframing of porn companies as public intermediaries – liberating them from conventional regulatory mechanisms. Understanding these changes is critical to understanding the social role of mainstream pornography. This chapter explores these developments and explains the ways in which they have changed pornography. Chapter 3 demonstrates how these transformations to the production, marketing, and consumption of mainstream porn have elevated the degree to which pornography contributes to social and cultural norms.

The Ubiquity of Porn Today

The manner in which pornography is produced, distributed, profited from, and accessed and consumed, has changed radically in the last sixty years. In the 1960s, porn typically consisted of magazines with pictures of partially nude women and feature-length films produced by "adult film" companies.[4] Access to these pornographic films required attendance at theatres, mostly (although not exclusively)[5] adult movie theatres. While the 1970s saw a growth in the production of pornography in some jurisdictions, the reluctance of many to attend public venues to view pornographic films or purchase sexually explicit magazines continued to limit the market.[6]

In the 1980s, with the advent of home video technology and adult entertainment cable television, porn videos became consumable in the privacy of one's own home.[7] Consumption increased dramatically.[8] But, the need to rent or purchase these videos from one's local video store, or the lack of anonymity involved in subscribing to a porn channel, continued to serve as barriers for some, and thus a limit on the market.[9] While consumption had moved to the private sphere, acquisition still occurred in public spaces or through subscription services discoverable by other members of one's household.

In the 1990s, the Internet, in part fuelled by the demand for pornography, became a mass medium.[10] And by the turn of the century, porn had moved online – with consumers initially paying to download video clips or subscribe to "adult content" websites.[11] This made it possible to not only view porn in private spaces, but also to access or acquire it privately. Consumers had a new level of privacy: changes in technology enabled anyone to watch nearly any sexually graphic depiction without having to reveal their practices to others (other than the corporations gathering and aggregating data about them).

As a consequence of this technology-facilitated quasi-privacy, combined with the growth of high-speed Internet and the ability to stream high-quality video, the market for porn grew substantially.[12] These developments were quickly followed by the rise of streaming platforms, or "tube sites" as they are sometimes called, largely nullifying the last of the traditional forces of regulation restraining mainstream porn consumption, to borrow from Lawrence Lessig.[13] Porn-streaming platforms, like other video sharing sites, allow users to upload, download, and stream content (including user-generated amateur videos, professionally produced content, and content pirated from other sources). Today, most mainstream pornography is distributed through, and consumed on, these platforms.[14] Often this content is free; much of it is stolen or pirated.[15] The companies that provide these platforms make most of their money by selling advertising on their free sites, and by using the free content on these platforms to promote and attract customers to their premium or fee-based content and subscription-based sites – a "business model [that] relies on the massive popularity of free pornography."[16]

This change in the business model – the move to mass streaming of free porn with revenue generation focused largely on the sale of advertising and efforts to drive users to sites and content that does require payment – means that, unlike in any previous era, millions and millions of pornographic videos are now freely available to anyone with an Internet connection.[17] Due to the reliance on advertising for revenue generation, the business model for platforms, including porn-streaming platforms, relies on volume of traffic, which means generating and keeping the attention of users. This has some very specific implications for the production, marketing, and content on porn platforms and the technological affordances designed to facilitate the ability of users to engage on these platforms. The result: a staggering explosion in the number of people consuming porn on a regular basis. It also has some specific implications for the sexual integrity of women and girls, as examined in chapters 5 and 6.

Consider the prevalence of pornography in our daily lives. We talk a lot about how much we watch Netflix or the Disney channel. Yet, more than a quarter of all video streaming on the Internet involves pornography.[18] Pornhub, one of the most well-known and highly trafficked porn-streaming platforms, reported 42 billion visits to its site in 2019 – an average of 110 million visits per day.[19] Over 80,000 users reportedly visit Pornhub every minute.[20] According to some reports, Internet users in the United States access Pornhub more frequently than Twitter, Wikipedia, or Netflix.[21] Globally this site has almost as many visits as Amazon.[22] According to its former chief executive officer, Pornhub is among the top five most visited websites on the Internet,[23] and in 2020 MindGeek reported receiving 4.5 billion visits per month to its various platforms, which is more than social media sites like Facebook.[24] xHamster, another major porn-streaming platform, reported over 13 billion visits in 2019 and 1,400 videos downloaded every minute.[25] In 2021, XVideos, yet another popular porn-streaming platform, was the thirteenth most frequently visited website on the Internet.[26]

The viewing audience on these platforms is pervasive. The results of one study suggest that 46 per cent of American men watch pornography in a given week.[27] Another study found that 91.5 per cent of American men and 60 per cent of American women reported consuming pornography in the past month.[28] In Canada, four million discrete users – more than 12 per cent of the country's population – visit Pornhub every day, according to the company.[29] While estimates vary, and are different for different age groups, every recent study confirms that pornography consumption today is incredibly common. Porn on the platform is mainstream.[30]

Yet, while a lot of people consume porn, few talk about it.[31] Even in academic and research spheres, pornography tends to be treated as a discrete and separate topic rather than a dominant feature of our social landscape – a part of many people's regular routine. As Rowland Atkinson and Thomas Rodgers note, "[t]he paradox of mass access to sexually explicit material alongside its relatively secretive engagement is a distinctive feature of today's cultural landscape."[32] However, there is one important exception to this observation: some consumers *are* talking about it, albeit anonymously, on the porn-streaming platforms themselves.

Networked Porn Communities

Removal of the practical inhibitions for consuming porn and the corresponding surge in consumption across demographics are important factors in understanding pornography's evolving social role. But these factors alone do not provide the full picture. The same technology that triggered a massive expansion in the number of people who consume and participate in porn by shifting the site of pornography acquisition and consumption from public spaces to private ones, from single consumption units (e.g., a magazine, a video) to multiple consumption units (e.g., a website with millions of concurrently available videos), from geographically limited locations (e.g., in one's bedroom, at the theatre) to ubiquitous ones (e.g., on the bus, in one's office, at the public library), and from long-duration formats that required planning to short-duration options obtainable spontaneously, also created online forums in which pornography consumers can commune.

Porn as Community

In her discussion of Internet porn, Professor India Thusi writes: "[t]echnology ... allows the audience to become a community and a forum for associating around various forms of speech."[33] Internet viewers, she observes, can discuss content with each other, unlike the passivity demanded of viewers in a movie theater, for example. Thusi concludes that "[t]echnology allows audiences around the world to connect with each other as fellow audience members and with content providers as part of their community and viewership"; not only that, she continues, "it generates movements and mobilizations around different forms of [pornographic] content."[34] As Professor Susanna Paasonen observes in *Carnal Resonance*, "[t]he sense of connectedness, interactivity, and presence facilitated by networked technologies renders online porn specific in the resonance it entails between the bodies displayed on the screen and those located at the keyboard."[35]

Constructing online forums, or communities, of this nature appears to be intentional on the part of some porn-streaming companies. The creators of xHamster reportedly imagined it as a social media site designed to bring together people who wanted to chat, exchange sexually explicit videos and pictures, share "amateur" porn with each other, and potentially meet others for intimate interactions.[36]

Similarly, Pornhub has explicitly branded itself with this community-building objective. Pornhub describes itself as a "social community" and as "the most inclusive and safe adult community on the Internet."[37] Its logo, which is shown at the beginning of videos on the site, is "Pornhub Community."[38]

The affordances, or mechanisms for interaction and use, available to a user on porn-streaming platforms are similar to the ones found on other social media platforms. Users can sign up to become "members" of these communities.[39] Like with Facebook and Twitter, members of the "Pornhub Community" can send friend requests and follow other users on this site.[40] The platform enables community members to interact with one another (and with the content).[41] It is possible to upload content, tag to other videos, "like" particular videos, and until recently download them and share them with others.[42] The platform allows its members to send each other messages and leave comments on specific videos for other viewers to read. In 2019, over 70 million messages were sent between members of the "Pornhub Community."[43] During that same year, 11.5 million comments on Pornhub videos were left by viewers for others to read.[44] According to the company, "[a]s Pornhub has grown from a video tube site to a social community of porn lovers, the number of video comments has increased exponentially in the last few years."[45] Unlike social media networks such as Facebook and Twitter, in which female-identified members outnumber male-identified members, the vast majority of Pornhub users who sign up to join this particular social media community as "members" self-identify as male.[46]

Assessing the social role played by pornography requires consideration of the ways in which porn-streaming platforms create this sense of community among users. Dana Rotman and Jennifer Preece describe online communities as "group[s] (or various subgroups) of people, brought together by a shared interest, using a virtual platform, to interact and create user-generated content that is accessible to all community members, while cultivating communal culture and adhering to specific norms."[47] Indeed, one of the functions of any community, online or otherwise, is norm setting.[48] Communities set, revise, and require adherence to specific norms.

As Professors Atkinson and Rodgers suggest, "[t]he world of online porn, even though differentiated, enables elective modes of experimentation with desire, through hyperlinks, suggestions and communities of users providing signposts to related or more extreme content – all of which facilitates the creation of implicit peer support communities."[49]

Accepting that members of virtual porn communities can anonymize themselves in ways not possible in an adult theatre or neighbourhood video store, it remains true that the same technology that created the opportunity for private acquisition and consumption of pornography has now also pushed porn and its consumers into new quasi-public spaces in the form of interactive, online communities. In this sense, technology, and in particular digital streaming platforms, have created what we might describe as male-dominated, networked porn communities. Indeed, the business model of porn-streaming platforms, just like that of other types of platforms, relies in part on users interacting with one another about the site's content.[50]

It has always been the case that pornography had "community" or group elements – think, for example, of the "stag film" screenings in brothels in the 1940s, group consumption of pornography films at fraternity houses, the bulletin board systems (BBSs) used to share content through phone modems, or mainstream media's engagement with the theatrical release of *Deep Throat* in non-adult theatres during the "porno chic" era of the 1970s.[51] However, the scale and explicit organization of connective communities, and the social media nature of engagement, on mainstream porn-streaming platforms does not have an analogue in previous eras. Moreover, as examined in further detail in chapters 3, 4, and 5, the interactions between users, and between users and the platform via data collection and circulation, play a different role on platforms, given their functionality, than content-based conversation between viewers could have played in earlier eras.

To be clear, if the data that companies like Pornhub provide (measuring annual visits in the billions) is accurate, then the majority of users in these networked porn communities fit within the category of what Rotman and Preece characterize as "tourists."[52] Tourists are those who visit sites and watch pornography without directly interacting with other users or registering an account.[53] That said, there are also millions of "residents" (in the form of those who sign up as members in order to create user profiles, comment on and rate content, and message other users) in these networked porn communities. Users are typically unable to use these types of platform functions without registering. Pornhub reports that close to one-third of its daily visitors are registered users.[54] In addition, while tourists vastly outnumber those who have become members on free porn platforms, tourists and residents nevertheless interact with one another indirectly. For example, the profiles on Pornhub created by those who do sign up as members have received approximately half a billion views – clearly these profiles are being viewed by users of both types.[55] Similarly, non-members can provide members with feedback on the videos they upload, through "likes" and comments, and, on some sites, by sharing them with others.[56]

In addition, all users, both members and tourists, have the ability to flag content that is unlawful, and users are informally marshalled by platforms to serve in this role.[57] As Tarleton Gillespie observes with respect to platforms generally, "[b]y shifting some of the labor of moderation to users (i.e., through flagging), platforms deputize users as amateur editors and police."[58] This creates a norm-setting and policing role for residents and tourists alike. Norms, of course, are set and revised not only by what users may flag as unlawful, or characterize in their comments as unacceptably misogynistic or racist, but also by the content that the community accepts or tolerates – the videos that are not flagged, that are viewed thousands or millions of times but are not commented upon negatively or reported to the company.

Networked porn communities generate, revise, and reinforce norms related to both the content of the videos streamed on these platforms and how users on these sites engage with the content and with one another. An assessment of pornography's social impact requires recognition of the normative role played by the interactions that occur in virtual porn communities.

Participatory Porn

There is another interactive element to mainstream pornography that did not exist in previous eras. One of the central features of any virtual community today is the extent to which its content is user generated.[59] Characterized as "Web 2.0," networked communities today are built on the participation of their users.[60] The online communities found on porn-streaming platforms are no exception. Pornhub reports that in 2018 alone 4.79 million new videos (with over 1 million hours of viewing) were uploaded to its site by so-called amateurs, models, and content partners.[61] In 2019 that number was 6.83 million.[62] While it is not clear what proportion of these videos come from studios, or involve professional performers versus actual amateurs, it is clear that there has been an exponential increase in the number of videos uploaded by individual users to porn-streaming sites in the past five years.[63] xHamster reported that almost two thousand videos a day were uploaded by its users in 2017.[64] Empirical work examining the practices of amateur uploaders to porn platforms indicates that "the motivations behind many [of these] uploaders is inextricably linked to the actions of those who view their content."[65] In this way, user-generated content is participatory and quasi-interactive, and iterative: users, or some users, consume content on platforms, which informs the content that they then create and upload.

Users can also interact with some of the performers captured in porn videos. Recall that the rise in streaming platforms, and the content piracy and user-generated content that came with it, resulted in a new business model in the mainstream porn industry that relies heavily on advertising for revenue generation, rather than simply on monetizing access to pornography itself. It may be that, as a consequence of this change, women who appear in professionally produced pornography are paid less than they were in earlier eras.[66] It is also the case that there is less professionally produced studio work for these performers. While porn-streaming platforms have found a way to profit despite the pervasive content piracy that now exists online, individual performers may be less immune from the economic impact of these copyright infringements. Indeed, the rise of porn-streaming platforms (whose business models rely on free content and who thus arguably *de facto* sanction content piracy)[67] has infinitely compounded the problem of copyright infringement for studios, such that there has been a drastic reduction in the volume of content they produce.[68] Many performers and content producers report that they are not able to financially support themselves solely on the money earned from appearing in this type of porn.[69]

This reality has presumably furthered the interactive aspect of networked porn communities by pressing those who perform in porn videos into new modes of revenue generation. Some performers rely on the videos they shoot, and which are posted on porn-streaming platforms, as marketing tools for other modes of revenue generation, several of which are directly interactive.[70] This includes custom performances for individual clients, escort services, web camming (in which a performance is streamed live for viewers who can interact with the performer through a chat function and pay to enter a "private room" with the performer, where customers pay by the minute to keep the live video streaming), and the sale of products.[71] Heather Berg provides an example of the latter: "performers post online wish lists, inviting fans to gift them lingerie, clothing and shoes. Fans can then see their gifts featured in porn scenes. Then, performers sell the lingerie and clothing they have worn in scenes to fans."[72] According to Berg, "twenty-dollar underwear might auction for fifty dollars once used."[73] The gateway to these interactive experiences with some of the performers appearing in the videos on porn-streaming platforms is through the platforms themselves. This too contributes to the interactive element of pornography.

The interactive element of porn on the platform is emphasized by Pornhub to performers who join its "model program" by encouraging them to engage with users. As noted, in addition to its free site, the platform has premium sites in which performers – or "models," as Pornhub calls them – can post their videos for users to access for a fee. The platform encourages them to connect their Twitter accounts to their Pornhub accounts so that they can "build [their] fan base, engage with the followers they already have, and most importantly drive views to [their] Pornhub content."[74]

The way in which many of the videos found on porn-streaming platforms are filmed also creates a quasi-participatory experience by facilitating the viewer's ability to place himself in the scene. Many videos are shot from a first-person perspective in which the male performer's face and much of his body – with the exception of his penis – are not shown. That is to say, the camera is positioned to reflect the user's point of view (POV), assisting his ability to imagine himself as performing the sex acts depicted. POV porn is paradigmatic of Peggy Orenstein's observation that in mainstream porn, "sex is portrayed as something men do *to* rather than *with* women."[75] In nearly all mainstream porn, the video culminates with a depiction of male orgasm. As Amia Srinivasan writes, "[c]anonically and near-invariably, the porn film ends with the penis ejaculating … onto the woman's body, which is pinned by the camera's gaze. If the viewer times things right – online, unlike in the cinema, one can always pause, fast-forward, rewind – it becomes his semen on her face and breasts."[76]

The development of virtual reality technology has both increased the popularity of POV videos and added an additional interactive, quasi-participatory element to the consumption of porn found on porn-streaming platforms. The connection between virtual reality and POV filming merited commentary in Pornhub's 2019 annual report. The platform commented:

with the rise of at-home virtual reality technology, POV (Point of View) was a search that defined 2019. Users looking for a more realistic porn-viewing experience could tune-in and unzip, getting everything they needed without all the real-world troubles. Who needs an IRL partner when you have POV Pornhub videos on your side?[77]

Increasingly popular, virtual reality pornography offers viewers a three-dimensional perspective.[78] As Thusi explains, with virtual reality porn "the aim is to simulate real sex in a way that two-dimensional representations do not. There is a sensorial component to the experiences … It also facilitates live action situations with other audience members and content creators."[79] She describes the "first interactive vibrating stroker," which incorporates a tactile element beyond self-stimulation, into the virtual reality porn experience.[80]

According to Pornhub, on average users spend slightly less than nine minutes viewing POV and virtual reality videos, which the company suggests is approximately two minutes less than the average time spent watching videos on the platform.[81] Pornhub seems to imply that this is because viewers take less time to reach orgasm watching these types of videos – an insinuation that users find POV and virtual reality videos more quickly arousing or more stimulating.[82] Research on how people experience watching virtual reality porn supports the company's insinuation that virtual reality porn is more engaging and arousing than two-dimensional porn.[83] One psychologist describes the experience of watching virtual reality porn as: "You aren't just watching and thinking about it. You are feeling it, and it's not just your genitals. There is literally a mind–body connection."[84]

While mainstream pornography has presumably always been used for purposes of self-gratification, technology has changed the nature of this masturbatory tool to facilitate the ability of male viewers in particular (because the point of view in these videos is almost always that of a male performer) to imagine themselves as participating in the sexual acts depicted, creating briefer, more targeted experiences.

Lastly, and as is explained in the next section, the iterative, data-driven nature of content production, distribution, and display in these networked porn communities means users are indirectly communicating with one another, and with the platforms, at all times.

Data-Driven Porn

In addition to recognizing the ubiquity of porn consumption, and the networked forums in which it occurs, assessing the contemporary social role of porn requires consideration of the ways in which mainstream pornography is shaped and reshaped on the basis of big data collected by porn-streaming platforms. The manner in which mainstream pornographic content is presented to viewers in networked porn communities, and even the type of pornographic content produced, is driven by the information that porn-streaming platforms collect about viewer preferences and online behaviour.[85] In a sense, and unlike earlier eras, porn providers are in constant digital dialogue with mainstream porn consumers. This dialogue informs both the types of porn presented to users on these platforms and the content of the porn produced. The result is a homogenizing feedback loop which reifies a narrow set of bodies, sex acts, and sexual scripts as desirable, and reinforces the sexist, ableist, phallocentric, and racist biases that underpin much of this content.[86] While it may be true, as one Internet meme suggests, that if it exists there is Internet porn of it, that does not mean that the millions of people consuming digital, mainstream pornography every day are viewing a broad, inclusive, and eclectic spectrum of sexually explicit content.[87]

Data-Driven Porn Marketing

In their examination of platform companies, Professors Kal Raustiala and Christopher Sprigman characterize the advent of mass streaming, coupled with the capacity of streaming platforms to gather vast amounts of data about consumer preferences and patterns of consumption, as a "digital disruption."[88] While their focus is on the implications of this digital disruption for the law of intellectual property rights, their work provides important observations for understanding pornography's social role. Streaming, they emphasize, is "fundamentally a two-way communications channel for data about content consumption."[89]

Video-streaming platforms record what a user watches, what time of day they watch certain content, whether they pause or rewind or fast forward a video, whether they watch all of it, what device they watch it on, how they rate it, whether they share it with others, what they search for, and their geographic location.[90] These companies, whether Netflix, YouTube, or Pornhub, use this data to categorize content for the viewer, to categorize the user for the platform, and to make suggestions to viewers about what to watch next, based on information about prior viewing.[91] They also use this data to curate and promote specific content to the viewer, such as by featuring it on their landing pages, or as suggestions for future viewing.[92]

There is, however, one noteworthy difference between porn-streaming platforms and other types of video-streaming platforms. Raustiala and Sprigman explain that, because the videos on porn sites are much shorter than those on platforms like Netflix or Prime Video (most are less than 15 minutes), because there are many million more videos, and because viewers tend to toggle through numerous videos during a visit to a porn-streaming platform, porn-streaming companies have "access to more, and more varied, consumer data than many other digital content providers."[93]

The data-driven algorithms used to determine what content to present to which viewers on these porn-streaming platforms are highly sophisti-cated. Algorithms learn user preferences and present viewers with similar types of content based on categories created by the platform.[94] They cat-egorize and define users in ways users might not have done for themselves. They also, as Srinivasan highlights, "give users what others in their demo-graphic like to watch, bringing their sexual tastes into conformity" with their demographic cohort.[95]

Similarly, search functions on these platforms, like other types of plat-forms, make suggestions based on user-generated data that is relied on to predict the most relevant choices in response to a user's half-typed search. For example, when I typed the letter "t" into the search function on Pornhub on 12 November 2021, the site suggested the following searches: "teacher," "teenagers fucking," "moms teach sex," and "tiny teen."[96] The search func-tions on porn platforms autofill perceived incomplete searches by relying on consumer preference data. On xHamster, for instance, when I typed the word "step," the search engine autofilled the search term "mom step son" and produced links to videos purporting to depict sex between mothers and their stepsons.[97] As Gillespie notes, in describing these same functions in reference to Google, the search engine "is in effect putting words in your mouth – did you mean *this*? The suggestion … seems to come from Google as a recommendation, and is then fitted onto your half-query, as if you were about to say it yourself."[98]

Through categorizing, curating, and selectively profiling content, porn-streaming platforms are actively engaged in guiding porn consumers to specific content based on the data that they collect about consumer preferences and consumption practices of both individual users and users in the aggregate.

Data-Driven Porn Production

It is not only that porn-streaming platforms use the immense volume of data that they collect to determine how and what to present to whom, thus shaping the consumption patterns of users. Raustiala and Sprigman note that, as a consequence of the extraordinary volume of data available, platforms are beginning to use the knowledge that they gain about consumer preferences to determine not only what content to disseminate and promote and how to promote it, but also what content to create or commission others to produce.[99] In the platform industry, and in the porn platform industry in particular, the use of extensive data is being incorporated into the creative process itself – a phenomenon called "data-driven creativity."[100]

In the mainstream porn industry this data-driven creativity is performed by a small number of companies. The business model of companies like MindGeek involves what is sometimes called "vertical integration," which means "having content creation and aggregation as well as content distribution under the same roof."[101] In addition to owning most of the largest porn-streaming platforms in the world, including Pornhub, MindGeek has also purchased many of the companies that produce porn.[102] The company, or its subsidiaries, produce countless videos every year to upload to its streaming platforms. As early as 2016, MindGeek maintained that it was producing 400 of its own videos per month.[103] Supplementing this, MindGeek's corporate offspring – such as companies like Pornhub and RedTube – reportedly partner with other professional content producers to have their videos distributed on the company's platforms.[104]

The content created and commissioned by MindGeek, and its subsidiaries, is directly informed by the user-generated data gathered by the company. In other words, MindGeek uses its massive trove of consumer preference data to determine what content it will produce, and what to commission from other producers.[105] In an interview with Raustiala and Sprigman, MindGeek executives emphasized that script decisions about numerous aspects of the videos they produce, including certain dialogue, the sex acts to occur, the particular positions of the actors, camera angles, and other visual elements of the scene, are based on the data mined from the online behaviour of viewers on their sites.[106]

This suggests that the more popular a genre of content is – the higher the number of views, comments, and shares it receives from both "residents" and "tourists" – the more popular it will become and the more likely companies like MindGeek will produce and commission videos with comparable content.[107] Presumably, over time, this iterative, data-driven "creativity," controlled by a small number of corporations that rely on a sophisticated set of confidential algorithms, impacts the range of content produced in mainstream pornography, progressively rendering some sexual scripts hegemonic.

Unsurprisingly, the sexual scripts being reiterated and reified tend not to accommodate minoritarian, diverse, or queer articulations of gender, sexuality, and sex. In their recent study of Pornhub, Ilir Rama et al. demonstrate how the platform's algorithm (in conjunction with reliance, for certain purposes, on an assigned gender identity for users) "significantly contributes to a heteronormative perspective on sexual desire and sexuality typical of a heterosexual, white, and hegemonic masculinity."[108] Content is distributed and videos are recommended by the platform based on their popularity; this privileges some bodies and sexual practices as ideal and inevitably flattens diversity of content over time.[109]

The content of mainstream porn is further homogenized by independent producers and small studios. With the advent of porn-streaming platforms and their algorithmic logic, "studios started making more content that would cater to keywords and search queries, to show up high in the search results on tube sites."[110] Similarly, influence over their content is exercised by platforms through the infrastructure used by porn platforms. For instance, Pornhub permits its models to create custom videos for "fans," who fill out request forms. The forms are generated by Pornhub, based on a set of selections made by the performer regarding the type of sex acts they are willing to perform, length of video, resolution, and delivery time.[111] Content producers of this sort are encouraged to tailor their products to the demands of major streaming platforms because these companies control distribution and access to consumers.[112] In this sense, "content producers are always in a position of dependency" vis-à-vis these large porn-streaming companies, which in turn guide and direct the content that these independent performers and studios produce.[113] As David Nieborg and Thomas Poell explain in their discussion of platforms generally, "algorithmic logic becomes gradually more central to cultural production, as content developers are progressively orienting their production and circulation strategies toward the recommendation, ranking, and other kinds of end-user facing algorithms of major platforms."[114]

A similar phenomenon occurs with respect to so-called amateur or user-generated videos uploaded to these platforms. Research examining the supply side of user-generated content on porn-streaming platforms indicates that factors such as "popularity effect" and "self-reinforcing behaviour" make users likely to upload the same type of content repeatedly.[115]

In their study of the behaviour of 85,000 uploaders to xHamster, and the 800,000 videos that these users have uploaded to the site over an approximately six-year period, Rishabh Mehrotra and Prasanta Bhattacharya show that "users are more likely to upload content if they perceive that the content they are uploading will be well-received by the content consumers," as measured by the number of views and/or comments a particular type of video receives.[116] This is what they mean by popularity effect.[117] The more popular a particular genre of content is on the platform, the more likely users are to upload videos that fit within that genre. Their work also suggests that "users exhibit strong predictable behaviours in terms of their affinity towards a particular genre-cluster. Quite frequently, a particular user consistently uploads videos belonging to the same genre."[118] They assert that this "self-reinforcing behaviour observed on the platform is ... a major factor governing the proportion of content in any particular [genre or category]."[119]

Relatedly, some research suggests that approximately 75 per cent of uploaders upload fewer than five videos and 40 per cent only upload one video.[120] This means that the vast majority of user-generated content on platforms like Pornhub and xHamster is uploaded by a small number of content producers oriented towards producing and uploading the same type of content – content that is perceived by them to be the most popular based on "likes" and views – over and over again.

Like with the algorithm-based content decisions made by the platforms themselves, research demonstrating that users tend to upload the same type of content repeatedly supports the contention that certain types or genres of porn on these platforms have become, and will continue to be, dominant. Atkinson and Rodgers assert that, rather than "generating a more authentic form of representation," the reams of user-generated content now available online have "tended to reproduce the scripts and tropes of male-dominated forms of mainstream pornography."[121]

Other research based on content analysis of user-generated videos on mainstream porn-streaming platforms supports this conclusion. In a 2010 study of free Internet porn, Stacey Gorman, Elizabeth Monk-Turner, and Jennifer Fish found that depictions of a woman being orally penetrated by a man were absent in only 16 per cent of videos.[122] In every video in their sample that included acts of submission it was a woman who played the submissive role.[123] Nearly half of the videos in their sample included at least one scene in which one or more men ejaculate onto the face of a woman.[124] Eran Shor's research produced the same result in a similar study in 2019.[125] In addition, he found that in videos featuring teenage girls, or women who were portrayed as teenagers, an even higher proportion included this particular act: in his sample over 65 per cent of videos involving teenagers included scenes in which men ejaculated on the face of, or in the mouth of, the girls.[126]

Similarly, in their 2013 study of the content on porn-streaming platforms, Sarah Vannier, Anna Currie, and Lucia O'Sullivan found that "free online pornography uses a fairly generic template."[127] They analyzed two commonly searched categories of online pornography: "teen" and "MILF" ("mother I'd like to fuck"). Their study revealed that a standard script is followed in both categories: "Videos from our Teen and MILF samples possessed remarkably similar characteristics across video type (e.g., actor race, pubic hair grooming, context, sexual behaviours)."[128]

Platforms encourage users to contribute to this homogenizing cycle when they upload content. For instance, in its directions to both professional performers/content creators and amateur creators on how to upload content to the platform, Pornhub provides users with access to a list of the most popular search terms on the platform, and reminds them that the highest-rated videos always include the ubiquitous "cum shot" at the end of the video.[129] The platform also encourages users to include the maximum number of tags permitted (sixteen) and suggests they might rely on Pornhub's autofill function to make recommendations to them on what tags to use.[130]

Moreover, the same critique that platform governance and media studies scholars offer regarding the ways in which the business models and algorithmic shaping of large social media platforms, such as YouTube, contribute to the production of harmful norms and social trends also pertains to porn-streaming platforms.[131] These researchers explain that the advertising-oriented business models of platforms mean that, because their economic interests are always oriented towards attracting and holding the attention of users, they are incentivized to amplify rather than remove shocking, attention-grabbing content. Pornhub's "PlayBook," which is offered to users on how to "make money with Pornhub" through the videos they upload, and includes the video titles "Step Sister Fucked by Brother While Talking on the Phone with Boyfriend" and "Hot Teen Blackmails and Fucks Panty Sniffing Step Dad" as examples, suggests the same is true of porn-streaming platforms.[132] Titles like "Gigantic Cock Rips Skinny Bitch" and "Teeny Booper Kidnapped by Huge Black Cock" are not uncommon on mainstream porn-streaming platforms.[133] Compare these to a sample of popular porn video titles in the 1970s: *Mona: The Virgin Nymph*, *Deep Throat*, *School Girl*, *Pretty Peaches*, and *Hot and Saucy Pizza Girls*.[134] Without making empirical claims that the content of porn videos has become more "hardcore" – films from the 1970s also included depictions of sexual assault and rape, whatever their titles – it is clearly true that the business model of mainstream porn today, due to its platformization, incentivizes promotional and marketing strategies that rely on shock value, just like other social media platforms.

One of the challenges with all social media platforms is that this financial incentive to capture the attention of users has permitted racist, misogynistic, transphobic, and homophobic content to remain, if not flourish, online. As Cynthia Khoo highlights, "media coverage has revealed how executives at both YouTube and Facebook ignored or shelved internal research at each company that demonstrated each platform's propensity to systematically amplify and promote abusive speech and hate-based rhetoric."[135] A recent study by British researchers examining 150,000 video titles on three of the world's largest porn-streaming platforms suggests that the same attention economics – in which content with shock value is amplified – operates in relation to porn platforms. Fiona Vera-Gray et al. found that one in eight titles of videos shown on the landing pages of these platforms to first-time users describes sexual activity that constitutes sexual violence.[136] That does not necessarily mean the videos themselves contain depictions of sexual violence. Moreover, it does not mean this is what porn consumers necessarily prefer. In fact, some research indicates that a majority of consumers prefer videos that do not include violence and that do depict mutual pleasure (which, as discussed in chapter 6, can present other challenges depending on the nature of the content and consent script relied upon in the video). Yet, titles on porn-streaming platforms frequently frame videos in terms that are deeply misogynistic, racist, or transphobic. For example, videos on Pornhub with titles such as "Trans Teen Slut Anal Fucked by Police Officer"[137] and "Little Slut Wanted to Leave but Was Fucked in Clothes"[138] raise questions such as why platforms would permit uploaders to frame videos this way if research suggests that many, if not most, users actually prefer content that depicts some degree of mutuality and less aggression. It is clear that platforms collect sufficient data to be well aware of what attracts viewers. One explanation may be that titles like this shock, compel, and hold the attention of users, regardless of the actual content of the videos. In the first nine months it was posted, "Little Slut Wanted to Leave but Was Fucked in Clothes" received two million views on Pornhub, and at the time of writing, "Trans Teen Slut Anal Fucked by Police Officer" had received three million views on Pornhub. As examined in chapter 3, the manner in which porn is framed – through titles, tags, and categorization – is important regardless of what the actual videos portray; titles, as Vera-Gray et al. explain, convey to users how to understand what they are consuming.

Some academics have suggested that the technologically facilitated opportunity for anyone to now produce their own pornography has democratized porn.[139] It is true that technology has radically reduced the cost of making videos, including pornographic ones, and made it possible for amateurs to access audiences for the sexually explicit material that they produce.[140] As Thusi explains, "the ability to create content is no longer limited to an elite subsection of the population that has access to the resources to make videos and connect to viewers."[141] No doubt technology has aided in the creation of new porn niches and representations of sexual desires and acts that did not previously exist. But, if what is meant by democratizing porn is a more diverse and inclusive representation of sexuality in mainstream pornography, then flattening access to the tools of porn production does not appear to have democratized porn. It seems to have done the opposite.[142] In *The Right to Sex*, Srinivasan urges us not to ignore the pornographic mainstream.[143] She notes that of the twenty most popular "porn stars" on Pornhub in 2017, all but one were White and all twenty were cisgendered, able bodied, slim, and feminine in their gender expression.[144] The online world of mainstream porn, she highlights, is not "a place of free idiosyncratic desire and personal kink."[145] Rather, it is a world of highly curated, relatively homogeneous content dictated either directly or indirectly (in the case of user-generated content) by algorithms developed by a small number of corporations with the objective of replicating over and over again what users are most likely to watch. (Chapter 3 examines in greater detail the ways in which the activities of users on porn-streaming platforms contribute to the social meaning ascribed to the content on these platforms and the relationship between this process and the shaping of sexual norms.)

If what is meant by democratizing porn is not a more diverse and inclusive representation of sexuality, but instead a more equitable division of profit, that too is an uncompelling claim. As Ruberg writes, "The future of the adult industry has yet to be determined, but it certainly appears that the production of content through the unpaid labour of amateurs, along with the underpaid labour of pirated professional porn, has become a standard *modus operandi* for pornography today."[146]

One further factor regarding the homogenizing impact of the mainstream porn industry's use of big data should be emphasized. As noted, MindGeek overwhelmingly dominates the digital porn market.[147] In addition to Pornhub and several other of the most highly trafficked sites that stream free porn (such as YouPorn, RedTube, and xTube), the company owns over one hundred subscription-based porn sites.[148] The business model that platforms generally (not just porn-streaming companies) are based upon has a tendency towards monopolization. As Nick Srnicek explains, large corporations with platform-based business models use data extraction to build monopolistic empires online.[149] He argues that "the more numerous the users who use a platform, the more valuable that platform becomes for everyone else ... this generates a cycle whereby more users begets more users."[150] In an interview on the impact of tube sites on the pornography industry generally, one studio owner told author Samantha Cole, "[i]t was the most horrific nail in the coffin ... The consolidation of free video porn into tubes. It was a perfect storm ... Those things all happening in 2008 changed porn forever."[151] He estimated that within four years of the introduction of porn-streaming platforms, nearly 70 per cent of the porn companies that had been in business closed.[152] The iterative, data-driven content distributed on porn-streaming platforms today surely does reflect a "two-way communications channel," as suggested by Raustiala and Sprigman.[153] But it is, to a significant extent, a channel between a small handful of multinational, monopolistic corporations and the whole world of mainstream, Internet porn consumers and producers.

The combination of this monopolistic, "data-driven creativity" with the creation of networked porn communities and the norm-setting function they perform progressively narrows the representations of sexuality depicted in the world of mainstream pornography. When combined with the algorithmic logic used by platforms to determine what content to feature and present to users based on the business need to attract the highest number of users possible, the homogenizing effect on the content of mainstream porn seems clear. In terms of the social role of pornography today, the implications of this data-driven approach adopted by the mainstream porn industry – and in particular the homogeneity it produces – are significant.

Porn as Publicly Private

There is yet another technological development that contributes to the contemporary social role of pornography. The vast majority of porn is consumed on mobile devices, primarily smartphones.[154] This means that it can be viewed almost anywhere, including, for example, in public parks, or on public transportation. It can be readily accessed on smartphones while one attends public school or university classes.[155] It can be viewed in workplace offices and public washrooms. Nearly half of Pornhub's 110 million daily visits occur between 9 a.m. and 6 p.m. – typical school and work hours for many.[156] As much as 20 per cent of American men report viewing pornography while at work.[157] Studies not reliant on self-disclosure indicate that between 30 per cent and 70 per cent of Americans access porn at work.[158] Similarly, research suggests it is not uncommon for students to consume porn on smartphones while they are at school.[159] There are a plethora of online stories told by women about their experiences of riding public transit beside a man who is watching pornography on his phone or laptop.[160] In most of them, women report an inclination not to complain or protest this behaviour due to their lack of clarity as to whether this is illegal, and an assumption that what people view on their mobile devices is private.[161] Without a doubt, Internet porn is regularly consumed on smartphones in public and semi-public spaces, such as on public buses, in airports and subway stations, in public parks, and in schools and offices.[162] This is true even as some jurisdictions pursue legal mechanisms to prohibit the consumption of pornography in public spaces.[163]

Porn is also consumed in public facilities that provide free Internet access on computers and tablets, such as public libraries and municipal recreation centres. Enough porn is being consumed in some public libraries that they have had to adapt their public computer policies.[164] In the interests of protecting free speech, public libraries typically do not prohibit porn consumption (other than child sexual abuse material) on their computers.[165] Instead, library staff may encourage patrons to view sexually explicit content in more discreet locations in the library, such that others are less likely to be involuntarily exposed.[166] Public libraries in New York City reportedly installed plastic hoods on some of their computers to respond to the problem of people viewing pornography in plain sight on library computers.[167] Some public libraries even have adult-only computer labs, where users are permitted to openly view porn.[168]

The use of mobile devices and public computers to consume pornography in public spaces muddies the public/private divide. Unlike in a movie theatre, one's screen is not necessarily (or intentionally) shared with others, making it private in a sense. But then watching it on the bus, at the library, at work, or in the airport is certainly more public than doing so in one's basement or bedroom.

While advances in technology mean that porn can now be acquired and consumed without any public interaction, the proliferation of smartphones and the rise of free Internet access in public facilities have created new intersections between public spaces and the consumption of pornography. The consumption of porn in these types of public spaces is relevant to our understanding of pornography's social role today.[169]

Not only has the consumption of porn moved into public spaces, but so too have porn companies. Whether it is Pornhub's Times Square billboard, its offer of a $25,000 "happiness scholarship" for one university student (a fairly modest contribution for a company with revenues of approximately $460 million per year), its promise to send two dozen snowplows to Boston during a storm (which the company claims to have done in 2017), or xHamster's three-day fundraising event for LGBTQ, trans, and sex worker organizations, the marketing strategies of major porn-streaming platforms have an undoubtedly public component to them.[170] While porn, and the consumption of it, may still linger at the margins of our public spaces, those margins have shifted.

Conclusion

Together, various technologically driven changes to the production, distribution, marketing, and consumption of pornography produce several factors that are essential to our understanding of the contemporary social role played by pornography. The number of people consuming pornography has risen substantially because it can be acquired for free and consumed without anyone knowing. At the same time, porn consumers can interact with one another and with (some of) those who appear in the porn videos that they view. Porn-streaming companies offer users a community in which to consume pornography while maintaining anonymity. In these communities, like any other, norms about what is acceptable, exciting, arousing, or offensive are established and maintained, as is further examined in chapter 3.

The content of mainstream pornography is largely determined by a small number of corporations that base their decisions on what is already popular – which has a ripple effect that narrows the type of content users decide to upload to these platforms. The logical result of this phenomenon is a narrowing of the scope of sexually explicit material on offer in mainstream porn. An understanding of the role that porn-informed sexual scripts play in today's social context requires recognition of the market dominance of companies like MindGeek. The consolidation of corporate power in this way, combined with the iterative, data-driven "creativity" that contributes to the content in mainstream pornography, undoubtedly renders some sexual scripts hegemonic.

For some, the consumption of porn now includes a sensorial experience that goes beyond two-dimensional sight and sound to include a three-dimensional experience, and in some instances even a tactile one.

Increased access to porn-streaming platforms through mobile devices and public Internet access means porn can be, and is being, consumed at work, school, on public transit, and in other public spaces. While new technology facilitated the ability to both acquire and consume pornography in private, it also created a new type of public space for porn, and a more public, and potentially impactful, role for porn companies.

Simply put, mainstream pornography today is ubiquitous, quasi-interactive and participatory, communal and dialogic, corporate, algorithmically determined, likely to become increasingly homogeneous, and privately public. And the vast majority of it is distributed and consumed on digital platforms.

CHAPTER 3

Porn Platforms as Social Meaning Makers

Pornography should interest us, because it's intensely and relentlessly *about* us.
– Laura Kipnis, "The Eloquence of Pornography"

In *The Platform Society: Public Values in a Connective World*, Jose van Dijck, Thomas Poell, and Martijn de Waal suggest that an emerging "global online platform ecosystem," driven by data and algorithms, and governed by large tech companies, has "penetrated the heart of societies."[1] This ecosystem is largely dependent on a small number of infrastructural platforms created and controlled by companies like Google and Apple. Together these networked platforms shape our everyday practices – economic, social, and political – regarding everything from hospitality and health to education and transportation.[2]

To date, feminist work seeking to understand or challenge the social impact of pornography may not have fully grappled with its "platformization."[3] Understanding the social role of pornography today requires understanding the mechanisms that drive platformization and the social role of platforms. Mainstream porn is ubiquitous, communal, quasi-interactive and quasi-participatory, data-driven, and likely to become increasingly homogeneous *because* of its platformization. That is to say, the paradigm shift in how mainstream pornography is produced, marketed, profited from, and consumed, described in chapter 2, is all about the "platform society."[4]

The insights and observations of those who study platforms must be brought to bear on considerations of the social role that pornography plays today. One facet of the social role played by platforms generally is of particular interest: far from serving simply as intermediaries, platforms, according to those who study them, constitute culture, public discourse, and behavioural norms.[5] There is an increasing degree of consensus across disciplines regarding the constitutive role that digital platforms play in shaping and reshaping contemporary culture, discourse, and norms. Insights about, and broad consensus on, the degree to which, and the ways in which, our engagements with and on digital platforms shape and constitute cultural, social, and economic relations provide an opportunity to consider the social role of mainstream porn from a different disciplinary perspective, without necessarily becoming enmeshed in debates about empirical claims specific to pornography's impact on the individual person. If we are living in a platform society, one in which our online behaviours and personal information is collected, amalgamated, and fed into algorithms designed to simultaneously predict and shape our future preferences and behaviours, it is not only our political, cultural, and consumer behaviours and norms that are perpetually shaped and re-shaped through these platforms but also, of course, our sexual ones. Indeed, if volume of traffic is any indicator, then mainstream porn-streaming platforms form a significant unit of the ecosystem in our platform society.

Platforms Constitute Culture

Van Dijck, Poell, and de Waal define platformization as "the transformation of an industry where connective platform operators and their underpinning logic intervene in societal arrangements."[6] They argue that online platforms – from Airbnb to Uber to Facebook – have transformed not only economic and labour relations but also social and interpersonal ones.[7] Similarly, in their consideration of the platformization of culture, Nieborg and Poell assert that "cultural production is progressively 'contingent on,' that is, *dependent on* a select group of powerful digital platforms."[8] Likewise, in their treatment of platform intermediaries and hate speech, Professors Danielle Keats Citron and Helen Norton note that platforms like Facebook, Twitter, and YouTube possess significant control over what we see and hear today.[9]

They argue that cyber hate has a major presence on social media sites and that "norms of subordination may overwhelm those of equality if hatred becomes an acceptable part of online discourse."[10] To summarize, platforms are producing culture, constituting social norms, and transforming social and interpersonal relationships. While platform studies and media scholars do not tend to focus on sexual norms, at least not directly and explicitly, in their consideration of the impacts of platforms on norms and culture, there is every reason to assume that their insights and analysis should be brought to bear on these particular aspects of our culture, social norms, and relationships.[11]

Van Dijck, Poell, and de Waal explain how the mechanisms used to build and drive these platforms shape our economic and social practices. For instance, they observe that when Facebook was criticized for its binary approach to gender and sexual orientation the company added a number of other identity options and the ability for users to reject gender and sexual orientation categorizations.[12] In addition to granting Facebook access to more detailed and nuanced data about the gender identity and sexuality of its users, this change "actively influenced social norms by expanding the conventional binary options."[13] Their example shows how the platform's mechanism for gathering data about gender identity in fact served to constitute social norms regarding gender identity.

The same can be said of porn-streaming platforms. In their study, researchers Rama et al. show how aspects of the structure of Pornhub's platform inscribe certain heteronormative social assumptions about sexuality and gender identity.[14] When a user registers on Pornhub they are asked to self-identify their gender identity and to specify a sexual interest by choosing between "I like…: Guys, Girls, or Guys and Girls."[15] The researchers created and registered a set of different users, with different identities and specified interests. They observed that changing a user's sexual interest did not on its own warrant a change in the content proposed or suggested to the user by Pornhub. In other words, "male-oriented, heteronormative content [was] assumed to be the norm regardless of stated interests."[16] This remained the case up until the combination of self-disclosed gender identity and sexual interests matched how the platform preconceives male homosexual relationships. The switch to categories and channels catering to homosexual males takes place only if the user's sexual interest is set to "Guys," and self-disclosed identity is either "Male," "Same-Sex Couple (Male)," or "Trans Male."[17]

Even more striking, once the switch occurs the user is redirected into an entirely separate section of the platform: "this 'website within the website,' while still retaining the same domain, underlines the interplay between the technical structure of the website, its affordances, and the specific social conceptions of sexual identity embedded within the platform."[18] As the researchers strikingly highlight, it is not possible to gain access to straight videos from the gay section of the platform and vice versa. Moreover, the ways in which these portals can be accessed and exited is telling: "[t]o get to homosexual content from Pornhub," a user must select the link from a drop-down menu in the list of categories; but to pass from the gay section to the heterosexual platform, "the link is clearly visible: the 'home' button from the 'standard' website is substituted by 'straight' on Pornhub Gay."[19] In this sense, norms of sexuality and gender identity as binary and static, and the primacy of heterosexuality and heterosexual desire, are both embedded in the platform's design and infrastructure, and reinforced in, for, and through the user's seemingly self-selected Pornhub sub-community.

In *Custodians of the Internet*, Tarleton Gillespie suggests that platforms "constitute a powerful infrastructure for knowledge, participation and public expression."[20] Platforms moderate content by filtering videos, creating suggestions for viewers based on the data that they collect about them and how they define and profile users based on that data, and by featuring particular content on their landing pages.[21] They perform these functions with the goal of increasing and sustaining viewership, user engagement, advertising revenues, and data collection opportunities.[22] But, as Gillespie notes, the impact of these activities by platforms also has a dramatic effect on public discourse.[23] He explains the ways in which platforms not only mediate, but in fact constitute public discourse:

[T]he moment that social media platforms introduced profiles, the moment they added comment threads, the moment they added ways to tag or sort or search or categorize what users posted, the moment they indicated what was trending or popular or featured, the moment they did anything other than list users' contributions in reverse chronological order, they moved from delivering content for the person posting it to constituting it for the person accessing it.[24]

This is how and why "our public culture is, in important ways, a product of their design and oversight."[25] These insights apply as much to porn platforms as they do to other forms of social media. But this design and oversight is not readily observable to the average user.

Van Dijck, Poell, and de Waal note that platforms use the data they collect to monitor "how users think, feel, experience and intend particular things."[26] But they do more than this: "Platforms do not merely 'measure' certain sentiments, thoughts and performances but also trigger and mold them."[27] Facebook's infamous experiment demonstrating that it could manipulate people's emotional state by confining their news feeds to either positive or negative content for a week, conducted on users without their consent, provides a striking example.[28] Van Dijck, Poell, and de Waal argue that the technologies used by platforms in their user interfaces – such as functions that allow users to rate, share, or comment, "greatly shape how users interact with each other and what kinds of data signals they produce."[29]

While these authors were referring to other types of platforms, porn-streaming platforms also perform these functions, and rely on these technologies, in their user interfaces. As examined in chapter 2, they too allow users to become members and create profiles. They offer comment threads and ways to rate, tag, and search content. Every video on these sites indicates the number of views it has received, revealing what is popular or trending every time a user arrives on the landing page of a porn-streaming platform or performs a search. Like other social media platforms, they do much more than serve as a conduit between user-generated content and viewers. As already explained, not only do porn-streaming platforms produce and commission their own content, they also actively categorize, curate, and selectively promote the content of others, creating a feedback loop between porn platforms and consumers (and user-generated porn producers), in an effort to maximize return visits and engagement. Porn-streaming platforms are involved in the same type of data-driven, iterative processes that other platforms deploy – processes that constitute public discourse, or to use Nieborg and Poell's framing, processes of cultural production. While those who study platforms generally do not tend to include consideration of porn-streaming platforms, the observations and explanations that they offer as to how platforms constitute public discourse and culture pertain as much to Pornhub, xHamster, and YouPorn as they do to Facebook, YouTube, and Twitter.[30]

Porn-streaming platforms contribute to public discourse, the production of culture, and the constitution of norms and social meaning at both macro and micro levels. This chapter considers some examples of the macro level contributions of porn-streaming platforms like Pornhub and xHamster to the cultural production of sexual norms. Chapter 4 examines more closely the ways in which the architecture and user interfaces of, as well as the gathering and constant circulation of data by, porn-streaming platforms constitute social meaning through a perpetual and iterative series of micro interpretations.

There is a growing expectation that major platforms of all sorts, given their magnitude, bear public responsibilities despite their private ownership.[31] Gillespie argues, for example, that the constitutive role major platforms play in public discourse gives rise to responsibilities. Social media platforms, he suggests, now "inhabit a new position of responsibility – not only to individual users but also to the public they powerfully affect."[32]

To some extent, platforms have embraced this narrative. Van Dijck, Poell, and de Waal observe that "[c]orporately owned and operated platforms often claim their online services benefit 'the public' in general."[33] The authors show how platforms purport to "make the world a better place" by facilitating and advancing the ability of people to self-organize online.[34] They argue that platforms claim this public role explicitly by characterizing their purpose as to empower people and enable citizens' self-expression and ability to act as "independent, autonomous individuals."[35] Their observations are as true of mainstream porn-streaming platforms as they are of other types of platforms. Like other platforms, when it serves their interests, the companies that own these platforms position themselves as public leaders with services that perform a public function.

Consider the following comment from MindGeek's then chief executive officer: "when [we] joined MindGeek in 2008, our goal was to create the most inclusive and safe adult community on the Internet. It was designed to celebrate freedom of expression, to value privacy and to empower adults from all walks of life."[36] This is not dissimilar to Facebook's articulated mission: to give people the power to build a global community, stay connected, and express what matters to them.[37]

The public leadership space that mainstream porn-streaming platforms have attempted to occupy plays a role in pornography's social impact. Porn-streaming platforms frequently make public statements announcing initiatives intended to present themselves as public leaders and porn consumption as an everyday, ordinary recreational practice. Pornhub arguably attempted to capitalize on both the COVID-19 pandemic and the Black Lives Matter (BLM) movement.[38] xHamster, in the face of #MeToo, issued public statements condemning rape, and announced no-tolerance policies with regard to content that depicts sexualized violence.[39] However, the narratives of public responsibility and leadership that major porn-streaming companies cultivate do not always align with many of the actions that they take, or fail to take, with respect to the administration of, and content on, their sites.

Porn Platforms as Sexual Meaning Makers

Porn-streaming platforms, like other platforms, seem to vacillate between pitching themselves as mere intermediaries who cannot be, or ought not to be, held responsible for the content on their sites, and global leaders dedicated to creating digital infrastructures that bring people together in new ways to form novel communities.[40] These communities are construed by platforms as safe and confidential spaces in which adult users can consume sexually explicit material that depicts consensual, perfectly legal sex. This latter self-characterization by platforms – advanced through user agreements and content moderation policies that purport to prohibit a broad swathe of potentially harmful content, or are inconsistent about what they prohibit – and their publicly expressed commitments to end rape culture and promote sex-positive expression presumably aide in the interpretation of porn by users. The disjuncture between these terms of service and publicly expressed commitments and some of the prominent content on these sites is problematic.

Users May Assume All Content Depicts Consensual Sex

As Vera-Gray et al. highlight in their study of video titles on Pornhub, xHamster, and XVideos, platforms' terms of service typically indicate to the user that "the material prohibited is not ... limited to 'real' acts of sexual violence, but includes simulations."[41] In other words, they suggest that user agreements with these types of provisions represent to the user that everything shown on these sites constitutes depictions of consensual sex.

Pornhub's policies serve as an example. The platform's Non-consensual Content Policy prohibits content featuring "real or simulated non-consensual acts."[42] The platform's Community Guidelines stipulate that any "actual, simulated or animated content" that "depicts, promotes or advocates" for illegal conduct of any kind is prohibited.[43] In its now annual transparency reports, Pornhub emphasizes that a "combination of human review and cutting-edge detection technologies" enables the platform to ensure that it remains free of content that is illegal, "unacceptable," or that otherwise violates its terms of service.[44]

Included in the company's Non-consensual Content Policy is a list of "sensitive themes and considerations for consent," one of which is depictions of sexual activity involving a person who is asleep.[45] Pornhub's policy on non-consensual content states that "where there is a component of sleep in the content, the person must wake up within a reasonable time from the start of any sexual act(s) and consent must be made clear by that person."[46] It is clear, across many jurisdictions, that as a matter of criminal law, people who are asleep, or otherwise unconscious, lack the capacity to consent to sexual acts.[47] Moreover, thankfully, courts (unlike many accused) have not struggled with drawing this line.[48] That someone might awaken (within whatever length of time Pornhub considers under its policy to be "reasonable") and retroactively sanction sexual acts that occurred while they were unconscious by expressing consent does not change this legal requirement, nor render acts which occurred while they were asleep legally consensual. Yet, countless videos on Pornhub with titles such as the following, depicting the perpetration of sexual assault on sleeping or unconscious women, are readily available on the platform:

- "Step Sis Gets Woke Up to Big Brother's Cock in Her"[49]
- "Teen Woke Up with Big Cock in Her Big Pussy"[50]
- "Accidently Woke Up My Step Sister With My Dick"[51]

The response that the women in these videos are depicted as offering when they "awake" to find themselves being penetrated is typically positive, if not orgasmic. They appear to be thrilled to find themselves being penetrated by their (step)brothers, best friends, or (step)fathers. The women and girls in these fictional depictions offer a very different response than that typically received by men whose (step)sisters, wives, (step)daughters, or friends do not accept being sexually assaulted by them in their sleep.

The problem of sexual predation perpetrated against women and girls who are initially asleep or unconscious (often due to intoxication) is as prolific as this genre of porn appears to be popular.[52] This is one reason why the disjuncture between Pornhub's articulated prohibition on non-consensual content in one part of its policy and its endorsement of this type of non-consensual sex in another section of the same policy is problematic and potentially harmful. Cases in which women awake, or regain conscious-ness after passing out, to find themselves being penetrated by husbands, boyfriends, fathers, brothers, friends, and strangers are incredibly common.

The disjuncture between, or contradictions in, what porn-streaming plat-forms say they prohibit and what appears on their sites is not limited to user agreements and content policies. It extends to the public statements and tes-timony given by the top executives and spokespeople of these companies. Consider the following example involving a public statement by xHamster in response to the 2016 sexual assault conviction and sentencing of former Stanford University student and varsity athlete Brock Turner.[53] Turner was caught behind a dumpster on campus sexually assaulting an unconscious woman. He was convicted of assault with intent to rape an intoxicated woman, sexually penetrating an intoxicated person with a foreign object, and sexually penetrating an unconscious person with a foreign object.[54] The six-month sentence that he received for these convictions generated signifi-cant public outrage.[55]

In response, xHamster announced that it was "shocked and appalled" by the light sentence, and said that it was "taking a stand against rape culture" by instituting what it referred to as the "Brock Turner Rule."[56] The company declared that it "does not condone any type of non-consensual sex," nor "tol-erate any type of violence," and that not only would the platform use its "size and influence in the online adult world to put an end to r@pe culture for good," it would encourage the rest of the porn industry to "follow suit and institute the Brock Turner Rule."[57] The company promised that any user who looked for a "r@pe category on xHamster" would be shown the follow-ing message: "If you are searching for this category, probably it's time you consulted with a professional psychologist."[58] According to xHamster, the user would then be redirected to a website offering free online help.[59]

Despite the platform's public commitment, the "Brock Turner Rule" does not appear to have been implemented by the company, or if it was put into effect, it was short lived.[60] Recall that Turner's victim was unconscious due to alcohol consumption when he assaulted her. She did not regain con-sciousness until several hours after the assault, while at the hospital.[61] It is true that typing the words "unconscious" or "rape" into xHamster's search engine does not yield any results. However, neither does either of these searches produce the message to users promised by the platform.[62]

More importantly, using the search term "wake up" *does* yield countless videos that portray men sexually touching and penetrating teenage girls and women who appear (at least initially) to be unconscious.[63] That is to say, the site contains innumerable videos *depicting* the sexual assault of women who are asleep or otherwise unconscious. For example, in December 2021 the first result yielded by this search on xHamster was a video entitled "Wake Up Sis" which showed a young woman asleep in bed when a young man creeps up next to her bed and begins to rub her leg, presumably to confirm that she is, indeed, "asleep."[64] When her eyes remain closed, he begins to perform a variety of sexual acts on her, including oral penetration of her mouth with his penis. This continues for more than two minutes before she "wakes up."[65]

Similarly, in an xHamster video entitled "Her Wake Up Call," which was also presented on the first page of results from this same December 2021 search using the words "wake up," a woman is shown unconscious and slouched in a chair with her head tilted at an awkward angle, wearing a short evening dress and high heels.[66] A man moves towards the ostensibly unconscious woman, acting as if he has just discovered her. He looks over his shoulder at the camera and addresses her as "Mrs," presumably to suggest to the viewer that he is a stranger to her and/or that he is looking to see if anyone is watching. He tries to wake her up by speaking to her and touching her. She remains "unconscious," at which point he lifts her dress and begins to touch her inner thighs and genitals. He then carries her to a bedroom and places her on the bed. Still, she appears to be unconscious. He penetrates her vagina with his penis for over two minutes before she is depicted as regaining consciousness – at which point she begins moaning and expressing pleasure. Later in the video he gives another man permission to "fuck her."[67] The video ends when one of the men ejaculates in her open mouth and on her face, while her drowsy, half-lidded eyes appear, at one point, to roll back in her head.[68]

The "wake-up porn" I am describing is not the portrayal of sleepy sex initiated by a cohabitating spouse, or an exploration between ongoing sexual partners of the border connecting the states of hypnopompia and wakefulness.[69] These are depictions of predation upon women who are represented, at least initially, as asleep or unconscious, often accompanied by titles that explicitly invite the user to understand them as sexual assault. Granted, the two videos I have just described appeared to be fictional depictions of non-consensual sex – "Wake Up Sis" more obviously so, to me, than "Her Wake Up Call." Regardless, surely a publicly expressed commitment not to condone sexual violence and to end rape culture for good is inconsistent with content that depicts this type of sexual violence, even if the depiction is fictional? Moreover, these two videos appeared on the first page of results in response to the search phrase "wake up." In other words, they were prominently featured in the search results on the platform. That search yielded twenty-two pages of results with approximately fifty videos per page. How many of these hundreds of videos also depict sexual assault?

xHamster's user agreement requires users to agree that the content on its platform *depicts* (not just constitutes but depicts) consenting adult models; the platform "strictly prohibits" content that is "unlawful, harmful, or hateful" or content "*involving* rape … drunk, drugged, passed out or sleeping persons."[70] Consider xHamster's policy in light of the description I gave of the xHamster video "Her Wake Up Call" – which, again, depicts the rape of an unconscious woman.[71] At best, policies and user agreements that promise content will be confined to depictions of consenting adults, and public declarations to end rape culture on platforms with readily available and promoted videos of non-consensual sex, feed a common, harmful social narrative about the supposed difficulty of distinguishing between consensual and non-consensual sex, or suggest that some ambiguity exists between the two.[72]

At worst, this disjuncture risks reinforcing erroneous understandings of the distinction between consensual sex, and rape and sexual assault. Indeed, it is possible that the juxtaposition between xHamster's publicly declared commitment to condemn rape culture and refuse to condone sexual violence, and the content of these "wake-up porn" videos encourages users to assume that these videos must not portray sexual assault, particularly given that pornography "involving rape or drunk or sleeping persons" is "strictly prohibited" on the platform.

The response by users to this type of content suggests this may be true. For example, "Her Wake Up Call" had been viewed 467,135 times as of 20 September 2022.[73] Ninety-eight per cent of those who rated it gave it a thumbs up.[74] Of the nine viewers who commented on the video, none raised any issues regarding consent. Instead, they offered comments such as, "waaaw very hot," "fucking love this sex woman!," and "love this … need to see more from her."[75]

Similarly, the xHamster video entitled "Wake Up Sis," which, as described earlier, portrayed a young man performing sexual acts on a young woman sleeping in a bed, including touching her genitals and penetrating her mouth with his penis, does not appear to have raised any flags for users.[76] Recall that the young woman in "Wake Up Sis" is depicted as "asleep" until approximately halfway through the five-minute video, at which point she appears to regain consciousness and become an active, and seemingly enthusiastic, participant. This video had been viewed 5.97 million times as of 20 September 2022, with 100 per cent of those who rated it giving it a thumbs up.[77] The comments on this video included the following: "wow super," "this is what I have been waiting to see," "I do this with my sister," "wish I had a sister that would let me fuck her like that," "love the way she behaves," and "I woke my little sister up that way many times when we were teens."[78]

None of the users who commented on these videos remarked on their depictions of non-consensual sexual activity or the fact that they were contrary to the terms of service in xHamster's user agreement or the company's "Brock Turner Rule."

User agreements that purport to prohibit all non-consensual sex, real or fictional, particularly when considered in conjunction with the publicly expressed commitments of corporate executives to put an end to rape culture once and for all, make it difficult not to speculate on how these prominent platformed depictions of sexual violence might perpetuate erroneous understandings of consent and what constitutes sexual assault, particularly among the sexually uneducated. While porn-streaming platforms are not the only social media sites, or platforms generally, that have been criticized for failing to consistently uphold their Community Guidelines or terms of service, this failure may be more harmful, or harmful in different ways, in the context of porn, given the supposed inability of some users to identify non-consensual sex in the porn they consume – a social phenomenon (with multiple explanations, misogyny, and willful blindness among them) that is replicated in the perceptions of some accused – and some judges – in sexual assault cases.

Users May Assume That the Content Is All Lawful

In testifying before a Canadian parliamentary committee in 2021, Mind-Geek's then chief executive officer stated:

We are very proud that we built a product that gets 170 million people visiting a day, four million Canadians, 30% of them women. Don't you believe if those four million Canadians who come to our site every day saw something so heinous and criminal, they would be calling the police? Wouldn't the police lines ... be ringing non-stop? We created a very good product that I and our 1,800 employees who have families and children are proud of.[79]

The answer to his questions seems to be no. People apparently interpret all, or most, of the pornography that they watch as lawful. In one study, 56.5 per cent of pornography consumers said that they had never seen behaviour in porn that they interpreted as non-consensual violence or aggression; another 17.5 per cent indicated that they had only seen such content once or twice.[80]

Vera-Gray et al. argue that the terms of service used by platforms like Pornhub and xHamster could lead to a misplaced assumption among users that what is offered on these sites must be lawful.[81] Content can be unlawful because of what it portrays or because it is produced or disseminated without the consent of those appearing in it, as has been alleged with respect to videos on both Pornhub and xHamster.[82]

A lawsuit filed against MindGeek in 2021 by women alleging that their intimate images were uploaded onto the platform without their consent (some of which they allege were created in the context of sexual assaults) suggests the potential disjuncture between Pornhub's policies and public statements and the content that is, or at least was, available on the platform.[83] The statement of claim describes a video of one of the plaintiffs, who alleges it was uploaded onto Pornhub by her ex-husband three years before she discovered it in 2020. The lawsuit claims that her ex-husband drugged her, and videotaped himself sexually assaulting her while she was unconscious. The title of the video disclosed that she was unconscious. According to the statement of claim, the video was tagged "sleeping pills," "while sleeping," and "hold her hands."[84]

Another plaintiff in the same lawsuit described a video of herself on Pornhub, entitled "Misadventures of a Drunk Girl," in which she was so incapacitated she could not walk or stand up and was ultimately "completely unconscious with her eyes rolled into the back of her head" while sexual acts were imposed upon her.[85] The lawsuit alleges that users offered comments on the video such as: "so hot. Love how drunk she is!"; and "I would take advantage of her all nite. dude's smart for trying get her to drink more. Bet he dumped loads in her stupid cunt. I know I would."[86]

GirlsDoPorn, discussed in chapter 7, victimized over one hundred women by coercing or forcing them to perform sexual acts while being videotaped and then uploading these videos onto porn-streaming platforms without their consent.[87] There was a subscription-based, dedicated GirlsDoPorn channel on Pornhub, and hundreds of other versions of these unlawful videos were allegedly uploaded onto MindGeek platforms.[88] Did the millions of users who allegedly consumed this content know that it was illegal?

Porn Platforms as Public Leaders and Norm Entrepreneurs

A disjuncture between their content and their policies is not the only means through which platforms contribute problematically to cultural landscapes. Porn-streaming platforms occupy public space in ways that may contribute adversely to the production of cultural norms at a macro level when they represent themselves as public leaders or "norm entrepreneurs."[89] Pornhub's response to the global spread of COVID-19 and the ensuing lockdowns caused by the pandemic in the spring of 2020 provides an example.

On 24 March 2020, Pornhub Premium announced that for the month of April, and in order to help models who were financially impacted by the health crisis, it would offer them 100 per cent of their video sales minus a 15 per cent processing fee.[90] Pornhub Premium also announced that it would allow users to sign up for a month of free access to Pornhub Premium (one of the paid sites it tries to drive users to from its free platform). That same week traffic to the British government's Revenge Porn Helpline nearly doubled.[91]

For the remainder of the month of free access to Pornhub Premium, "more cases were opened [at the Helpline] ... than in any previous four-week period" in the five-year history of the organization.[92] Similarly, Safer-Net in Brazil reported a 154.9 per cent increase in the non-consensual distribution of intimate images in April 2020 as compared to April 2019, according to research conducted by the Centre for International Governance Innovation.[93]

There are many factors that could have contributed to such a dramatic rise during this period in what is (problematically) referred to as "revenge porn." (It is problematic to refer to it as "revenge porn" both because this implies that the victims of this non-consensual distribution of intimate images may have done something worthy of being avenged and because it misleadingly suggests that the motive for this harmful behaviour is always, or even often, spite, when it may just as likely be, for example, profit or misogyny.) Whether this nearly complete overlap in timing is merely a coincidence remains a matter of speculation. However, that this particular marketing strategy on the part of Pornhub was aimed at positioning the company as a public leader is clear.[94] For instance, the press release announcing this offer also included a list of donations of personal protective equipment that the company had donated to fire stations and hospitals, excerpts of statements by fire fighters and others about how grateful they were to Pornhub for its donations during this time of crisis, and a $25,000 donation to a sex workers outreach project to meet the needs of sex workers impacted by the pandemic.[95] Less clear is what, if any, steps were taken by the company to mitigate the risk that its marketing strategy could, in incentivizing users to upload videos by offering them more money, also encourage the non-consensual distribution of intimate images during a time in which the social conditions for this harmful offence were ripe.

More than half of the cases reported to the British Revenge Porn Helpline during this period arose in the context of abusive and controlling relationships.[96] The non-consensual distribution of intimate images – such as by uploading sexually graphic videos and images onto platforms without the consent of the women captured in them – is frequently perpetrated by abusive partners or ex-partners.[97] Statistics from many jurisdictions suggest an increase in the number of reports of domestic violence received by police, and calls to intimate partner violence service providers during the COVID-19 pandemic.[98] This is an unsurprising trend given the connection between abusive, controlling behaviour by men and their level of stress, job loss, relationship breakups, and/or alcohol and drug consumption – all of which were elevated during the pandemic.[99] Among other forms of intimate partner violence, an increased prevalence of so-called revenge porn is a predictable consequence of the lengthy economic and social lockdowns imposed around the world in response to COVID-19.

Again, many other factors disconnected from Pornhub's promotional offer could explain this drastic rise in reports of non-consensual distribution of intimate images during this period. That said, there is no publicly available evidence to suggest that Pornhub, in the public leadership role it had assumed to assist porn performers, took any specific steps before making this offer to mitigate the risk that its promotion might incentivize this harmful activity.[100] Instead of publicly available evidence of steps taken by the company to mitigate against this particular risk when it announced its offer, there is evidence, based on Pornhub's practices at the time, to suggest the company may have done the opposite. In the spring of 2021, the Canadian House of Commons Standing Committee on Access to Information, Privacy and Ethics held hearings on MindGeek in response to the revelations (described in chapter 1) in the *New York Times* in December 2020 regarding the company's role in facilitating and profiting from the distribution of videos that depicted child sexual abuse, and videos that were uploaded to Pornhub without the consent of one or more of the people captured in them. The Committee heard testimony from women who said that they had repeatedly attempted to have videos of themselves removed from Pornhub.[101] One witness testified that it took several weeks after filing a request for Pornhub to remove a video of herself in which she was thirteen – only to have it re-uploaded a week later.[102]

Pornhub did not stop the ability of users to download videos (which could then be subsequently re-uploaded even if a victim was successful in having it removed in the first instance), or prevent unidentified, anonymous users from uploading videos, until December 2020 – close to a year after their COVID-19 offer but only four days after the *New York Times* exposé and threats by Visa and Mastercard to cut ties with the company.[103] Performers, whose economic interests do not always align with those of the platforms that host their content had been lobbying platforms like Pornhub for years to adopt measures to prevent unverified users from downloading videos, and to permit only verified users from uploading videos, in order to prevent piracy and promote safety.[104]

A lawyer who represented some of the victims of Pornhub testified that MindGeek's response to the public scrutiny it was now facing had been to "conduct a gaslighting campaign in the media and social media to discredit victims and deflect from the issue."[105] He spoke of numerous examples of videos on Pornhub of children and young teenagers being raped.[106] He testified that it took the company weeks or months to remove some of these videos when complaints were made, all the while garnering thousands or hundreds of thousands more views and downloads.[107]

Pornhub's response to the BLM movement provides a similar example of the platform seemingly attempting to capitalize on a social issue by purporting to act as a public leader. In the aftermath of the murder of George Floyd by White police officers, and the subsequent protests motivated by his death, the company declared on Twitter that it "stood in solidarity against racism and social injustice," and urged others to donate to organizations fighting anti-Black racism, like the National Association for the Advancement of Colored People (NAACP).[108] At the same time, BLM pornographic videos flourished on the platform.[109] A December 2021 Google search of the words "Black Lives Matter" and "Pornhub" yielded numerous links to Pornhub landing pages that featured videos relying on imagery and narratives of slavery and toxically racist anti-Black stereotypes, while simultaneously invoking the BLM movement.[110] For example, a video entitled "Sexy Cotton Picking Field Slave Gets Fucked for Freedom" depicts a man penetrating a Black woman from behind, while referring to her as a "slave" and a "bitch."[111] Another is entitled "Thick White Girl Getting Stuffed with BBC Black Lives Matter!"[112] The thumbnail image for this video depicts what appears to be the erect penis of a Black man and the vagina of a White woman.[113] Critics pointed out that while Pornhub promised to donate $100,000 to the NAACP, "the donated money was raised, in part, from videos containing sexualized depictions of African American women in antebellum slave scenes with their 'white masters' and the Confederate flag as a backdrop."[114]

Numerous researchers have identified the racist content and themes in some mainstream pornography featuring Black performers.[115] In considering this exploitation of Black women, it is important to heed the observations of scholars like Duke University professor Jennifer Nash. She explains that it is not sufficient to simply highlight pornography's "differential" treatment of Black women.[116] To do so is to be inattentive to the ways in which pornography mobilizes "*particular* racial and ethnic differences."[117] The differential exploitation of Black women in pornography relative to White women is not a difference in degree but in kind.[118] To be clear, Nash's work moves beyond mainstream porn's injuries, including those implicated by its racism, to also challenge feminists (most particularly Black feminists) to consider and claim racialized porn's potential for pleasure and agency.[119] By invoking her analysis, I am not intending to implicate her in the politics of respectability or the dominant feminist narratives about racial porn that her work seeks to challenge. But as Nash observes, examining the possibilities of pornographic representations for "black female sexual subjectivity," and pleasure and desire, requires attending to the "social, historical, and technological specificity of pornography's racialized meanings."[120] Pornhub's BLM tweet, its invocation of George Floyd's murder and the NAACP, and its platformization of both "BLM Porn" and "Ebony Porn" are part of that specificity.

Porn has a deep history and ongoing praxis of anti-Black racism.[121] The racism in porn extends not only to the nature of sexual representations found in mainstream porn, but also to the ways in which porn performers are differentially treated by the pornography industry. In *A Taste of Brown Sugar*, Mireille Miller-Young examines the ways in which Black women in the porn industry are confronted with the same forms of systemic marginalization and discrimination that Black women in other occupations face.[122] Similarly, Angela Jones highlights the ways in which sexual racism in the camming industry operates at structural and cultural levels to thwart the success of Black women performers by structuring the sexual market in ways that privilege Whiteness and hold in place norms of white supremacy.[123] Heather Berg documents the explicitly anti-Black racist pay rates in porn (which compensate Black women less than White women and which pay White women more to appear in videos with Black men).[124] Miller-Young's research reveals similar findings: "Black women earn half to three quarters of what White women make. The difference in earnings involves a lot of overt and covert racism."[125] Berg explains how, as is the case in other labour markets, pay rates in pornography are structured by normative ideas about sexuality, including norms underpinned by racist stereotypes.[126] Black women are paid less because of a discriminatory social assumption that, unlike White women, they are "always, already [sexually] available."[127] White women are paid more to have sex with Black men because of taboos against this type of "interracial sex."[128] These taboos are premised on racist stereotypes about the predatory nature of men of African descent. Berg also documents racism in casting (which means fewer opportunities for Black women), poorer working conditions, and anti-Black racism in satellite industries such as webcam businesses and sex toy companies (which privilege White women).[129] Porn performer Betty Blac, who identifies as an "African American Big Beautiful Woman (BBW)" performer, describes how White friends are offered more scenes because they are considered more "marketable" by some producers, and suggests that White performers are more likely to be given the covers and promoted in ads following photo shoots related to a video, and offered more prestigious, higher paying shoots and feature opportunities relative to Black performers.[130]

Far from disrupting the racist norms and practices in the porn industry, companies like Pornhub arguably advance them. Despite Pornhub's public assertion that it stands in solidarity against racism, the platform continues to include and celebrate a category of videos under the classification "Ebony" (in addition to the newly created BLM category).[131] Indeed, a year after George Floyd was murdered and Pornhub made its public declaration about BLM, the company boasted that "Ebony" was its third most searched category in 2021.[132] Carolyn West and Stephany Powell note that "despite Pornhub's terms and conditions that do not allow 'racial slurs or hate speech' – a search for the n-word turned up thousands of user-uploaded videos with the word in the title, description, or comments."[133] Asian stereotypes and racist norms regarding Asian women are also common. The taxonomy of racist hatred created through the platform's use of metadata, which curates content on the basis of anti-Black racist titles and tags is examined in chapter 7.

This serves as yet another example of the disjuncture between a platform's terms of service and public-facing policies, and the content found on its site. Pornhub purports not to "tolerate hate speech in any form" and promises that the platform is "committed to its eradication" under its hate speech policy.[134] Included in Pornhub's definition of hate speech is "any communication or material that promotes, calls for, supports, or advocates for the delegitimization" of any person or group on the basis of race.[135] Again, videos, including their titles, are not posted on Pornhub until they have been approved by its human moderators. This means Pornhub, in the face of its zero tolerance hate speech policy, has approved countless videos with racist titles and descriptions using racist slurs that would unquestionably be considered hate speech under the platform's own definition.

This same type of effort to present itself as a public leader can also been seen in Pornhub's response to the rise in fake celebrity pornography, sometimes created with the use of artificial intelligence, and without the consent of the celebrities whose images are coopted. When artificial intelligence is used to create this type of sexually explicit content, it is referred to as "deepfake porn." The prevalence of deepfake videos has risen significantly in the last several years. Like other online technological advances,[136] the ability to use machine learning to create this type of synthetic media developed in the context of porn. Deepfake technology involves using artificial intelligence to exchange the face of one person in a video with someone else. It can be used to create highly realistic videos in which someone appears to be in a video in which they were never actually filmed. Approximately 96 per cent of deepfake technology is used to create non-consensual deepfake porn, virtually all of it of women.[137]

Victims of deepfake porn are clear about the profound harms they have experienced on an individual level.[138] Creating and distributing deepfake porn of someone without their consent is a severe violation of their autonomy, privacy, and equality rights. It poses risks to their physical, economic, psychological, and professional safety. The individual harms are experienced in ways that parallel the non-consensual distribution of intimate images not produced through artificial intelligence.[139] Research suggests that while not all victims of this type of violation will want to engage legal systems for other recourse, having this content removed as quickly as possible and censored will be of central concern to nearly every victim of deepfake porn.[140]

Moreover, deepfake porn is being used as a tool of misogyny to silence outspoken women, such as feminist journalists and activists.[141] Professor Suzie Dunn notes that "while many deepfakes seem to be made for purely pornographic purposes, impacting the sexual autonomy of those non-consensually featured in the videos, some [are] specifically weaponized to attack female journalists, activists, and social commentators."[142] As Jane Bailey et al. have explained more generally, the use of artificial intelligence to perpetuate gender inequalities ought to be framed in the language of human rights and responded to as a mechanism of structural gender-based oppression.[143]

Pornhub announced in 2018 that it considered deepfakes to be non-consensual porn and banned these videos.[144] In an interview with journalist Samantha Cole, the platform's spokesperson told Cole that "we do not tolerate any non-consensual content on the site and we remove all said content as soon as we are made aware of it."[145] According to the spokesperson, this type of content directly violates the platform's terms of service.[146] Indeed, as Cole points out, Pornhub's terms of service prohibit content that "impersonates another person or falsely state[s] or otherwise misrepresent[s] your affiliation with a person."[147] But as Cole also highlights, despite the platform's public statements, the site remained loaded with examples of deepfake videos. She reports being able to easily find dozens of deepfake videos uploaded since Pornhub's declaration, including ones with the term "deepfake" and the names of celebrities included in the title.[148]

But the disconnect between Pornhub's public position on deepfake porn and some of its platform activities, as highlighted in a follow-up article published by Cole, is more profound. In its 2019 annual "Year in Review" report, published a few months after proclaiming the ban on deepfakes and highlighting its policy prohibiting content that impersonates another person, Pornhub celebrated and promoted the very content it purported to ban: "If you follow our Pornhub Insights blog, you already know that 2019 was a juicy year – jam-packed with celebrities."[149] The 2019 "Year in Review" included a list of the thirty most popular celebrities that year on Pornhub, and while many, or most, of them had not been involved in producing porn, searches of their names yielded links to fake porn videos of them. The "Year in Review" goes on to boast that "[w]hen celebrities are in the news and on everyone's mind, they tend to drive a lot of Pornhub searches."[150] Not only had Pornhub enabled users to search for fake porn videos of celebrities on its platform, contrary to its terms of service, the company was boasting about how successful it had been at leading users to this non-consensual content – even after publicly proclaiming its prohibition months earlier. The 2019 "Year in Review" exclaimed:

Cardi B was the most popular music artist in 2019 with 11.8 million searches, followed by Ariana Grande at 9 million and Nicki Minaj at 8.4 million. Miley Cyrus trailed behind with almost 5 million searches in 2019. Coincidentally, the day that Miley allegedly split from Liam Hemsworth, her searches spiked by 102% – do Pornhub users love a single lady?[151]

While the platform stopped including information about so-called celebrity porn after its 2019 "Year in Review," a search for the names of any of these women on 1 April 2023 yielded countless fake porn videos of them on the first page of search results, some of which appeared to be synthetic or artificial intelligence–generated media, and others explicit impersonations. At the bottom of the page of these search results, Pornhub maintains tags with the names of other celebrities, directing users on how to find fake porn videos of these women. For example, a search using Ariana Grande's name produces fake porn videos of Ariana Grande, and at the bottom of the page Pornhub maintains tags with names like Jennifer Lopez, Nicki Minaj, and Miley Cyrus.

Recall from chapter 1, ECP vice-president Sarah Bain's endorsement of Pornhub: "We are confident that the MindGeek team and all MindGeek platforms operate with trust and safety at the forefront of everything they do."[152] According to Bain, the issue for the company is "a misalignment between how MindGeek operates and what the public perceives about this industry and these platforms."[153] In fact, when it comes to the platformiza-tion of porn, it appears that the much more significant misalignment is be-tween the commitments and principles articulated in the public statements, terms of service, and user agreements of these platforms and some of the readily available content on their sites.

To be clear, attempts by pornography producers and distributors to lever-age social justice movements in an effort to buoy their public reputations is not a twenty-first century invention. *Playboy* offers a paradigmatic example of this strategy. In the 1970s, the magazine positioned itself as a de-fender of the women's liberation movement and a promoter, if not a vision-ary, of gender equality and sexual liberation for women.[154] *Playboy* advocated for abortion rights and advanced the notion that women, too, were inter-ested in sexual experiences that would not anchor them in the domestic ob-ligations imposed upon them by heterosexual marriage.[155]

Nor is the hypocritical disjuncture between such positioning and some of the activities engaged in by pornography companies new. For example, *Playboy* was promoting a particular framing of women's equality while sim-ultaneously affirming the sexual violation of women and contributing to rape culture by, for example, publishing jokes and articles on how to use alcohol to inhibit a woman's ability to resist sexual advances.[156] *Playboy*, too, had its disconnects.

There are, however, factors that make this phenomenon different today. First, given the volume of Internet traffic to mainstream porn-streaming platforms, it seems plausible to suggest that the public profile of companies like Pornhub and xHamster is greater than was the case for pornography companies in the pre-digital era. It is true that *Playboy*, for example, ex-panded into other markets such as nightclubs and hospitality. Nevertheless, at its 1972 peak the magazine's circulation was seven million.[157] Contrast that with the 42 billion visits that Pornhub reported receiving in 2019.[158] Today, the profile of a pornography company's public commitments to social justice is amplified due to the expansive, globalized reach of porn-streaming plat-forms. In terms of understanding the social impact of the contemporary pornography industry, this makes the public leadership role that these com-panies attempt to occupy and the disjuncture between the content and the interpretation of this content by its distributors more important factors than perhaps was the case in earlier eras. Regardless of how famous Hugh Hefner and his Playboy mansion became during the height of his celebrity and the peak of the magazine's circulation, the company's reach is dwarfed in comparison to that of today's porn-streaming companies.

Second, when it suits them, porn-streaming platforms, like other platforms, position themselves as neutral intermediaries whose function is to connect users who produce, in this case, pornography, with users who consume pornography.[159] While this framing is inaccurate, it provides a narrative that porn-streaming platforms rely upon to distance themselves from content on their sites that the public purports to oppose, or that is unlawful.[160] This is a narrative that was not available to pornography companies in earlier eras. When Hefner was challenged by Susan Brownmiller and Sally Kempton (who asserted that *Playboy* magazine degraded women) on the *Dick Cavett Show* in 1970, Hefner could argue, as he did, that women and men are physically different and that these differences should not be elided, but rather enjoyed.[161] He could reject the proposition that paying women to be photographed naked was degrading. Hefner could even have argued that publishing rape jokes or articles on the use of alcohol as a date rape drug was in some way consistent with his articulated commitment to gender equality through sexual liberation.[162] What he could not have done is suggest that it was someone else, and not him or his company, that was responsible for the public dissemination of this content. *Playboy*, unlike Pornhub or xHamster, could not disavow and distance itself from the content from which it profited, regardless of whether that content was consistent with the public image promoted by the company.

Porn-streaming platforms attempt to protect the public reputations that they nurture by absolving themselves of responsibility for content on their sites that receives public criticism. They assert, as MindGeek's former chief operating officer did when questioned by Canada's parliamentary ethics committee, that what their companies do is provide a "safe environment for people to consume adult content" and that problematic or unlawful content is a function of "people out there who are trying to misuse these platforms."[163] They maintain, as xHamster's user agreement stipulates, that under no circumstances will they accept any liability for any of the content on their sites.[164] These platforms disavow any connection between their companies and content that garners public criticism or legal censure.

The public profile nurtured by companies like MindGeek impacts the degree to which pornography is relied upon as a resource for the development of sexual norms and social understandings of sexuality. As Susanna Paasonen, Kylie Jarrett, and Ben Light emphasize in *#NSFW: Sex, Humor,* *and Risk in Social Media*, this effort to reframe porn consumption as ubiquitous, fun, ordinary, and socially safe is intentional on the part of companies like Pornhub.[165] Arguably, the more successful porn-streaming platforms are at achieving legitimacy and respectability, the more influential they become in a particular social environment. For example, some research suggests that many young people turn to digital porn to learn how to perform sexual activities.[166] As Amia Srinivasan writes, "[p]orn is not pedagogy, yet it often functions as if it were."[167] She highlights a study by the British government from 2013 in which male youth reported that they looked at porn to "see the way [sex] is done" or to "learn more things."[168] Similarly, in their study of pornography use among a sample of low-income, racialized youth, Emily Rothman et al. found that twenty-one of the twenty-three youth they interviewed reported learning how to have sex by watching pornography.[169] As one young woman in their study put it: "I never knew how to, like, suck dick, basically, and I went on there to see how to do it. And that's how I learned."[170] To be clear, youth report several motivations for watching porn – curiosity, sexual gratification, and because their peers do so are also among the most frequently cited motives – but learning "how to have sex" is consistently identified as one of their reasons.[171] Chapter 8 engages with how we might, more productively, think about porn as pedagogy. The point is that the more public credibility a mainstream porn-streaming company achieves, the more likely the sexually inexperienced – among others – are to turn to it as an educational resource.

To state it in more general terms, the more a porn-streaming platform can position itself as a cultural institution, the more authority its content has and the more impactful its role is in constituting norms regarding, for example, who is desirable, and what is arousing. For instance, Pornhub's release of its annual "Year in Review Insights Report," documenting the most searched for terms that year, the categories of porn that are trending, and demographic data on who is watching what on the platform, has become an event worthy of coverage by mainstream media.[172] Journalists rely on these reports to declare to their readers that women in Ohio are into foot fetish porn and those in Kentucky love stripteases.[173] Every year mainstream media reveals who the most popular "porn stars" are on Pornhub and confirms for us that "lesbian" and "MILF" remain among the most searched-for types of porn on the platform.[174] In this way, data on user activities gathered by Pornhub are reflected back to us in mainstream media as "news" about our sexual preferences. The credibility of this information turns on the degree to which, and how widely, the platform is accepted as part of our cultural infrastructure, rather than marginalized as a purveyor of smut targeted at the prurient few.

Conclusion

Again, the consumption of mainstream porn is common. As explained in chapter 2, its content is algorithmically determined based on data-driven feedback loops between platforms and users. It is consumed in virtual communities in which users set norms and provide implicit peer support regarding content.[175] If we agree that we are living in a platform society, one in which public values are shaped and reshaped in digitally connected communities,[176] then we must accept that porn-streaming sites and the networked communities that they produce are unquestionably a constitutive part of our social landscape – and in particular, a contributive part of the socially acquired aspects of our sexualities. The contemporary social role of pornography, given its platformization, contributes to and is constitutive of public discourse and culture. As it happens, and as is examined in the next chapter, this is a conclusion that is strongly supported not just by platform studies and media studies experts, but also by the work of cultural criminologists and those who study sexual script theory.

CHAPTER 4

Are We Living in the House That Porn Built?

Pussies are bullshit.
– porn producer John Stagliano, interview with Martin Amis in the *Guardian*

Platform studies scholars agree that platforms are constitutive of public discourse – that they contribute to the production of culture and structure social interactions. This consensus is strikingly contrasted with the highly contested and long-standing scholarly debates about the societal impact of pornography. Feminists, let alone researchers more generally, have never found common ground on porn's social function. There have been conceptual and theoretical debates about what pornography "is," voluminous and competing empirical studies and claims regarding the possibility of a causal relationship between pornography consumption and violent sexual behaviour, and equally contested efforts to prove or disprove correlative connections between the consumption of porn and individual sexual behaviours, relationships, and attitudes generally.

Rather than continued attempts to demonstrate a direct causal or correlative relationship between the consumption of pornography and the individual perpetration of sexual violence, a growing body of research focuses on how pornography may inform and even constitute aspects of our social environment. Two strands of work in this area are sexual script theory and cultural criminology.[1]

Sexual script theory starts from the premise that sexuality is, like many human behaviours, at least in part socially constructed, rather than an exclusively biological construct.[2] (Sexual script theory is, of course, not the first or only body of scholarship to conceptualize sexuality as socially constructed.[3]) According to sexual script theory, societal norms, exposure to media, public institutions like law and education, personal experiences, and pre-existing values and attitudes contribute to the construction of a person's sexuality: "it is not the physical aspects of sexuality but the social aspects that generate the arousal and organize the action, or, in other words, provide the script."[4] In this sense, sexuality is socially acquired: "Individuals develop their understandings of sexuality through resources in their social environment."[5] These resources are relied upon to attach meaning to sexual behaviour, to delineate the parameters of acceptable and inappropriate sexual behaviour, and to understand within the context of a sexual encounter what one's role is, how a sexual interaction is to proceed, and what the reaction of others and the predictable consequences of particular sexual behaviours are likely to be.[6] Taken as a whole, the learning that is acquired through one's social environment forms a metaphorical script.[7]

There are cultural, interpersonal, and intrapsychic levels of sexual scripting. As Michael Wiederman explains, cultural norms function at the most abstract level of scripting but are still necessary: "[i]n a sense, cultural scenarios lay out the playing field of sexuality; what is deemed desirable and undesirable, and where the broad boundaries lie between appropriate and inappropriate sexual conduct."[8] It is this cultural layer of scripting that seems most pertinent to an examination of porn's social role. Think of it in much the same way that gender, gender expression, and sexuality are deeply informed by, and constituted through, hegemonic norms. To use the example of sexuality specifically, and drawing on the insights of queer theory, as Gayle Rubin famously observed, "sexuality is as much a social product as are diets, methods of transportation, forms of labor, types of entertainment, [and] processes of production."[9] The social meaning and norms derived from cultural scripts, including those sourced in porn, inform and constitute our understandings of our sexual behaviours and our interpretations of others' sexual behaviours, of what is "normal," of what is hot and what is not.

In their study of the titles used on mainstream porn-streaming platforms, Vera-Gray et al. draw sexual script theory together with the insights of cultural criminology.[10] Cultural criminologists, they note, "have outlined a nuanced model where social meanings flow into and out of the media

landscape, able to 'reverberate, and bend back on themselves.'"[11] An understanding of the relationship between porn and sexual behaviour premised
on the insights of cultural criminology and sexual script theory rejects a
linear relationship between the consumption of pornography and particular
sexual behaviours. Adding the lens of cultural criminology to sexual script
theory, the authors note, avoids claims focused on the direct impact of particular sexual scripts (or pornography) on individual behaviour.[12] It is not,
they assert, that individual people take in information, process it, and then
act it out in the social world.[13] But at the same time, this understanding of
the relationship between pornography and sexual behaviour "also challenges notions of pure fantasy divorced from any real world impact."[14] The
authors rightly point out that rejecting a causal relationship "is not the same
as rejecting any relationship."[15] Instead, their claim is that the development
of sexuality is an iterative, reciprocal process in which "we are influenced
by, and in turn influence, the resources" in our social environment.[16] They
argue that "drawing sexual script theory and insights from cultural criminology [and I would add queer theory, as above] together in this way and
applying them to questions about sexual violence in pornography brings
forward an understanding of pornography's social function."[17] It provides
insight into "how sexuality and what counts as 'sexual' in our social environment mutually shapes and is shaped by pornography."[18] Sexuality is
developed through an iterative, complex set of interactions and interpretations, both at a societal level and an individual level.

This iterative, reciprocal process in which sexuality and sexual meaning
are developed echoes the constitutive social role played by platforms. Recall
from chapter 2 that, in their examination of platforms, van Dijck, Poell, and
de Waal conclude that platforms do not simply connect users but "fundamentally steer *how* they connect with each other."[19] In other words, platforms
structure social interactions. They shape social norms. For example, platforms do not only measure users' "sentiments, thoughts, and performances
but also trigger and mold them" through the design of their user interfaces.[20]
Providing users with features such as the ability to rate, "like," share, and
comment significantly shapes how users interact with one another and what
kinds of data they generate for the platform.[21] Van Dijck, Poell, and de Waal
observe that while the "technological and economic elements of platforms
steer user interaction [they] simultaneously shape social norms."[22] In this
way, "platforms do not reflect the *social*: they produce the social structures
we live in."[23] In their analysis, platforms are performative.[24]

That said, users are not mere puppets: "while platform mechanisms filter and steer social interactions, users also define their outcome."[25] The authors note that "any major platform is a recalibration laboratory where new features are constantly tested on users" and subsequently refined.[26] In this sense, there is a constant feedback loop between platforms and users with respect to the architecture of the platform, including the technology employed by platforms to structure social interactions. Where on a page to place a "like button," whether or where to include a link to a performer's profile, or how many tags to permit per video will impact if, or how, such features are used, which will in turn have a bearing on how the platform's user interface is refined by the company, and subsequently used in the future.

As explained in chapter 2, there is also a constant feedback loop between platforms and users with respect to what content is presented to users, how it is promoted, and even what content will be produced in the future. Recall Tarleton Gillespie's explanation of the mechanisms through which platforms constitute public discourse.[27] He argues that the moment platforms began curating, categorizing, and selectively promoting content to users they shifted from delivering content provided by one user to constituting it for other users.[28]

Chapter 2 highlighted the central features of contemporary mainstream pornography: consumption of it is ubiquitous, its production is data driven, it is communal, it is likely to become increasingly homogeneous, it is quasi-participatory and interactive, and it is produced and marketed by and through, and consumed on, digital platforms. Chapter 3 explained how platform companies position themselves as public leaders in ways that may amplify the profile of these companies in social spaces. Chapter 3 also examined the disjuncture between the public statements and interpretations these platforms offer about the content on their sites and the *depictions* of non-consensual sexual activity readily available on these platforms.

As one might expect, the way in which porn today is produced, marketed, and consumed – the platformization of mainstream pornography – informs its role as a resource in our social environment that shapes and is shaped by sexual norms. This is the principal claim in this chapter: pornography is both informed by and constitutes social and sexual norms. Porn on the platform contributes to the formation and re-formation of our sexual scripts – at least at the cultural level.

An examination of the platformization of mainstream pornography supports the contention that porn serves as a resource in our social environment from which sexual meaning is shaped and sexual norms are formed. In fact, the platformization of porn elevates or amplifies the degree to which pornography performs this function. This chapter establishes that porn "does things in the real world."[29] Chapters 5 and 6 explain some of what, more specifically, it is that mainstream, contemporary pornography is "doing in the real world."

Porn Sows Our Social Fabric

Feminist author and legal theorist Catharine MacKinnon opened a 2021 *New York Times* opinion piece with the line: "We are living in the world pornography has made."[30] MacKinnon has been making this claim about the social impacts of pornography for decades.[31] In *The Right to Sex*, Srinivasan revisits MacKinnon's contention that pornography, more than just a reflection of women's oppression, in fact constitutes women's oppression.[32] What if, Srinivasan asks, MacKinnon was not wrong but rather prescient – a bit before her time?[33] She discusses one of legal theorist Ronald Dworkin's main critiques of MacKinnon's claim.[34] Dworkin dismissed MacKinnon's thesis on the grounds that pornography could not possibly have the widespread, negative social effect MacKinnon suggested because viewing it is not sufficiently pervasive.[35] He argued:

> No doubt mass culture is in various ways an obstacle to sexual equality, but the most popular forms of that culture – the view of women presented in soap operas and commercials, for example – are much greater obstacles to that equality than the dirty films watched by a small minority.[36]

Srinivasan rightly notes that even if that were true in 1993 when Dworkin asserted it, it is certainly not true today.[37] Indeed, today pornography *is* mass culture. As documented in chapter 2, the creation of porn-streaming platforms has resulted in an exponential growth in the consumption of pornography. The degree to which porn consumption was pervasive might have been debatable in 1993. It is not debatable today.[38] Evangelos Tziallas's articulation of porn consumption is apt. In describing his morning routine on Tumblr, he writes, "no longer a discrete entity, porn is woven into the fabric of the digital media assemblage, an integral part of our daily media consumption – sometimes more so than traditional sources."[39] Pornography as quotidian ritual.

The societal impact of contemporary, mainstream porn must be assessed on the basis that consumption of it, and participation in it, is widespread. If one accepts that pornography is one of the resources that shapes the meaning of sexuality in our social environment, it seems reasonable to suggest that its contemporary omnipresence will amplify this role. The more ubiquitous porn is, the more likely it is to help shape sexual norms.

Pornography Is Sex

In *Only Words*, MacKinnon argued that "what pornography does, it does in the real world, not only in the mind."[40] In her analysis, pornography is performative.[41] That is to say, porn does not merely reflect or give voice to the sexual, political, and economic inequality of women; it structures and constitutes this oppression.[42] Rather than merely speech, or only words, pornography, she observed, is used as, and therefore is, sex:

> What is real here is not that the materials are pictures, but that they are part of a sex act. The women are in two dimensions, but the men have sex with them in their own three-dimensional bodies, not in their minds alone. Men come doing this. This, too, is a behaviour, not a thought or an argument. It is not ideas they are ejaculating over.[43]

MacKinnon's theoretical framework for an assessment of pornography's social function was assailed by critics, often on grounds that were explicitly gendered, and in some instances severely misogynistic. Writer Carlin Romano began his review of *Only Words* with: "Suppose I decide to rape Catharine MacKinnon before reviewing her book. Because I'm uncertain whether she understands the difference between being raped and being exposed to pornography."[44] He went on to describe how he would imagine raping her – the physical logistics, what her face looks like, how much she protests, her disgust and despair.[45] *Washington Post* columnist George Will described MacKinnon as "the leader of the most radical assault on free speech in American history."[46] Prominent United States Court of Appeal judge Richard Posner accused her of being "obsessed with pornography" and described her book as "a verbal torrent that appeals ... to elemental passions (fear, disgust, anger, hatred) rather than to the rational intellect."[47]

Dworkin suggested her book was "disingenuous."[48] She was called "militant," "[ir]rational," and "reckless" by these men.[49] One reviewer speculated about her sexual relationship with her partner.[50]

The main intellectual argument marshalled in reviews that were critical of *Only Words* is a common one: MacKinnon's work, they contended, posed a profound threat to freedom of speech.[51] The tone of and personalized attacks in these reviews were less common. Why did these critics respond with such passion and contempt?

One of the key arguments relied upon in response to so-called anti-porn scholarship is that porn is fiction, or mere fantasy.[52] People, by which critics typically mean adults, despite studies demonstrating prevalent consumption of pornography by adolescents and to some extent children,[53] know the difference between the symbolic and the real – between the supposedly fantastical depictions of sex in pornography and "sex in real life." The vitriolic and at times misogynistic response to MacKinnon's assertion that pornography constitutes acts, not just thoughts and ideas, may have been fuelled by a strong interest in defending the claim that porn is fantasy, not reality.

The conceptualization of pornography as speech, and not speech act as MacKinnon would have it, is a necessary presupposition to the assertion that consumers of pornography understand it as fantasy, distinct and separated from the real world. Even platforms attempt to maintain this distinction. xHamster's user agreement, for instance, requires anyone who accesses the platform to agree that all materials and content on the site constitute expressive content (and that this expression may be fully protected by the First Amendment to the United States Constitution and other similar principles).[54]

It becomes impossible to rely on a distinction between fantasy and reality to defend or justify one's porn consumption practices or preferences if pornography is, as MacKinnon suggests, behaviour not thought, active not passive, constitutive not only connotative. By resoundingly rejecting the proposition that pornography is the depiction of sex, not sex itself, MacKinnon threatened the fantasy/reality distinction at a conceptual level. Perhaps these reviewers attacked her personally because they took it personally? I am not suggesting that the consumption of (all genres of) mainstream porn is indefensible, but rather that justifications which rely on the fantasy/reality distinction do so precariously.

One need not embrace every aspect of MacKinnon's analysis in order to draw on her insight that pornography is more than just expression. Her contention that what porn does, it does in the real world, advances our understanding of pornography's social function. Accepting this does not require us to condemn all pornography, and embrace censorship as the only possible legal response to porn's social impact, nor accept Robin Morgan's (in)famous declaration that "pornography is the theory, and rape is the practice."[55] That pornography *is* sex, that is to say that it constitutes sex, does not mean that sex and pornography must be wholly coextensive. Rejecting the latter does not require a wholesale rejection of MacKinnon's contributions to our understanding of pornography's social impact. Nor must we accept that because the production of some porn is coercive and violent, the production of all pornography is coercive and violent. And finally, to say that the consumption of mainstream porn contributes to the constitution of sexual norms that are dangerous for women and children does not mean that all porn consumption is always and only dangerous and oppressive – that porn can never constitute pleasure for women or serve a liberatory function. The "sex wars" or porn debates that erupted at the 1982 Barnard Conference on Sexuality (but which were simmering well before then) left feminist academics of that generation polarized, and for some even traumatized.[56] This division was compounded by the failure of some feminists (typically straight, White, cisgendered, privileged ones) during this era to advance a vision of equality that was inclusive and that could account for, and accommodate, the racial, economic, sexual orientation and gender identity–based diversities that intersect in ways that contradict the idea that there was ever a monolithic women's movement.[57] While those debates served important functions, there is no reason to confine our engagements with issues of pornography today to battle lines drawn in an earlier era.[58]

Features of the platformization of pornography, such as the participatory and interactive opportunities it offers, support and in fact strengthen MacKinnon's claim that recognizing the social impact of pornography "requires understanding it more in active than in passive terms, as constructing and performative rather than as merely referential or connotative."[59] That is to say, the manner in which pornography is produced, distributed, marketed, and consumed today belies the notion that pornography is merely thoughts and ideas, and thus does not cause harm because porn consumers identify it as fantasy (rather than identify with it as fact).

Like with Dworkin's assertion that porn could not have the social impact MacKinnon claimed because it is an activity engaged in by only a small minority, several features of the platformization of pornography provide new challenges to the claim that porn is merely expressive activity and the passive consumption of this expression.

Distinguishing Fantasy from Reality in an Online Participatory Culture

Chapter 2 identified several participatory/interactive elements of the consumption of porn on streaming platforms. Recall that on some porn-streaming platforms, users can interact with the performers captured in some of the videos they view by hiring them as escorts, visiting them in chat rooms, watching them on camming platforms where they can request and pay for specific sexual acts, or purchasing items for them from performers' digital wish lists.[60]

Consider the example of camming. In camming, users log on to a site hosted by a "cam model," who live streams a sexual performance for viewers once a certain threshold of tips, set by the performer, has been reached.[61] A cam site will typically include a menu stipulating the tip threshold for a particular type of performance, and a comment section in which users can make requests or offer other comments. Some cam performers also conduct private shows with clients.[62]

In camming, as Emily van der Nagel writes, "[t]he candid nature of the cam performance is highly valued as a form of intimate connection, and cam performers are often placed in contrast to professional porn performers, regarded by their audiences as more authentic and accessible."[63] Van der Nagel's characterization of the intimacy of the connection between performer and consumer in the camming context is compelling – the distinction that consumers may draw between cam performers and professional porn performers or content producers perhaps less so. Often the cam performer and the porn performer are one and the same. As Heather Berg highlights, and as noted in chapter 2, because the pay rates for appearing in studio-produced porn videos have decreased due to the advent of porn-streaming platforms, some women appear in videos in order to promote their camming businesses or other methods of revenue generation.[64] Betty Blac makes this same point in her interview with researcher Mireille Miller-Young.[65]

Regardless, when a user visits the camming site of a woman whose Pornhub video he has consumed, and contributes to the public tipping pool to commission her to perform particular sex acts while he watches and masturbates, whatever basis one might have for asserting the line between fantasy and reality, act and thought (as well as that between pornography and sex work), disappears.[66] Clearly this user is not merely indulging in a fantasy. He is engaging in sexual activity with the woman he has commissioned, as is she. That this activity is occurring online rather than in a motel room or the backseat of a car does not render their activities fantastical or imaginary. Similarly, that he may harness his imagination in pursuit of sexual gratification does not render the acts engaged in any less real than when one uses their imagination to maintain sexual arousal while engaged in sexual acts not mediated digitally.[67]

The rise of camming platforms demonstrates one of the new opportunities to act on and through pornography presented by its platformization, but it also helps to elucidate the point that even absent these new participatory opportunities the consumption of pornography is active, not passive. It is clear that during the camming session, the orgasm this user achieves (if he achieves one), the ejaculate he expels, are real, as are the sexual acts engaged in by the woman he pays to perform them. But neither his orgasm and ejaculate, nor the acts she performs in real time, are *more* real than when they occur asynchronously. The ability to interact provided by chat rooms and camming creates an additional act or set of acts – an interaction or interactions that do not exist in asynchronous forms of porn – that may well make the experience feel more authentic than traditional porn, a point Angela Jones makes in her work on the significance of embodied authenticity to camming.[68] But it cannot be said that the ability to interact transforms the very same bodies, engaged in the very same physical movements, from fantasy to reality. They were always real.

Consider another example. Porn-streaming platforms, like other social media networks, facilitate a new form of "participatory culture" in which groups of people are "shaping, sharing, reframing and remixing media content" and distributing it widely through their networked communities.[69] Video editing technology allows users to extract, remix, and modify brief segments of videos to create (micro)porn, as it is sometimes called, which can then be shared across the creator's digital networks.[70] Some users take clips from longer videos on sites that require payment and post these excerpts on platforms like Pornhub or xTube.[71] This is an example of the type of "contextual sexual meaning making" that Katrin Tiidenberg and Emily van der Nagel explain is produced through the "entanglement of creation, consumption, and interaction" of people's sexual social media practices.[72]

There are two ways in which this practice can be said to challenge the supposed distinction between fantasy and reality. First, the process of selecting a particular excerpt from a longer porn video, and re-titling it, which means reframing and presenting the content in a new way for other viewers, changes the role of porn consumer into the role of (micro)porn producer. Whatever one might argue about the nature of the excerpted content, the act of producing the (micro)porn and sending it into the digital universe is undeniably real.

In addition to longer excerpts, as Joseph Brennan notes, users sometimes further shorten pornography into sexually explicit "gifs" – suitable, he suggests, "for the porn feeds of [users'] daily, scrolling, social media rituals."[73] Helen Hester, Bethan Jones, and Sarah Taylor-Harman argue that the creation of these pornographic gifs allows consumers to choose for themselves "the bodies and fragmented sexual inter/activities they desire to see presented."[74] Here, too, porn consumer becomes (micro)porn producer.

Some porn-streaming platforms offer to assist users with the creation of these porn gifs. Pornhub, for example, includes a page highlighting the month's top-rated gifs, encouraging users to share them with their friends, and offering to teach users how to make them:

Everyone loves to look at porn gifs. Let's face it you're here for the best sex gifs and animated porn to share on your social media accounts and with friends. Nothing makes users happier than seeing gif porn and the hilarities that ensue from seeing an illustration of them. We are your number one source for NSFW gifs and gif maker options especially when it comes to sex. When you want to add some animation to your gif you can learn how to do so with such ease here that you will keep coming back to do it again and again.[75]

Like paying someone to perform specific sexual acts after watching them in a video, hiring them as an escort, or purchasing items for them that will then appear in their next video, these acts of excerpting, modifying, and disseminating pornography are real, not fantasy.[76] When users engage in the production of (micro)porn they are not passively consuming porn. They are engaged in an activity that produces content that then exists in, and has impacts on, our social environment.

Second, (micro)porn producers may offer a reframing of the content that they excerpt in a way that explicitly characterizes it as real, even if the original content is clearly presented as fantasy. In his consideration of (micro)porn, Brennan examines the potential impact of the loss of context that can occur when users excerpt clips from longer commercial videos, and re-title and post them on free porn-streaming platforms.[77] He uses the example of a scene that he says was cropped from a "commercial website" explicitly dedicated to the "fantasy of 'bareback sex addiction'" and posted on Pornhub.[78] Brennan observes how the excerpted clip is stripped of any reference to the production company that made it, the safe sex disclaimer that accompanied it, or its explicit acknowledgment that it was created to appeal to those with a bareback fantasy.[79]

The original video was shot in the "gonzo style" commonly used in porn production today to represent or convey its realness.[80] Brennan argues, based on an analysis of the comments about the excerpted clip posted by Pornhub users, that once removed from an explicitly commercial context (such as a paid site) in which it was marketed as a fantasy, and due to the gonzo style in which it was filmed, viewers assumed or at least speculated that the video had captured real sex. He notes comments by viewers on its seeming authenticity: "seems real enough"; and the comments of viewers who connected the video with their own sexual experiences: "'I've done something similar.'"[81] Brennan's conclusion is that this type of (micro)porn can convert content that was originally explicitly presented as fantasy into reality in the eyes of the viewer.[82]

The effect is similar to content that is presented as the inadvertent or surreptitious capture of sexual activity without the knowledge of those being videoed, such as so-called up-skirting clips and hidden camera videos – another relatively common phenomenon on porn-streaming platforms.[83] It is also worth noting that those users who liken the sexual acts depicted to their own sexual experiences seem to be relating to the content as more than mere fantasy.

Porn producers are attuned to this preference for, or perhaps even preoccupation with, authenticity. Porn producer John Stagliano's comment, "pussies are bullshit," quoted at the beginning of this chapter, was made in reference to his preference for filming acts of anal penetration over vaginal penetration.[84] He explained that with vaginal penetration the viewer is more likely to question the authenticity of the performance – to ask whether it is "real" or "bullshit."[85] But with anal penetration the female performer's response is more likely to be guttural, more animal like (possibly due to the pain caused). And thus, "assholes are reality. And pussies are bullshit."[86]

Think about this statement in light of the constitutive role porn plays in shaping our social landscape. Again, porn on the platform is performative.

Some platforms reportedly also cater to this demand for authentic or so-called amateur porn – including through allegedly unlawful means. According to a lawsuit filed against MindGeek in 2020, a company insider alleged that MindGeek purchased content from human traffickers in Eastern Europe in order to ensure a supply of this type of video. The videos allegedly captured trafficked young women who were coerced, threatened, or blackmailed into participating. According to the lawsuit, these videos were then uploaded onto the site in a manner which made it appear as if they had been provided by an individual user. The insider is reported as stating:

MindGeek owns studios and works with studios. These studios produce high quality porn at high cost. MindGeek determined that high quality porn doesn't convert well on tubesites. Most people want to see the girl next door and videos that seem more realistic. To get this content they run networks of advisors who run agencies that acquire porn and cam videos from high trafficking areas like Czech Republic and sell in bulk to MindGeek entities all over the world or license companies that all actively feed the videos into the tube sites as user uploads.[87]

Setting aside for the moment the important issue of trafficking, this preoccupation of some pornography consumers with content that is real, as opposed to professionally produced, is worthy of closer consideration. In her examination of the distinction between professional and amateur porn, Susanna Paasonen suggests that the appeal of amateur porn revolves around "notions and promises of real bodies, real pleasures, real people and real places."[88] Whether the content is actually amateur or whether it is what is sometimes called "pro-am porn" (content produced using professional performers or by studios but made to look amateur), we might ask what underpins the preference by some, or perhaps many, for content that purports to have captured real sex engaged in by real people that was not conducted for the purposes of producing pornography. The preference for depictions of so-called real sex must reveal something about the relationship between porn consumption and this supposed fantasy/reality distinction. Perhaps users find it easier to insert themselves into the scene, and thus more arousing, if the sexual acts do not appear overly scripted or choreographed and the performers overly manicured. Perhaps pornography that purports to capture real sex is perceived by the viewer as more instructive than professionally produced porn.

Regardless, this "real sex with real people" discourse reflects an untenable distinction. To begin with, a good deal of the pornography on tube sites is, or makes a claim to be, real, homemade, amateur porn. Moreover, as Aidan McGlynn, a senior lecturer at the University of Edinburgh, demonstrates in his interrogation of the claim that pornography is fiction not reality, the distinction is actually quite blurred – as it is with all fiction.[89] This leads him to conclude that it can bear little weight in terms of assessing porn's social impact. First, he observes that "the storylines of most works of fiction take place against a background of facts about the non fictional world. For this reason, a work of fiction has been likened to 'a patchwork of truth and falsity.'"[90] Second, unlike with written text, with videos the fact that a work is unambiguously fictional does not mean that its creation was not real. Drawing an analogy to live action fiction films, McGlynn notes the distinction between a movie in which the actor performs his own stunts and one in which the stunts are computer generated. In both, the "nominal portrayal" is fictional, but in the former this portrayal is depicted by "non-fictional people, objects, places and behaviour" – what he terms the "physical portrayal."[91]

McGlynn uses the example of *Mission Impossible: Ghost Protocol* to demonstrate his point: "Tom Cruise's character Ethan Hunt scales up the side of the Burj Khalifa. The nominal portrayal here – Hunt's dangerous climb – could have been depicted by mostly computer generated images, but in fact it was not; Tom Cruise really did film the scenes while dangling off the side of the Burj Khalifa."[92] As he points out, *Ghost Protocol* is clearly a work of fiction. "But we would have missed something out," he argues, "if we stopped there, given that the way that it represents its fictional content depends on recordings of the physical portrayal."[93]

For the most part, and with exceptions like animated porn, synthetic or deepfake porn, and some/most depictions of female orgasm (at least those in mainstream porn),[94] the sexual acts captured in videos produced by professional studios and amateurs alike are real, as are the women (and men) performing them.[95] Whether the nominal portrayal of a porn video is fictional or real, its physical portrayal almost always relies on recordings of actual acts by real people. The production of pornography, whether it be professional or amateur, requires the use of real people's bodies.[96] Whether it is homemade or professionally produced, women may act like they are enjoying it, but they are not acting like they are being, for example, orally, vaginally, and anally penetrated. They really are being orally, vaginally, and anally penetrated (sometimes all at once), and men really are, for example, thrusting into their anuses or ejaculating on their faces. Moreover, some unknown proportion of porn, the nominal portrayal of which is fictional – for instance, a rape video that is portrayed as fantasy – is in fact the capture on film of non-consensual sexual acts or a recording of the sexual assault of a trafficked woman, a point emphasized by MacKinnon in some of her earlier essays on pornography.[97]

To offer a further example of the participatory nature of porn on the platform examined in chapter 2, users can now consume virtual reality, point-of-view pornography in which they experience the content in a three-dimensional format.[98] As noted in chapter 2, this mode of consumption may even include external tactile stimulation if they have the right technology.[99] MacKinnon's concession in 1993, that "the women [in pornography] are in two dimensions," is not always true today.[100] This increasingly popular genre of online pornography facilitates the viewer's ability to place themselves in the scene; to perceive the women in these videos in three dimensions.[101] It enhances their ability to experience the sexual acts depicted in the content that they consume not only through self-stimulation but by performing these acts virtually.[102] This is a viewing experience that further challenges the distinction between fantasy and reality. Indeed, that is the objective of virtual reality media generally: "Virtual reality environments strive to be as close as possible to physical environments; for the subjective mind of users present in a simulated environment, virtual reality is in that moment their only reality."[103]

The understandable concern expressed by performers and content producers regarding the security of their identity and personal information further challenges the suggestion that porn consumers engage with porn solely in the realm of fantasy, separated and apart from real life. Porn performers and content creators have a heightened need to ensure that their personal information is never leaked due to the risk that viewers who obtain this information will, indeed, contact them, harass them, or perhaps even stalk them in their real lives.[104] Lawsuits against platforms brought by women who have been the victims of the non-consensual distribution of intimate images indicate that these concerns may be far from baseless. Plaintiffs have sued MindGeek on the basis that photos and/or videos of themselves as children and teenagers were uploaded to MindGeek platforms without their knowledge or consent. They report having received repeated, unsolicited social media requests, being sexual propositioned, being asked for further videos and photos, or being harassed in public and called a slut and whore by people unknown to them but who appear to have seen their photos and videos.[105]

In her research on technology-facilitated gender-based violence, Suzie Dunn references cases in which people have used facial recognition software to discover the identity of porn performers by matching their faces to their other social media profiles. As Dunn notes, "[o]nce a person's personal information is made public, harassers can then show up at their workplace, threaten them at their home or send harmful messages to their phone, email address or social media accounts."[106] Whether or not efforts by a viewer to interact with a performer in real life are intended to be threatening, or are experienced as threatening by a particular performer, they most certainly transcend any supposed divide between the fantastical and the real.

Finally, users can and do make their own sexually graphic videos, and upload them for others to watch.[107] Platform technology enables anyone with a cell phone to create pornography and share it around the world. While amateur porn is not new, it is a defining feature of the pornography industry today.[108] As already explained, the sense that porn consumers prefer videos of real sex means that even a significant proportion of professionally produced pornography today attempts to present as homemade or amateur.[109] Both the consumption and the production of so-called amateur, user-generated porn that purportedly depicts an authenticity that porn which is explicitly professionally produced is devoid of contribute to the sense of participation created on porn-streaming platforms.

Contemplate first the *consumption* of amateur porn on the platform. Brandon Arroyo argues that "[t]he inclusion of amateur content alongside studio-produced videos suggests that tube sites are fostering a pornographic community beyond just turning viewers into consumers. Being able to see other users as an active part of the site suggests a type of continuity between site and user."[110] Presumably, this continuity enhances the user's sense of belonging to, and participation in, the pornographic communities Arroyo describes. The networked porn communities fostered by porn-streaming platforms (through, for example, free memberships, user profiles, and message functions, as described in chapter 2) enhances this sense of continuity, connection, and participation. Like any community, it also enhances or amplifies the norm-setting function of the platform.

Now consider the *production* of user-generated pornography. Clearly this too exemplifies a participatory element to contemporary pornography. As Arroyo writes, "[f]or those submitting videos to tube sites, their performance may be understood as part of a desire to take part in the wider circulation of pornographic affects."[111] (As an aside, this could also be said of those who produce [micro]porn.) Surely the production of user-generated amateur pornography, if motivated by a desire to "take part" in the digital world of porn, transcends the supposed divide between fantasy and reality. Recall from chapter 2 that users who upload videos to porn-streaming sites are likely to reproduce what they perceive to be the most popular content on these platforms.[112] In other words, these users record and upload videos of themselves, or others, replicating the sexual activity that they watch on porn-streaming platforms. For this subset of users, mainstream porn serves as a literal script. The fantasy/reality distinction can do very little, if any, analytical work with respect to this aspect of contemporary pornography.

Taken together, the participatory opportunities created by the platformization of mainstream porn challenge the supposed distinction between fact and fantasy. These participatory and interactive elements must be characterized as acts. Those who would reject MacKinnon's proposition that the consumption of pornography constitutes sex acts not thoughts must contend with the interactive and participatory elements of mainstream porn-streaming platforms – both in terms of the implications of these opportunities in their own right, and in terms of what they reveal about how pornography constitutes sexual norms more generally.

It is not that the participatory nature of porn on the platform renders individual users unable, in some novel manner, to distinguish between fantasy and reality, consciously or unconsciously. It is that the participatory opportunities on porn-streaming platforms make obvious the active character of porn consumption, and in doing so illuminate the untenability of the fantasy/reality distinction relied upon by some, including MacKinnon's critics, to deny pornography's social function. Not only that, platforms offer porn consumers new forms of participation, from directly interacting with women who appear in pornography, to virtual reality, point-of-view porn, to producing and disseminating porn themselves.

Consuming Porn and Shaping Norms in a World of Platform-Driven Sociality

The participatory nature of contemporary, mainstream pornography extends beyond micro(porn) producers and user-generated videos. Platforms enable a connectedness and thus a digital collectivity not possible prior to the emergence of Web 2.0.[113] As explained in chapters 2 and 3, the user interfaces, or "affordances" as they are sometimes called, on most platforms, including porn-streaming platforms, encourage user engagement and interaction.[114] Porn-streaming platforms market themselves as public infrastructure that allows users to form communities and that provides them with the mechanisms to contribute to, and interact in, these communities. As highlighted in the introduction to this chapter, the devices that platforms have developed to encourage user engagement and interaction, combined with the role that data plays in these online communities, do more than promote connectivity. They structure social interactions. As noted, and like porn itself, platforms are performative.[115] Platform mechanisms and the communities they constitute and promote create a type of platform-driven sociality that elevates mainstream pornography's contribution to sexual meaning making in our social environment.

Users on porn-streaming platforms continually establish and revise sexual norms through their interactions with one another, their activities on the platform, the data they provide to the platform, and their responses to the data that the platform provides back to them. Together, users and porn-streaming platforms constitute the social meaning attached to the content of the videos on a platform, as well as the content itself.

First let us examine the role of users. Each time a user rates, comments on, shares, or reports or fails to report a video on a platform, they create a data point for the company. Data, remember, function as the economic engine of porn-streaming platforms, but also inform decisions regarding the type of content on these platforms – this is the notion of data-driven creativity described in chapter 2. But these activities also contribute to the platform community's interpretation of the content in that video in a way that structures sexual norms. Each of these acts conveys to the platform community a user's perception of, or response to, the sexual depiction that they have just consumed. Similarly, each time a user chooses a title for and tags content that they then upload to the platform, they contribute to the community's interpretation of, and response to, the content in that video by contextualizing it for other users.

Even the act of clicking on, and viewing, a particular video contributes to the social meaning attached to its content, as well as the likelihood that similar content will be produced in the future. Watching a video increases the number of views that certain content receives – a data point that is revealed to other users and that may influence the content selection of other users. In addition, watching a video tells the platform what this user, or other users, may be willing to consume in the future.

Each of these platform activities might be characterized as an interpretive act that contributes to the formation of sexual norms regarding what is desirable, what is acceptable, and what is to be rejected. Together, the community's activities regarding the content in the pornography it consumes, structured through the platform's architecture, shape the social meaning of that content, and the content of future porn.

Now consider the platform's contributions. As already explained, platforms collect the activities of their users, such as how many views and the ratings a video receives, search activities, or whether a user who watches a video then clicks on the tags that direct them to other videos by the same performer or other videos with similar content, along with many other data points, to generate a massive volume of consumer information. The platform relies on some combination of the individual user's activities and an amalgamation of the activities of other users to determine what next to present to the user based on what the platform's confidential algorithm concludes is most likely to keep that user engaged.

While these determinations are particularized to each individual user based on how the platform categorizes them, the algorithms that make them are neither neutral nor benign.[116] As Safiya Umoja Noble demonstrates in *Algorithms of Oppression*, they reflect the values and biases (including race and gender biases) of the humans who design them.[117] A platform's algorithm and the human biases embedded in it contribute to the interpretation of, and production of, the content on that platform. Ariadna Matamoros-Fernández explains the ways in which the design and function of social media algorithms (in addition to user engagements with platform affordances, and the business policies and content moderation practices of platforms) shape and contribute to a form of "platformed racism" in which not only is racist discourse amplified by the platform, but racial inequality is reproduced through platform governance.[118] Algorithms shape and constitute social discourse and they do not do so in a neutral manner. A disproportionate number of the world's algorithms have been designed, built, and trained by affluent, White men.[119]

Data performs an additional function on platforms. As van Dijck, Poell, and de Waal note, "while datafication can be understood as a techno-commercial strategy deployed by platform owners, it can concurrently be regarded as a user practice."[120] Platforms reflect back to users a version of their interpretations in the form of data.[121] The authors observe that "[p]latforms systematically collect and analyze user data; they also constantly *circulate* these data to ... end users."[122] Porn-streaming platforms do this by reporting the number of views a video garners and its ratings. In addition, porn-streaming platforms publicize reports that include detailed data on the most popular search terms; the performers and categories of porn that are trending; the number of visitors they receive per day and year; the number of video uploads; the number of gigabytes of data streamed per second, hour, and day; the number of messages sent between users; the number of comments on videos; the videos with the most views; a breakdown of the type of porn consumption by city and country; the average number of minutes spent per user visit; and on and on.[123] This data informs the future platform activities of its users. In other words, a user's decision regarding what to search for or watch next is informed by the continual flow of data that the platform reflects back to the user.

Together, these user activities and platform functions continually establish, reinforce, validate, reject, and revise the social meaning of a porn-streaming platform's content, and define and categorize the user's characteristics and circulate them back to the user. In this way, norms about which sexual acts and bodies are desirable, what types of sexual activities are popular and among whom, how sexual activity is to proceed, and where the boundaries lie between appropriate and unacceptable sexual behaviour are constituted within, and reflected back to, the platform's community. As van Dijck, Poell, and de Waal explain in reference to platforms generally, platforms "trigger and filter user activity through interfaces and algorithms, while users, through their interaction with these coded environments, influence the online visibility and availability of particular content."[124] Those involved in the porn industry recognize the iterative, data-driven process through which the content of contemporary porn is constituted. In explaining the explosive demand for incest-themed porn (which is examined in the next chapter), Tasha Reign, a porn performer and director, comments, "[w]e are the supply to your demand ... all of us have a lot of power in creating content that paves the path for what is accepted and popular."[125] Together, users and platforms shape and reshape content, and the meaning ascribed to that content.

It is helpful to reflect on this phenomenon by focusing on an example. Consider again the search conducted on xHamster using the words "wake up" that I discussed in chapter 3. One of the other videos produced on the first page of results for this search was entitled "My Step-Father Loves to Fuck Me without Protection."[126]

The video begins with what appears to be a teenage girl or young woman asleep on her side, in a bed in a darkened room, under the covers, with her back to the camera. After a few seconds, a man's hands reach into the frame and begin rubbing her buttocks and lower back. She remains asleep. After a few more seconds, the man's mid-torso and erect penis enter the frame. He then places his hands on the young woman's buttocks again and she tries to sleepily push them away. After a few more seconds of him groping her body while she, in a seemingly semiconscious state, tries to push his hands away, he penetrates her vagina with his penis. At this point she appears to awaken and makes an ambiguous noise that could be interpreted as an expression of either pain or sexual pleasure. She is wearing a sleeping mask, and so her face is partially obscured, but her facial expression appears to be one of mild pain and displeasure. For the next several minutes the male performer penetrates her. Multiple times she places her hands on his stomach or legs and pushes at him, with only modest force. He responds by holding her arms down. At one point he briefly holds her down by the throat, again with only modest force. Throughout this latter part of the video she continues to make ambiguous noises, and her facial expression suggests she may be experiencing mild discomfort or slight pain. The video ends with a close-up of his penis ejaculating into, and on the exterior of, her vagina.

As of 12 September 2022, this video had been viewed over 81,000 times. Of those users who rated it, 99 per cent gave it a thumbs up. As with all videos on this site, this rating is indicated below the title of the video and the thumbnail image used to promote the video on the search results page. The video has several tags, including "Homemade," "Amateur sex," "Latina teen (18+)," "Latina amateur homemade," "Sex without condom," "Small boobs," "Step daughter," "Step father," "Stepfather," "Wake up," and "Wake up sex." Each of these tags can be clicked on to discover other videos on xHamster that share that tag. In this way the tags categorize the videos. For example, if you click on the tag "Step father," it directs you to a page with links to other videos categorized by the platform as "Step Father Porn Videos."[127]

One of the tags at the top of the screen is a link to a page which invites you to sign up for free to become a member of xHamster so that you can "save your favorites; enjoy video recommendations and sexting and post comments."[128] This page appears to include a running total of the number of users who have signed up to become members of xHamster. The number of members on 15 January 2022 was over 46 million and increased every few seconds. Three months later, on 8 April 2022, an additional 2.5 million users had signed up to be members of xHamster. By September 2022, membership had reached over 53 million.[129]

As of 15 January 2022, four users had left comments on the video for other users to read. Their comments were:

- "Good girl. Fight it but take it after all."
- "I can't even blame him for constantly fucking you, because I'll be STICKING AND DROPPING my dick in you every chance that I get lol. You are sexy as hell no cap!"
- "She pushed him aways, but her legs would open wider, what a good girl …"
- "My stepdaughter loved to fuck me! We started fucking after her mom put her on the pill at 16. And we were still fucking when she was 28. The only reason we stopped was her getting married."[130]

Let us start with the title chosen by the uploader of this video: "My Step-Father Loves to Fuck Me without Protection."[131] The choice of title contextualizes the sexual activity for the user. This influences the user's interpretation of what they view. As Eran Shor notes in his study comparing Pornhub videos featuring teenage performers and adult performers, "[w]hen a title promises that teenagers will be 'ravished,' 'destroyed,' or 'fucked hard,' this may affect … sexual scripts about what is considered acceptable/normative in having sex with young women and adolescents."[132] Vera-Gray et al. explain that "titles … [play] a key part in shaping understandings about what is and is not sexual, not necessarily what the user actually sees but *how* they are encouraged to make sense of it."[133] Titles help the user to interpret the video. The authors note that porn-streaming platforms themselves recognize the important interpretive function of these titles.[134] Pornhub, they observe, instructs uploaders to use the title to explain to users not simply what they will see but how they will see the content.

Titles also tell the user what to expect. The user in our example is told to expect a video of sex between, or the depiction of sex between, a stepfather and his stepdaughter, and that this sex will be without a condom. The user knows this before choosing to watch the video. Presumably, the title is part of the reason why he selects this video. Put otherwise, if the user clicks on the link and watches the video, he knows he has selected for himself a video that purports to depict a stepfather "fucking" his stepdaughter without a condom. He also knows that 81,000 other users have made the same choice. He is not alone.

What else does he learn from his community of users? He learns that nearly every one of the users who rated this depiction of a stepfather groping his sleeping stepdaughter, holding her down, and penetrating her gave this video a thumbs up. The ratings, the fact that 81,000 other users viewed this video, and that it remains posted on the site indicate to him that none of the other users seemed to have objected to the video or reported it to the platform on the basis that it depicted non-consensual sexual activity. Perhaps he assumes from this that very few, if any, of these 81,000 users identified this as a depiction of sexual assault, or that if they did identify it as such this did not deter them from viewing the video. Perhaps *he* fails to identify the video as a depiction of sexual assault. Recall the disjuncture, discussed in chapter 3, between the purported prohibition of non-consensual depictions of sexual activity by mainstream porn-streaming platforms and the content on these sites. Recall the research indicating that a majority of users report having never, or seldom, seen depictions in pornography that they interpreted as non-consensual.[135]

When a user tags a video that they have uploaded, they influence how subsequent users will respond cognitively and physically to its content.[136] The tags tell the user what features of the video the uploader considers important. The same is true when a platform permits a search term that produces pages of content entitled "Step-father porn videos." Our hypothetical user sees that this video has been tagged as "Homemade," "Amateur," "Amateur Latina homemade," "Latina teen (18+)," "Step father" "Step daughter," and "Wake up." This may tell him that what he watched was not made in a professional studio and that the young woman in the video is a teenaged Latina girl. While the video itself appears to be an effort at creating the amateur aesthetic already discussed and is not obviously fictional, it is evident from other aspects of the presentation, such as links to the female performer's other videos and a reference to her website, that it is a fictional depiction. And so the user may notice the link to the female performer's other videos and conclude that while this was not actually an amateur video, whoever uploaded it wanted users to think or imagine that this was a homemade video featuring a Latina teenager. Our user learns from these tags that this is supposed to be a depiction of a stepfather perpetrating sexual acts on his stepdaughter while she is asleep, and that the uploader thinks other users will want to find other videos that depict stepfathers engaging in sexual acts on their stepdaughters while they sleep. Like titles, the tags selected by the uploader aid the user in how to make sense of the video. He also learns from these tags that the depiction of sex between stepfathers and stepdaughters is a genre of porn on this platform. He might think to himself that there must be a lot of people who like to watch depictions of stepfathers "fucking" their stepdaughters.

If the user scrolls down to read the comments after watching this video, he will learn that other users find this teenager "sexy as hell." He discovers that other users think she is a "good girl" because she put up a fight but then opened her legs "wider" and took "it after all."[137] He learns that, from the perspective of these users, following the stereotypical heterosexual script of female resistance in response to male sexual aggression, followed by female acquiescence, made her a "good girl," and that this seemed to be arousing for these users.[138] It seemed to please them. (Of note, girls and women who watch this video and read these comments will also learn that these users found it arousing and pleasing to see a depiction of a young woman initially resisting but then acquiescing to sexual acts initiated while she was asleep.)

Our hypothetical user will learn that one of the men who commented on the video claims his "stepdaughter loved to fuck" him and that she did so for many years. If he believes this user's claim to be true then he will have discovered that this man engaged in sexual acts with his teenage stepdaughter for years and that his stepdaughter loved "fucking" him, or at least this man thinks that to be the case. If he believes this man is fabricating his claim then presumably the user still learns that this man considers it appropriate, or arousing, or reputation enhancing, or perhaps funny to tell the xHamster community that he "fucked" his stepdaughter for years.

If the user views the videos and reads the comments on some of the other videos featured on the first page of search results using the words "wake up," he will find other users who connect the sexual acts depicted in the videos with claims about their real-life sexual activities.[139] He will learn that the comments on videos that purport to depict fathers engaging in sexual acts with teenage daughters or stepdaughters, or brothers engaging in sexual acts with sisters or stepsisters, frequently include claims by users to have themselves engaged in sexual acts with their daughters, or sisters, or to know of others who have done so, or who claim a strong desire to do so in the future.[140] Recall the xHamster video, described in chapter 2, that depicts a young man surreptitiously groping and penetrating a teenage girl who is presented as his sleeping sister. One of the users who commented in response to that video claimed to have woken his "little sister up that way many times when [they] were teens."[141] Similar comments can be readily discovered in response to other videos on the site depicting this type of content:

- "I have three daughters the youngest one, shes [sic] 28 now but when she was 19, and back for the summer fromn collage [sic], wanted me to pop her cherry, it was great, i fucked my daughter."
- "I'd love to absolutely destroy my daughter's pussy and asshole!!"
- "if she was my step daughter I'd have to fuck her no doubt"
- "I have talked with so many women who admit they were getting it on with daddy growing up willingly."
- "There is no reason a man shouldn't fuck his stepdaughter, especially if she is a small tittied cutie like this little blonde piece"
- "My pretty brunette stepdaughter had small, but nice tits, and a little bush on her sweet pussy, and NO shitty tattoo's [sic]. And she loved to walk around the house in her bra & panties when her mom wasn't home, we fucked many times"[142]

Whether such comments reflect these other users' actual life experiences or their fantasies, they contribute normatively to the interpretation of the content on the platform.

As Nadine Desrochers and Daniel Apollon write regarding the function that these platform activities and the data they reflect back to users produce (what they describe as "paratext"):

[t]hese statistics and comments from user-generated peritextual elements literally frame the films of Pornhub. Such user contributions give these texts a significant, and essential, new meaning: legitimacy

… Users are assured that they are indulging in a titillating activity in which millions of other people are unashamedly engaged.[143]

Having considered what the platform and community of users communicates to, and how they interpret this video for, our hypothetical user, we must now ask how this user's platform activities will contribute to how other users interpret this video. What does he tell his community of users about this video? Even if all he does is watch it – even if he does not rate it, does not comment on it, does not share it, does not click on the performer's profile or any of the tags – he tells the platform's algorithm that this is content he will watch, content he will not flag as inappropriate or in violation of the platform's user agreement. The platform will rely on this information, in part, to determine what type of content to next present to this user.

Even if all our user does is watch this video, he adds to its number of views. The next user who clicks on this link will learn that 81,001 members of his porn-streaming community chose to watch a video depiction of a stepfather "fucking" his stepdaughter without a condom while she was asleep, and that these 81,001 users did not flag this video for the platform or for other users as a depiction of sexual assault, or if they did the platform did not respond by removing the video because it was in breach of the company's policy on non-consensual content.

Now think about what our hypothetical user contributes if, after watching the video, he gives it a thumbs up, comments positively on it, shares it with other users, or clicks on the tags associated with it and consumes other videos with similar content. Each of these acts contributes to the meaning ascribed to this video: sex with one's teenage stepdaughter is arousing; penetrating a teenage girl without a condom and ejaculating in and on her makes a sexual interaction more exciting, as does her physical resistance, her initial state of unconsciousness, and the fact that she is Latina. The community of users who consume this video provide implicit and explicit peer support to other users who choose to view the video. It is okay to be aroused by, and masturbate to, this depiction of sexual assault. Lots of men fuck, want to fuck, or like thinking about fucking their daughters and/or stepdaughters. Sexual norms within the community are established, re-visited, revised, and reified.

Finally, consider what the platform does with all of this data. These user contributions are shaped into the categories maintained by the platform's infrastructure – categories which are intended to serve the corporate ends of the company. As Desrochers and Apollon note: "instead of the users re-shaping the texts to better reflect their desires, their desires come to be defined by what a porn site offers … in their tagging, commenting and uploading, [users] are simply legitimising and bolstering the values and attitudes of [the platform]."[144] The result: a set of values and attitudes aimed at ensuring a stable, predictable, and marketable product that can be "commercially controlled."[145]

While it is true that men could always share stacks of *Playboy* or *Hustler*, discuss particular movies with friends, or make recommendations to co-workers, the opportunities for pornography consumers to connect with others, to share in their experiences and interpretations of pornographic depictions, to provide implicit – and sometimes explicit – peer support for the pornography they consume, and to collectively shape, and be shaped by, the content of mainstream pornography vastly outnumber those from an era in which most mainstream porn was made by professional studios or publishers using professional performers and distributed in a manner similar to other types of movies and magazines.

Likewise, gathering consumer preference data on one's audience is not a new business model for media companies. But the ability to do it with such precision and in such detail, and to analyze that data and tailor the promotion of content based on it in real time, is a business tool that was not available to Hugh Hefner or Larry Flynt but is very much relied upon by companies like Pornhub and xHamster.[146] As technology and communications scholars have observed, the breadth and depth of corporate data collection in a digital era is different in kind, not just in quantity.[147]

Conclusion

Pornography, both in its consumption and in its production, is a cultural practice. Platformization has made this if not more true, then at a minimum more apparent. As is the case with other practices in which people in a community commonly participate, widespread participation in pornography helps to shape a community's norms. As an analogy, compare norms related to the relationship between human and non-human animals in a community in which many or most of its members are hunters, farmers, or ranchers, with those in a community in which very few participate in hunting, farming, or ranching. Norms related to the consumption of animal flesh, or the degree to which non-human animals are treated as members of the family by humans, are likely to be different in these two communities. This analogy is, of course, only partial because unlike participation in hunting or ranching, there is a complex public/private dynamic to one's engagement with pornography, and a complicated relationship between pornography, desire, shame, and stigma – as there often is when it comes to sex.

Clarissa Smith and Feona Attwood observe that common sense has sometimes problematically been relied upon in the context of porn debates as sufficient to establish academic claims.[148] While accepting that common sense alone is not adequate to ground empirical claims, we are not required in our engagements with this topic, as with any other, to refuse ourselves rational logic. It would be odd to assume that the capacity of platforms to draw a wide swath of a community's members into an interactive, quasi-participatory engagement with porn has no impact on that community's sexual norms – just as it would be surprising to discover that veganism is as common in hunting and farming communities as it is in highly urban settings.

Arguably, participation augments the capacity of a particular activity to serve as a resource relied upon to guide practices and help us understand our social world. In this sense, the participatory opportunities created by porn-streaming platforms, like the prolific growth in porn consumption that platformization facilitated, elevate the role of pornography as one of the resources in our social environment relied upon to develop and refine norms regarding sexuality, notions of desire, the manner in which sexual activity proceeds, and the parameters of acceptable sexual behaviour: our sexual scripts.

It is not necessary to demonstrate that men who consume porn go on to act out in "real life" what they masturbate to online, in order to accept that pornography, depending on what it depicts, has problematic social consequences. While causal or even correlative claims seem impossible to prove, surely it is wrong to assert that the widespread consumption of and participation in porn has no social impact. Our social and cultural engagements with pornography, like our practices connected to language, art, food, work, and family, have constitutive impacts on our social environment.

An assessment of pornography's social impact that focuses on how porn contributes to social understandings of sexuality and sexual norms should help to avoid claims about the effect of porn consumption on the beliefs or behaviours of specific individuals. Instead, it raises questions about the potential adverse effect of some pornography on legal and social systems, cultural norms, sexual scripts, and relationship dynamics. For instance, how does mainstream pornography's depiction of female sexual passivity followed by acquiescence to male persistence inform understandings of what it means to be heterosexual? In what ways does prolific consumption of mainstream pornography that relies on racist tropes assist in replicating or reinforcing discriminatory power structures that already exist? Are workplace gender dynamics affected in male-dominated offices with coworkers who watch videos before coming to work of multiple men ejaculating on a woman's face? Or who watch such videos in the office once they get to work? How are familial relationships or parenting styles affected in a community in which many of its members masturbate to videos that purport to depict men having sex with their daughters and stepdaughters? In a community in which this is common, does this shape whether suspected cases of intra-family child sexual abuse are reported, or by whom? Are adult stepdaughters in such communities less, or more, likely to be believed by their family and friends, or by the legal system, when they accuse their stepfathers of sexual assault? How does this practice impact the way a community educates its children about sexuality? Similarly, are sexual assault complainants who allege that they did not consent to sexual activity that was initiated while they were asleep or passed out less likely to be believed by healthcare workers, law enforcement, judges, and educational institutions in communities in which "wake-up porn" is widely consumed? Before we can attempt to address questions of this sort, we need to consider more closely the content of mainstream pornography. What are some of mainstream porn's contributions to our sexual scripts?

This chapter demonstrates that porn is one of the resources in our social environment from which sexual meaning is shaped, that it is not merely or only representational, and that its platformization has rendered more visible, and perhaps enhanced, both the connotative and constitutive aspects of its social function. The next two chapters consider some of the sexual norms mainstream porn is helping to shape, reinforce, and reject, and what this might mean for law. Chapter 5 examines the incredible popularity of incest-themed porn on mainstream porn-streaming platforms, and the replication of the sexual scripts in a subset of this genre of porn that appear to also inform the offending patterns of sexually abusive (step)fathers and (step)brothers, as well as those represented in child sexual abuse material. Chapter 6 assesses the relationship between the sexual scripts that dominate mainstream pornography and the legal "rough sex" scripts that appear to inform some contemporary sexual assault prosecutions: the so-called rough sex defence to allegations of sexual assault.

CHAPTER 5

The Problems with Incest-Themed Porn

I think this stuff is hot, and it's important to normalize it.[1]
— porn performer Tasha Reign on incest-themed porn

Depictions of men penetrating their "stepdaughters" vaginally and anally, of brothers ejaculating on their sisters' faces, or of stepsons convincing their stepmothers to fellate them have gone mainstream. The consumption of incest-themed pornography is not an anomalous phenomenon indulged in by a niche market. Rather, portrayals of sexual activity between family members have become a mainstay of contemporary mainstream pornography. Almost half of the most popular online mainstream pornography consumed in New Zealand, according to a 2019 government study, involved depictions of sex between (step)parents and their (step)children, or between (step)siblings.[2] Indeed, according to the Government of New Zealand, 43 per cent of the most popular videos on Pornhub in New Zealand involve incest-themed porn.[3]

New Zealand is not an outlier. According to Pornhub's annual reports, of the several billion searches conducted on the platform every year, searches related to mothers and sisters are among the most frequent.[4] For instance, Pornhub reported twenty-five billion searches on its platform in 2017; "step sister" was the fifth most common search performed that year; "step mom" and "mom" were the fourth and sixth most frequently searched words.[5] In early 2022, Pornhub advised its content partners – porn studios that the platform partners with by driving traffic to the studios' paid sites in exchange for a portion of their revenues – that "step mom" was trending and was the number one search term, with "step sister" at number two. The platform urged partnered studios to upload videos with content related to these search terms as soon as possible.[6]

According to one study, "daughter" is the sixth most common role for female porn performers and "sister" is the tenth most common role.[7] Another study reveals that the words "mom" or "mother" are present in the titles of 37 of the 100 most watched videos on xHamster.[8]

While incest-themed pornography is not a new phenomenon, its growth in popularity in the last ten years has been exponential.[9] Far from relegation to some deep corner of the dark web, incest-themed porn has become one of the most popular and common genres of pornography available on mainstream porn platforms. What explains its increased popularity?

For starters, porn-streaming platforms have been actively involved in presenting incest-themed porn as popular and mainstream. Indeed, depictions of sexual activity between family members are prominently marketed on the landing pages of these sites.[10] Porn producer Bree Mills explains the radical growth in demand for incest-themed porn:

> I think [porn websites] were able to spot trends in family role play, pump out a lot of content that met that demand, and then put that into all of their advertising, which influenced what people were watching … It became a closed loop – go to Pornhub and all the ads are about family stuff. That helped propel it to the mass popular interest it is now.[11]

Others in the porn industry both agree that incest-themed porn has become incredibly common, and echo Mills's explanation for why this has occurred.[12] Commenting on the popularity of incest-themed porn, performer and director Tasha Reign notes, "What we create has a lot to do with what is popular. It is a business. But all of us have a lot of power in creating content that paves the path for what is accepted and popular."[13]

As the demand for this type of pornography grows, so too does production, which, given the functionality of platforms, creates further demand.

This exponential growth in the production and consumption of incest-themed porn exemplifies the iterative, data-driven process through which the content of porn on the platform is shaped, as described in chapters 3 and 4. It also exemplifies the homogenizing effect that this process has on the content of contemporary mainstream porn. As performer Whitney Wright commented in a 2018 interview for *Esquire* magazine, "You can ask any young female performer what bookings she has this month, and she'll tell you she's playing 17 step-daughters."[14] Some professional performers who in the past refused to do this type of porn, regularly find themselves performing these roles today; others suggest that their refusal to perform these roles has meant a reduction in work opportunities.[15] Porn performer Ashley Fires reportedly stated, while on a 2016 panel on the topic, that the high demand for incest-themed porn led her to let go of the reservations she had about appearing in videos that depict blood-related family members having sex.[16] "Now, I'm fucking my 'son' all the time," she commented.[17]

Oddly, the popularity of producing and consuming incest-themed porn has not inspired a robust academic engagement with this type of pornography. For example, *Porn Studies*, an interdisciplinary journal created in 2014 and dedicated to the work of scholars who study porn, has no articles that examine the popularity of incest-themed porn. In fact, I could find only thirty-five articles in total (out of 388 at the time of writing) that even mention incest.[18] Even content-based research specifically focused on the depiction of relationships in mainstream porn does not address portrayals of intra-family sexual activity.[19] The dearth of scholarship on incest-themed porn is both puzzling and unfortunate. This genre of mainstream pornography raises important issues. Two of them will be addressed in this chapter: first, public discourse on incest-themed porn typically fails to acknowledge the degree to which it eroticizes not simply incestuous sexual activity but incestuous sexual violence; and second, incest-themed porn frequently replicates the same sexual scripts reflected in the offending patterns of sexually abusive fathers and brothers, and that are also represented in child pornography. Mainstream porn's eroticization of incestuous sexual violence and reification of sexual scripts that tend to operate in the context of intra-family sexual offences are an important aspect of contemporary pornography's social function.

Public Discourse about Incest Porn: It's All about Fantasy and Taboo

While consideration of this type of sexually explicit material is largely absent from scholarly discourse, mainstream media and pop culture have taken stock of the increased popularity of incest-themed pornography.[20] However, there are problematic aspects to the way this genre of porn is typically portrayed in pop culture and mainstream media. For instance, it is sometimes characterized as a niche genre aimed at serving those with a particular fetish.[21] As just demonstrated, the demand for, and consumption of, incest-themed porn is not limited to a niche market; it is a staple of mainstream pornography widely consumed by general porn audiences.

Perhaps more importantly, public commentary on incest-themed pornography is almost never straightforward about the actual content in a significant subset of this type of porn. It is often described as humorous or silly. The following description typifies this characterization: "As a quick browse of the most-viewed videos on any tube site will show, fauxcest is typically shot in a schlocky, fluffy, comical manner – a busty step-mom helping her step-son with homework or a step-daughter in pigtails spanked by her step-dad for failing school."[22] In fact, this characterization of the genre fails to capture an important and seemingly prominent subset of incest-themed porn: content that depicts the sexual assault of girls, boys, and young women by their (step)fathers and (step)brothers. Layered on to the incest theme in many of the videos in this genre of porn are depictions of intra-family non-consensual sexual activity. Instead of reckoning with this aspect of incest-themed porn, those who write about it often frame it as titillating because of societal taboos about incest.[23] Mainstream media typically fails to address the degree to which incest-themed porn eroticizes not only the taboo of incest but also the sexual assault of family members.

Indeed, as will be examined next, in a prominent subset of this type of porn the narrative device used to create a sexual charge is not the taboo of incest per se but rather the depiction of child sexual abuse and the sexual assault of incapacitated teenage girls and young women. Public commentary that does make reference to, or acknowledge in some manner, the violent aspect of incest-themed porn as a genre typically does so in veiled language with references to its "edgy" or "dark" side rather than through consideration of its non-consensual nature.[24]

In addition, incest-themed porn is often characterized in public discourse as pure fantasy, something that those who consume it would never want to do in real life.[25] As Reign offers in her comments on incest porn, "There are many things we like to watch that we would never want to do in our personal lives ... I think that's what is positive about the adult industry: We give you an outlet to channel these feelings in a safe environment."[26] This type of content is often framed as an effort to push boundaries, to "depict the very outer edges of sexual behavior."[27] Discussions of V.C. Andrews's novel *Flowers in the Attic* – which involved graphic descriptions of an incestuous (and initially violent) relationship between siblings locked in an attic for years by their mother – exemplifies this type of public commentary.[28] In a 2014 article on the appeal of the book's incest theme, James Twitchell asserted: "It's one of the few things along with cannibalism that we don't have any interest in doing, but we have a great interest in reading about ... or watching ... onscreen."[29] In these accounts, incest-themed porn is fantastical and actual incest "unthinkable."[30]

In the same vein, recent media articles have tried to explain the increased popularity of porn that depicts family members having sex by pointing to the portrayals of incest found in the popular television series *Game of Thrones*.[31] This is an inapt and problematic comparison. *Game of Thrones* is set in the fantastical land of Westeros, in which royal members of society marry their siblings in order to keep their blood line pure so as to maintain their ability to control dragons.[32] Yes, dragons. The depictions of sexual activity between family members found on porn-streaming platforms bear little, if any, resemblance to the incest themes found in *Game of Thrones*. As explained next, depictions of incest on porn-streaming platforms are more likely to resemble the offending patterns of men who sexually assault their daughters and stepdaughters, and brothers who sexually assault their sisters and stepsisters, than the fantastical royal marriages depicted in *Game of Thrones* (or the elaborate incestuous rape plot in *Flowers in the Attic*). In addition, efforts to attribute the explosive popularity of incest-themed porn to pop culture trends like *Game of Thrones* rarely include a key aspect of the incestuous sexual activity depicted on the television series: much of it, too, was rape.[33] Characterizations of incest-themed pornography that invoke analogies or references to the television series *Game of Thrones* exemplify precisely the problems with the way in which this genre of porn is frequently portrayed in public discourse: the coercive and violent nature of many of the incestuous interactions depicted are obscured, and the myth of pure fantasy is promoted.

Teenage girls are more likely to be sexually assaulted than any other demographic.[34] In the United States over 30 per cent of sexual assaults are perpetrated against teenagers between the ages of eleven and seventeen – the vast majority of these teenagers are female.[35] As many as one in four American girls have experienced sexual assault by the age of seventeen.[36] Not only are teenage girls more likely to be sexually assaulted than any other demographic, research suggests that these assaults are often perpetrated against them by male family members.[37] Studies indicate that the latter is also true with respect to children.[38] Indeed, a high percentage of sexual assaults against children and teenage girls occur in the victim's home.[39] In addition, some research indicates that the harmful effects of child sexual abuse are aggravated when the abuse involves incest.[40]

Law professors Janine Benedet and Isabel Grant conducted a study of over six hundred reported judicial decisions in Canada over a three-year period involving prosecutions of sexual assault against teenage girls between the ages of twelve and seventeen.[41] They found that in almost half of all cases the accused was a male family member of the complainant, and that in more than 25 per cent of sexual assault prosecutions in which the complainant was a teenage girl, the accused was the girl's biological, adoptive, step, or foster father.[42]

While less is known regarding rates of sibling sexual assault, it is clear that the most common form involves brothers sexually assaulting sisters and that this type of sexual offence is also far from rare.[43] In a 2017 study of university students in Portugal, 11 per cent of male students reported engaging in sexually coercive behaviour towards their siblings during their childhood.[44] Some research suggests a relationship between this type of sibling abuse and patriarchal families in which male members are accorded more power.[45]

Again, incest is often constructed in public discourse as taboo and unthinkable, and incest porn as pure fantasy.[46] But for a vast number of children, teenage girls, and young women, sexual activity (and in particular non-consensual sexual activity) with their fathers, stepfathers, brothers, and stepbrothers is very real. For them, sexual activity between family members may be unspeakable, but it is very likely not unthinkable. Indeed, there is reason to believe that this is the case. The difficulty and length of time it takes for survivors of sexual assault perpetrated against them by parents, particularly those who live with them, is well documented.[47] Rates of reporting for sibling sexual assault are even lower.[48] Incest may be indescribable, unreported, kept secret, for many children, adolescents, and young women – but for them, it is tragically real. Public discourse about incest-themed porn that perpetuates the notion that its erotic charge comes simply from its taboo nature, and that actual incest is unthinkable, is both inaccurate and harmful, for reasons not the least of which include because it is certain to contribute to the barriers which make it so difficult for survivors of intra-family sexual abuse to report (and thus access social services or the modest legal protections available), and because it is so common for us not to believe them when they do come forward.

Considering the Content of Incest-Themed Porn on the Platform

There are fantastical and/or comical incest-themed videos on platforms like Pornhub and xHamster. There are videos that depict consensual incestuous sexual activity between adults. There are many videos that invoke an incest theme through either the title or a line or two at the beginning of the video, but which are otherwise indistinguishable from non-incest-themed porn.[49] However, a prominent subset of this genre of mainstream porn draws on narrative devices that, far from campy and silly, instead replicate the relationship dynamics, the factual settings, the grooming patterns, and the power imbalances that facilitate, perpetuate, and conceal the sexual assault of children, teenagers, and young women by their family members. Videos in this latter category are not relying on the theme of incest as a "simple and expedient way to introduce a 'taboo' element to an otherwise simplistic porn narrative."[50] These videos are relying on narratives of child sexual abuse, rape, and the sexual assault of sleeping or unconscious teens to create an erotic charge.

So, how common are depictions of non-consensual sexual activity in incest-themed porn on the platform?

In its study of digital pornography, the government of New Zealand found that videos on Pornhub involving incest themes were more likely to include depictions of non-consensual sexual activity than videos generally.[51] The study also indicated that "[e]ven when consent is clearly established and given without pressure or coercion, the narratives tend to raise problematic issues around power dynamics and inappropriate sexual behaviour within a family context."[52]

One of the challenges with assessing more precisely the degree to which the incest-themed pornography found on mainstream porn-streaming platforms involves depictions of non-consensual sexual acts is that very few of the content-based studies of porn, by those who are either anti-porn or pro-porn, have focused on incest-themed material. Indeed, as noted, academic consideration of incest-themed porn generally is extremely sparse, and research on mainstream sexually explicit material that eroticizes not simply the taboo of incest but also, or rather, the sexual assault of family members is almost non-existent.[53] As discussed in chapter 6, content analysis research on all sides of the porn debate tends to focus on depictions of aggression. The definition of aggression articulated by content analysis researchers, even those who do not employ a consent-based demarcation, rarely explicitly includes depictions of incest, unless such depictions incorporate some other form of aggression.[54] This challenge is compounded by the difficulty, as an individual researcher, of ascertaining the frequency of any particular type of content on porn-streaming platforms. Platforms begin to gather data about users from the moment they visit the site. Subsequent to that first visit, videos presented to a user either on the platform's landing site or in response to a search are algorithmically determined based, in part, on whatever data has been gathered. This makes it difficult to draw empirical conclusions about what proportion of videos on a given platform contain particular content, such as, for instance, depictions of non-consensual sexual activity between family members.

One exception to this observation is a recent British study conducted by Vera-Gray et al. These researchers examined the titles of videos most likely to be advertised to first-time users on the landing pages of porn-streaming platforms like xHamster, Pornhub, and XVideos. They developed a software-based methodology which produced a sample of 150,000 video titles that appeared on the landing pages of these platforms over a specified period of time prior to a user having interacted with any of these sites.[55] In other words, they were able to create a sample of the video links provided to a user on each of these platforms before a platform had gathered any data about the user's viewing practices and preferences. They found that one in eight video titles on these platforms described a form of sexual violence, and that references to sexual acts between family members was the most common form of sexual violence promoted to first-time users in the titles of videos on the landing pages of these platforms.[56] While their study does not tell us what proportion of incest-themed content on porn-streaming platforms generally includes depictions of sexual assault or other sexual offences, it does indicate that such portrayals are commonly marketed to new users.

The videos discussed in this chapter appeared on, or were linked to videos that appeared on, the first two pages of results on Pornhub and xHamster when I conducted searches using basic terms like "(step)father," "(step)-brother," "(step)sister," "(step)daughter," and "(step)mom." These latter three terms are ones that the platforms themselves report on in their annual announcements as among the most popular in the past several years. I also conducted related searches by relying on the autofill function provided by the platform. For example, typing the letters "s-t-e-p-d" in the search function on Pornhub produces the suggested search "Stepdad Fucks Step-daughter." Some of the videos included in this chapter involve incest-themed porn that appeared in the first two pages of results when I conducted searches using the term "wake up," discussed in chapter 3.

This methodology is subject to the vulnerabilities that come with any content-based research on these platforms (other than that which employs the type of software-based methodology used by Vera-Gray et al.) and thus cannot be relied upon to make definitive claims about prevalence. That said, neither can the content that appears at or near the top of search results, using popular incest-themed search terms or terms taken from the metadata connected to the most popular videos using these terms, be dismissed as anomalous or extraordinary. The depictions of sexual violence described in the next section of this chapter are, indeed, reflective of some of the content that a user is presented with when they search for porn using the most popular terms and prominent metadata on mainstream porn-streaming platforms.

So then, what do porn videos with this type of content portray?

Sister/Stepsister Porn and the Sexual Assault of Incapacitated Teenagers

Consider first the example of sister/stepsister pornography. As noted, "step sister" is among the most popular searches performed on mainstream porn-streaming platforms.[57] Many of the videos produced on the first two pages of search results on mainstream porn platforms, using the term "sister" or "step sister," have titles that are silly or humorous, such as "Truth or Dare with Hot Step Sister."[58] Some of these videos depict sexual activity between adult stepsiblings that appears to be consensual and non-exploitative.[59] But using either of these terms – "sister" or "step sister" – also produces videos with titles that imply or describe sexual assaults, such as "My Little Step Sister Lets Me Do Everything," "Step-Father Demands Me to Fuck My Step-Sister… in Front of Him," and "Accidently Woke Up My Step Sister with My Dick."[60] Moreover, it is not only that these types of titles suggest or describe sexual assault and/or rape; many of the videos with such titles in fact depict sexual offences.[61]

The most common depiction of sexual assault in stepsister and sister videos on Pornhub and xHamster feature men surreptitiously entering the bedroom of a (seemingly) teenage girl and engaging in sexual acts while she is (depicted as) asleep or unconscious. In some of the videos the teenage girl is depicted as asleep or unconscious throughout all of the sexual activity captured in the video. In other videos, she "awakens" at some point (typically following repeated penetration) and becomes an active participant. Videos of this nature, such as "Step Sister Gets Woken Up by a Hard Cock," "Step Sister Woke Up When She Felt a Dick," and "Step Sister with Perfect Ass Woke Up When I Fucked Her," have been viewed hundreds of thousands, and in some instances millions, of times on platforms like Pornhub and xHamster.[62] Such videos typically receive very high approval ratings.[63]

A video on Pornhub entitled "My Little Stepsister Lets Me Do Everything" provides an example of this type of content.[64] The video is shot from the male subject's point of view. It starts with him entering the darkened room of a "sleeping" teenage girl. He pulls the bedcovers off of her, takes her hand, and places it around his penis. She remains unconscious. He then begins to grope her and insert his penis into her mouth and vagina. She is unresponsive and motionless as he repeatedly penetrates her vagina and mouth with his penis. She is depicted as unconscious or asleep, until the very end of this video (which is twelve minutes and forty-three seconds long), at which point her mouth partially opens and he ejaculates onto her face.[65]

An xHamster video entitled simply "Step-Sister" depicts virtually the same scenario. A young man enters the bedroom of his sleeping "step sister" and begins masturbating and touching her to see if she is awake. She remains "asleep" or "unconscious" on her stomach while he touches her, removes his clothing, and then climbs on top of her. He penetrates her vagina for nearly six minutes before she begins to "wake up."[66] This video had been viewed over six million times and had a 99 per cent approval rating.

A similar Pornhub video entitled "Stepbro Surprises Stepsis with Cock in Her Mouth," produced using these same search terms, also begins with a point-of-view shot of a man entering a darkened room in which a teenage girl or young woman is depicted as asleep on the bed.[67] He removes her bedcovers and hovers over her while standing near the bed masturbating. He then rubs his erect penis on her face and presses it to her mouth until she "wakes up" and begins to perform fellatio on him.[68]

The depictions of sexual assault in these videos are representative of the type of non-consensual sexual activity portrayed in several of the videos produced on the first two pages of search results on these platforms using the terms "wake up," "sister," or "step sister." In other words, a search using any of these terms yields multiple videos that depict brothers sneaking into their sisters' or stepsisters' bedrooms to grope and/or penetrate them while they are depicted as sleep or unconscious (at least initially). While the proportion of sister and stepsister videos that depict sexual offences is unknown, it would appear that these videos are not uncommon.

The legal definition of consent to sexual touching varies. However, criminal laws across jurisdictions consistently prohibit sexual contact with someone who is asleep, unconscious, or otherwise incapacitated.[69] While the videos I have just described seem to be either professionally produced or simulated amateur performances, suggesting the female performers appearing in them were not actually asleep, these portrayals of men entering the bedrooms of sleeping or unconscious teenage girls and young women, removing their clothing, touching their genitals, and penetrating them, are inarguably depictions of sexual assault and rape. Videos in which women are in fact unconscious or asleep when sexual touching is imposed upon them would be, of course, recordings of actual sexual offences.

Daughter/Stepdaughter Porn and Child Sexual Assault

Like (step)sister porn, some mainstream (step)daughter pornography also features depictions of men surreptitiously entering the bedrooms of sleeping girls, teenagers, or young women and engaging in sexual acts upon them. Conducting searches on Pornhub and xHamster yielded videos with titles such as: "Waking Up Stepdaughter with a Cock Inside Her," "Ahh Ahh Don't Scream! Stepdaughter Gets Fucked by Her Stepdad While She Was Taking a Nap," and "Daddy Dominates Stepdaughter While She Is Resting."[70]

In addition to depictions of (step)fathers sexually assaulting their (step)-daughters while they are asleep or unconscious, using the search term "daughter" or "step daughter" also yielded videos with an additional sexual assault theme that is not as prominent in results using the term "sister" or "step sister."[71] Some videos on the first two pages of search results on these platforms using the term "daughter" or "step daughter" depict fathers engaging in sexual acts with teenage girls or young women who are portrayed as children.[72]

Consider the following example from a video on the first page of search results, using the term "step daughter," on xHamster. The video is entitled "Daughter Creampied by Stepfather in Her Bedroom."[73] It is filmed from the point of view of the male subject. It is filmed in a room staged as a little girl's bedroom, on a bed with purple sheets, a bright childlike comforter, and Lego and a lollipop on the nightstand beside the bed. Asleep in the bed is a teenager or young woman holding a large pink stuffed animal. She is wearing knee-high socks with pink stripes and onesie pyjamas with a rainbow heart on the front and a snap at the crotch, like the type worn by infants, and toddlers still in diapers. The pink teddy bear she is clutching and the hood on her pyjamas cover her face, making it difficult to discern her precise age.[74]

After creeping into the room, the male subject pulls the covers back and touches her, eventually groping her breasts. He wraps her hand around his penis and moves it up and down. She remains "asleep." He unfastens the snap on her pyjamas which reveals her hairless genitals. She is portrayed as asleep until six minutes and forty-five seconds into the video, when he says, "Wake up, there you go, good girl, good morning," and whispers to her, "We need to be quiet, okay?"[75] He penetrates her vagina with his penis while repeatedly saying "shhh" as she starts to moan. After he ejaculates while penetrating her vagina, he tells her she is a good girl and again quiets her as one would a young child. He then tucks her teddy bear in beside her, puts her blankets back over her, and leaves the room. At the time the search was conducted, this video had been viewed 802,440 times and had a 99 per cent approval rating.[76]

A similar video on xHamster, on the first page of search results using the term "step daughter," entitled "Stepfather Gets Stepdaughter Pregnant with Accidental Creampie," is also set in a little girl's bedroom.[77] A teenage girl or young woman in pigtails, wearing a pink tank top and little girl underwear with a unicorn on them, is lying on the bed. She is holding a stuffed animal. The video begins with her reading aloud using a childish voice, reading slowly such as would commonly be associated with someone who has just learned to read:

> Dear Diary. Today I found out that I am pregnant. It all started a few weeks ago when Mommy was at work and Daddy came to wake me for dinner. We snuggled like we normally do and we used protection so I don't know what went wrong.[78]

The video then cuts to the point of view of a male subject who reaches out a hand and opens a bedroom door to reveal this teenage girl or young woman "sleeping." He peers in and begins masturbating. He then enters the room, shakes her, and says, "Scarlet, are you asleep?" She does not awake. He says, "Perfect," and starts rubbing her body while whispering, "Daddy's little girl is sleeping." He pulls down her unicorn underwear and she rolls over. He says, "Shhh, it's just Daddy, go to sleep." She rolls over and continues sleeping, at which point he begins to sexually abuse her. He takes off her unicorn underwear and masturbates with them. The next scene cuts to him putting on a condom and penetrating her vagina while stating, "Yeah, daddy doesn't want to get you pregnant," and, "Oh, your pussy is so much tighter than your mommy's." At this point she "awakens" fully and says with a slight degree of alarm, "Daddy, what are you doing?" He quiets her and tells her, "Daddy's just giving you a massage." He then continues to penetrate her vagina with his penis while she moans with pleasure. He tells her, "It's okay, Daddy is wearing a condom," but surreptitiously removes the condom. There is a close-up of him ensuring that his ejaculate enters her vagina. The video ends with a shot of her diary, in which she has written that she is very scared to tell her mother what has happened.[79] This video had been viewed over 300,000 times, with a 99 per cent approval rating.

A video on Pornhub, on the first page of results using the search term "stepdaughter father," is entitled "Giving Step-Daddy Her Virginity for Step-Father's Day – What More Could a Man Ask For?"[80] The female performer in this video is depicted as being in the early stages of puberty: her supposed "stepfather" grabs her chest in the first scene and expresses surprise that she has begun to grow breasts; in the second scene she is depicted in her bedroom, lying on her bed using felt pens to make a Father's Day card, and wearing a pink headband and the clothing of a young adolescent girl.

The narrative in this video is that her mother has died and she does not know what to give her stepfather, with whom she is living, for Father's Day. He tells her that he has an idea and then grooms her for sex, teaching her about the difference between a flaccid and erect penis, and encouraging her to kiss his penis and then put it in her mouth. The sexual abuse escalates from there. This video had also been viewed over 300,000 times, with a 90 per cent approval rating.

The popularity of incest-themed porn extends to the "gay sections" of mainstream porn-streaming platforms.[81] Intra-family child sexual abuse is relied upon as the narrative device in a prominent subset of this genre of porn as well. For instance, the video "Young Twink Step Son Morning Family Fuck Step Dad," found on the first page of search results on xHamster using the search term "father step-son," shows a man enter the bedroom of a seemingly adolescent boy to rouse him in the morning. The seemingly adolescent "stepson" is wearing onesie pyjamas. The man tells him a few times to get out of bed, which the son resists in typical teenage fashion. His "stepfather" then initiates sexual touching that culminates in anal penetration.[82]

A similar video, also on the first page of search results, featuring the same performers and following a similar narrative, with the seemingly adolescent performer represented as the adult male performer's "stepson," is entitled "My Step-Father Usually Fucks Me Before Bed."[83] The stepson in this video is also wearing child-like onesie pyjamas. The video begins with him cuddled next to his "stepfather" on the couch, watching television. Eventually he lays down with his head on the man's lap as a child would and falls asleep. His stepfather begins to rub his back and buttocks and touch his own genitals. In the next scene the man has removed his penis and the stepson is performing fellatio on him. The sexual abuse progresses to anal penetration, with the stepfather penetrating the son to ejaculation – after which he tells him, "It's time to go to bed."[84] This video also appears on Pornhub.[85] It received high approval ratings on both platforms.

A video on the first page of search results on Pornhub, using the same search terms, entitled "Father and Son Re-connect with Buttplug and Breeding," opens with a large, middle-aged man and a seemingly adolescent, smaller male wrapped in a blanket, cuddling in front of a Christmas tree. Cozied together in their pyjamas, in front of the fire, the "father" says "Merry Christmas, kiddo," and hands his "son" a gift. His son asks him what it is, and the father tells him that he has checked his browser history and seen that he was looking up how to have sex. The son unwraps the gift, and not knowing what it is – a butt plug – his father offers to teach him how to use it. From there the father leads him in a series of acts of sexual abuse.[86] This video had been viewed almost half a million times and had a 92 per cent approval rating.

Age of consent laws vary across jurisdictions. Apart from certain close-in-age exceptions, the age of consent in Western countries is typically between sixteen and eighteen years old. Sixteen is the age of consent for purposes of sexual activity in England and Canada.[87] In the state of New York the age of consent is seventeen.[88] It is eighteen in California.[89] Some jurisdictions also have sexual exploitation laws that prohibit adults from engaging in sexual acts with a young person over the age of consent over whom they are in a position of trust or authority, or with whom they are in a relationship of dependency, or with whom they are in a familial relationship.[90] Prohibitions on incest, which in some jurisdictions is defined to include only blood relatives, vary significantly across jurisdictions, and while not all countries or states have them, those that do prohibit incest often distinguish (for purposes of either the offence or the penalty) between incestuous acts involving young people below the age of consent and incestuous acts involving only adults.[91]

It is not always possible to discern the age of the performers in videos on these platforms – some of the "daughters" and "sisters" in these videos appear to be adult women or older adolescent girls. Others look as though they could be below the age of consent – particularly in jurisdictions with ages of consent as high as seventeen or eighteen. In other words, in some of these videos, in some jurisdictions, the physical portrayal may itself be a sexual offence. Moreover, the nominal or fictional portrayal in this subset of incest-themed porn generally is of an adult male, in a parental role, engaging in sexual acts with a female child (or in the case of the "gay-cest porn" a male child) who is under the age of consent. The (step)daughters (and sometimes sisters and sons) in these videos are portrayed as children or early adolescent teenagers. Some of them are depicted as asleep when the sexual activity commences. Unquestionably, the nominal portrayal in these videos is of sexual assault, rape, and/or other sexual offences. Those in which the "daughter" or "son" is, in fact, under the age of consent in the jurisdiction in which the video was made, if that occurred, are recordings of actual sexual offences.

Moreover, regardless of the actual age of the performers, in Canada, section 163.1(1)(b) of the *Criminal Code* defines child pornography to include any visual representation that "advocates or counsels sexual activity with a person under the age of eighteen years that would be an offence under this Act."[92] This advocacy or counselling can be explicit or implicit. As the Court of Appeal for Ontario determined in *R v Beattie*, "[m]aterial that describes sex with children as enjoyable, normal and beneficial, and the children as willing may send the message that sex with children can and should be pursued."[93] In other words, content that expresses the notion that children want and enjoy sex with adults constitutes child pornography.[94] Presumably, users who produce and upload this type of pornography, and platforms that knowingly permit or fail to remove this type of content, do so in contravention of Canada's child pornography laws.

This type of content also meets the definition of "content that sexually victimizes a child or revictimizes a survivor" under the federal government's recently tabled *Online Harms Act*.[95] Bill C-63 defines such content to include a "visual representation that shows a child, or a person depicted as a child, who is engaged in or is depicted as engaged in sexual activity."[96] The bill, if enacted, would impose a duty on platforms to make this type of content inaccessible in Canada. Unfortunately, unless the government passes regulations stipulating otherwise, at least in its current form the bill specifically excuses platforms from proactively searching their sites to identify (and remove) such content.[97]

Daughter/Stepdaughter Porn and the Use of Physical Force

In addition to depictions of men sexually assaulting incapacitated teenage girls and young women, and videos depicting the sexual assault of seemingly compliant or aroused (female) children by their fathers and stepfathers, a smaller subset of videos produced by the search terms "daughter" and "step-daughter" yield videos with titles that explicitly frame the content of the video as coercive and/or physically violent sexual activity. For example, the first two pages of search results on xHamster and Pornhub, using these terms, included videos with the following titles:

- "I Take Advantage of My 18 Year Old Step-Daughter"[98]
- "Step-Daughter Horrified by Step-Daddy's Monster Cock"[99]
- "Step-Father Tricks Step-Daughter into Perverted Photo Shoot and First Facial"[100]

- "Step-Daughter Fucked in the Ass" (with a thumbnail image attached to the title that shows a pigtailed girl holding a stuffed animal, along with the caption "Daddy I am so scared")[101]
- "Dad Manipulates Step-Daughter into Sex"[102]

Perhaps contrary to common assumption, sexual assaults perpetrated against teenage girls often involve the same forms of physical force and physical violence imposed upon adult women, in addition to and sometimes rather than the grooming and manipulation associated with the sexual assault of children and youth.[103] In their study of father–daughter sexual assault, law professors Janine Benedet and Isabel Grant found that "[w]hen girls resisted or objected … fathers simply forced themselves on their [teenage] daughters."[104]

Some of the videos produced in the first two pages of search results on xHamster using the term "daughter" depict this type of violence. For example, a video on the first page of search results on xHamster entitled "Daddy Forces Stepdaughter ***" depicts an older man raping a teenage girl or young woman for nine minutes and fifty-five seconds as she cries, struggles against him, begs him to stop, calls out for her mother, and repeatedly yells, "Papa, no."[105] He holds her down and repetitively forces his penis into her mouth and vagina. This video had a 98 per cent approval rating. It had been viewed 1,100,000 times. The forty comments on this video included, "sounds like he was teaching you how to be a good girl," and "Sometimes you just gotta #Metoo the bitch."[106] At the time the search was conducted, the video had been posted for more than a year.

Another xHamster video, this one on the second page of search results, is entitled "Stepdad Fucks and *** His Crying Daughter ***."[107] The video is a two-minute depiction of a brutal rape by a stepfather of his daughter. She cries and appears terrified throughout the multiple penetrations of her mouth, throat, and vagina that he forces on her. The video depicts her gagging and choking on his penis, painful vaginal penetration, and her sobbing and crying while he ejaculates repeatedly on her face. The video had been viewed 2,244,353 times and had a 99 per cent approval rating. The sixty-three comments by users on this video were positive and enthusiastic, and included the following: "beautiful," "Doin the public service. Thank-you," and "Good Girl."[108]

Mother/Step-Mother Porn and the Agency of Their "Sons"

"Mom" and "step mom" continue to be among the most popular search terms used on platforms like Pornhub.[109] Unlike what is produced using the search terms "(step)daughter" and "(step)sister," videos on the first two pages of search results using the terms "mom" and "stepmom" do not include depictions of (step)mothers sneaking into their sleeping sons' bedrooms and groping and penetrating them, nor do they include depictions of moms engaging in sexual acts with little boys. Instead, these videos tend to portray consensual sexual activity between adult men and adult women, often initiated by the "son." Titles include "Sexy Step Mom Turned On after Catching Her Step Son Sniffing on Her Panties,"[110] and "Mommy Gives In and Gives Up the Pussy."[111]

Titles of videos on the first two pages of search results using these search terms that do suggest coercive or non-consensual sexual activity often portray the (step)son as the aggressor. For instance, in "He Couldn't Help Himself and Started Hitting on Mother," a "son" gropes his "mother" while she is asleep.[112] When she supposedly wakes up, she half-heartedly resists physically and verbally for several minutes while he persists. Ultimately, she becomes participatory, aroused, and orgasmic.

In "Extra Thick Stepmom Emily Addison Fucks Horny Stepson to Make Him Keep Her Sinful Secrets," an adult "step-son" extorts his "step-mother," whom he calls a "slut" and a "bitch," into engaging in sexual activity with him when he finds out she is cheating on his father. He tells her, "I get to use you freely," "I get to use all your holes as much as I want," and "I want you to blow me if you want to keep me silent."[113] He coerces her into engaging in multiple sexual acts with him over the course of a week by threatening to tell his father that she has cheated on him.

There is one common theme in several of the videos produced in the first two pages of search results on these platforms using the search term "mom" that could suggest exploitative sexual activity on the part of mothers: (step)mothers giving (step)sons lessons in sex education. While videos with titles such as "Moms Teach Sex – Step Mom Says 'You Dreaming About Your Step Moms Big Titties Again?'" are clearly invoking an exploitative narrative, the male performers in these videos tend to exhibit an agency and autonomy that is not present in the (step)father–(step)daughter and (step)sister–(step)brother genres.[114] In "Moms Teach Sex," for example, the "son" cajoles his "step-mother" into performing fellatio on him. He slaps her buttocks multiple times, hard enough to leave significant red marks on her. He penetrates her roughly for several minutes, and the video ends with him ejaculating on her.[115]

It seems that even porn that intentionally invokes narratives involving power differentials in favour of female characters portrayed as mothers and stepmothers still imbues the male subjects with a type of sexual agency that is much less commonly depicted or possessed by women in incest-themed mainstream porn (or mainstream porn generally). What explains this difference? Perhaps the distinction can be explained by the lack of proxy in the "real world." Recall the authenticity obsession discussed in chapter 3. The sexual assault of (step)sons by their mothers is very rare.[116] Moms sneaking into their sleeping sons' bedrooms and perpetrating non-consensual sexual acts upon them is not a sexual script with which we are particularly familiar. As examined next, the same cannot be said with respect to (step)fathers and (step)daughters.

Regardless, nearly all mainstream porn is skewed towards men's sexual pleasure.[117] Thankfully, and unlike as appears to be the case with respect to girls and young women, depictions of teenage men being sexually assaulted by their sisters while they sleep, or little boys being raped by their mothers, has not been similarly constructed as arousing or pleasurable for boys and adolescent men in mainstream porn. (Although, as described, *men* sexually assaulting their sons and stepsons has been represented in this way, in a subset of so-called gay-cest porn.)

The Sexual Assault of Daughters and Sisters: Reality, Not Fantasy

An examination of statements by survivors and perpetrators of childhood sexual assault, the fact patterns in reported judicial decisions involving prosecutions for the sexual assault of teenage girls, and user responses to incest-themed porn depicting the sexual assault of daughters and sisters by their family members, reveals significant similarities between the titles of, and content in, this subset of incest-themed porn and the factual circumstances, the tactics of abuse, and the relationship dynamics prevalent in cases of intra-family sexual assault.

Far from unthinkable, intra-family sexual assault is tragically common. As Benedet and Grant observe, the family "is the most powerful social institution implicated in sexual violence against girls."[118] It is from this horrible reality that the incest-themed porn on platforms like Pornhub and xHamster that depicts the sexual assault of children, teenagers, and young women by their fathers and brothers appears to draw its inspiration, not the world of dragons and royal marriages, or blonde-haired siblings locked away for years in an attic.

The Parallels between Mainstream Porn Narratives and Intra-Family Sexual Abuse

The Canadian Centre for Child Protection surveyed 150 survivors of childhood sexual assault as part of the organization's study on child pornography (or child sexual abuse material, as it is more aptly called).[119] Participants in the survey came from countries around the Western world, including from North America, Europe, Britain, and Australia. The results of the organization's survey indicate that in the majority of cases of sexual assault involving children and adolescents (in which some of the abuse is either photographed or videotaped), the abuser lived with the victim.[120] Other studies, not focused on child sexual abuse material, have made similar findings.[121] Survivors were asked, as part of this survey, about the strategies abusers used to facilitate these offences. One of the most common tactics reported by survivors involved family members seizing, and capitalizing on, opportunities to be alone with them, and in particular, acting upon times when the victim's mother was not present.[122] Survivor responses included the following:

- "My mother would sometimes go visit her mother for a few days or went on holiday for a week ... At those times a lot could happen at home."
- "My mother was nearly always at work."
- "When my mother was not present, for instance went to parents' evenings or was in a different room. Every free moment [nobody's around] was made use of."
- "My biological father lived with me and my adopted mother for some time. When she went out, he and I were left home alone."

- "My mom worked twelve hours shifts ... so my dad worked opposite shifts to her and was our caregiver."[123]

Interviews with men who have been convicted of sexually assaulting and/or raping their daughters and stepdaughters reveal the same pattern. Patricia Phelan interviewed forty men – fathers and stepfathers – who had engaged in incestuous acts against their daughters.[124] Like survivors, abusive fathers also describe capitalizing on opportunities when the child's mother was out of the house to sexually assault their daughters. One father stated, for example:

My daughter would come in in the morning and climb into bed with us. One day she came in ... My wife was gone [had already left for work] and I started molesting her. At first it involved fondling and cuddling, [later] I became more aggressive sexually.[125]

Compare these accounts of the circumstances surrounding intra-family sexual violence to the following titles of videos found on Pornhub and xHamster on the first page of search results on each platform, using the term "daughter":

- "Step-Dad Fucks Stepdaughter While Mom Is Away at Work"[126]
- "Alone with My Slut Teen Daughter"[127]
- "Daddy Fucks Stepdaughter Everytime Mommy Leaves" (sic)[128]
- "Step Sister Fucks with Step Daddy, Mom at Work!!!"[129]

As already noted, sexual assault against teenage girls is also frequently perpetrated by brothers and stepbrothers. According to an American study, one in seven sexual assaults perpetrated by adolescent men occurs on school days between the hours of three and seven, with the peak time being between three and four o'clock.[130] This is a time when many parents are still at work and teenage siblings are home alone. Recall that in 2017, "step sister" was the fifth most popular search term on Pornhub.[131] Videos on the first page of search results on Pornhub using the highly popular term included videos with these titles:

- "My Step Sister Suck My Cock While My Parents Aren't Home"[132]

- "Stepbrother and Step-Sister Home Alone"[133]
- "Fucked My Step Sis While Parents Are Not at Home"[134]

It is not surprising that sexual offenders use opportunities to assault their daughters and sisters during moments when the girls' mothers or other adults are not present. While the evidently common construction of the mother as sexual safeguard, or protectorate, in this genre of porn is noteworthy, it too is unsurprising. Women are often constructed as the gatekeepers to men's sexual access.[135] The more notable observation here is that these titles reveal prominent, incest-themed porn on mainstream platforms that relies on a narrative device that, far from fantastical, parallels precisely the factual circumstances in which the sexual assault of (step)daughters and (step)sisters by their (step)fathers and (step)brothers tends to occur.

Consider another example of the same observation. One of the most common locations reported by survivors of child and adolescent sexual assault is in their bedroom when other members of the household are asleep or out of the residence.[136] Survivors who completed the survey by the Canadian Centre for Child Protection reported the following:

- "The hands-on abuse happened at night, and/or when my mother wasn't home, or when he had time one-on-one with me in the house."
- "At night, when house was asleep."
- "Pulled into an empty room, visiting me at night in my own room."
- "My father simply at home when he put me to bed, he raped me then, that happened almost as long as I know."[137]

The fathers in Phelan's study reported similar patterns of behaviour. Fathers and stepfathers offered these descriptions of the sexual activity they perpetrated against their daughters and stepdaughters:

- "I would hug her and then I would put her to bed, I would give her a goodnight kiss, and another hug, and then little by little I started touching her."
- "So I would go into her bedroom, talk to her, wake her up ... I started rubbing her back and stuff and it expanded from there."
- "On nights when my daughter was deeply asleep I could do just

about anything … I could move her around, pull blankets down and roll her onto her back."
- "She'd be asleep or faking sleep and there was never a response."
- "I could do with her when she was asleep almost anything I wanted. She was very cooperative."[138]

As part of the same study, Phelan also interviewed the abused daughters of these forty men (or the daughters' therapists).[139] Their accounts were consistent with the statements offered by survivors in the Canadian Centre for Child Protection survey:

- "Just one night I woke up and he was fondling me."
- "It would be at night in my bedroom in my bed … And he would come in my room and pull up my night gown and he'd start touching my breasts and down here [points to vaginal area] and I would, like, move around."[140]

Compare these statements by survivors and abusers with the following titles from PornHub and xHamster, again found on the first two pages of search results on each platform using the search term "daughter":

- "Father Sneaks into Daughter's Bedroom and Touches Her Pussy"[141]
- "Daughter Snuggles with Step-Father in Bed and Gets Fucked"[142]
- "Waking Up Stepdaughter with a Cock inside Her"[143]
- "Scared Stepdaughter Gets Fucked While Wife Sleeps"[144]

These titles invoke factual contexts for the sexual activity depicted in the videos that match the descriptions of intra-familial sexual assault provided by survivors and abusers. Likewise, the videos portraying the sexual assault of girls by their (step)brothers and (step)fathers described earlier in this chapter – such as "My Little Stepsister Lets Me Do Everything," "Daughter Creampied by Stepfather in Her Bedroom," and "Stepfather Gets Stepdaughter Pregnant with Accidental Creampie" – replicate the factual circumstances described by survivors.[145]

Recall that these videos depict men, cast as brothers and fathers, sneaking into their daughters' and sisters' bedrooms while they sleep, removing their covers and night clothes, testing to see if they are awake, touching them, and then eventually imposing a variety of sexual acts upon them. Compare this type of porn to the frequent accounts of survivors of child sexual assault who describe awaking to find their fathers groping or penetrating them or who report having pretended to be asleep until it was over, to how abusers themselves describe their offending patterns, or to Benedet and Grant's finding that in nearly 25 per cent of cases involving sexual assaults by fathers and stepfathers, the assault was perpetrated while their daughters were asleep or intoxicated.[146] The fodder for this subset of incest porn is not fiction, fantasy, and flirtation with the taboo. Its inspiration is drawn from the horrific, albeit commonplace and persistent, reality of intra-family sexualized violence.

One need not spend long reviewing judicial decisions regarding sexual assault prosecutions in which the accused is a family member to confirm that the plot, setting, and narrative devices used in this type of incest-themed porn invoke, parallel, and replicate the realities of incestuous sexual violence. Sexual assault case law is replete with, for instance, descriptions of men sneaking into the bedrooms of their daughters, sisters, granddaughters, and nieces while their wives are at work or asleep, of girls and teenagers awaking to discover a family member groping and penetrating them, or of children and teenage girls testifying that they pretended to remain asleep until the assault was over. Compare the facts in the following recent cases to the videos described earlier in this chapter:

At the time of the first alleged assault, the complainant said she was sleeping in the basement of V——'s house, lying on her stomach, when she felt [her father] touch her vagina over her clothes, shift her underwear to the side, and then penetrate her vagina with his penis.[147]

The offender entered the bedroom, and after checking to make sure K was asleep, would grab the victim's breasts, and put his hand down her pants, both underneath her pyjamas. He would also make her touch his penis, at times, to the point of orgasm.[148]

The victim in this matter was the 14-year-old daughter of [L's] girlfriend. L entered the bedroom of the victim, M.R., while she was sleeping. M.R. testified that she was asleep in her room, lying on her stomach and did not initially hear L enter her room. M.R. testified that L moved the covers off of her and pulled her pants down her legs. M.R. testified that "[h]e was pushing my head down and he put his private area in mine's [sic]."[149]

Mr [G] approached her at night, while she slept on the living room sofa. Everyone else in the home was asleep. He held her down and vaginally penetrated her with his fingers, tongue or writing instruments … The complainant variously struggled, "disassociated" or "spaced out." In these latter cases of disassociation or spacing out, she would simply lie there and wait for it to end.[150]

An additional commonality between the actuality of intra-familial sexual assault and the content of this type of porn should be highlighted. The sexual assault of young people is facilitated by, and often even reliant upon, the abuser's ability to instill in his victim a sense of fear, shame, and humiliation at the prospect of getting caught.[151] One of the most consistent aspects of reports from survivors of childhood incest involves the demands placed upon them by their abusers to keep secret the sexual violence to which they were subjected.[152] Incest-themed porn also relies on this actuality to develop the narratives featured in these videos. Fathers whisper, tell their daughters to be quiet so their mothers will not hear, and sneak in and out of their bedrooms.[153] Daughters are portrayed as frightened that their mothers will find out what they have done and be angry with them.[154] Titles frame relationship dynamics as punishment oriented or fear based, and secretive, as in the video "Father Punishes His Daughter," in which a "father" is depicted as punishing his teenage "daughter" after he catches her reading a sexually inappropriate book by forcing her to fellate him.[155]

In their review of case law involving the sexual assault of teenage girls by their fathers, Benedet and Grant found numerous cases in which fathers attempted to use their daughters' supposed promiscuity to control them or normalized the sexual abuse as sex education.[156] Here, too, the titles of incest-themed videos on mainstream porn-streaming platforms appear to echo or replicate real life. For example, a common theme involves policing the sexuality of teenage girls by engaging in sexual acts with them when they are caught masturbating or with their boyfriends:

- "Stepdad Caughts [sic] Stepdaughter Naked and Cums All over Her"[157]
- "Naughty Stepdaughter Ep. 6: Caught by Stepdad Making a Video for My Boyfriend"[158]
- "Step Daddy Caught Me Playing with My Pussy and Fucked Me Hard"[159]

Similarly, sex education, punishment for bad behaviour, and coercion through threats and/or bribery are common tactics used by incestuous abusers and common themes in incestuous porn videos:

- "Stepdad Gives Me a Sex Education Lesson"[160]
- "Step Dad Pays 18 Year Old Step Daughter Money for Intimate Intimacy – Homemade Porn"[161]

As already explained, in videos involving sex education themes depicting (step)mothers and (step)sons, the (step)sons tend to be grown men and exhibit significant sexual agency throughout the interaction. In sex education–themed videos depicting (step)fathers and (step)daughters, the (step)-daughters are often depicted as children, and/or the object of male sexual exploitation.[162] Sex education themes between (step)mothers and (step)-sons seem to be about (often male-initiated) sexual exploration, whereas the same themes involving (step)fathers and (step)daughters are more likely to be presented as (step)fathers teaching their (step)daughters a lesson and/or punishment for their supposed indiscretions with boys or other men.[163]

Consider another parallel. Children and adolescents in state custody are sexually assaulted at even higher rates than those who live with a parent or other family member.[164] Research suggests that children in foster care are more likely to be sexually assaulted than those who are not in state custody.[165] In their study, Benedet and Grant found that "the foster father cases were particularly tragic cases with some girls who had been sexually assaulted in multiple homes by different foster fathers."[166] The search term "foster parents" produces videos on Pornhub with titles, on the first page of results, that include "Skinny Teen Fucked by Controlling Foster Parents" and "My Foster Daughter Wanted Some Dick before the Social Workers Came for a House Visit."[167]

Pornography producer Bree Mills is atypically forthcoming about the degree to which the reality of harmful sexual behaviour serves as the source material for the porn, including incest-themed porn, that she produces.[168] Her incest-themed videos have been described as "dramatic realism."[169] A 2018 article in *Jezebel* in which Mills was interviewed describes how "she approaches [producing porn] with a realism and degree of emotional gravity that she says goes against accepted wisdom about how to handle such a [topic]."[170] Equally unusual within public discourse about this type of porn, the article candidly acknowledges that while Mills's videos "dwell in the realm of fantasy, they also have painful counterparts in the real world."[171] Mills's candour is unusual. Not uncommon is her reliance on the reality of this type of sexual violence as inspiration for the pornography she produces. Clearly, the sexual scripts prevalent in the context of intra-family sexual assault are relied upon, or paralleled, in depictions of incestuous sexual assault on mainstream porn-streaming platforms.

Some Users Who Comment Relate Their Experiences and Desires to the Behaviours Depicted

The comments on videos containing portrayals of (step)fathers and (step)brothers sexually assaulting their (step)daughters and (step)sisters reveal users who relate to these depictions of sexual assault not as taboo fantasy, but rather as fictional renderings of their own sexual behaviours, fantasies, or desires. For these users, videos with this type of content seemingly depict a form of sexual activity that they have engaged in or fantasized about, or a form of sexual behaviour in which they would like to engage.

Recall, for instance, the video "Daughter Creampied by Stepfather in Her Bedroom," in which a male performer engages in vaginal intercourse with a young woman wearing onesie pyjamas and clutching a pink teddy bear.[172] Comments on this video (which were overwhelmingly positive and enthusiastic) included the following:

- "My stepdaughter wears the same type of onesies, just for me. It makes it so easy to finger her when I tuck her in each night. She also has pajamas with feet on them. They have a zipper that goes from her chest all the way down to one ankle."
- "Used to sneak in and jack on step daughter when she was little."
- "The first time I creampied my stepdaughter was when we were riding our bikes on the trails in the park behind our house… We fucked on the picnic table, and … went into the port a john to clean up her pussy. We did that almost every Sunday all summer long. My wife thanked me for spending so much 'quality time' with my stepdaughter."[173]

Similarly, the xHamster video depicting a young girl reading aloud from her diary, in which she has written that she was impregnated by her father, had eighteen comments, all enthusiastic. One user said, "This is like watching myself sneaking into my stepdaughter's room early in the morning after her mother had left and fucking her before I went to work."[174]

The video "Father Sneaks into Daughter's Bedroom and Touches Her Pussy," which also depicts a young girl asleep when her father creeps into her room and gropes and penetrates her, had comments that included:

- "I love doing this to my daughter."
- "I worked on night shift, so when I got home in the morning my wife was getting ready to go to work, and my stepdaughter had to get up and get ready to go to school. She was still a virgin, but she liked me licking her pussy & sucking her clit to wake her up. But after her first boyfriend popped her cherry… I woke her up with my cock in her furry pussy."[175]

Comments on the xHamster video "Daddy Forces Stepdaughter to Suck and Fuck," which depicts the rape of a teenage girl or young woman by her father, as she cries and calls out for her mother, included:

- "I'd love to do this to my 21yo."
- "I did the same thing with my step [granddaughter], she wasn't old enough to get pg."[176]

The video "Horny Stepdad Fucked His Stepdaughter" features a point-of-view depiction of a father sneaking into a child or very young teenage daughter's bedroom, reaching out to make sure that she is asleep and then exposing his penis and masturbating it near her face until she wakes up, at which point he penetrates her orally and then vaginally. User comments on this video included "I would love to do this with my stepdaughter" and "I need a daughter like her."[177]

Recall, also, some of the comments left by users about their daughters, discussed in chapter 4:

- "I have three daughters the youngest one, shes [*sic*] 28 now but when she was 19, and back for the summer fromn collage [*sic*], wanted me to pop her cherry, it was great, i fucked my daughter."
- "I'd love to absolutely destroy my daughter's pussy and asshole!!"
- "if she was my step daughter I'd have to fuck her no doubt."

- "My pretty brunette stepdaughter had small, but nice tits, and a little bush on her sweet pussy, and NO shitty tattoo's [sic]. And she loved to walk around the house in her bra & panties when her mom wasn't home, we fucked many times."[178]

Similarly, the video "Wake Up Sis," examined in chapter 3 (which depicted a young man sneaking into the bedroom of a sleeping teenage girl and engaging in sexual acts while she was still asleep), included these comments by users: "Wish I had a sister that would let me fuck her like that" and "I woke my little sister up that way many times when we were teens."[179]

Users who leave comments on these platforms represent a very small fraction of those who have consumed the platform's videos. We do not know the extent to which their seeming tendency to relate these videos to their personal experiences and/or desires reflects the response of users more generally, or even the veracity of the comments. However, we do know that the content of these videos mirrors many of the relationship dynamics, grooming practices, power imbalances, and factual circumstances prevalent in cases involving the sexual assault of children, teenage girls, and young women by their family members. We also know that users' descriptions of their own sexual offences, or fantasies, echo the details in the statements made by survivors describing the sexual violence imposed upon them by their (step)-fathers and (step)brothers, as well as the disclosures made by (step)fathers who have sexually assaulted their (step)daughters. We know that videos with these types of depictions have been viewed on porn-streaming platforms millions of times, and that their approval ratings tend to be extremely high. And finally, we know that the sexual assault of children, teenage girls, and young women by their fathers, stepfathers, brothers, and stepbrothers is heartbreakingly common. Taken together, this knowledge suggests, compellingly, that at least some consumers of this type of content are not relating to these depictions as pure fantasy and unthinkable in real life. The parallels, the overlapping narratives, and descriptive accounts, between what is depicted in this genre of porn and the sexual offences regularly perpetrated against children, teenagers, and young women by their family members are too similar to conclude otherwise.

Moreover, it is not only abusers, and potential abusers, who relate to this type of content as fictional depictions of their real lives, desires, and fantasies. It is clear that some survivors of sexual assault by a family member see themselves or their experiences in this type of pornography. The first comment on the video "Daddy Forces Stepdaughter to Suck and Fuck" was "my stepdad did this to me when I was 12."[180] When asked what they would like the public to know, one of the survivors of child sexual abuse and child pornography surveyed by the Canadian Centre for Child Protection responded: "they should … understand that a lot of regular porn with adults has themes similar to child abuse and can be highly triggering to survivors."[181] Consider also this comment by a reader in response to the *Jezebel* article describing the "realism" relied upon by Bree Mills in the incest-themed videos she produces:

I'm a straight woman of color and my dad sexually abused me. Let me spell out to you what incest meant to me. I can remember only a very few moments of my childhood ever being happy. There are no childhood photos of me smiling. I spent much of my childhood in my bed, under a blanket, crying. I was completely disconnected from my body – sports, dance, music … I was a strange, intense child and had a really hard time making friends … My path to having a family of my own – requires a partner and a child, which meant having sex which was impossible for me. So I never was able to get what I want the most. I still struggle with men and dating in my forties … Too bad the writer couldn't bother to ask actual incest survivors about how they feel about this. These are the people this woman is making money off of. This is what people are getting off o[n].

It's time for #metoo to put a light on us, the most damaged and vulnerable survivors. Otherwise all the movement will do for us is create an incredibly triggering environment without providing an outlet.[182]

Characterizing This Type of Porn as Fantastical Denies the Reality of Routinized Patriarchy and Its Relationship to Incestuous Sexual Violence

Phelan's interviews with sexually abusive (step)fathers also reveal the types of age- and gender-based familial power struggles, enforcement of patriarchal family norms, and surveillance of, and proprietary attitudes towards, the sexuality of adolescent girls that create the conditions for incestuous sexual assault. Many of the perpetrators in her study maintained that they believed that what they were doing to their daughters was much less serious than sexually assaulting someone else's daughter:

- "It's worse if you molest a neighbor's child, because the neighbor's child would not be related to me – she's not *my* daughter."
- "I guess I was feeling, it was all right, 'it's *my* daughter, I've got all the rights.'"
- "[I] would never have considered approaching somebody else's child … I guess the biggest thing to me is the right of other parents to raise their children the way they want to."[183]

Benedet and Grant made a similar finding regarding male sexual entitlement: "We saw many cases in which fathers assumed an entitlement to control their daughter's sexuality."[184]

Phelan's conclusion from the interviews she conducted with fathers and stepfathers and the (step)daughters they had sexually assaulted and raped, was that "it is exactly the ordinary, routine, patterned family interactions out of which … incest grows."[185] She was referring to (step)fathers whose grooming behaviours involved reading bedtime stories to their children, tucking them in at night, caring for them while their mothers were at work, back rubs, tickle fights, and waking kids up from their naps, and to the patriarchal context in which these interactions unfold.[186] It is these quotidian elements of family life – massages, bedtime rituals, childish games – layered onto patriarchal family structures, gendered power dynamics, and narratives of secrecy or fear, that provide the factual set-up in many of the incest-themed videos depicting sexual assaults found on mainstream porn-streaming platforms.[187] It is these prosaic details – the "lint of people's lives"[188] – combined with these power structures, that bring this subset of incest-themed porn the sense of realism to which Mills was likely referring.

Were it not for the horrifying trauma and profound, long-lasting harm caused by men who impose sexual acts upon their daughters, sons, and sisters, the narratives and factual circumstances depicted in porn of this genre would be almost banal.[189] These videos are not pushing the boundaries of human sexuality. They are, sadly, not edgy. The porn I am describing is not "age-play porn," such as content addressed to the "adult baby/diaper lover" (AB/DL) community.[190] These are videos being consumed by a strikingly mainstream audience, depicting a disturbingly common occurrence: the sexual assault of children, adolescent girls, and young women by their family members. We ought not to confuse fiction with fantasy. These portrayals, while nearly all seemingly fictional, are not remotely fantastical. In fact, it may be that their appeal is a function of the element of realism that they capture. That is to say, perhaps these videos are popular not because they represent an exciting, fantastical, unbroachable account of human sexuality – they do not – but rather because, other than their wives and girlfriends, it is (step)daughters and (step)sisters to whom men most frequently have access. Indeed, the appeal of this genre of porn may be related to how achievable this type of sexual activity is for some men. Recall, again, the privileging of the "authentic" when porn is evaluated, rated, valued, and recommended.[191] Perhaps it is a combination of male sexual entitlement rooted in patriarchy, and the realism and feasibility that real-world access adds to these fictional depictions, that renders this type of porn so appealing to its consumers.

Regardless, when we talk of incest as fantastical, as something no one would want to do in real life, we reinforce a social narrative that makes us, as a community or society, less willing to believe child sexual abuse survivors. Public discourse that reinforces this narrative by explaining the incredible popularity of incest-themed porn as an indulgence in a taboo fantasy of the unthinkable is harmful in this regard. As it stands, it is already incredibly difficult to convince legal actors that allegations of incestuous sexualized violence are true.[192] As Benedet and Grant note, cases involving allegations of sexual assault by a father are, at their core, nearly always about credibility, not reliability.[193] Often allegations of incestuous sexualized violence are not disclosed by the complainant until many years after the abuse, adding to the difficulty of prosecuting these offences.[194] In the cases they studied, Benedet and Grant found a "strong undercurrent" of belief that teenage complainants who alleged sexual assault by their fathers and step-fathers were "fabricating their stories."[195]

Not only is it harmful to characterize incest as unthinkable and incest porn as pure fantasy, it is also inaccurate. Likening social barriers to, and societal condemnation of, incest to those pertaining to cannibalism, for example, perpetuates an erroneous assertion about the rarity of the former.[196] It is true that both acts are illegal and are subject to societal taboo, but there is a lot more incest in our communities than cannibalism.

Efforts to devise appropriate social and legal responses to this type of porn may be distorted if we are not clear about the relationship between the depictions in incest-themed porn and incestuous sexual offences. Consider, for example, the attempt in mainstream porn to distinguish between biological relatives and incestuous acts between family members who are not blood relations. While there certainly are videos depicting sexual activity between biological fathers and daughters, and biological brothers and sisters, more of the videos on the first two pages of search results on these platforms purport to depict stepfathers and stepdaughters, and stepbrothers and stepsisters.[197] Porn producers/uploaders suggest that incest-themed videos are often framed in this way either to avoid obscenity charges, or to remain in the good graces of credit card companies (which are relied upon to facilitate payments to the fee-based aspects of their businesses).[198] In other words, the perception is that some financial institutions will continue to allow a site to use its services if it depicts incest between stepparents and their stepchildren or between stepsiblings but not if the site includes depictions of sex between a biological parent and their child or between biological siblings.[199] As a result, there are more stepparent and stepsibling videos on these platforms, or videos that at least gesture towards a step relationship in some part of the title or metadata, than videos and/or titles that explicitly purport to depict biological family members.

This trend may mirror relative rates of sexual abuse by stepfathers and biological fathers. For instance, Benedet and Grant found that stepfathers are among the "most likely sexual abusers of teenaged girls."[200] In this sense, the policies of credit card companies and the interpretation of obscenity laws steer those who make incest-themed porn towards content that may even more closely parallel real-world intra-family sexual violence. This is a perverse result and one that likely stems, in part, from a lack of clarity regarding the degree to which incest-themed porn is eroticizing the circumstances surrounding, and tactics used in, intra-family sexual violence. It reflects a didactic approach to this genre of porn that is focused on the supposed immorality of sex between blood relatives rather than the harm of intra-family sexual assault. It is also an approach that misses its mark – at least if that mark is aimed at rejecting socially harmful porn.

To be clear, urging a more accurate recognition of the extent to which incestuous sexual assault is perpetrated against (step)daughters and (step)-sisters is not the same as normalizing this harmful sexual behaviour. Indeed, one of the problems with incest-themed pornography, and in particular porn of this genre that depicts sexual offences, is that it risks reinforcing, perpetuating, and/or normalizing sexual scripts that, for example, eroticize sex between adults and children, construct the possession of one's daughter or sister as arousing, and incorporate intra-family dynamics of coercion, fear, secrecy, manipulation, and punishment into social understandings of how to pursue sexual desire. The aim should be to recognize and discuss more openly the reality of intra-family sexual violence, and depictions of it in mainstream porn, without normalizing it or failing to condemn harmful sexual behaviour of this nature. The failure to do this, particularly in favour of public discourse about the unthinkability of these sexual abuses in so-called real life, reinforces a social narrative that encourages us to respond to allegations of intra-family sexual assault with suspicion and disbelief.

Another Problem with Incest-Themed Porn

There is one important distinction between the actuality of intra-family sexual violence and the portrayal of it in incest-themed pornography. This distinction evidences one of the potential harms arising from the widespread consumption of this type of porn. Recall that a seemingly common depiction of sexual assault in incest-themed porn on popular platforms like Pornhub and xHamster involves men engaging in sexual acts with daughters and sisters who are, or are depicted as being, asleep or unconscious. In mainstream porn videos of this genre, the response of the sisters and daughters to the sexual acts being imposed upon them while they are asleep or unconscious is typically portrayed in one of two ways: they either remain asleep or unconscious for the duration of the video, or they "wake up" at some point after the sexual activity has commenced and begin to participate in the sexual acts and express sexual pleasure and arousal. There are exceptions, such as the depictions of rape by physical force described earlier in this chapter. But in most portrayals of incest-themed sexual assault on the first two pages of search results on these platforms, the victim is presented as either orgasmic or unaware of what is happening. These depictions constitute a grossly inaccurate representation of how survivors of incest report experiencing these incidents of sexual violence. But importantly (and problematically), they do parallel the reported perceptions of, and justifications relied on by, those who perpetrate this type of sexual violence.

Children and Teenage Daughters Experience Sexual Assault by Their Family Members as Profoundly Harmful

Contrary to the depictions in porn, survivors of childhood incest report that, while they may have been asleep or unconscious when an incident of sexual assault commenced, they did not remain unaware of what was happening to them. In their study of survivors who were sexually abused by brothers and fathers, it was clear to Jane Rudd and Sharon Herzberger that the women they interviewed "knew that they were being victimized."[201] What these survivors did sometimes do, however, was pretend to be asleep or unconscious. Indeed, some survivors report that they persistently faked being asleep when the assaults were occurring – "I often pretended to be asleep" – or that they disassociated or tried to distract themselves.[202] One woman in Rudd and Herzberger's study commented, "I would just go deep inside myself and pretend it was not happening."[203] Some of the survivors in Phelan's study described the strategies they used to avoid further sexual violence: "I just did anything to stay away."[204] Benedet and Grant reported cases of teenage girls staying awake all night in an effort to protect themselves from their fathers or stepfathers.[205]

The pornographic depictions of daughters and sisters who respond with orgasmic delight to the sexual violations imposed upon them by their fathers and brothers are equally inaccurate. Women whose family members engaged them in sexual activity as children and teenagers (whether through force, coercion, manipulation, and/or grooming) almost universally characterize these experiences as intensely unwanted, and profoundly harmful. In Phelan's study, none of the survivors reported "enjoying what was happening" to them.[206] Instead, they described themselves as initially confused and in disbelief that their (step)fathers would do this to them, followed by feelings of disgust, pain, and betrayal as the sexual assaults progressed.[207] One daughter stated: "Just one night I woke up and just he was fondling me. I remember I woke right up. The next day I went to school and I felt sick 'cause I could not believe it happened."[208] Another described the first incident and her reaction to it as follows: "I remember exactly how it started. He was reading this book to me and my stepsister. She was older. He was reading this story and he was tickling our stomachs and he started fumbling my breasts. I hated it."[209]

Many women who were sexually assaulted as children and teenagers by family members report depression, suicidality, addictions, nightmares, and flashbacks.[210] Participants in Rudd and Herzberger's study indicated that even as adults they think about the abuse more than once a day.[211] Some described a continual daily struggle to deal with its impacts.[212] One of the participants in their study reported wanting to die both at the time the sexual assaults were occurring and now, as an adult: "I think I hated life, God, family, myself so much all I wanted to do is end it all. Very often I [still] feel that same way."[213] Survivors who responded to the Canadian Centre for Child Protection survey gave comments like these:

- "I cry every day. Do things every day to keep me on track: daily exercise, going outdoors, making sure to take rest breaks. Can't cope with a full-time job. Resolution requires lots of effort and energy."[214]
- "From the moment I wake up in the morning until I go to bed I have to put in a lot of effort to keep myself going. There are many daily issues I am confronted with, thresholds I have to pass, and anxiety I have to fight to lead a somewhat livable life. Of course the night is full of nightmares, re-experiencing and panic attacks. There are periods when my life is livable. But there are also many periods when my life is only mere survival. That is difficult, I only have one life ... I suppose it has affected all aspects of my life: relationships, family, career, finances, addiction problems, body perception, intimacy, trust, sexuality."[215]
- "My experiences impact (and have impacted) virtually every possible area of my life. My relationship with my body is always disturbed, and I live with enormous hatred towards myself. I'm constantly absorbed with death and it's a very tough struggle not to give in to suicidal thoughts or destructive behaviours (such as cutting). For fifteen years, right from childhood, I've had an eating disorder ... I have difficulty with men, setting limits, sexuality, intimacy, trust, and I often suffer anxiety and nightmares. I feel extremely ashamed of myself and of my experiences."[216]

It is eminently clear that girls, teenagers, and young women who are subjected to the sort of sexual interactions depicted in this type of incest-themed porn experience these interactions not as pleasurable but as confusing, upsetting, shame inducing and deeply, life-alteringly harmful. For daughters and sisters who have experienced the type of sexual activity depicted in this prominent subset of incest-themed porn, the restful unawareness or orgasmic desire exhibited by the sisters and daughters in these videos could not be further from their own experiences. However, for the perpetrators of incestuous abuse, these pornographic representations of how girls and young women respond to sexual acts imposed upon them by their fathers and brothers does appear to reflect either their purported perceptions of how their victims responded, or, more likely, their wilful blindness to their victims' responses.

Perpetrators of Incestuous Sexual Abuse Describe Their Victims as Asleep, Unaware of, Aroused by, or Active Participants in the Abuse Imposed upon Them

While there is a profound disjuncture between the experiences of incestuous sexual assault survivors and the portrayal of girls and women in incest-themed mainstream porn, there is a disturbing parallel between these pornographic depictions and the reported perceptions of those who perpetrate this type of sexual violence. Many of these men maintain that they perceived reactions and behaviours by their victims that correspond strongly with how girls and young women are depicted in incest-themed porn. In Phelan's study, more than half of the (step)fathers she interviewed asserted that their child initiated the sexual activity and/or enjoyed it.[217] Fathers and stepfathers commented:

- "When she would come to me for something I would hug her and then I would put her to bed. I would give her a goodnight kiss, another hug and then little by little I started touching her and caressing her and I found her more affectionate all the time."[218]
- "I told her it was natural to have intercourse, that it would probably hurt but it would give her pleasure too ... I knew she was enjoying this because she would orgasm and lubricate."[219]
- "She seemed to accept it and it would be okay for her as far as she was concerned."[220]
- "I started seeing her as an adult woman. I saw her as a sexual being other than a child."[221]

Sexually abusive fathers in a study conducted by Linda Williams and David Finkelhor maintained similar perceptions regarding their victims' responses. One of the men in their study commented, "I felt that at five years old she was able to be stimulated by the same things I was."[222] Another described "how he convinced himself that his daughter was also aroused so that he could molest her while driving the guilt from his mind."[223] In many of the cases Benedet and Grant examined, fathers blamed their daughters for initiating the sexual activity or coming on to them.[224] The authors note that based on the facts reported in these cases, these were clearly cognitive distortions on the part of these offenders.[225]

In addition to perpetrators' purported perceptions that their victims, if aware of what was happening, enjoyed what was being done to them, some of the men that Phelan interviewed maintained that they were surprised or shocked when they were caught.[226] They purported to have believed that their daughters were asleep and unaware of what they were doing to them, paralleling the second common response depicted in incest-themed porn that portrays the sexual assault of sleeping or unconscious daughters and sisters. They offered statements such as the following:

- "On nights when my daughter was deeply asleep I could do just about anything – she became a rag doll … I thought it would not affect her because she was asleep, not aware, therefore not a lot of damage."[227]
- "For the most part I thought she was asleep."[228]
- "I truly thought she was sound asleep. I never thought it was damaging."[229]

Several of the daughters of these men told Phelan that they were not asleep, but rather would try to make themselves believe it was not happening by not opening their eyes or moving.[230]

Incest-Themed Porn That Depicts Sexual Assault, Child Pornography, and Perpetrators of Intra-Familial Sexual Violence All Seem to Be Running the Same Scripts

Accepting that these perpetrators' statements about their daughters' seeming arousal or lack of awareness are presumably motivated by a self-interest in excusing their own behaviour, and in most instances reflect wilful blindness and a refusal to accept responsibility for their harmful conduct, the parallels between their reported perceptions and the representations in incest-themed porn of sleeping and unconscious daughters and sisters is still important. Pornographic representations like the ones described earlier in this chapter present the same sexual scripts that perpetrators appear to rely upon to justify or rationalize their behaviour. This is true with respect to how "sisters" and "daughters" respond in these videos and also true, as explained earlier in this chapter, with respect to the factual circumstances surrounding the sexual acts, as well as the strategies "fathers" and "brothers" in these videos use to gain access to and compliance by their supposed family members. Regardless of one's views on the social function of pornography, it is impossible to deny the similarities between the sexual scripts relied upon in these prominent, widely viewed, and popular incest-themed porn videos, and the sexual scripts that appear to inform the factual circumstances, relationship dynamics, and gendered assumptions surrounding the sexual assault of girls, adolescents, and young women by their family members.

Moreover, accounts by survivors of child pornography – photographed and videoed recordings of the sexual assault of children (often by their family members) – indicate that child pornographers also invoke and rely on these same scripts. Survivors of child sexual abuse material consistently report that they were instructed to either smile and pretend for the camera that they enjoyed what was being done to them, or pretend that they were asleep and unaware of what was occurring.[231] For instance, when the Canadian Centre for Child Protection asked survivors of child pornography whether their abusers gave them instructions, they reported that they were told to:

- "keep silent and smile. Sometimes I had to play-act, show that I was enjoying it and having pleasure in it."
- "play-act that I really want this"
- "pretend to sleep"
- "pretend I liked being raped"
- "smile as if I was enjoying it"
- "above all not [show] … any misery"
- "behave like an adult porn star"
- "keep silent and smile"[232]

As appears to be the case with consumers of adult pornography, the overwhelming consistency of comments like these from survivors of child pornography suggests that men who consume child sexual abuse material must also prefer depictions of child sexual assault in which the victims seem to either enjoy the sexual violence perpetrated against them or are depicted as unaware of what is being done to them.[233]

This Type of Porn Reinforces Injurious Sexual Scripts – and the Cognitive Distortions, Wilful Blindness, and Harmful Sexual Norms That Underpin Them

In order to assess the social impact arising from the widespread consumption of the type of porn examined in this chapter, we must account for the fact that it often relies on the same sexual scripts that appear to inform incestuous sexual violence, and that within virtual porn communities (as described in chapter 2) these scripts are being celebrated, not challenged or disrupted. The users of porn-streaming platforms belong to, or regularly visit, digital communities in which millions of viewers watch videos that portray girls, teenagers, and young women either respond enthusiastically or remain oblivious to sexual offences perpetrated on them by their supposed fathers and brothers. These are communities in which virtually no one comments negatively about the content they are viewing, or notes for other users that these are depictions of sexual assault and rape. Instead, comments on videos with this type of content provide implicit and explicit peer support for viewers who purport to have engaged in, or would like to engage in, similar behaviour towards their sisters and daughters. Relatedly, those in these communities who offer an assessment of the content of this type of porn through a platform's "like" button or "thumbs up/down" function, rate these depictions very highly. These platforms promote incest-themed videos, including ones that portray sexual assault, even to new users who have not provided any data to the platform suggesting an interest in incest-themed porn or depictions of sexual violence.

As explained in chapter 2, the algorithmic logic that drives the content on porn-streaming platforms means that the more frequently videos are viewed, the more frequently they will continue to be viewed, and the more likely it is that more videos with the same type of script will be produced and consumed. In this way, the norms that underpin these particular sexual scripts are held in place by this type of porn. That is to say, the sexual scripts informing the perpetration of intra-family sexual violence inspire the scripts relied upon to produce incest-themed porn. Incest-themed porn, in turn, helps to hold in place, and reinforce, the norms that underpin these sexual scripts. It is an iterative cycle. And it is important to be clear about precisely what these norms are, about what exactly the social contribution of this incredibly popular "faux-cest porn," as it is called, offers us. The social meaning making offered, reinforced, and re-offered by the platformization of incest-themed porn includes:

- the construction of girls and women as a set of orifices to which male family members are sexually entitled;
- the sexual desirability of prepubescent and pubescent girls;
- the construction of men as sexual aggressors and girls and women as passive, if not unconscious, recipients/receptacles;
- the construction of children as either asexual or pre-sexual objects incapable of understanding what is being done to them, or as hypersexual and precocious initiators of the sexual abuse they endure;
- the paramountcy of male sexual pleasure and sexual entitlement;
- the notion of women, and mothers specifically, as sexual gate-keepers; and
- the desirability of sex that is obtained illicitly through manipulation, coercion, duplicity, force, and perhaps most importantly, patriarchy.

Together these norms create social conditions in which intra-family sexual violence not only is tolerated but thrives. They help to write the backdrop for a set of harmful sexual scripts. The platformization of incest-themed porn, combined with the widely and ignorantly embraced public narrative about the unthinkability of incest "in real life," imposes a profoundly unjust paradox on women and girls: massified consumption of sexually explicit content that normalizes the sexual assault of (step)daughters and (step)-sisters by their (step)fathers and (step)brothers in a society that is disinclined to believe women and girls when they tell us they have been sexually assaulted by their (step)fathers and (step)brothers. How is that for a truly unfair social circumstance?

While it may, at first instance, seem shocking to claim that incestuous sexual violence is socially tolerated, recall that the videos described earlier in this chapter are approved by human moderators, receive very favourable ratings, and are viewed hundreds of thousands or even millions of times without being reported, or if they are reported, without being taken down by these platforms. And recall that the sexual assault of children and adolescent girls by their family members, far from being fantastical and fictional, is horribly, tragically common. It is neither sensational nor fantastical to observe that intra-family sexual violence is socially tolerated within our platform society. On platforms like Pornhub and xHamster it is celebrated.

If we think of sexual integrity as a shared interest – an aspect of our interactions and relationships with one another that is capable of promoting joy, pleasure, and human flourishing but that in its diminishment is equally able to cause pain, indignity, and human suffering – it should be obvious that porn that holds in place norms like these causes serious social harms. The first-order harms caused by the reinforcement and reification of norms that support the "cultural scaffolding"[234] of incestuous sexual violence is to this (and the next, and the next) generation of daughters, sons, and sisters sexually assaulted by their (step)fathers and (step)brothers. But the collateral, and secondary, damage caused by the perpetuation of these sexual norms ripple and echo throughout the entirety of our sexual landscape. Joyful, fun, hot, loving, adventurous, or exploratory sex requires sexual actors with the capacity to experience sex as joyful, fun, hot, loving, adventurous, or exploratory. Harmful sexual norms, and porn that reinforces and perpetuates them, diminishes and destroys this capacity both for individuals and communities.

Conclusion

This chapter advanced two central claims. The first claim is that the manner in which incest-themed porn is often characterized and understood is harmful and inaccurate. Public discourse about incest-themed porn often reflects a lack of either awareness or candour regarding the degree to which a subset of this genre of porn depicts dysfunctional power dynamics, coercion, and the sexual assault of unconscious or sleeping teenagers and young girls. A prominent subset of incest-themed porn eroticizes not incest per se but incestuous sexual assault. A lack of openness regarding incest-themed depictions of sexual violence in mainstream porn causes harms. Discourse that characterizes this type of porn as pure fantasy or as an unthinkable taboo ignores its often non-consensual nature and obscures the degree to which this type of sexual violence is, in fact, relatively common. This makes it harder to believe survivors of incest when they do come forward. Moreover, efforts to devise appropriate social and legal responses to this type of porn and to this type of sexual violence may be distorted if we are not clear about the relationship between the depictions in incest-themed porn and incestuous sexual offences. Incest-themed porn is very much consistent with Aidan McGlynn's work, discussed in chapter 4, in which he observes that "the storylines of most works of fiction take place against a background of facts about the non fictional world."[235]

The second main claim in this chapter is that the content in this subset of incest-themed porn invokes and relies on the same harmful sexual scripts that appear to inform intra-familial sexual violence (and the sexual assault of children generally). There is a profound contradiction between abusers' purported perceptions of the response and impact on their victims, fictional portrayals of these same reactions in incest-themed porn, and portrayals in child pornography, and how this harmful sexual behaviour is actually experienced by its victims. This means that the justifications, wilful blindness, and cognitive distortions that sexually abusive family members may adopt to excuse their behaviour are repeatedly represented in incest-themed porn. Likewise, broader sexual scripts informing incest-themed porn, particularly porn that portrays the sexual assault of (step)daughters and (step)sisters, replicate and perpetuate the sexual scripts that appear to operate with respect to incestuous sexual offences. As a result, the harmful sexual norms that underpin these scripts are reinforced by this type of porn. This is not good for anyone, and is acutely detrimental to children, teenage girls, and women.

The sexual scripts informing this prominent subset of incest-themed porn are not mainstream porn's only contribution to harmful sexual norms and the diminishment of sexual integrity as a shared interest. Chapter 6 examines the implications for the legal system of the widespread consumption of "rough sex porn" without adequate consent scripts, a circumstance that also reinforces and perpetuates sexual norms that are dangerous for women.

CHAPTER 6

Do Judges Watch Porn? Porn, Sadomasochism, and the So-Called Rough Sex Defence

"slap that bitch," "slap her pussy," "fucking fist that bitch bro"
– excerpts of a transcript of a video of three men sexually assaulting "Sara"

Crown attorney: But up to that point ... She's crying, you're not paying
attention to what's going on with [Sara]?
Accused: No. Why... why would I be paying attention to what [Sara] is thinking
or saying? How am I supposed to know that she's going to cry?
– excerpts of a transcript of an accused being cross-examined in prosecution for
sexually assaulting "Sara"[1]

Media attention, cultural awareness, and rising public interest in experimenting with sadomasochism (s/m) have led some to proclaim that s/m, perhaps not unlike incest-themed porn as discussed in chapter 5, has gone mainstream.[2] Indeed, research suggests that a substantial minority of the population have fantasized about, or experimented to some degree with, s/m – or bondage, discipline (or domination), sadism (or submission), and masochism (bdsm), as it is sometimes called.[3] In addition, there is an empirical basis upon which to conclude that "rough sex" – slapping, spitting, forceful penetration, strangulation, gagging, and biting – has become more common.[4]

s/m and so-called rough sex have also hit the courts. Criminal courts, for instance, have seen an increased prevalence of legal narratives about either s/m or rough sex in recent years.[5] In particular, courts are increasingly confronted with people who defend themselves against allegations of sexual assault by claiming that the impugned acts constituted consensual s/m or that they honestly, but mistakenly, believed that their accuser had communicated consent to engage in s/m or, the more prevalent claim in legal cases, consensual rough sex.

In Canada, the vast majority of reported sexual assault cases in which the prospect of consensual rough sex has been raised have occurred in the past ten years.[6] In the reported cases from twenty years ago, this "rough sex defence" was nowhere to be found.[7] In the United Kingdom, law reformers have adopted amendments to the *Domestic Abuse Act* to respond to a reportedly 90 per cent increase since 2010 in the number of criminal cases involving violence against women in which the so-called rough sex defence is invoked.[8]

Rough sex shows up not only in our pop culture and legal narratives – it is readily observable in mainstream porn. However, there is considerable discrepancy among assessments of the proportion of mainstream porn that includes "aggression."[9] For instance, there is significant debate about whether porn that depicts consensual acts of physical aggression should be coded as violent or nonviolent. At one end of the spectrum are researchers who code pornography as aggressive only if it includes acts that are presented as intentionally causing harm and which are met with resistance.[10] Conversely, studies that find that the vast majority of mainstream porn depicts aggression tend to include not only physical acts of aggression but also verbal aggression and acts of what these researchers code as degradation (such as scenes in which men ejaculate on the faces of women).[11] Some acts that would otherwise be recognizable as physically aggressive or violent may be genuinely s/m or bdsm, although in those circumstances the consent script is likely to be robust and the overall portrayal of activities perhaps less likely to resemble much of the content found in the "rough sex" category on mainstream platforms like Pornhub and xHamster.

The heavy focus on content that depicts aggression is perhaps somewhat misplaced. Sexual acts that violate another's sexual integrity do not always include activity that is readily identifiable as aggressive. Sexual violence includes acts that are coercive, fraudulent, exploitative, and deceptive. So does some mainstream porn. For instance, videos with titles indicating depictions of sex that include the surreptitious removal of condoms ("stealthing," as it is sometimes called), or "surprise anal," in which women are "surprised" by anal penetration that they were not expecting and therefore did not consent to, following consensual vaginal penetration, can be readily found on mainstream porn platforms.[12]

Similarly, as evident in several of the examples examined in earlier chapters, some of the common depictions of sexual assault found on porn-streaming platforms involve portrayals of the sexual violation of women and teenage girls who are asleep or unconscious, and depictions of the sexual assault of (step)daughters and (step)sisters by their (step)fathers and (step)brothers. Some examples of this latter genre of porn replicate the grooming patterns and opportunistic offending patterns often seen in intra-family sexual violence, and may be less likely to include acts of physical aggression. Moreover, in porn the response to these acts, coded by some researchers as aggression, is most often positive or neutral.[13] As Eran Shor and Kimberley Seida have documented, depictions of non-consensual sex in mainstream porn that are explicitly labelled as such are less common and are less popular.[14] Likewise, there is significant disagreement on what constitutes degradation and whether depictions of degradation are categorically violent.

While content-based porn researchers may not agree on the proportion of porn that includes depictions of aggression, or even what constitutes aggression, or on what percentage of mainstream porn depicts sexual violence more broadly, inarguably a significant proportion of the videos on mainstream porn-streaming platforms, even beyond those that are specifically categorized as rough sex, contain depictions of women being coerced into sex, slapped, pulled by the hair, choked, strangled, and/or very forcefully penetrated – with the only portrayal of their consent being that which is implicit in their seemingly positive or neutral response to what is being done to them.[15] In a 2020 study of 4,009 heterosexual scenes on Pornhub and XVideos, Niki Fritz and Paul Bryant found that 45 per cent of Pornhub scenes and 35 per cent of scenes on XVideos included acts such as spanking, gagging, slapping, and hair pulling; that women were the targets of these acts in 97 per cent of the scenes; and that their responses were either neutral or positive in 97 per cent of the Pornhub videos and in 92 per cent of the videos on XVideos.[16] In his 2019 study, Shor found that 43 per cent of videos in his sample of mainstream porn included acts of biting, pinching, kicking, hair pulling, choking, forced gagging, rough handling, and/or forceful penetration, albeit in his research only 13 per cent of the most popular videos contained such content.[17] Shor also found that teenage performers (or those who appeared to be teenage girls or adolescent women) were five times more likely than older women to appear in videos featuring forceful anal penetration, and three times more likely than adult women to appear in videos with titles that described what he identified as aggression.[18] To be clear, porn with this type of content is not depicting safe, sane, and consensual s/m or BDSM.

For the purposes of this discussion there are three key points emanating from this content analysis–based research: (1) depictions of rough sex are common in mainstream porn; (2) in mainstream porn that does include rough sex, it is virtually always girls and women, not men, who are the targets of the hitting, gagging, hair pulling, forceful penetration, etc.; and (3) the adolescent girls and women performing in these videos are almost always depicted as responding neutrally or positively to whatever is being done to them. One further, and related, point should be made at the outset of this chapter: like the depictions of rough sex in mainstream porn, the so-called rough sex defence is deeply gendered. According to research conducted by Elizabeth Sheehy, Isabel Grant, and Lise Gotell, in Canadian cases it is *only* men who have relied on this defence in an effort to exonerate themselves from charges of sexual assault, assault, and homicide, and in nearly every case their alleged victims have been women.[19] This fact alone – that it is only men relying on a particular legal defence in response to a crime perpetrated almost always against women – reveals the need for law reform in response to this supposed rough sex defence.

• • •

Is there a relationship between the types of sexual scripts featured in mainstream porn and the legal rough sex scripts that appear to inform some contemporary sexual assault prosecutions? Perhaps it is not a coincidence that the appearance of porn-streaming platforms and the marked emergence and rise of this so-called rough sex defence occurred over the same time period? It seems reasonable to speculate that a considerable increase in the consumption of sexually explicit material that depicts seemingly consensual rough sex would raise the profile of, and thus the tendency of accused individuals to rely on, legal narratives of consensual rough sex in response to allegations of violent sexual misconduct. If this is true, what does it mean for legal systems charged with responding to allegations of harmful sexual conduct? Is the plausibility of the "she consented" defence, or the "he honestly thought she was communicating consent" defence, in the face of allegations that include non-consensual sexual touching combined with, for example, strangulation, slapping, and hitting, increased by the reality and impact of mainstream porn-streaming platforms? Are jury pools impacted in a community in which many of its members visit virtual porn communities with highly rated content that depicts women responding positively to being gagged with penises, spit on, and forcefully penetrated in the anus and vagina, and that tag, categorize, and curate similar content for the user? Are legal fact finders more likely to accept that it is at least *possible* that a complainant was a willing participant in the sexual acts that occurred, or that an accused believed this, because of the platformization of porn? What is the relationship between (1) the social media character of mainstream porn platforms (including the inevitable norm setting and iterative evaluation and re-evaluation of norms that occurs in any platform community that comments on, "likes," shares, tags, uploads, downloads, and algorithmically amplifies content); (2) the rough sex scripts in some mainstream porn; and (3) and the consensual "rough sex defence" that has emerged in contemporary sexual assault law?

We do not know the answers to these questions. However, we do know that judges and juries are increasingly required to adjudicate allegations that mirror the sexual scripts followed in some, if not a good deal, of mainstream pornography. For example, in Canada between 1996 and 2020 there was a more than 250 per cent increase in the number of reported judicial decisions involving allegations of non-consensual anal penetration.[20] Between these same dates there was an almost 200 per cent increase in the number of reported sexual assault decisions involving allegations of choking, or as it is more appropriately labelled: strangulation.[21] Likewise, there has been a 200 per cent increase in the number of reported decisions involving allegations that the accused urinated on the complainant without her consent, and a 250 per cent increase in the number of cases involving allegations that the accused spit on the complainant during the sexual assault.[22] Similarly, and as already noted, the vast majority of reported sexual assault cases in which the prospect of consensual rough sex is raised by the accused have occurred in the past ten years.[23]

An even more striking pattern exists with respect to the growth in reported cases involving allegations of the surreptitious, non-consensual removal of a condom.[24] The Supreme Court of Canada recently confirmed in *R v Kirkpatrick* that "sex with and without a condom are fundamentally and qualitatively distinct" and that a woman who consents to sex with a condom has not consented to sex without a condom.[25] In *Kirkpatrick* the accused engaged in vaginal penetration of the complainant in a darkened room in the middle of the night, knowing that she would only consent to intercourse on the condition that he wear protection. She believed he was wearing a condom until after he had ejaculated inside of her vagina. When she asked him the next day in a text message why he had done this to her, and whether he knew that this was a sexual assault, he indicated that he found it humorous and sent the complainant a porn video entitled "Oh My God, Daddy Came inside Me."[26]

These statistics alone are not sufficient to draw conclusions regarding changes in offending patterns. Numerous factors might contribute to the increased number of cases, or reported decisions, with these types of fact patterns. Although reporting rates for sexual assault have not increased over this period, which means these increases are not explained by a rise in overall reporting. It is possible these statistics reflect differences in the types of sexual assaults being reported. But recall that this radical increase in reported decisions with these fact patterns is paralleled by research demonstrating that strangulation (choking), slapping, spitting, hair pulling, and gagging are remarkably common sexual practices today[27] and are frequently experienced as unwanted by the women subjected to them.[28] This makes it difficult not to speculate that this drastic rise in reported decisions indicates that these types of sexual assaults have become more common. This is not to revive the long-standing and intractable empirical debate about causal relationships between porn consumption and individual sexually violent behaviour.[29] Perhaps porn is imitating life ... Whatever might explain such overlapping trends, it seems clear that the same sexual scripts are operating in both of these contexts.

Do judges watch porn? While we do not know whether judges spend more, less, or about the same amount of time on porn-streaming platforms as other members of our communities, we do know that, increasingly, judges who preside over sexual assault trials have to watch sexually explicit video material as part of their job.[30] We also know that judges and juries today may more regularly be called upon to adjudicate factual claims in cases of sexual violence not as commonly presented to them twenty or thirty years ago, but which closely resemble the depictions of sex readily found in some mainstream porn today.

The issue of this so-called rough sex defence inevitably raises challenging legal questions regarding autonomy, liberty, and equality. Largely, this is because it is often wrongly conflated with s/m and bdsm practices. Feminist reflection on s/m requires consideration of the relationship between protecting human health and safety, preserving personal autonomy, and promoting the social conditions in which the good of sex might flourish. There are tensions between ensuring legal protection for the sexual integrity of women (in particular) and the criminalization of consensual sexual acts on the basis of heteronormative or "vanilla" attitudes about the (un)desirability or worthlessness of certain marginalized sexual minorities and practices.[31] Katherine Franke argues that legal feminists have focused exclusively on the dangers of sex at the cost of properly recognizing the female body as a site of pleasure and desire.[32] She suggests that implicit in this focus of legal feminism is the problematic assumption that before sexuality can be explored positively, harmful, dangerous sex must be eliminated.[33]

Waiting until the dangers of sex have been eliminated to embrace the capacity of sex to promote human flourishing does seem ill advised.[34] That said, ensuring that legal protection of the right and ability to say "no" is effectual seems necessary to facilitate and expand women's capacity to pursue pleasure – to say "yes."[35] In other words, women's ability to say "yes" requires robust legal protection of their right to say "no." Both as a matter of theory and practice, s/m throws this circumstance into relief.[36] However, the consensual rough sex scripts that are increasingly being invoked in sexual assault prosecutions? These seem more like a parasitic effort to coopt a fractional aspect of a minority sexual practice and misrepresent it in service of a legal justification for what is a very different sexual practice – one which in virtually every prosecution, at least in Canada, the complainant alleges that she did not consent (often to anything).[37] Her sexual liberty is, indeed, at stake in these cases – but it is not the state that has put it in jeopardy.

The potential relationship between the sexual scripts in mainstream pornographic depictions of women being choked, strangled, slapped, spit on, and very forcefully penetrated; the conflation of these depictions with the practice of safe, sane, and consensual s/m; and legal scripts that rely on consent to rough sex, or a mistaken belief in communicated consent to rough sex, complicates and diminishes the capacity of women to pursue pleasure.

That these depictions are offered and consumed in platform communities in which users are in constant digital dialogue with one another, and with the algorithms used to determine the marketing and production of future porn, emphasizes the potential significance of this relationship. That is to say, widespread, quasi-participatory and quasi-interactive, data-driven, and communal consumption of pornography that includes the nominal and/or physical portrayal of consensual rough sex has specific implications for our legal responses to harmful sexual behaviour.

A legal regime that properly and consistently delineates between consensual and non-consensual acts in adjudicating rough sex defences could help to promote freedom from oppressive, harmful sexual experiences. Confidence on the part of women that such a regime was in place would facilitate women's freedom to pursue more sexual creativity and greater exploration of desire and pleasure. One of the many harms of sexual violence is that it diminishes the capacity of adolescent girls and women to seek self-fulfilment, develop their identity, and pursue desire, pleasure, and joy through sex. While Franke's call to legal feminists to "theorize yes" should be heeded, it would be foolish not to recognize that the capacity to say "yes" to sex in all of its complexities, to pursue erotic activities adventurously, is furthered by, and arguably reliant on, the right and ability to say "no."[38]

Unfortunately, judges still fail to consistently and properly delineate between consensual and non-consensual sex. The realities are that some courts, as Karen Busby notes, continue to struggle with the "did she consent" question in sexual assault cases, and that this struggle may be heightened in cases in which accused individuals invoke s/m, or more often consensual rough sex, in response to allegations of non-consensual sexual contact.[39] In other words, some judges continue to err when answering the "did she consent" question, let alone the "can she (legally) consent" question. The contributions that mainstream porn-streaming platforms make to both our sexual scripts and our legal ones may aggravate this legal circumstance.

Legal systems have to account for the likelihood that some of the scripts reflected in rough sex porn likely contribute to legal scripts, either explicitly through the invocation of doctrine such as the so-called rough sex defence, or implicitly as a consequence of the iterative, norm-setting social function through which widespread consumption on porn-streaming platforms and participation in platform communities contribute to social understandings of sexuality more generally and consent specifically. Protecting the capacity to say "yes" through upholding the right to say "no" requires recognition of the extent to which the consent scripts invoked in courts could be increasingly informed by widespread public engagement on, or at a minimum attendance in, mainstream porn communities with significant proportions of content that depicts adolescent girls and women being slapped, choked, strangled, spit, urinated and ejaculated on, and penetrated vaginally, orally, and anally with significant force by men (and almost never the reverse). A lot turns on the legal definition of consent relied on by courts in response to this so-called rough sex defence. This chapter explains why our social engagement with porn on the platform that depicts rough sex magnifies the need for both a legal definition of consent that is subjective, communicative, affirmative, specific, and contemporaneous, and a judicial system that consistently and rigorously applies this definition.

The platformization of porn also supports the conclusion that, when it comes to the "can she (legally) consent" question, in relation to sexual acts that cause "significant bodily harm," as in long-lasting or permanent injury, the answer should be "no."[40] In this context, and as the Court of Appeal of Alberta rightly concluded recently, sexual violence causing significant bodily harm that is objectively foreseeable ought not to be conflated with safe, sane, and consensual BDSM. In virtually all of these type of cases, the women subjected to this violence, if they are still alive, do not claim to have "said yes," and there are sound policy reasons related to protecting the health, safety, and lives of women that support vitiating consent in these circumstances.[41]

Scripting Consent in Rough Sex Porn

Before explaining in more technical terms what it means to use a subjective, communicative, affirmative, specific, and contemporaneous legal definition of consent, it is helpful to consider some examples of consent scripts in mainstream pornography. How do mainstream porn platforms tend to script consent?[42]

At the time of writing, there were close to 50,000 videos in the "Rough Sex" category on Pornhub and another approximately 13,000 in the "Bondage" category. To be clear, there are depictions of rough sex in many, if not most, categories on mainstream porn platforms. That is to say, such depictions are not limited to videos in categories explicitly labelled as rough sex.

Moreover, according to some researchers, a good deal of supposedly s/m-themed mainstream porn lacks any depiction of the explicit communication that experienced s/m practitioners engage in both prior to, during, and after a s/m or bdsm scenario.[43] As a result, there is sometimes a conflation in mainstream porn between what is characterized as bdsm porn and what is in reality rape-themed pornography, or at a minimum depictions of rough sex with paltry and insufficient consent scripts that fail to articulate the key attribute of a bdsm scene: a carefully negotiated, rigorous, and detailed mutual articulation of consent.[44] As already explained, and as is demonstrated in the two cases examined in this chapter, this same conflation shows up in the legal reasoning in some sexual assault decisions. Busby hypothesizes that "increased social openness to bdsm may permit defendants to claim a bdsm practice by relying on judicial ignorance about bdsm practices and, thereby, raise doubt about consent" in cases in which that doubt is not warranted.[45]

Several of the videos on the landing page for the "Rough Sex" category on Pornhub depict men engaging in physically aggressive, extremely rough sexual acts with women without any discussion of consent, or any depiction of negotiation and communication regarding the parameters of what is to occur. In fact, in several of the videos on the landing page when I visited this "Rough Sex" category on Pornhub for the first time, the sexual activity had commenced before the video began, which meant there was no depiction of consent or of communication and negotiation between the sexual actors.[46] For example, "Busty Teen Step-Sister Skylar Vox Gets Pussy Pounded by Frustrated Step-Brother" is a twelve-minute-and-forty-eight-second video of extremely vigorous, forceful penetration in a variety of positions. The sexual activity in this video begins with the male performer grabbing his (according to the title) stepsister by the throat and telling her, "You want to fuck your brother, don't you?"[47] She quickly goes from startled to orgasmic as she gets "pounded by [her] frustrated step-bother."[48]

Consider the consent script used in another video found on the landing page during a first visit to the "Rough Sex" category on Pornhub entitled "Daddy Makes Petite Newcomer Lilli Chanel's Pussy Squirt."[49] The video employs the "casting couch" trope as its narrative device. Casting couch, which has been described as a "metonym for the skewed sexual politics of show business," is a genre of mainstream pornography.[50] In terms of consent, the casting couch trope is itself problematic, regardless of any other aspect of the content in a particular video. It invokes a dynamic of coercion, manipulation, and exploitation, intentionally aimed at undermining the sincerity and voluntariness of any articulation of consent that is depicted in a video that relies on this trope. One need only reflect on the grotesque impact of the gendered power imbalances in the entertainment industry, which was the context in which the #MeToo movement gained its global momentum, to appreciate the disturbing connotation of this trope.[51] As director Sarah Polley observes, in reflecting on the articulated misogyny of the film industry (from which the casting couch porn trope draws its inspiration): "Harvey Weinstein may be the central-casting version of a Hollywood predator, but he was just one festering pustule in a diseased industry."[52]

This particular video – "Daddy Makes Petite Newcomer Lilli Chanel's Pussy Squirt" – starts with a female performer sitting on a couch directly in front of a camera as a male voice from off-screen asks her why she is there. She tells him that she wants to get "face fucked." He replies that "Daddy is going to do a lot more than face fuck you today. He is going to do everything to you." She whispers, "Okay." The significantly larger male performer enters the frame, asks if she has "ever gotten it rough before," and she indicates that she has not. With the exception of what seem to be intended as depictions of pleasure on her part (but which are not convincing) during some other parts of the remainder of the video, this exchange is the extent of the depiction of consent in this video. After she whispers "okay" to his vague assertion, he places her in a choke hold, followed by which, for the remaining eleven minutes of the video, the female performer is repeatedly slapped on the face and hit on the breasts, buttocks, and genitals. The male performer spits directly into her mouth and on her face multiple times. He twists and slaps her nipples. He places his hands around her throat and squeezes at several points. She is repeatedly gagged and choked with his penis and violently penetrated in the vagina with his penis and hand. She has difficulty breathing at times. The degree of force used by the considerably larger male performer in thrusting his penis and hand into her vagina makes it difficult not to speculate that she would have sustained vaginal injuries filming this video. It ends with a close-up of her face covered in ejaculate.[53]

The sexual norms held in place by a script such as the one reflected in this first video include the construction of male sexuality as aggressive and violent, and female sexuality as passive and acquiescent; male desire and sexual pleasure as pre-eminent and female desire and sexual pleasure as secondary, if not irrelevant, and experienced, if at all, through subjugation and submission; and male bodies as subject actors and female bodies as inexpressive objects to be acted upon, or receptacles for male sexual violence.

Now consider the consent script followed in a second video. The second example is a video on the landing page during a first visit to the "Bondage" category on Pornhub. It is called "Diviyne Does Vegas Mayhem Extreme in Las Vegas Bondage Assisted Masturbation."[54] This video also starts with a female performer sitting on a couch and a male voice, off-screen, who confirms with her that she wants to make a "BDSM video." He then asks her a series of questions: "Okay, so you are fully willing to be controlled, even blindfolded." She replies, "Yes, absolutely." He asks her to confirm that she is willing to be tied up. She says, "Yes." That she has told him that she likes this? "Yes." That she wants to be sexually played with while tied up? "Yes." He asks her whether she wants all of her body parts played with? "Yes." He asks her to confirm that she is not under the influence of alcohol or any mind-altering drugs. She confirms that she is not incapacitated in any manner. She does not appear incapacitated. He confirms again that she wants to "experience this BDSM." She indicates, "Yes." She agrees that she has been given "safe words and safe actions" to protect her safety. The remainder of the video contains a series of scenes with her and a hooded and clothed man who uses various BDSM-associated devices to seemingly stimulate various parts of her body in ways that appear to cause her a combination of significant sexual pleasure and some modest physical pain. She is blindfolded, wearing a ball gag, and tied up throughout most of this part of the video.[55] She is penetrated vaginally while tied up, blindfolded, and nipple clamped. Her genital area and breasts are slapped and hit with various devices. Unlike in the first video, the depiction of female sexual pleasure is a convincing one of agency, some autonomy, and genuine gratification and delight.

The depictions of consent in these two videos are very different. In the first video the female performer is told (not asked) by the male subject that he is "going to do everything" to her. He does not specify what "everything" entails. She quietly utters the word "okay" in response. This is a depiction of broad, advance, and unspecified consent. There is no suggestion in this video that they have agreed upon safe words or safe actions. They do not establish, for instance, a signal or gesture she might make to indicate her lack of consent if she is unable to do so orally because he has thrust his penis so far down her throat that she can neither speak nor breathe. Her capacity to consent is not assessed or ascertained.

In the context of BDSM a standard of consent that requires contemporaneity, as explained next, must include the negotiation of, and agreement upon, safe words and safe actions that can be invoked in order to cease the

activities immediately. Without these terms of engagement, parties are relying on an articulation of advance consent to assess one another's voluntariness. A legal standard that accepts broad, advance consent does not
sufficiently protect women's right to say "no," diminishing the ability to say
"yes." Legal reasoning that relies on consent scripts of this nature risks perpetuating and instantiating the same sexual norms that porn of this nature
problematically articulates and reinforces.

Unlike with the first video, the consent script followed in the second
video does invoke several of the elements demanded by a communicative,
affirmative, specific, and contemporaneous definition of consent. The video
depicts communication that is unequivocally affirmative – the female performer responds "yes, absolutely" when asked whether she wants to be controlled and blindfolded. There is a degree of specificity regarding the
particular acts to be engaged in: he asks her to confirm whether she wants
some or all of her body parts played with by the "master." There is confirmation of her capacity to grant the consent depicted. There is confirmation
that the parties involved have identified safe words and safe acts, which aids
in ensuring that consent will be contemporaneous with the sexual acts engaged in during the video. Again, a failure to identify a safe word and safe
act (in circumstances in which speaking is not possible, such as when someone is wearing a ball gag) makes it impossible to ensure that consent is ongoing, particularly if role playing is involved.

The consent script followed in this second video is not perfect. For
example, it, too, relies on the trope of the casting couch and the sexual
exploitation dynamic that this trope invokes. It does not depict a negotiated
exchange; she simply agrees to everything suggested to her. In addition, to
avoid depicting broad, unspecified consent, the acts to be engaged in could
have been further specified, and the devices to be used should have been in-
dividually specified and agreed upon. That said, a comparison between the
consent scripts followed in these two videos reveals both the severe deficiencies in the first script and the significant strengths, in terms of protecting
sexual integrity, of the depiction of consent in the second video. Unfortunately, in adjudicating the so-called rough sex defence, some judges rely on,
or accept, a construction of consent that more closely resembles the consent
script followed in the first video than that of the second video.

Before considering legal cases of this sort, let us return briefly to the description of the first video: the one that shows a large man hitting, twisting
the nipples of, spitting on, strangling, and forcefully penetrating the throat

and vagina of a much smaller woman. There is one further aspect of the sexual depiction in this video that I have not yet touched upon: the female performer's response. The woman in this video responds positively to what is being done to her. As a representation of female sexual pleasure, it is not a convincing performance, and her pleasure is very much not a centred aspect of the video. But when she is not gagging up spit and saliva, choking on his penis, or gasping for air, the woman in this video is depicted as neutral or even smiling in response to the acts imposed upon her. This is not surprising. Recall that research suggests most male viewers who consume mainstream porn want the women in it to be depicted as responding positively, no matter what is being done to them.[56]

That the representation of female pleasure in the first video is unsurprising does not make the implications of it unimportant. Indeed, this aspect of the first video demonstrates precisely why it is so necessary to employ a legal definition of consent in sexual assault law that does not rely on an accused's perception of, or assumptions about, what his alleged victim wanted, or resisted but then appeared to enjoy. As feminists have long recognized, the protection of women's sexual integrity requires a legal definition of consent that turns on the complainant's subjective experience of the sexual activity at the time that it occurs and not the accused's perception of whether "she wanted it." A definition of consent that turns on this is better able to counter precisely the problematic consent scripts, and underpinning sexual norms, that mainstream rough sex porn perpetuates – norms such as the notion that a woman's initial resistance or reluctance likely masks an underlying desire to consent, or that women's sexuality manifests primarily as a receptacle for male sexual fulfillment, or that some women will consent to anything.

A Subjective, Affirmative, Contemporaneous, and Communicative Definition of Consent

When assessing whether a particular sexual act was consensual for purposes of criminal law, courts typically consider the perspectives of both the person who alleges being subjected to non-consensual sexual acts and the person accused of engaging in non-consensual sexual behaviour. In other words, at least with respect to adult complainants, the legal definition of consent typically includes these two parts. The complainant's perspective is assessed in order to determine whether the sexual act was, in fact, non-consensual. (This is referred to as the *actus reus* – the guilty act of sexual assault.) If the sexual act at issue was non-consensual from the perspective of the complainant, then the accused's perspective is assessed in order to determine whether he knew that it was non-consensual. In other words, can he be blamed for the non-consensual sexual act in which he engaged? (This is often referred to as the *mens rea* – the guilty mind.)

There are different ways to make these assessments of the complainant's perspective and the accused's perspective. Canada was one of the first common law jurisdictions to incorporate a subjective, contemporaneous, affirmative, and communicative standard into this assessment. What does this mean? To say that a legal definition of consent is subjective and contemporaneous is to say that for the purposes of determining whether the sexual act was, in fact, non-consensual, the complainant's perspective – her subjective state of mind, her experience of the act at the time it was occurring – will determine whether the act was, in fact, non-consensual.[57]

If the sexual touching was, in fact, non-consensual, then the analysis turns to the accused's state of mind to determine whether he is blameworthy. To say that a definition of consent is affirmative and communicative is to say that assessing whether the accused knew that he was engaging in a non-consensual sexual act will be determined by whether he can point to evidence that the complainant communicated "yes" – either through her words or actions. In other words, for the purposes of determining whether an accused is blameworthy for the non-consensual act, the assessment is not based on his assumptions about whether the complainant was consenting, which risk being informed by his assumptions regarding her gender, attire, earlier flirtation, sexual reputation, race, age, level of capacity, or relationship status; rather, it is his perception of what the complainant was communicating to him at the time the act occurred that is determinative of his moral blameworthiness.

While all of this might seem a bit technical or lawyerly, this definition of consent, when properly applied, reduces the likelihood of gendered social assumptions and sexist and/or racist norms about women, sex, and consent – such as the ones sometimes depicted in mainstream pornography – from infecting legal analysis in sexual assault prosecutions. It also precludes accused individuals from relying on these assumptions to exonerate or justify their coercive or violent sexual behaviour. For example, when properly applied, this construction of consent precludes legal conclusions about the presence of consent based on outdated and discriminatory assumptions that women, or some types of women, secretly want to be raped; will consent to anything; convey consent by what they wear; enjoy being slapped, hit, and spit on despite denying it; will do anything when they are drunk; or need to be forced but will eventually succumb and respond pleasurably to whatever is being done to them.

This legal approach to consent is critical to protecting women's right to say no. Consent scripts, whether in porn or in court, that invoke the notion of consensual rough sex bring the need for this definition sharply into focus. Closely examining cases in which courts fail to apply a subjective, contemporaneous, affirmative, and communicative definition of consent demonstrate why such a definition is critical, particularly in cases involving this supposed rough sex defence. In Canada, one of the first jurisdictions to adopt a legal definition of consent with these components, sexual assault case law provides an opportunity to perform this type of close examination.

The remainder of this chapter examines the trial proceedings in two recent cases, *R v Hunter* and *R v AE*, in which trial judges in Canada failed to apply this definition, and instead accepted or adopted an account of consent that more closely resembles the consent script followed in the first video examined earlier ("Daddy Makes Petite Newcomer Lilli Chanel's Pussy Squirt") than that of the second video ("Diviyne Does Vegas Mayhem Extreme in Las Vegas Bondage Assisted Masturbation").[58]

Two Case Studies: *R v Hunter* and *R v AE*

There are many similarities between both the facts in *R v Hunter* and *R v AE* and the legal errors in these two cases.[59] Both cases involved reliance on the so-called rough sex defence by the accused. In both cases the incidents involved sexual interactions between more than two people. Both involved sexual acts – slapping, choking, hitting, strangulation – similar to those depicted in the first video. Both involved interactions that seemingly commenced with consensual sex, and as noted, in both cases the trial judges arrived at acquittals, having accepted or followed a consent script that more closely resembled the one depicted in the first video than that of the second video. In doing so, the trial judges in both of these cases failed to apply the subjective, contemporaneous, affirmative, and communicative definition of consent required under Canadian law. In *Hunter*, this legal error was not corrected because the Crown failed to appeal the decision. Thankfully, the Crown did appeal in *AE* and the legal errors made by the trial judge in that case were corrected by the Court of Appeal of Alberta.

The Case of Her Majesty the Queen and Logan Hunter

The complainant in *Hunter*, A.G., had a hearing disability that made it difficult for her to understand someone speaking unless she was lip reading.[60] She and the accused, Logan Hunter, arranged through an online messaging app to meet for what they both described as a "dominant–submissive" sexual encounter involving the two of them and another woman, S.D.[61] The accused and A.G. agreed that she would take the bus from Halifax to Cow Bay, Nova Scotia, where the accused would pick her up. Due to difficulties with A.G.'s bus route, it was 10:30 p.m. before Hunter collected her from the bus stop and drove her to S.D.'s residence, a trailer in a wooded area of rural Nova Scotia. The complainant had never been to, and was unfamiliar with, this location.[62] S.D. was a long-time friend and "somewhat regular" sexual partner of Hunter.[63] A.G. had never met S.D. and did not know the accused's real name. Hunter used a pseudonym in their communications on the messaging app. The accused significantly outweighed A.G.[64] All of which is to say, there were numerous factors contributing to the significant power differential between A.G. and Hunter that night.

A.G., Hunter, and S.D. all testified. A.G.'s evidence was that the incident began with a series of consensual sexual acts between the three of them. Her allegation was that, following these consensual acts, the accused engaged in several acts to which she did not consent. She alleged that he, without her consent, repeatedly choked her with his penis by shoving it so far into her throat that she could not breathe, slapped her face, grabbed and twisted her breast, and partially strangled her with his hands while penetrating her vagina with his penis. Some of the sexual acts at issue in *Hunter* closely resemble the depiction of rough sex in the first video we examined.[65] Hunter was acquitted.

The Need to Consider Whether A.G. Subjectively Wanted to Choke on Hunter's Penis

A.G.'s evidence was that as the sexual interaction started, she and S.D., the third participant that night, took turns performing oral sex on Hunter while kneeling in front of him. She testified that "he wanted me to have his penis all the way down my throat until I threw up and I didn't like that so I was hesitant in letting his penis go all the way back, but I uh, but it was still consensual. Um, during this point he would also pull on my hair."[66] Following some further consensual sexual acts between the three, Hunter then instructed A.G. to lie on the bed and hang her head off the edge of the bed. From this position he would be in "complete control" of how far he could push his penis down her throat.[67]

·In assessing the trial judge's conclusions regarding A.G.'s consent, it is helpful to consider the evidence he heard. A.G. testified in direct examination that while she was in this position on the bed:

A.G.: [the accused] inserted his penis into my mouth and he went so far back, to the back of my throat, and I remember feeling like I couldn't breath [sic] and his stomach was pressed up against my face, and he …

Q: Okay, carry on.

A.G.: Um, so he did this about twice, and I started to panic because I couldn't breath [sic] and I lifted my hands up above my head and started to try to push him off me. So I was pushing on his stomach area to try to push his penis out of my mouth because I could not breath while he was doing this. Um … I remember I started to cry, and there were, um … visible tears at that point, um … and then …

Q: And were you … at this point were you consenting to what was going on with the oral sex, with the insertion of the penis further down your throat so that you couldn't breathe?

A.G.: No. No.

Q: Okay, carry on, Ms. G.

A.G.: So, um … he did, after I tried pushing him off of me, he did back his penis out of my mouth, and I shook my head and I told him "no," that I did not want to do it anymore, and at this point I was still crying and he slapped me across the face, and the female, she said, "just do it one more time and then Daddy will fuck you again." Um … and then as response Logan [Hunter] said he won't go as far down this time and just for me to do it one more time. Um … I did give in and agree because by that point I was feeling scared and like he wasn't going to listen to anything I had to say. Um … though he did agree and not go as far down my throat this time. Um … this lasted maybe ten minutes.[68]

S.D. testified under cross-examination that A.G. was "kind of resistant" during the "oral sex."[69] She agreed that she had told the police that A.G. either said "stop" or "no" to the accused or otherwise indicated a lack of consent during the "oral sex."[70]

Hunter testified that "there were multiple insertions" of his penis down A.G.'s throat and that at "no point did she say 'no' or push against" him.[71] He stated that "each time there was a longer pause between each [insertion] because of the gagging. You tend to, like, lose your breath and, you know, your nose becomes stuffy and things so I would give her a break between each insertion."[72] He testified that:

> each time she's catching her breath her mouth is not available for oral sex. So, you know, she's breathing heavily and she's just laying there ... So there's just a longer pause each time before she eventually opened her mouth. But I didn't threaten her. I didn't smack her ... and I did not make any threat about, you know, not driving her home or any type of violence.[73]

Hunter testified that A.G. was gagging and coughing, had lost her breath, her nose was running, her eyes were glassy, and her face was turning red, and then asserted that he did not see or hear any indication that "she was in any state of discomfort."[74] If gagging, coughing and gasping for air, watery eyes, and reddening face do not amount to signs of discomfort in response to having a penis thrust into the back of one's throat, what *would* constitute a sign of discomfort?

Hunter's perception of how the complainant responded between these acts of choking her with his penis is reminiscent of the content in the first video we examined. The editing cuts in that video moved directly between scenes in which the female performer was being choked by a penis or gagging on her own saliva, to ones in which she was smiling, back to ones in which she was again gagging and choking as the male performer thrust his penis (and hands and fingers) into the back of her throat.

Regarding these acts of choking A.G. with his penis, Hunter agreed on cross-examination that:

> Q: ... there were times when Ms G. squirmed, correct?
> Hunter: Yes.

Q: There were times when she gagged?
Hunter: Yes.
Q: There were times when she clearly couldn't breathe and needed air?
Hunter: Yes.
…

Q: And the reason for that particular position with her lying on her bed with her head [hanging] over the bed is that it allows you to push your penis deeper down her throat than you would otherwise be able to do?
Hunter: In an upright position it doesn't, it's not able to go as far. So, yes.
Q: And that position also allows you to control … the situation more. You're kneeling over her head as it dangles off the bed. You're in control of how far the penis goes down her throat?
Hunter: Yes.[75]

Hunter told the police, "there may have been tears, because when you gag, your eyes water and your nose tends to run. But I wouldn't say, like, she was crying, I guess. It's just, like, the involuntary response of coughing that hard or something."[76] When pressed on this point during cross-examination, Hunter agreed that he was simply guessing when he suggested that the tears were from gagging and not because she was upset or in distress.[77]

Despite A.G.'s evidence that she did not want to be choked by the accused's penis, despite S.D.'s evidence that A.G. showed resistance when the accused was pushing his penis down her throat, and despite the accused's evidence that A.G. was squirming, gagging, coughing, and could not breathe, Justice Duncan was "not satisfied beyond a reasonable doubt that A.G. was not consenting to the acts of fellatio."[78] While he accepted that "at one point [A.G.] decided that she did not want to have Mr. Hunter's penis so deep in her throat that it caused her to gag and tear,"[79] he was left with a reasonable doubt regarding her evidence that she did not consent to any of these acts of being choked by Hunter with his penis while in this position on the bed.

How could evidence from A.G. that she did not want to have this man's penis repeatedly thrust so far down her throat that she could not breathe, combined with evidence from Hunter himself that she was gagging, coughing, tearing up, and turning red, and evidence from S.D. that A.G. was at times resistant, not be sufficient to conclude that she had not consented to this act? The answer is that Justice Duncan failed to properly apply the subjective element of the definition of consent. Recall that the subjective element of the definition means that determining whether the sexual act at issue was, in fact, non-consensual turns on A.G.'s subjective state of mind at the time the act occurred.

Justice Duncan expressed doubt about "A.G.'s evidence that she attempted to push the accused away."[80] He reasoned that "if she did that it was not apparent to the accused. This could be explained by the fact that he is a large man and she may not have used enough force to make her intentions known to him."[81] His emphasis on what the accused saw and knew – on what was apparent to him – suggests that Justice Duncan may have relied on Hunter's perspective to determine whether this was, in fact, consensual, rather than on A.G.'s state of mind. Justice Duncan's repeated emphasis on the accused's perceptions – particularly his explanation as to why the accused may not have been aware of A.G.'s resistance – suggests that his doubt of A.G.'s claim that she did not consent to being choked in this manner by Hunter's penis was informed by an assessment of Hunter's state of mind at the time of the incident.

Recall that the accused's assumption or belief as to whether A.G. was consenting is not relevant for purposes of determining whether the sexual act was, in fact, consensual.[82] Under Canadian law, this part of the analysis is supposed to be determined exclusively by the complainant's subjective experience of the incident at the time it was occurring. To instead objectively construe consent based on, for example, a woman's compliance or failure to (adequately) resist would be wholly ill-suited to protecting women's sexual integrity.[83] Why? Because an objective standard requires inferring or implying consent based on factors external to the complainant's state of mind. Notions of implied consent are highly susceptible to empirically unsound and potentially discriminatory social assumptions about, for example, sex, gender, race, class, or Indigeneity. Reforms aimed at eliminating legal doctrine that rely on implied consent reflect a recognition that these problematic and discriminatory social assumptions exist; that they are fed by gendered as well as racial, economic, colonial, and ableist power imbalances; and that they are factually unreliable. The platformization of porn makes this recognition even more important. Widespread public participation on porn-streaming platforms in which women are almost universally depicted as enjoying, or at least accepting, virtually any act being done to them has not ameliorated the social circumstances that motivated these law reforms.

Again, in mainstream porn that does feature hitting, slapping, spitting, urination, choking, strangulation, and forceful penetration, it is virtually always girls and women upon whom these acts are imposed.[84] Recall from chapter 4 the notion that platform mechanisms and the collectivity that they promote create a type of platform-driven sociality that elevates porn's contribution to the meaning of sex in our social environments. Norms about which sexual acts and bodies are desirable, what types of sexual activities are popular and among whom, how sexual activity is to proceed, and where the boundaries lie between what is appropriate and unacceptable, desirable and undesirable, are constituted and reinforced within these platform communities. It seems reasonable to suggest that the platformization of porn amplifies the need for a legal norm that accounts for discriminatory social assumptions about sex, sexuality, and the gendered power imbalances that underpin them. A legal definition of consent in which the determination as to whether the act was, in fact, non-consensual that turns exclusively on a complainant's subjective state of mind at the time the act occurred is such a norm. Determining whether a woman consented to having a man choke her with his penis in this manner, through an assessment of whether he thought she did not want that to happen, or whether he realized she was trying to push him away, reflects a significant failure to uphold this norm.

Justice Duncan also pointed to A.G.'s failure to provide the accused with "verbal cues" indicating her lack of consent to being choked with his penis.[85] Recall again that the question of whether the act was, in fact, non-consensual is determined based on the complainant's state of mind at the time of the incident, not the accused's state of mind.[86] In the face of evidence from both A.G. and the accused that she was gagging, coughing, and, at times, could not breathe because Hunter was shoving his penis down her throat, a lack of verbal cues indicating non-consent is not particularly probative of her state of mind at the time of the incident. She testified that she was unable to speak while she was trying to push him away because "his penis was all the way down [her] throat, as well his stomach was blocking over [her] nose area."[87] Presumably, this type of act, which was also depicted in the first video described in this chapter, would make it difficult if not impossible to provide verbal cues indicating lack of consent. This is why in the second video (in which the female performer was wearing a ball gag once the sexual activity commenced) a safe act, in addition to a safe word, was identified and agreed upon.

Following the incidents of choking A.G. with his penis, and other sexual acts involving the three parties, Hunter penetrated her vaginally with his penis. A.G. testified that while this was occurring, he "grabbed my, my breast … and then he was squeezing it incredibly hard, [to] the point where it was painful, and I told him 'ow' but he continued having sex with me."[88] She testified that the accused "then put his hand over my neck, while having sex with me … and at that point I panicked again and I didn't want it to continue anymore."[89] Her evidence was that she tried to remove Hunter's hand from her throat and said "stop" but that he continued penetrating her, keeping his hand around her throat, until he ejaculated shortly after that.[90]

Justice Duncan concluded that the Crown had failed to prove that the complainant "did not consent to the fondling and pinch of her breasts."[91] His basis for this conclusion included that "pinching" of the breasts is "within the scope of BDSM activities"[92] and that the accused saw no indication that A.G. was either not consenting or wanting to withdraw consent to this type of conduct.[93] As occurred in his analysis of the incidents in which the accused pushed his penis down A.G.'s throat, the trial judge's focus on what Hunter perceived suggests he may have based his assessment on, or in part on, what Hunter, rather than A.G., was thinking. Again, relying on an accused's perception of what the complainant wanted or whether she was enjoying herself to determine whether the act was, in fact, consensual is an error of law and does not adequately protect the sexual integrity of women.

Consider Hunter. According to his testimony, he maintained he had not interpreted her gagging, coughing, runny nose, and tears as signs of discomfort. The point is, and this was the insight driving the legal reform three decades ago, *his* perception of what she wanted is not reliable. What I would add to this is that the platformization of mainstream porn is likely to have made it more unreliable.

Guilty Minds in the Context of the "Rough Sex Defence" in the Era of Porn on the Platform

Justice Duncan did conclude that A.G. did not consent to having Hunter's hand around her throat while he was penetrating her vagina. This raised the issue of *mens rea* – whether Hunter had a guilty mind, was morally blameworthy, for the non-consensual sexual act (partial strangulation during intercourse) in which he engaged. As documented earlier in this chapter, allegations of non-consensual strangulation have also become much more common in reported sexual assault decisions in Canada in the last ten years.[94]

In *Hunter*, the issue of *mens rea*, or moral blameworthiness, turned on whether Hunter honestly but mistakenly believed that A.G. had communicated consent to having his hand around her throat while he penetrated her vagina with his penis. Again, this part of the definition of consent, properly applied, requires that the accused's belief be based on evidence of words or actions indicating a willingness by the complainant regarding the specific act, at the time the act occurred. This is what it means to have a communicative, specific, and contemporaneous definition of consent. Justice Duncan also got this wrong.

Consent to "Rough Sex" Must Be Communicated, Not Implied

Under the Canadian definition, it is the accused's perception of what the complainant *communicated* that drives the analysis of the honest but mistaken belief in communicated consent defence. As the Supreme Court of Canada highlighted in *R v Barton*, "the principal considerations that are relevant to this defence are (1) the complainant's actual communicative behaviour, and (2) the totality of the admissible and relevant evidence explaining how the accused perceived that behaviour to communicate consent."[95] The accused must point to some evidence to support his belief that the complainant contemporaneously communicated a willingness to engage in the specific sexual act at issue: "contemporaneous, affirmatively communicated consent must be given for each and every sexual act."[96] This requirement is the same whether the parties are engaged in "vanilla," s/m, or any other type of sexual activity.

Key to the legal standard, "in order to make out this defence, the accused must have an honest but mistaken belief that the complainant actually communicated consent, whether by words or conduct."[97] Why is the focus on *communication* so important? It is the focus on communication that protects against reliance on implied consent. Again, reliance on implied consent, by men in their sexual interactions with women, and by courts in sexual assault prosecutions, does not sufficiently protect women's sexual integrity. In a world in which porn has been platformed, implied consent becomes even more dangerous for women. Indeed, the focus on communication is sufficiently critical such that the majority of the Supreme Court of Canada in *R v Barton* directed lawyers and judges to refer to the defence as "an honest but mistaken belief in *communicated* consent."[98] Far from trifling semantics, the Supreme Court's direction was intended to "focus all justice system participants on the crucial question of *communication* of consent and avoid inadvertently straying into the forbidden territory of assumed or implied consent."[99]

Justice Duncan's reasoning in *Hunter* did not focus on communication. Unsurprisingly, the "territory of assumed or implied consent" is precisely where this part of the decision in *Hunter* landed.[100] Justice Duncan stated:

> It was the first and only time that a choking action was attempted. It was an escalation of *what was seen by Mr. Hunter as within the range of permissible* BDSM *conduct*. I accept that it could be within the range of such conduct as the infliction of pain or other forms of discomfort are *implied by the* BDSM *construct*.[101]

Determining whether Hunter was morally blameworthy for partially strangling A.G. without her consent should not have been based on what was seen by Hunter "to be within the range of permissible [sexual] conduct," or on what a judge considered to be *implied* by a particular sexual "construct." In *Hunter*, the accused was permitted to rely on implied, advance consent as a defence to partially strangling A.G. while penetrating her vaginally because Justice Duncan decided that this was implied by the range of sexual activity that Hunter thought was permissible. Instead, Justice Duncan should have focused on what Hunter perceived the complainant to have communicated to him at the time the sexual activity was occurring.

Justice Duncan went on to state that:

> Mr. Hunter honestly and reasonably believed that his conduct in putting his hand on A.G.'s throat, in the way he did, was within the bounds of permissible conduct contemplated by the mutual agreement that the activities that night were to be governed by the BDSM parameters of conduct. This was a defined context for the activities that night.[102]

One consents to sexual acts, not sexual constructs. An accused who seeks exoneration on the basis of an honest but mistaken belief in communicated consent must point to some evidence to support a belief that the complainant communicated consent for the particular sexual act at issue, at the time the act occurred. That there was a general agreement in advance to engage in an S/M-themed threesome does not remotely meet this requirement.

Think for example of the difference between the consent scripts depicted in the two videos examined earlier: the first a vague and unspecified general consent and the second a detailed, quite specific articulation of consent that confirmed both types of acts and body parts.

In providing an "overview of [the accused's beliefs]," Justice Duncan stated:

> It is important to remember how this began. It was a plan that had been discussed previously and one that A.G. appeared to be interested in pursuing. She knew and agreed to participate in a BDSM-governed sexual experience with two persons, in a place she had never been and with one person she had never met. She showed considerable determination to make her way to Cow Bay to participate.[103]

A specific and contemporaneous definition of consent means that evidence of broad, advance consent, which is what Justice Duncan invoked, cannot be relied upon as the basis for an honest but mistaken belief in communicated consent, regardless of whether the parties contemplated S/M. There was no evidence that A.G. and the accused had discussed what was to occur, beyond the broad-stroke suggestion of a threesome that would involve, in the complainant's words, a "dominant–submissive kind of relationship."[104] Indeed, Justice Duncan specifically found that the three had not discussed what was to occur; that they had left unstated "the parameters of what might be permitted."[105] This is the opposite of what occurs in a carefully negotiated and explicitly communicated BDSM scene. The lack of a common understanding of this supposed "BDSM-governed sexual experience," as Justice Duncan described it, was starkly evidenced by the fact that the complainant and Hunter and S.D. did not share a view regarding even the most basic elements of the "scene."[106] For example, the complainant testified that she was the submissive and that S.D. and the accused were the dominants.[107] S.D. testified that she and the complainant were both submissives and that Hunter was the dominant, which appears to have also been the accused's understanding.[108]

Similarly, while there was a text message between Hunter and the complainant (subsequent to the incident) in which he reminded her that he had told her she was "going to learn to take it deep," there was no evidence to suggest that the complainant and the accused discussed him repeatedly choking her with his penis while she lay in that position on the bed.[109] Nor was there any evidence of a discussion about him inflicting pain upon her and bruising her by grabbing her breast, nor any evidence of a shared plan for him to place his hand around her throat while penetrating her vagina with his penis. Nor was there any evidence that they had discussed how consent was to be communicated with respect to each of these acts. Justice Duncan specifically found that the complainant, S.D., and Hunter had not discussed and agreed to the sexual acts that took place.[110] There was no "plan."[111] In fact, A.G. and S.D. had never met, nor spoken, let alone discussed a plan for sexual activities.[112] At trial, S.D. did not appear even to know the complainant's name.[113]

The importance of applying a communicative definition of consent in response to legal scripts that invoke this so-called rough sex defence cannot be overstated. Think of it this way: if we do not demand a legal norm that requires this type of communication, what chance have we of instantiating a communicative norm of this nature at a social and cultural level?

As Cara Dunkley and Lori Brotto observe, explicitly negotiated consent is the single universal characteristic in BDSM sexual interactions and is considered a fundamental tenet in the BDSM community.[114] Maneesha Deckha suggests that proponents of s/m assert that it is marked by "extensive consultation and contracting beforehand and respect of boundaries during the power play."[115] At a minimum, a plan in *Hunter* (or reasonable steps, as it is described in law) would have required detailed discussion, very proximate in time to the incident, confirming that the complainant wanted the accused to engage in each of these acts, as well as discussion and agreement on how consent would be communicated for each of these acts during the "scene," confirmation that the complainant had the capacity to provide consent both during this discussion and during the "scene," and agreement on, and ascertainment of, some form of contemporaneous confirmation by the accused of ongoing consent based on the complainant's words or actions during each of these acts.[116]

As already explained, invoking the notion that one consents to a sexual construct invites judicial reliance on implied consent. Reliance on implied consent opens the door to reasoning based on stereotypes and discriminatory social assumptions. And indeed, discriminatory thinking does appear to have seeped into the reasoning in *Hunter*. The trial judge's assertion that the complainant knew and agreed to participate in a "BDSM-governed sexual experience" in an unfamiliar place with unfamiliar people raises the spectre of discriminatory stereotypes and victim-blaming attitudes about women who make so-called risky choices – such as to consume alcohol, dress provocatively, allow themselves to be alone with men, or who, as in the case of *Hunter*, agree to a threesome in a remote location with someone they do not know.[117] For example, Justice Duncan's comment that A.G. "showed considerable determination to make her way to Cow Bay" may suggest a perception that she was, to borrow from arguments advanced by Sheehy, Grant, and Gotell, "'up for anything' and presumed to be consenting."[118]

Hunter involved a complainant, with a hearing disability, who took a bus from the city where she lived to a mobile home in a wooded area in a rural part of Nova Scotia where she had never been, at night, in the winter.[119] She had no way to leave this location without the accused (who had not told her whose residence they were at) and did not even know the accused's real name.[120] Without discussion of what acts the complainant was willing to engage in, and how consent to engage in them would be contemporaneously communicated, the significantly larger accused choked this woman repeatedly with his penis, wrenched her breast painfully, and placed his hand around her throat while penetrating her vagina with his penis. Yet the failure to properly negotiate and communicate about consent, and to establish safe words and actions was characterized by Justice Duncan as a mutual one.

The court's application of the law to these facts was almost exclusively focused on what Logan Hunter desired, perceived, and thought reasonable. Assessing the absence of consent based on whether an accused perceived resistance or noticed signs of discomfort, or determining the moral blameworthiness of an accused who has engaged in acts of non-consensual sex based on what he assumed to be within the parameters of a particular sexual construct, echoes the almost exclusively male point of view in which the majority of mainstream porn is filmed.

The complainant in this case appears to have been seeking some form of sexual pleasure for the sake of pleasure. She was not bound by the shackles of domestic obligation, gendered economic power differentials, or love narratives. When she boarded the bus to Cow Bay, she left a boyfriend waiting for her at home. A.G.'s initial consent cannot be questioned by challenges to legal liberalism based on women's lack of choice. This was not a decision forced by a familial power imbalance or economic vulnerability. Indeed, the complainant may have been disbelieved by the court and arguably held responsible for her own victimization, precisely because this was, at the outset, an exercise of choice on her part.

Again, confidence in the law's capacity to protect women's sexual integrity would promote women's sexual autonomy. Decisions like the one in *Hunter* suggest that, at this point, such confidence would be misplaced. Instead of sending the message "proceed with extreme care, negotiate s/m scenes carefully and in a detailed way, and learn the rules and follow them," the reasoning in cases like *Hunter* has the opposite effect.

Judges who avoid relying on common sense or their own incomplete knowledge of s/m practices to assess a complainant's credibility, and who apply the doctrine of consent and mistaken belief in communicated consent rigorously and strictly in assessing so-called rough sex defences, contribute to a legal landscape that promotes sexual liberty for women. Judicial reasoning that fails in this regard has the opposite effect. Not only does the latter fail individual complainants, it also makes it less safe – less possible – for women to pursue self-fulfilment and pleasure through desire, in all of its complicated forms.

As a matter of law, and contrary to Justice Duncan's conclusions, the failure in *Hunter* was not mutual. Had the definition of consent been properly applied, the legal risks flowing from the failure to establish a safe word, to negotiate carefully the parameters of conduct, and to ascertain consent for each specific sexual act would have been born by the person interested in choking a woman with his penis, wrenching her breast, and strangling her while penetrating her vaginally. This is a modest concession given that A.G. seems to have assumed nearly all of the other risks in this encounter. It is an absolutely necessary allocation of risk, given what we know about the relationship between notions of implied consent, discriminatory legal reasoning, and the gendered reality of both rough sex porn and the so-called rough sex defence. While the concept of risk allocation is a problematic, neoliberal framing of what is in fact a social problem,[121] if consent is framed in this manner and risk is to be allocated, then any concept of sexual justice must account for the social conditions adolescent girls and women confront in their sexual encounters.[122] These are social conditions, to be clear, that allocate risks differently for men and women, and which are shaped by the constitutive impact of the platformization of mainstream porn.

The Case of A.E., T.F., and M.M.

This case involved a brutal sexual attack on a teenaged woman by three young men with whom she had attended high school. The men videoed significant portions of the assault on their cell phones, without her knowledge or consent. The incident commenced with what may have been consensual sexual acts between the four, followed by a series of non-consensual sexual acts and other physical and verbal attacks perpetrated by the three men against the complainant (who was given the pseudonym "Sara" in media reports on the case).[123] The accused penetrated her vagina and mouth with their penises and an electric toothbrush. They repeatedly slapped her face; punched her head, breasts, and groin area; called her a bitch, slut, and whore; and told her to "suck [their] fucking dicks."[124] They laughed at her as she yelped and cried. They urged each other on with comments such as "slap that bitch," "punch that pussy," and "fucking fist that bitch bro."[125] They told her to "shut the fuck up" and slapped her when she cried out in pain.[126]

One of the men, still a youth at the time of the offence, pleaded guilty to sexual assault. He admitted to sexually assaulting Sara with his sister's electric toothbrush by repeatedly thrusting the handle of it into her vagina, punching and slapping her in the vagina repeatedly, and directing the other two men to perform specific sexual and physical acts upon her. Judge O'Gorman, the sentencing judge in the youth's case, viewed the cell phone videos as part of the sentencing hearing, and described this evidence as "the most appalling acts of human depravity [he had] had the displeasure to witness as a judge."[127] He stated that there was not one part of the videos that "show[ed] a scintilla of consent."[128] He emphasized that the complainant was "visibly shaken and frightened" and that "to suggest otherwise is simply ignorant."[129]

The two adult males pleaded not guilty to sexual assault and sexual assault with a weapon, and were tried together in front of Justice Scott Brooker. Their defence was that this was consensual rough sex. Justice Brooker acquitted both men of sexual assault, despite the videos showing them slapping and punching Sara, verbally abusing her, punching her vagina, slapping her, yelling at her to "suck their cocks" *after* she had cried out "No," and penetrating her mouth while a foreign object (the handle of the electric toothbrush) was being painfully thrust into her vagina and she was crying out "no."[130] Justice Brooker found that, with the exception of A.E.'s acts of penetration with the toothbrush, Sara was a "willing and consenting participant" in all of the activity that occurred.[131] One of the two accused (T.F.) was acquitted of all charges and the other (A.E.) was acquitted of sexual assault, but convicted of sexual assault with a weapon, for penetrating her with the toothbrush.

Justice Brooker viewed the same video evidence that Judge O'Gorman described as "the most appalling acts of human depravity" he had ever had the misfortune of watching, videos that he asserted showed not "a scintilla of consent."[132] How could Justice Brooker watch these same cell phone videos and arrive at such a stunningly different legal conclusion regarding what occurred? The answer, at least in part, is that he failed to apply a contemporaneous, specific definition of consent. Instead, he relied on evidence of the complainant's broad and unspecified advance consent to engage in sexual activity with these three men to acquit T.F. and A.E. of these acts of sexual violence.[133]

Like the outcome in *Hunter*, Justice Brooker's faulty reasoning in the trial decision in *AE* (which was thankfully overturned on appeal) is of precisely the sort that occurs when courts follow or accept the type of consent script reflected in the first video examined earlier, rather than that of the second.[134] Justice Brooker acquitted these men of sexual assault because he accepted their evidence that Sara had, according to him, "expressed a desire or willingness to engage in rough sex" with them earlier in the evening before the videos were made.[135]

Justice Brooker's analysis was deeply flawed. The accused testified that Sara had asked for rough sex. The approximately ten minutes of video do not depict her asking for rough sex. She does not indicate a willingness to be slapped or punched in the videos. To the contrary, the videos show her crying and saying "no" multiple times.[136] Indeed, her evidence was that she did not consent to being slapped, hit, and punched, having her hair pulled, or being videotaped or penetrated in the vagina with a foreign object, or penetrated orally while being penetrated in the vagina with a foreign object. With the exception of the penetration by a foreign object (the toothbrush), Justice Brooker did not believe her. He identified as problematic the fact that the videos only covered ten minutes of the incident. T.F. testified that the incident lasted approximately fifteen minutes. A.E. estimated it was twenty to twenty-five minutes.[137] Despite devastating cross-examinations of the accused, despite their multiple lies to the police, and despite the fact that the evidentiary record included video recordings of this group sexual assault, Justice Brooker believed the accused's evidence that Sara asked for rough sex before the videos were taken, and from this determined that, therefore, everything that happened on the videos (with the exception of the use of the toothbrush) was consensual. His reasoning was faulty in two fundamental respects, both of which are relevant to our consideration of the relationship between legal rough sex scripts and the consent scripts articulated in mainstream porn on the platform.

First, Justice Brooker's decision, one of his last before retirement, reveals a literal example of the "she asked for it" response to allegations of rape and sexual assault.[138] Under a specific, contemporaneous definition of consent, it does not matter whether Sara asked for rough sex in advance of the incident. He relied on the conclusion that she gave broad, advance consent to rough sex to acquit T.F. and A.E. The Court of Appeal of Alberta overturned his decision, in part, on the basis of this legal error.[139]

Second, his assessment of Sara's credibility was profoundly problematic and deeply troubling. Justice Brooker watched videos of this sexual assault. He had video evidence of Sara repeatedly saying "no" and "ow," and crying or whimpering in pain, which the accused responded to by slapping her, telling her to "shut the fuck up," to "suck [their] dick[s]," and threatening to hit her again, followed by further physical violence, oral penetration, and other sexual touching.[140] He watched ten minutes of videos that included Sara being punched, slapped, and verbally abused, that showed her crying out and whimpering and saying no. He heard Sara's testimony asserting that she did not want to be punched in the vagina, verbally abused, slapped in the face, and treated in this manner while being penetrated orally and vaginally, and touched all over her body by these three men. And yet, he decided that he did not believe her when she said she did not consent to this treatment. He decided that, in her mind, at the time the punching, slapping, and other ill treatment was occurring, as she was being penetrated and touched by these three men, crying out "no" and whimpering, she "wanted it": "while the complainant says that in her own mind she was not consenting to these sexual activities, I do not believe her."[141]

There were issues with the complainant's credibility, as there often are in sexual assault cases. She was not forthcoming about whose idea it was to purchase alcohol and she deleted text messages to her friend that indicated that she was originally contemplating consensual group sex with the three accused. The point is this: Justice Brooker had videos. As Justice Pentelechuk noted in her decision to overturn the acquittals, "this is a case of a trial judge seriously misapprehending the objective video evidence."[142] Consider Judge O'Gorman's description of this "objective video evidence":

> The videos depict, in graphic detail, three male individuals degrading the victim in a most sadistic fashion. In addition to the name calling, they yelled at her to do a better job on the oral sex and struck her repeatedly in such a vicious manner that not even an animal should be treated in such a way. The punching of the victim in her vagina with a closed fist as hard as possible, as they simultaneously ridiculed and laughed at her as she pleaded for it to stop, is not youthful impulsivity or bad decision making. This was a prolonged brutal and vicious assault.[143]

That Sara was not forthcoming about the degree to which she was initially interested in engaging in sexual activity with these three men, or her role in securing alcohol for their get-together, or how they ended up in M.M.'s basement in the first place, should have been of no consequence in a trial in which there were videos of the sexual assault that showed the complainant repeatedly saying "no" and "ow," and whimpering and crying, to which the accused responded with further sexual and physical violence. On what basis did Justice Brooker not believe her? Did he think she was performing? What did he see in these videos?

Life Imitates Porn? Or Porn Imitates Life?

In both literal and more figurative ways, the cell phone video evidence in this trial mirrors aspects of mainstream porn on the platform. To begin with, parts of the accused's dialogue with one another in the videos, a transcript of which was entered into evidence at trial, read as if this could be the script of a video one might find in the "rough sex" category on a porn-streaming platform like xHamster or Pornhub. Some of the dialogue by the accused in the videos seems contrived and performance oriented. For instance, one of the early videos, before the complainant withdrew her consent, captures the complainant being asked, "Do you like that?" to which she replies, "Yeah, I like that, Daddy"; the youth involved then instructs her: "Call him Daddy. Call him Daddy."[144]

It was evident at times that the accused were performing for the camera. For example, T.F. acknowledges the camera at one point – breaking the fourth wall, so to speak – by looking directly into the camera, smirking or laughing, and making a "hang ten" signal with his hand as he penetrates Sara vaginally with his penis.[145] The youth, M.M., who was filming at this point, urges him on, saying, "Fuck her, T———. Go rail her."[146] Had these men uploaded these videos to a platform like Pornhub (which is alleged to have platformed videos of girls and women being raped at the time this offence was recorded),[147] the videos might have been considered user-generated content or amateur porn, and commodified by the platform.

One of the notable elements of the assault, as captured on the videos, is the degree to which these three men were oriented towards, and communicated primarily with, one another rather than with Sara during the sexual acts. They frequently spoke about Sara in the third person while they perpetrated this assault on her. They concerned themselves with who had, and had not yet, ejaculated.[148] They spoke to each other directly throughout the sexual interaction, even demanding that they watch what one another was doing, as if they were performing for each other (and the camera) rather than having sex with Sara. For example, the youth, M.M., repeatedly told the other two, "I'm going to wreck her. Watch here … I'm going to wreck her, bro."[149]

A.E.'s testimony is also striking in this regard. Even in his direct evidence – the testimony he provided in response to questions from his own lawyer – it is clear that these three men were primarily interacting with one another *on* Sara rather than *with* her:

Q: Okay. And so did you ever hear anybody say "titty fuck her"?
A: Yes, M.M. told me to "titty fuck" her.
…
Q: Okay. Is it possible you might have said, "I'm going to titty fuck her" or something like that?
A: Yes.[150]

Similarly, A.E. testified that M.M. told him to "Punch her pussy, bro. Punch her pussy, bro."[151] The youth also told him to "rail her with that toothbrush," to which A.E. responded by repeatedly penetrating her vagina, with increasing force and speed, with the handle of the electric toothbrush as she whimpered and cried out. The three men urged each other to "punch that pussy," "get that fucking pussy," "fucking rail her," and "wreck her."[152] When they did speak to Sara, rather than to each other, it was violent and directive, not interactive. For example, at one point the complainant asked A.E. if they were videotaping the incident, to which he falsely replied: "No. Shut the fuck up and suck my dick."[153]

In addition to speaking about Sara in the third person, other aspects of their testimony reveal the degree to which these men constructed Sara as an object. During his direct evidence, T.F., who was the only one of the three to penetrate Sara's vagina with his penis, offered this description of his participation in the sexual acts that occurred:

Q: Did the positions change from that?
A: They did, yes.
Q: And how or why did the positions change?
A: She actually – she wanted to go on her back so we could make it more accessible in case intercourse wanted to happen, so she moved onto her back herself.[154]

Intercourse, of course, does not have wants. In addition to anthropomorphizing the act of penile–vaginal penetration (which allowed T.F. to conceptually abdicate his own responsibility for that act of penetration), he used the word "it" to refer to Sara's vagina. Similarly, M.M. repeatedly referred to Sara's vagina as an object, as in "punch that pussy" – as did T.F., as in "get that fucking pussy."[155] In the same vein, earlier in his testimony T.F. referred to her vagina as a place – rather than saying that he penetrated her vagina with his fingers, he testified:

Q: Did you do anything else, other than rub her vagina?
A: I – my fingers went in *there* as well.[156]

In addition to their focus on one another and the degree to which this was a sexual interaction between these three men imposed on this woman-object, another notable feature of this incident was their post-facto construction of Sara's sexual pleasure and/or physical experience of the physical and sexual acts to which they subjected her. For example, during his testimony, A.E. admitted that he punched Sara in response to M.M.'s direction. In cross-examination he characterized it as a "fake punch," but agreed that when M.M. told him to "punch that pussy," M.M. wanted A.E. to really punch the complainant hard in her vagina.[157] A.E.'s evidence was that he made a fist and punched Sara lightly twice, between her legs beside her vagina, because he "thought she would enjoy it."[158] In describing the video evidence, Judge O'Gorman asserted that she was punched hard in the vagina. There was no indication in the videos that Sara had asked him to punch her vagina or that he had any reason to believe that she would enjoy being punched in her vagina.[159] A.E. testified that while the transcript of the videos made references to Sara "moaning" at certain times and "whimpering" at other points, he did not "know the difference between the two … to [him] it just sounded the same."[160]

T.F.'s evidence offers a similar example. While M.M. and A.E. were raping Sara with the handle of the electric toothbrush, encouraging each other to "fucking rail her" and "wreck her," T.F. was penetrating her mouth with his penis.[161] The Crown read the following excerpt from the video transcript of this part of the incident during her cross-examination of T.F.: "So you call her a 'fucking little whore,' she cries out 'No, no, ow,' and you say, 'keep sucking my fucking dick, you fucking bitch.' Correct?" T.F. answers: "Correct."[162] In his testimony, T.F. characterized her whimpering during this part of the assault as "moaning," and asserted that he thought she was enjoying what they were doing to her.[163]

Conversely, after watching the videos, Judge O'Gorman (the sentencing judge in the youth's case) indicated that it was simply "ignorant" to interpret this young woman's response as anything other than shaken and frightened.[164] It is possible, perhaps even likely, that T.F. was simply lying on the stand about his perception that she was enjoying what they were doing to her. But reflect for a moment on the sexual norms articulated and reinforced in mainstream porn, with scripts like that found in our first video: the construction of male sexuality as aggressive, if not violent, and female sexuality as passive, if not a passive receptacle for violence; male desire and sexual pleasure as pre-eminent and female desire and sexual pleasure as secondary, if not irrelevant; and male bodies as subject actors and female bodies as inexpressive objects to be acted upon.[165] It would be difficult to find an example of a sexual interaction that more aptly reflects or manifests these same sexual norms than the acts of these three men, captured on the cell phone videos taken, in conjunction with their subsequent testimony about what occurred. Is it, as Judge O'Gorman suggested, ignorance that would permit some viewers to watch a video of this type of human interaction and not see the brutal sexual assault that he and the justices of the Court of Appeal of Alberta saw? Or is it that for some, or many, viewers their interpretation of this content is informed by the same normative lens that underpins videos on porn-streaming platforms like our first video, "Daddy Makes Petite Lilli Chanel's Pussy Squirt"?[166] Was it ignorance that informed these men's assertions about what Sara might find pleasurable, or was it the same normative perspective that informs this type of porn?

Regardless, when judges accept or rely on a definition of consent that follows this same script, as the trial judge did in *Hunter* and Justice Brooker did in *AE*, we are left with judicial decisions that condone, if not reify, this set of sexual norms. This is a corpus of norms that is antithetical to women's sexual integrity.

The Misogynistic Norm of Indifference towards Women

Whatever their normative frameworks regarding sex, gender, and women's sexuality during the trial proceedings, T.F. and A.E. explicitly articulated an indifference towards Sara's subjectivity and experience that mirrored what occurred the night of this sexual assault and that is frequently depicted in some mainstream porn on the platform. For instance, when the Crown suggested to T.F. that he knew Sara would go with him that night because she had a long-standing crush on him, he responded, "How am I supposed to know what she thinks?"[167] A more striking example can be found in the following excerpt from the Crown's cross-examination of A.E.:

Q: You and I have a different definition of "foreplay." This is not foreplay … this is sex, correct?
A: Well, then I'll – I'll say the sex games. I mean, foreplay/sex games, is the same thing, or a sexual fantasy; whatever you guys want to call it.
Q: But nobody talked to [Sara] about a sexual fantasy.
A: I'm sorry. I don't – I don't understand that – that question. Like, how would I … How would I know what [Sara] wants in a sexual fantasy?[168]

A.E. admitted that at no point did he or either of the other two men give any hint or suggestion to Sara that they were going to penetrate her with a foreign object.[169] Later during the cross-examination he was asked:

Q: But up to that point when T[F] says, She's crying, you're not paying attention to what's going on with [Sara].

A: No. Why – why would I be paying attention to what [Sara's] thinking or saying? How am I supposed to know that she's going to cry?[170]

There is a profound indifference towards Sara's experience, sexual pleasure, even subjectivity generally, underpinning this testimony by A.E. The Crown's question was whether he was paying attention to "what's going on with Sara" while he was imposing this act of vaginal penetration on her, as his friend penetrated her mouth with his penis.[171] His response was: why would he be paying attention to what Sara was thinking or saying while he was thrusting the handle of an electric toothbrush into her vagina? How was he supposed to know?

Prior to his sentencing, M.M. undertook a sexual arousal assessment test, which involved answering a set of open-ended questions. In response to one of these questions, he denied being aroused by Sara. When pressed on this response, due to the fact that he ejaculated in her mouth during oral penetration, suggesting a higher level of arousal than he had admitted, he responded: "Just because I ejaculated doesn't mean I was aroused, I wasn't turned on by her, I was turned on by how it feels, the sexual act."[172] Here, too, the level of objectification and dehumanization articulated in the accused's post-incident reflections are both revealing and akin to the sexual norms articulated in mainstream porn.

The sexual activity ended when, as the complainant was being penetrated orally by T.F., she lifted herself up to stop the oral penetration and was pushed back down by A.E., who slapped and punched her.[173] A.E. stopped only when M.M., in response to her cries, told him, "Stop, stop, stop."[174]

It is significant that their indifference towards Sara was evidenced not only by what was captured in the videos, but also by what these accused articulated years later at trial. For example, more misogynistic than calling her a "fucking bitch" and a "little whore," perhaps even more revealing of the human shortcomings on display in this case than their non-consensual slapping, hitting, and penetrating of Sara, is A.E.'s seemingly genuine failure, even after the fact, when the stakes were high and it was in his interest to present himself in the best light, to recognize this woman's subjectivity, her humanity.[175] Even then, months or years later, after a police interview, and conversations with family, friends, and his lawyer, after time to reflect on what had transpired, after watching these videos himself, it had not occurred to him that, indeed, he was supposed to pay attention to what the woman he was penetrating wanted; he was, at a minimum, supposed to pay attention to what Sara was saying.

Similarly, in sentencing M.M., Judge O'Gorman noted that he "had almost consistently demonstrated a lack of remorse."[176] Prior to the hearing, a pre-sentencing report was produced for the court. The psychologist and psychiatrist who prepared it noted that M.M. blamed Sara for what occurred. He maintained that the incident was consensual and that she only reported to the police because her boyfriend found out what had happened and was upset. Even after watching the videos, being interviewed by the police, pleading guilty, receiving counselling, and receiving advice from his lawyer, M.M. indicated that he had no feelings for Sara and did not agree that she had been sexually assaulted. He said he thought that what they were doing was "funny."[177] In what was ostensibly a "letter of apology" addressed to the court, M.M. stated, "I was a 16 year old who was caught up in all of the fun."[178]

What caused such a drastic failure in empathy and human understanding in these three young men – none of whom had a prior criminal record, at least one of whom purported to be a virgin (A.E.), and one of whom was only seventeen years old? It is not possible to know. But we could speculate. Perhaps these men, like many men their age, belonged to or visited mainstream porn-streaming platforms and were impacted in some way by the readily available point-of-view videos that depict women who seemingly welcome being "wrecked," "railed," and "destroyed," to the "thumbs up" of thousands or millions of other users. Perhaps these accused had never set eyes on porn, but were nevertheless in some regard a reflection of the normative impact of having grown up in a social environment in which a significant proportion of their community regularly visits platform communities in which titles like "My Stepbrother and I *Destroy* a Teen with Our Huge Cocks While My Friend Films It on His iPhone," "Tiny 18 Year Old Teen Gets *Wrecked* by Muscular Stud," and "18 Year Old College Slut Getting *Railed* from Behind" receive high approval ratings.[179] The titles of these, and many other readily available videos on Pornhub, are certainly evocative of the "wreck her" and "rail her" discourse employed by the accused in this case. All three accused admitted that they referred to "girls who get around … or sleep … with a lot of guys" as "sluts" and "hos."[180]

Perhaps the profound lack of empathy that they demonstrated – their seeming failure to recognize Sara's humanity – had absolutely nothing to do with the ubiquitous nature and reality of mainstream porn-streaming platforms, the social media character of these online communities, and the fact that upon these platforms, videos with titles that frame sex as women and teenage girls ("sluts" and "fucking bitches") being "wrecked," "railed," and "destroyed" while friends film it on their phones are both readily available and overwhelmingly celebrated. But does this not seem unlikely?

The accused in these proceedings raised two main questions in their "consent to rough sex" defence: (1) How were they supposed to know what Sara was thinking, wanted, or desired? and (2) Why would they be paying attention to what she was thinking or saying? Men who turn to mainstream porn to answer the first question are unlikely to obtain reliable answers. Men who embrace the indifference embedded in the second question, particularly men interested in engaging in rough sex, do so at their own legal peril – at least in jurisdictions that require a subjective, specific, contemporaneous, communicative definition of consent, and judges that apply it properly.

An indifference towards the subjectivity of women, towards female sexual pleasure and women's sexual agency, is one of the norms that a subjective, communicative, affirmative, and specific legal definition of consent seeks to resist and disrupt. The sexual scripts that dominate a good deal of mainstream porn – in which consent is assumed, implied, or erased, and sexual pleasure is disproportionately represented from a male perspective – make displacing this norm more difficult. It is true that in mainstream porn with the kind of content reflected in the first video examined earlier, no one would be paying attention to what Sara was thinking or feeling – not in any real, substantive way. But in law, what Sara was thinking and feeling when the sexual acts occurred determines whether the activity was, in fact, consensual. And upon a proper application of law, an accused who fails to attend to what Sara was thinking and feeling (based on what she communicated through her words and/or actions) does so at his own legal jeopardy. Upon a proper application of the law, a failure to pay attention to what Sara was thinking and feeling is fatal to the defence of honest but mistaken belief in communicated consent. In law, upon a proper application of the contemporaneous, subjective, communicative, and specific definition of consent, all that mattered in terms of whether this was a sexual assault was "what was going on" for Sara, and whether these three men were willing or able to "pay attention" to "what was going on" for Sara.[181]

Conclusion

In both *Hunter* and *AE* there was evidence that the complainants initially consented to sexual activity that could be said to fall beyond the bounds of monogamous heteronormativity. In *Hunter* the complainant initially consented to a threesome with two other people, neither of whom was her boyfriend. In *AE* there was evidence suggesting that the complainant initially consented to a sexual encounter with the three men, despite being in a heterosexual, ostensibly monogamous relationship. In *Hunter* the trial judge permitted the accused to rely on implied consent to partial strangulation because the complainant had consented to a dominance–submission-themed threesome. In *AE* the trial judge himself implied the complainant's consent to being slapped and punched in the face and vagina, and to being called a "fucking bitch" while being double penetrated because she may have consented to a "gang bang" earlier that evening.

If legal feminists are to follow Franke's appeal to take up projects beyond the use of "law to tame sexual danger," if we are to embrace an account of female desire that includes contradictions, complexity, and the erotic potential of loss of control, then trial judges must do much better than what occurred in cases like *Hunter* and *AE*.[182] The platformization of porn makes this all the more true.

The proper interpretation and application of legal doctrine, and in particular the definition of consent for the purposes of sexual assault, must be calibrated to our social context. Today, our social context includes porn on the platform. In the overwhelming majority of mainstream porn that does depict hitting, slapping, forceful penetration, hair pulling, spitting, urination, ejaculation on the face, biting, punching, choking, and strangling, it is women being subjected to these acts, and almost always by men.[183] Porn-streaming platforms have created virtual communities visited by broad swaths of the public in which videos depicting women seemingly responding with pleasure to men forcefully thrusting their penises into the back of their throats, slapping their breasts, or squeezing their throats with their hands while they penetrate them, are commented on favourably, rated highly, and viewed transparently by millions – this seems likely to contribute to social understandings about what is desirable and pleasurable for women (and men). Protecting women's sexual integrity in this social context demands a legal approach to consent to sexual touching which does not rely on male perceptions of women's sexual pleasure. It requires an approach which, in the context of sexual acts that cause serious bodily harm, does not leave women's sexual safety solely dependent on men's ability to recognize the risk of harm posed by their behaviour.[184]

What does it mean to calibrate the law to this new aspect of our social context? For one thing it means that, to facilitate the ability of women to pursue sexual desires that extend beyond, or that subvert, norms of monogamy, reproductive sex, and romantic ideals, without either uncritically replacing them with the sexual scripts depicted in mainstream porn or forfeiting women's legal protections under criminal law, it is essential that determinations of whether the sexual acts at issue were, in fact, non-consensual be based exclusively on the complainant's experience in the moment. It also means that assessments as to the moral blameworthiness of an accused who has engaged in the types of acts alleged in these two case studies be based not on what the accused assumed a complainant wanted or thought was within the scope of a particular type of sexual activity, but on evidence of what she communicated to him at the time the acts occurred.[185] It is essential that uncontrolled, physical and sexual dominance not be mistaken for, or conflated with, the practice of BDSM – which demands a carefully, precisely negotiated, and genuine consent script. This is as important for women who seek pleasure through S/M or other forms of kink as it is for women who do not want to be choked, strangled, slapped, spit or pissed on, or penetrated with incredible force. The legal errors in *Hunter* and *AE* highlight the importance of this approach.

An affirmative, subjective, and contemporaneous definition of consent was a critically important development in the legal protection of women's sexual integrity well before the advent of porn-streaming platforms and consensual rough sex legal scripts. Its incorporation into Canadian law was considered a feminist victory, albeit one that has subsequently required persistent reassertion and safeguard.[186] And now it is a victory that must be defended in a world in which judges appear to be increasingly confronted with consent defences in response to allegations that mirror some of the content found in mainstream porn. The legal norm that underpins this definition of consent serves as a fundamental counterpoise to sexual scripts that eroticize the degradation and subjugation of women by men. Responding to the potential harms of mainstream porn on the platform, the topic of chapters 7 and 8, requires more than only that we hold tight to this legal norm. But it certainly starts there.

CHAPTER 7

What to Do about Unlawful Porn on the Platform?

> You understand and acknowledge that you are responsible for any Content
> you submit or contribute, and you, not us, have full responsibility for such
> Content, including its legality, reliability, accuracy, and appropriateness.
> – Pornhub, terms of service[1]

Platform intermediaries are not known for their inclination towards assuming legal liability, or even lesser forms of responsibility, for the content distributed on their sites.[2] Porn-streaming platforms are no exception, as the above excerpt from Pornhub's terms of service exemplifies. One of the steps necessary to respond to the harmful aspects of the platformization of porn is to identify clearly the circumstances in which it is both feasible and defensible from a policy perspective to impose liability not simply on the users who rely on platforms to distribute harmful content, but on the companies that both provide them with the digital platforms to pursue this objective and perpetrate harms separate and apart from those of their users.

Three possible legal interventions, in terms of what to do about porn on the platform that is unlawful, include the use of human rights legislation against porn-streaming platforms that engage in discriminatory practices by classifying, organizing, and promoting sexually explicit content in a manner that creates a taxonomy of misogynistic and racist hatred; the application of the *Criminal Code* against corporate actors and platform companies who knowingly distribute porn that promotes intra-family sexual violence or that was created or uploaded without consent; and the adoption of civil statutes to create expedited, easily accessible take-down and de-indexing remedies for victims of non-consensual distribution of intimate images and other illegal content such as child sexual abuse material.

This chapter examines human rights, criminal, and civil law frameworks for holding porn-streaming platforms liable for, and responsible for expeditiously removing, the unlawful pornographic content on their sites. Chapter 8 considers law and policy strategies for mitigating the potential harms and enhancing the potential benefits of porn on the platform that is lawful.

In Canada, unlawful sexually explicit content can be organized into four legal categories: content prohibited as obscene under the *Criminal Code*, content that violates hate speech prohibitions under either criminal law or human rights legislation, child sexual abuse material, and content produced and/or distributed without the consent of those appearing in it. (Material that violates intellectual property laws, such as copyright legislation, is also unlawful – regardless of its content.) Given my focus on the platformization of porn and legal interventions targeted at platforms themselves, primary consideration in this chapter is on the distribution of content that meets the criminal law definition of obscenity, the distribution of (rather than the possession of) child sexual abuse material, discriminatory platform practices (such as the construction and use of metadata and algorithms in a manner that constitutes hate speech), and the distribution of content by platforms that captures any other type of non-consensual sexual activity, or content that is distributed without the consent of any of those appearing in it.

To summarize, chapter 7 recommends:

- that the federal government re-enact a version of the hate speech provision formerly included under the *Canadian Human Rights Act* but targeted at platforms, rather than individual users;
- that under this new provision the financial penalties for porn-streaming companies that engage in hate speech by marshalling metadata and training algorithms to create taxonomies of racist and misogynistic hatred be severe;
- that systemic remedies aimed at remediating the structural and systemic harms caused by hate porn that perpetuates discrimination against marginalized groups be imposed against porn-streaming platforms under the *Canadian Human Rights Act*;

- that where possible, corporate actors and platform companies should be prosecuted under the *Criminal Code* for distributing pornography on their platforms that promotes or celebrates intra-family sexualized violence;
- that all provinces in Canada enact protection of intimate images legislation based on the *Uniform Non-consensual Disclosure of Intimate Images Act (2021)*;
- that platforms be held liable under such legislation for non-consensual distribution of intimate images unless they have taken reasonable steps to prevent this distribution; and
- that assessing whether a porn-streaming platform has taken reasonable steps to prevent the non-consensual distribution of intimate images be strictly premised on the specific types of risks that porn-streaming platforms in particular create.

Obscenity Laws Have Not Served Women Well

The Supreme Court of Canada's 1992 definition of obscenity in *R v Butler* turns on a standard of what the community would tolerate others viewing in light of the harm it poses, and the notion of undue exploitation of sex as constituted by either sex and violence, or depictions of sex that are dehumanizing and degrading to women.[3] The majority in *Butler* noted that:

[a]mong other things, degrading or dehumanizing materials place women (and sometimes men) in positions of subordination, servile submission or humiliation. They run against the principles of equality and dignity of all human beings. In the appreciation of whether material is degrading or dehumanizing, the appearance of consent is not necessarily determinative.[4]

The court concluded that explicit sex that is degrading or dehumanizing to women will be "undue" and thus obscene if the risk of harm is substantial.[5]

It seems problematic to conclude that all sex that places women in positions of subordination or submission is, by definition, degrading or dehumanizing. Regardless, the reasoning in *Butler* sounds almost quaint today. There are prominent genres or categories of mainstream porn specifically dedicated to the degradation of women. Take bukkake, for example, which is a category of porn on mainstream platforms. Bukkake involves a group of men gathered around one person, masturbating and ejaculating on their face. In mainstream porn the person ejaculated on is virtually guaranteed to be a woman. "Cum play" is a fetish for some people, and while bukkake itself is presumably not inherently degrading, its representation in mainstream porn – which involves a unidirectional flow of ejaculate that is gendered – does suggest a problematic, gender-based degradation. Titles on the first page of search results on Pornhub, using the search term "bukkake," on 16 May 2023 – including "Swallowing Bitch,"[6] "Slutty Black Serving Group of 5 BBC,"[7] "Nasty BBW Slut Gangbanged in Bowling Alley!,"[8] and "Hardcore Slut Takes It Rough"[9] – support this conclusion. The thumbnail image promoting most of these videos is a close-up of a woman's face, typically covered in ejaculate, surrounded by a set of erect penises. Labelling the women repeatedly ejaculated on in these videos as "nasty sluts" and "bitches" makes the gendered degradation in this genre of porn clear. Sexist, racist, or ableist depictions of sexual submission are degrading because they are discriminatory.

An examination of the metadata on mainstream porn-streaming platforms more generally reveals content in mainstream porn that would meet the first branch of the definition of obscenity in *Butler*, without even considering the content of the videos that this metadata classifies and contextualizes. Regardless of the sexual content in these videos (some of which itself clearly depicts women in ways that are contrary to the principles of equality and dignity of all human beings), the metadata framing and contextualizing these sexual depictions is itself degrading and dehumanizing. Consider, for example, that "dumb bitch" is a permitted search term on xHamster and that it yields videos on the first page of search results, with titles such as "Slapped, Facialed Then Pissed on ... Dumb Slut,"[10] "Dumb Piss Slut Gets Pissed On,"[11] "Dumb Black Bitches,"[12] and "Dumb Slut Needed to Learn Her Place. On Her Knees Sucking Dick."[13] "Dumb bitch" is also a permissible search term on Pornhub, which produces videos, on the first page of results, with titles such as "Dumb Bitch Gettin Fucked Real Good"[14] and "Dumb Bitch!!! Get's [*sic*] Facefucked for Lying."[15] The former video is of a sexual interaction between a Black woman and a White man. The latter video depicts a Black woman performing oral sex on a man while repeatedly being called a "dumb bitch" and told to apologize for lying.[16]

Content that invokes entrenched sexist and racist stereotypes, such as that women, or Black women, are of inferior intellect,[17] particularly through reliance on well-known phrases intended to have this effect, such as "dumb slut" and "dumb bitch,"[18] or when applied to racialized women, such as with the phrase "dumb Black bitch," clearly amounts to material that is degrading and dehumanizing – as contemplated by the *Butler* definition of obscenity. Similarly, content that represents women as useless or worthless beyond serving as receptacles for male ejaculate – so-called cum dumpsters, another classification on Pornhub – "runs against the principles of equality and dignity of all human beings," as articulated by the definition of obscenity in *Butler*.[19]

In addition to videos that depict women being choked, slapped, strangled, and penetrated without consent (accepting that non-consensual content is not the majority of the content in mainstream porn),[20] porn with metadata (in the form of titles, tags, and classification) that invokes discriminatory stereotypes, and/or represents women as sub-human, meets the definition of obscenity in *Butler*.

However, despite the ready availability of such content, the prohibition on distributing obscenity, found in section 163 of the *Criminal Code*, has not featured in the legal response to the platformization of porn. Indeed, the contemporary application of Canada's obscenity provision has been infrequent. The criminal law definition of obscenity, when it has been invoked post-*Butler*, has more commonly been relied upon by border officials or film review boards to censor queer, non-conventional representations of sexuality in porn, rather than marshalled against misogynistic mainstream pornography.[21] There are no reported decisions in which users or mainstream platforms have been charged with, or convicted of, distributing the type of obscene materials just described on the basis that the content of their communications degrades and dehumanizes women. Why?

Is it because, to be characterized as obscene, an undue exploitation of sex, material that combines sex with the degradation of women and adolescent girls must pose a substantial risk of harm, at a level the community will not tolerate – a requirement that may be difficult to prove? A comparison between the application of law to hate speech, child pornography, and commercial expression on one hand, and obscenity on the other, does not support this contention. In the former contexts, the law has repeatedly been brought to bear to respond to communication said to pose a risk of harm to marginalized or vulnerable communities. Not so with respect to obscenity laws.

In several legal contexts, including hate speech, tobacco advertising, child pornography, *and* obscenity, the Supreme Court of Canada has been willing to presume that exposure to certain types of content can cause harm by changing social attitudes and beliefs. But only in these first three legal contexts – hate speech, tobacco advertising, and child sexual abuse material – has the law subsequently been brought to bear in any meaningful way to protect segments of our communities. That is to say, there are virtually no modern cases in which the obscenity prohibition has been invoked in the context of mainstream pornography in response to the type of misogynistic porn just described. Again, why?

It could be because, unlike as is the case with child pornography, hate speech, or commercial expression, the legal definition of obscenity stipulates that demeaning and degrading sexually explicit content is only undue, and thus unlawful, if it presents a substantial risk of conduct which society will not tolerate because it is incompatible with its proper functioning.[22] What does this mean? Either society does not recognize the proliferation of this content as posing an undue risk of harm because, unlike these other types of expression, its target is women (albeit often most vehemently aimed at racialized or otherwise marginalized women), or because its contributions to our social and cultural norms, our sexual scripts, are in fact not deemed intolerably incompatible with society's proper functioning. In other words, our society tolerates this type of gendered oppression or inequality.

In *R v Ronish*, a 1993 case and one of the only reported appellate decisions post-*Butler* to deal with obscenity in mainstream porn, the Court of Appeal for Ontario, in assessing whether the Crown had met its burden with respect to proving that the material posed a risk of harm the community would not tolerate, placed significant weight on whether the Ontario Film Review Board had approved the films. The court commented: "this evidence, particularly when unrebutted, can be taken as a significant indication of the community's perception that films of this genre are not incompatible with current standards of tolerance in this country."[23] In *Ronish* and its companion cases, the court concluded that the material was not obscene because it did not combine sex with violence, and the Crown had not offered proof of harm.

This case was, of course, decided in a different era. How do we assess what the community will tolerate in the digital era, and in light of the platformization of porn? How do we define the community? Should weight be given to how a platform's community of users, or the Canadian segment of a platform, responds to this type of content? Mainstream porn-streaming platform communities, like Pornhub and xHamster, clearly tolerate, and widely approve of, content of this nature. For example, at the time of writing, the xHamster video "Dumb Slut Needed to Learn Her Place. On Her Knees Sucking Dick," classified as a "Dumb Bitch" video on the platform, had 11,241 views and a 92 per cent approval rating.[24] Presumably the 11,241 users who viewed this video tolerated the link between and connotation of this classification, its title, and the content of this video, as did those who rated it positively.

Similarly, the Pornhub video "Nothing but a Useless, Toothless Cum Dumpster Slut Sucking Dick on the Porch," classified as part of the "Cum Dumpster" section of the platform, had received 45,600 views and an 88 per cent approval rating.[25] It would seem that Pornhub's human moderator who approved the upload of this video and its title;[26] the thousands of users who failed to report it to the platform as a violation of the platform's terms of service; the users who offered comments such as "easy to score with crack hoes," "white women make the best sex slaves," and "PRO. Wish I had one of those"; the close to three hundred users who added it to their "favorites list"; and the users who gave the video a "thumbs up" considered this expression tolerable.[27]

A legal framework that includes a community tolerance standard, even a harm-based one, requires a societal commitment to insistently defend the sexual integrity of women and girls; combat gender inequality and gendered, ableist, and racist inequalities and the cultural norms that underpin them; and resoundingly reject the intersecting discriminatory attitudes that fortify these norms. Our societal commitment to these projects, it would seem, is not that robust. It is less threatening, conceptually easier, and more politically palatable to target "perverts and pedophiles," to borrow from Katrin Tiidenberg,[28] through narratives that construct the figure of the child molester or pedophile as a deviant outsider, than to pursue the types of social renovation necessary to respond to more common, everyday threats to our sexual integrity. Recognizing these everyday threats requires understanding sexual harm as a function of the dysfunction produced by our patriarchal, colonial, and heterosexist family and social structures. Directing attention to, and an obsession regarding, this "evil other" ignores, and thus holds in place, the hierarchies that produce the prolific sexual victimization of children by their fathers, stepfathers, uncles, and older siblings.[29] It is this phenomenon that permits the dissonance of a society obsessed with rooting out "pedophiles" and "child pornographers" while simultaneously propelling "stepdaughter" and "sister" to the top of the list of the world's most popular porn search terms.

On this view it is unsurprising that post-*Butler*, the concept of obscenity was more likely to be marshalled against queer, alternative representations of sexuality – which pose more of a threat to the classist, racist, patriarchal, and heterosexist hegemonies upon which society currently functions – than against the sexist and misogynistic expression reflected in these types of mainstream porn.

The law of obscenity and its reliance on a community standard of tolerance – again, even a harm-based one – is a poor framing for responding to the platformization of porn. Our community tolerates misogyny. The weaponization of the definition of obscenity post-*Butler* against queer folks by censor boards and customs officials,[30] and the failure to use criminal law obscenity prohibitions in any significant way to respond to misogynistic, racist mainstream porn post-*Butler*, suggests it was *never* a suitable framing; its inadequacy in the digital era makes this undeniable. A better legal response to this type of content is to recognize and respond to it as a human rights violation.

Hate Porn as a Human Rights Violation

In Canada, legal prohibitions on hate speech occur through both criminal and human rights law instruments. Human rights legislation in provinces such as British Columbia, Alberta, and Saskatchewan prohibit the display or publication of materials that expose others to hatred on the basis of a prohibited ground of discrimination.[31] In addition, former section 13 of the *Canadian Human Rights Act* stipulated that communication of matters likely to expose persons who are identifiable on the basis of a prohibited ground of discrimination to hatred or contempt constituted a discriminatory practice.[32] While that provision was repealed by the Conservative government in 2014, the Liberal government attempted to re-enact it under Bill C-36. This bill died when Parliament was dissolved in June 2021.[33] However, at the time of writing, the federal government had re-tabled a version of the provision as part of its commitment to address online harm more broadly under Bill C-63. If enacted, section 34 of the *Online Harms Act* would amend the *Canadian Human Rights Act* to add a provision stipulating that using the Internet to "foment detestation or vilification of an individual or group" on the basis of a prohibited ground of discrimination constitutes a discriminatory practice.[34]

Section 319(2) of the *Criminal Code* also prohibits anyone from wilfully promoting hatred against an identifiable group.[35] However, combined with other limitations of relying on criminal law to respond to the harms of mainstream porn on the platform outlined below, the requirement that the hatred be wilfully promoted, as in intentionally brought about,[36] suggests that this *Criminal Code* offence may be difficult to prosecute, particularly against platforms (as opposed to individual users).

There are additional advantages to relying on a human rights, rather than a criminal law, response in this context.[37] Human rights laws have a quasi-constitutional character in Canada, and are typically afforded a large and liberal interpretation such that they have primacy over other statutes. Unlike with section 319 of the *Criminal Code*, hate speech provisions under human rights legislation in Canada have not required that the expressor intend to promote hatred. The standard of proof is the lower balance of probabilities one, and the orientation of human rights legislation generally is both more systemic in nature and more ameliorative than that of criminal law. A human rights approach to hate porn might, as Jane Bailey argues regarding online hate speech generally, afford the opportunity for more proactive, remedial remedies not available through criminal law.[38] In addition, human rights prohibitions on hate speech are supported by international human rights instruments to which Canada is a signatory.[39]

Perhaps most importantly, human rights legislation offers the possibility to impose systemic remedies against porn-streaming platforms.[40] Systemic remedies allow a tribunal to monitor an entity on an ongoing basis to ensure that its orders are effectively implemented. Unlike an individual financial penalty, a systemic remedy is aimed at addressing discriminatory practices that have "become normalized."[41] In this sense the Canadian Human Rights Tribunal could play the type of detailed, supervisory role necessary to ensure change where the practice of discrimination is complex and ongoing. Systemic human rights remedies can be "dialogic" in nature.[42] Dialogue can be between the tribunal and the rights offender, in this case a platform, but might also include consultation with affected groups. For instance, in this context, that might mean a remedy that demands consultation with and response to the input of sex workers, and survivors of intra-family sexual violence, or victims of non-consensual distribution of intimate images and sexual assault generally. Systemic remedies are future oriented rather than aimed only at returning a claimant to their original position.[43]

The leading precedent outlining a constitutionally justifiable approach to legal limits on hate speech in Canada is the Supreme Court of Canada's decision in *Saskatchewan (Human Rights Commission) v Whatcott*.[44] As explained next, the *Whatcott* definition of hate speech could be used to apply human rights remedies against porn-streaming platforms that train algorithms and marshal metadata into taxonomies of hatred, activities that ought to be understood as a discriminatory practice.

In terms of proving that hate speech causes harm, the court in *Whatcott* and earlier cases has adopted a "reasonable apprehension of harm" approach.[45] As the court in *Whatcott* noted, "this approach recognizes that a precise causal link for certain societal harms ought not to be required. A court is entitled to use common sense and experience in recognizing that certain activities, hate speech among them, inflict societal harms."[46] The court recognized in *Whatcott* that this approach is justified when proof of a particular type of harm, such as the effects that expression will have on those exposed to it, is not possible: "Canadians presume that expressions which degrade individuals based on their gender, ethnicity, or other personal factors may lead to harm being visited upon them because this is within most people's everyday experience."[47] This is a notably different approach to the issues of harm and causation than courts have taken in the context of obscenity, as I have already explained.

The court in *Whatcott* observed that "[r]epresentations vilifying a person or group [are those that] seek to abuse, denigrate or delegitimize them, to render them … unworthy or unacceptable in the eyes of the audience."[48] Hate speech involves accusing a person or group of "disgusting characteristics, inherent deficiencies or immoral propensities which are too vile in nature to be shared by the person who vilifies."[49] The court confirmed that "delegitimizing a group as unworthy, useless or inferior can be a component of exposing them to hatred."[50] Unsurprisingly, the court concluded that "such delegitimization reduces the target group's credibility, social standing and acceptance within society and is a key aspect of the social harm caused by hate speech."[51] Drawing on previous case law, the court noted that "one of the most extreme forms of vilification is to dehumanize a protected group by describing its members as … subhuman."[52]

Given that it is the world's largest free mainstream porn-streaming platform, Canadian owned, and, according to it, frequented by millions of Canadians every day,[53] Pornhub is a logical example to use to examine how Canada's definition of hate speech ought to be applied in the context of mainstream porn-streaming platforms, and to consider what shape a re-enacted provision prohibiting the perpetration of online hate as a discriminatory practice under the *Canadian Human Rights Act* should take.

Recall that videos classified as "Dumb Bitch" on Pornhub include titles such as "Dumb Black Bitch Squirts" and "Dumb Bitch!!! Get's [*sic*] Face-fucked for Lying."[54] In addition to "Dumb Bitch," Pornhub offers a number of "Searches Related to 'Dumb Bitch,'" which include links to libraries of videos on the platform tagged under phrases such as "Stupid Bitch," "Dumb Blonde," "Stupid Cunt," "Dumb Slut," "Cum Dumpster," and "Stupid Slut," all of which produce hundreds or thousands of videos, depending on the phrase.

Clicking on Pornhub's link for "Stupid Slut" yielded 377 videos on 15 June 2023, including videos with the titles "Stupid Slut Used,"[55] "2 Stupid Sluts Getting Their Faces Fucked by 1 Guy While He Slaps Them Around,"[56] and "Two Stupid Sluts Degrading Themselves"[57] on the first page of search results. The latter is a video of two young women with words written in lipstick across their naked bodies. One has written on her body in lipstick "moron skank trash," with arrows pointed at her face; written on the body of the other woman are the words "dumb pig" and "garbage."[58]

Clicking on the platform's link for "Cum Dumpster" yielded 1,382 videos on 7 June 2023. The titles in this section of Pornhub include "Desperate for Money Cum Dumpster College Teens Fucked,"[59] "Slutty Step Daughter Is a Cum Dumpster,"[60] "This Stupid Whores Only Good for One Thing,"[61] and "Nothing but a Useless, Toothless Cum Dumpster Slut Sucking Dick on the Porch."[62] The latter video depicts an older woman who, after removing her dentures, performs oral sex on a man who denigrates her throughout the interaction; she appears mildly physically uncomfortable and mildly unhappy throughout the sexual activity.[63]

Other sexually explicit videos on the first two pages of search results in the "Cum Dumpster" section on Pornhub include titles such as "Crack Whore Fresh from Jail. She'll Run the Streets. In a Few Months, She'll Be Strung Out and Skinny,"[64] and "Crackhead Shows Up to Suck and Fuck for More Money."[65] The thumbnail photo promoting the latter is of a naked, decimated female body.[66] Other content classified on Pornhub in connection with these "crackhead" videos includes videos with titles such as "Strung Out Crack Slut Fucks While Boyfriend Has to Wait Outside,"[67] "Homeless Skank Sucks and Fucks Me in My Bathroom,"[68] and "Crackhead Slut Expertly Sucks My Cock. Best Blowjob of My Life."[69]

In assessing whether the metadata based classifications and algorithmic promotion in the "Stupid Slut," "Dumb Bitch," "Stupid Cunt," and "Cum Dumpster" sections of Pornhub constitute hate speech in Canada, the test in *Whatcott* asks: would this content risk exposing women, or a subset of women, as a group, to hatred?[70] Is it, more than simply repugnant or offensive, content that incites a level of abhorrence, delegitimization, and rejection that risks causing discrimination or other harmful effects to women?[71] In determining whether the platform activities occurring in these sections of Pornhub constitute hate speech, the platform's intention, or that of the users who upload, title, and tag videos designated to these parts of Pornhub's taxonomy, is irrelevant.[72] The focus under *Whatcott* is on whether this activity is likely to expose its targets, the women in the videos, women generally, or a subset of women (perhaps Black women, sex workers, women living in precarious housing, or women who consume drugs), to discrimination or other types of harm. The issue is whether this activity is likely to lower their social standing in the eyes of those exposed to it.[73]

Users who employ the types of titles described above to label sexually explicit videos are obviously perpetuating discriminatory stereotypes, and in some instances are engaging in expressive activity that meets the legal definition of gender, race-based, or other prohibited grounds of discrimination under the hate speech definition articulated in *Whatcott*. Critics have raised concerns with imposing this measure on individual users, such as the risk that the *Canadian Human Rights Code* might be used to weaponize human rights complaints or that it could result in a tidal wave of individual complaints;[74] my focus is not on whether individual users should be made subject to an online hate speech provision, which, for now, I leave for others to debate. It is the role that platforms play, the discriminatory practices of platforms, that I want to focus on. (I would note, however, that if the concern regarding a tidal wave of complaints is well founded, it suggests that there is a plethora of hate speech circulating in our platform society – which strengthens my argument that what is really needed is a systemic remedy targeted at the platforms responsible for disseminating and amplifying this hatred.)

Pornhub clearly aids in the perpetuation of discriminatory stereotypes by permitting users to employ tags like "Cum Dumpster" and "Stupid Cunt." But platforms do more than simply allow users to engage in expressive activity that risks causing discrimination. Platforms classify and categorize content, and link concepts. They create taxonomies, through the use of metadata and reliance on the algorithms they write, aimed at attracting and sustaining the attention of users. In other words, Pornhub produces and maintains a taxonomy of misogyny and racism, and the discriminatory sexist and racist stereotypes underpinning this taxonomy, when its IT technicians, either manually or through the algorithms they write, train, refine, and correct, link and/or maintain the link between "Stupid Cunt" videos, "Cum Dumpster" videos, "Dumb Bitch" videos, "Dumb Blond" videos, and "Stupid Slut" videos. Even if the company's algorithm initially connected these terms based on users' behaviour on the platform, it is the company that maintains and perpetuates the links between these terms and promotes videos classified by and within these sections of the platform. In other words, it is Pornhub, not its users, that maintains and promotes not only the classification of these video titles and/or the women depicted in them into "Stupid Slut," "Dumb Bitch," and "Cum Dumpster" categories, but also the relationships between these classifications. It is Pornhub, not its users, that created the platform for and maintains the conceptual links between, for instance, "stupid" and "cunt"; between "dumb" and "Black" and "bitch"; between "stupid cunt" and "dumb bitch"; and between "homeless skank," "crackhead slut," and "cum dumpster." And ultimately, it is Pornhub that maintains and promotes the relationship between depictions of women engaged in sexual activity and the classification of them as, for example, "stupid cunts," "dumb bitches," "crackhead sluts," "homeless skanks," and "cum dumpsters." And it is Pornhub that then uses this taxonomy to promote videos to users in a way that further exposes them to metadata with similar content.

In other words, the way in which metadata is designed and deployed on platforms like Pornhub to create this taxonomy of misogyny and racism – to organize, index, and algorithmically promote videos with titles and tags that convert these terms into linked classifications – is itself a discriminatory practice. Through the design and operation of this type of taxonomy, and through the videos the platform selects to promote to users based on this type of metadata, Pornhub engages in a form of hate speech. Put another way, the platform does more than simply perpetuate others' hatred; it perpetrates its own hate.

Now, as I will explain, it matters that the metadata – the titles, classifications, and tags – pertain to sexually explicit videos. And it matters that it is mainstream heterosexual porn in which this is occurring – given the tendency of mainstream porn to depict hierarchically gendered sexual interactions in which women often play sexually subordinate roles, in which women (rarely men) are penetrated, in which women (almost never men) are ejaculated on, and in which women (less frequently men) perform oral sex. However, whether the sexual depictions in videos associated with this type of metadata are consensual is irrelevant to the determination that, for purposes of assessing the platform's conduct, this constitutes hate speech. If the depictions in videos in these taxonomies of hatred portray non-consensual sexual activity, the hate speech is more egregious. But even if the depictions are of consensual sexual activity, hierarchically gendered sexually explicit content, with the type of metadata relied upon to create a taxonomy of misogyny and racism, such as the one Pornhub has created, constitutes hate speech under *Whatcott*.

To explain further, Pornhub's decision to maintain, link and intersect, or maintain the link between for instance, "Dumb Bitch," "Stupid Cunt," and "Cum Dumpster" videos that contain hierarchically gendered, sexually explicit content within its platform's classification system is a platform, not a user, activity: the platform connects these concepts, or maintains the connection between these concepts, for users and connects these concepts to certain types of video titles. Pornhub tells users that "Dumb Bitch," "Stupid Cunt," and "Cum Dumpster" videos are, to use Pornhub's word, "related."[75] Pornhub tells users these terms are "related" to each other and are "related" to videos with titles that feature "crackheads," "whores," and "homeless skanks."[76] This is activity engaged in by the platform. Again, it is Pornhub that represents these terms as "related." In doing so, Pornhub delegitimizes a protected group, women, or a subset of women, as useless, intellectually inferior, subhuman, and inherently deficient. This is the very definition of hate speech under *Whatcott*.

Classifying and maintaining a link between videos that have titles such as "this stupid whores only good for one thing,"[77] "2 stupid sluts getting their faces fucked by 1 guy while he slaps them around"[78] and "nothing but a useless, toothless, cum dumpster slut sucking dick on the porch"[79] as "Cum Dumpster" videos and "Stupid Slut" videos reinforces the message that women are intellectually inferior to men and useless (apart from the sexual services they perform for men). This is also true with respect to Pornhub's classification of videos that characterize women as "crackhead sluts" and "homeless skanks."[80] The term "crackhead" (itself a signifier of America's 1980s "war on drugs" moral panic, which saw Black crack cocaine drug users disproportionally criminalized for drug possession relative to White cocaine users)[81] has racist and classist connotations. When combined with the term "slut" or "crack whore," and linked with other videos in Pornhub's "Cum Dumpster" section of the platform, the intersection of class, race, and gendered de-humanization and degradation is manifest.

Again, Pornhub's taxonomy linking and/or maintaining the link between videos with these types of titles and these types of classifications – telling users they are "related"[82] – combined with the platform's initial approval of these video, titles, and tags, *in conjunction with* the presentation of sexually explicit content that is hierarchically gendered – that has women consistently performing sexually subordinate roles – constitutes hate speech pursuant to the human rights definition articulated by the court in *Whatcott*. This is not merely activity on the part of Pornhub that is offensive or hurtful. This is activity that "denigrate[s] and delegitimize[s]" women – that denies our basic humanity.[83] Moreover, Pornhub's privacy statement confirms that it collects information on how "users interact with [its] content … in order to develop and display content and advertising tailored to [users'] interests."[84] In other words, the platform not only creates this taxonomy of misogyny and racism, its algorithm presumably relies on it to promote to users who are interested in watching videos classified in this manner, with these types of titles and tags, other videos in these sections of the platform, with this type of hateful metadata. Pornhub appears to intentionally use its data to categorize users who it identifies as interested in a particular type of content, and then relies on the taxonomies it creates to steer them towards similar content. In this context presumably that means steering users towards more of Pornhub's own hate speech.

The hate speech analysis in Canadian jurisprudence is effects based. To constitute hate speech under Canadian law, the activity must not only denigrate and dehumanize the target group; it must also pose a risk of causing discrimination or other harm.[85] Linking and/or maintaining the connection between these various terms, telling users that they are "related," for example, clearly meets this legal standard. For instance, one would be hard-pressed to deny that representing women as "stupid sluts," "useless cunts," or "cum dumpsters" – whose only real value is sucking dick – is as likely to result in discrimination towards women as are statements that portray Jews as conspirators seeking to steal property and promote communism and drug use,[86] or that represent gay men as dirty, filthy sex addicts.[87] These expressions of antisemitism and of homophobia were recognized as hate speech by the Supreme Court of Canada.

As the court noted in *Whatcott*, hate speech has societal impacts. Under *Whatcott*, it is very clear that representing women as useless, beyond whatever sexual function they might serve for men, risks causing the type of discriminatory harm contemplated under Canada's definition of hate speech: "If a group of people are considered inferior, subhuman ... it is easier to justify denying the group and its members equal rights or status."[88] It is not difficult to imagine the discriminatory impact on equal employment opportunities and pay equity for women caused by the perception that they are intellectually inferior. It is not difficult to recognize the discriminatory impact on intellectually disabled women caused by the belief that they are useless, beyond their capacity to serve as a receptacle for male ejaculate. It is not difficult to contemplate the discriminatory impact on sexual assault survivors in the criminal justice system caused by the perception that women, or sexually active women, are worthless sluts and whores willing to do anything, and thus untrustworthy or undeserving of criminal law's protection. Indeed, fifty years of feminist-motivated law reforms have been aimed at renovating the laws of evidence and the substantive law of sexual assault in an effort to reduce the degree to which this type of discriminatory thinking distorts the truth-seeking function of the criminal trial process in Canada.[89] This taxonomy of hatred constitutes hate speech under the *Whatcott* definition.

Similarly, hierarchically gendered, sexually explicit videos, such as "Crack Whore Fresh from Jail. She'll Run the Streets. In a Few Months, She'll Be Strung Out and Skinny,"[90] and "Homeless Skank Sucks and Fucks Me in My Bathroom,"[91] linked by Pornhub to each other and identified in the "Cum Dumpster" section of the platform's taxonomy, represent the women targets of this expression, as disgusting and vile, with subhuman propensities not shared by the male sexual actors in these videos, and unworthy of human dignity and respect. By linking these videos to each other, or maintaining the link between them created by users, and classifying them as part of, or maintaining their classification in, for example, the "Cum Dumpster" section of the platform, and linking this classification to others – such as Pornhub's "Stupid Slut" and "Dumb Bitch" classifications – Pornhub represents to users that women living with addictions are useless or worthless, beyond serving as receptacles for male ejaculate, and that women with addictions or without secure housing can be treated as subhuman. This type of thinking is likely to support and perpetuate discrimination against sex workers, homeless or economically marginalized women, and women living with addictions. To use an example drawn directly from the reasoning in *Whatcott*, representing women in this way denies them their ability to fully participate in our democracy: before women who are working as sex workers, or women living with addictions or in precarious housing, can participate in broader public debates or advocacy regarding the right to housing, addictions treatment, or safe working conditions for sex workers, they must first defeat the absolutist position that they are intellectually incapable of participating in these debates and displace the assumption that they can be treated as subhuman and thus not entitled to such rights.[92] This is hate speech under the *Whatcott* definition. The same analysis applies to a video title which refers to a woman as, for example, a "dumb bitch," with video content that invokes racist stereotypes about women of colour and that links this video through metadata to the classifications of "Stupid Slut" or "Dumb Bitch." The discriminatory impact of any individual user's video, or title and tags, is different in kind from the effect of the platform's taxonomy of hatred.

As noted, Bill C-36, which was tabled by the Liberal government in 2021, would have re-enacted a provision in the *Canadian Human Rights Act* that makes the online communication of hatred a discriminatory practice. The problem with the bill, as it was contemplated, was that it would have exempted those who "host or cache hate speech or information about the location of hate speech" from the scope of the act.[93] The government's newly tabled *Online Harms Act* contains the same problematic exemption for platforms. It stipulates that one does not communicate hate speech by reason only that they indicate the existence or location of hate speech, or cache or store hate speech.[94]

It is true that, upon a proper interpretation, this exemption from liability should not include the discriminatory practices engaged in by porn-streaming platforms that collate, organize, curate, and promote content through the use of metadata and algorithmic amplification in a manner that itself perpetuates hate. As Tarleton Gillespie argues,[95] and as was explained in chapter 3, when platforms engage in these activities they are not merely indicating the existence or location of content, but rather contributing substantively to the content on their sites. However, based on the efforts of porn-streaming platforms to absolve themselves of any responsibility for the content on their sites,[96] it seems certain that they would attempt to avail themselves of an immunity provision like the ones contained in Bill C-36 and C-63. If there is to be an exemption from liability, it should be for individual users, given both the concerns regarding their expressive interests, the possibility of a tidal wave of individual complaints, and the broader, systemic impact of a platform's discriminatory conduct relative to that of any individual user. The use of these types of misogynistic and racist terms by an individual user to tag and title a video will not alone always constitute hate speech. Titling and tagging, in this manner, sexually explicit content that is consensual but involves subordinate, degrading, and/or dehumanizing depictions of women may, but will not always, meet the *Whatcott* definition; this will depend more on the content of a particular video and the context in which it is distributed or communicated. Unlike as is the case with respect to a platform, which when it deploys this type of metadata to operationalize, train, and refine its algorithm creates a taxonomy of hatred and puts it to work on a community of users, the risk of discrimination posed by any one individual video, title, or set of tags will depend to a greater extent on the video's content. This is why it makes more sense to target a human rights–based hate speech prohibition at platforms, not individual users. Likely the drafters of these bills were thinking about the broad and largely unrestrained immunity for platforms in the United States, granted under section 230 of the *Communications Decency Act*, not platforms like Pornhub, when this immunity clause was included. Offering porn platforms immunity from liability for the hate speech communicated through the marshalling of metadata into a taxonomy of hatred on their sites, will not encourage porn-streaming platforms to take responsibility for this type of human rights violation or the systemic risk of discriminatory harms that it poses.

Emily Laidlaw argues that "platforms be held accountable for their systemic risks of harm and their responsibility to respect human rights."[97] This requires recognizing that platforms have the capacity to, and sometimes do, cause systemic harms by enveloping users in a fascia of hatred through the metadata and algorithms they use to classify, organize, curate, and promote content. While algorithms generally are susceptible to reinforcing decades-old relations of oppression in less explicit ways, as Safiya Umoja Noble documents in *Algorithms of Oppression*,[98] what I am describing here involves explicitly harnessing metadata to buttress, maintain, and promote hatred. It is the discriminatory practice of the platform, which I have described using the taxonomy that Pornhub creates, as an example, and not the content uploaded by any particular individual user, that creates the connective tissue of hatred within a subset of the platform's community.

Canada should re-enact a hate speech provision under the *Canadian Human Rights Act*, such as is included in Bill C-63, but it should focus on liability for porn-streaming platforms for what are, in fact, their own discriminatory practices. Moreover, in addition to the systemic remedies already addressed, the Canadian Human Rights Tribunal should be empowered to impose significant financial penalties for porn companies that operationalize metadata and algorithms in this manner.

What about a chilling effect on Pornhub's freedom of expression? Corporations enjoy the freedom of expression protections of section 2(b) of the *Charter of Rights and Freedoms* (and are subject to its limitations). However, whether the output and representations of the algorithms these companies develop, train, and release onto the public is protected activity under section 2(b) is very much debatable.[99] But even if these platform activities do constitute expression for purposes of *Charter* analysis, even if harnessing metadata to create these taxonomies of hatred is treated under the law as expressive activity, the limits imposed by the human rights liabilities I am suggesting are ones that Canadian courts have already recognized as constitutionally justifiable. To be deemed justifiable under the *Charter*, limits on freedom of expression must be properly tailored based on the entity, and type of speech being moderated, and in relation to the objective that underpins the law placing the limit.[100] The more important or valuable the expression, the more carefully tailored to its objective a law must be.[101] In Canadian constitutional jurisprudence, hate speech (and commercial speech), like obscenity, is considered very low value expression, far from the core values of truth seeking, individual self-fulfillment, and democracy that the constitutional freedom of expression guarantee is intended to protect.[102] The government has a pressing and substantial objective in this context: to protect the sexual integrity, equality, and human dignity of women and vulnerable minorities.[103] Imposing this type of narrowly tailored liability on platforms, if these particular platform practices do fit within the scope of protection under section 2(b), in relation to commercial activity that also constitutes hate speech, in order to pursue these important objectives, would be justifiable.

What impact would imposing this type of human rights protection on platforms have indirectly on the expressive rights of individual users? This raises a few issues: (1) the right of individual users to express themselves by uploading videos to (porn) platforms and attaching the types of titles and tags I have described (and the corresponding right to access such content), (2) any arguable right users might have to the amplification of their expression that occurs when the metadata they attach to it raises its profile online, and (3) the risk that imposing this type of liability would cause platforms to over-remove content. Consider first those who would be prevented from labelling their pornographic videos in misogynistic and racist terms, in an effort to have them properly classified and thus promoted within a porn platform's taxonomy of misogyny and racism. Renée DiResta puts it well: "there is no right to algorithmic amplification."[104] The *Charter of Rights and Freedoms* primarily protects state-based interferences with a person's expressive interests; but for narrow exceptions it does not protect a positive claim to a particular platform,[105] let alone access to the amplification mechanisms of a private company.[106]

But what about users who seek to post content and attach metadata that uses these same types of terms but that does not constitute hate speech under *Whatcott* and is not posted in a context that contributes to a platform's infrastructure of misogyny and/or racism, or other discriminatory taxonomies, such as on a platform that does not use metadata in this manner? Would imposing liability on platforms create a risk of over-removal of content that is neither contributing to a platform's taxonomy of hatred nor itself an incident of hate speech? It could. This is why it matters that we not try to solve all of the Internet's problems with one solution. At least when it comes to content moderation and sex, a law without specificity will likely end up targeting and censoring the speech of sexual minorities rather than misogynistic mainstream hate porn.

For instance, it is clear that some of the arguments companies like Facebook make suggesting that hateful content would drive away users and advertisers (and thus it is not true that all content is good content for them)[107] cannot be made by a company like Pornhub in the same way. Facebook certainly facilitates its share of hatred, including for instance by providing a platform for the type of hate groups discussed by Danielle Keats Citron and Helen Norton in "Intermediaries and Hate Speech."[108] Citron and Norton suggest that online intermediaries can "foster digital citizenship" by inculcating norms of respect through well-developed, transparent, thoughtful policies that explicitly target the hate speech that they consider harmful, rather than through state-imposed measures and the collateral censorship that the latter risks.[109] Encouraging voluntary action on the part of platforms seems like it could be part of the solution for some platforms, particularly in a jurisdiction that may have fewer tools than Canada. They are writing in the context of the American First Amendment, with its more limited protections against hate speech, in a jurisdiction in which platforms enjoy incredibly broad legal immunity under section 230 of the *Communications Decency Act*. Moreover, Pornhub *has* an explicit and transparent hate speech policy that stipulates clearly the type of hateful content that it prohibits: "any communication or material that promotes [or] supports ... the delegitimization, dehumanization, or discrimination ... of a person or group of persons" on the basis of their sex or gender.[110] The policy prohibits speech that "expresses the belittlement or dehumanization of groups" and content that includes "stereotypes, tropes, expressions, slurs, and/or epithets, including other words or phrases used pejoratively toward or in reference to persons based on protected characteristics" such as sex and gender.[111] Like other platforms, it just does not seem to follow or uphold the policy, or at least not consistently or effectively. Instead, Pornhub, through this taxonomy of hatred, promotes hate porn to those users who it categorizes as being interested in hate porn.

Citron and Norton acknowledge that their strategy will not work for sites that base their businesses on encouraging hatred, citing the example of the social network site Hate Book, a website that encouraged users to post something they hated.[112] The subset of content on a porn-streaming platform like Pornhub that constitutes hate porn is analogous to their Hate Book example. Encouraging intermediaries to voluntarily foster digital citizenship in this subset of porn on the platform by instead promoting norms of respect seems highly unlikely to work.

It may be that in order to properly tailor limits, and strike a constitutional balance between shielding equality and dignity interests while protecting the freedom of expression of individual users, hate speech laws will need to become more particularized than they have been in the past. We have different regulatory frameworks for the sale of bubble gum and cannabis because they pose different types and levels of risk, and involve different considerations. Different types of platforms may require different legal responses. Balancing the expressive interests of individual users (threatened by over-removal incentivized by the imposition of a human rights liability) with the dignity and equality interests of women and children may be different when addressing a mainstream porn streaming platform than when regulating an online shopping platform or a platform that facilitates short-term vacation rentals, or even one that involves a broader spectrum of user-generated content, such as YouTube or TikTok.

Criminal Liability for Platforms under Non-consensual Distribution of Intimate Images and Child Pornography Laws

While obscenity provisions under criminal law are not effective and hate speech prohibitions are better housed in a human rights framework, there are circumstances in which criminal law may be the best legal tool to hold platforms responsible for unlawful porn on the platform. Criminal law prohibits individual users from producing, distributing, and in some instances possessing non-consensual sexually explicit content (which would include any content involving children, and non-consensual content involving adolescents or adults). With the exception of synthetic media,[113] criminal law in Canada also now clearly imposes individual liability for the non-consensual distribution of intimate images. But in addition to individual users, platforms that knowingly distribute non-consensual content should be liable under the *Criminal Code* prohibitions on child sexual abuse material and non-consensual distribution of intimate images.[114] Where possible, platforms that encourage users to upload non-consensual content (such as those dedicated to so-called revenge porn sites)[115] should be held directly liable under criminal law.

In addition, in cases in which the Crown can prove that a platform refused to take down and de-index non-consensual content upon being properly notified of it, which would require a notice of sufficient precision, platforms should be prosecuted as either principals or parties to the offence. For example, porn-streaming platforms that knowingly permit content that advocates sex with children, such as the content in some of the (step)father/(step)daughter and (step)brother/(step)sister videos examined in chapter 5, and some of the comments by users in response to these videos, such as those that seem to celebrate the sexual assault of their own daughters, younger sisters, stepdaughters, and stepsisters, should be prosecuted for distributing, or as parties to the offence of distributing, child pornography contrary to section 163.1 of the *Criminal Code*.[116] (Of note, this type of content, even if fictional, would also be prohibited under the government's proposed *Online Harms Act* – which defines content that sexually victimizes a child or revictimizes a survivor as including content in which a person is depicted as being a child engaged in sexual activity.)

Whether a platform will be considered to have "knowingly" permitted such content is not a straightforward issue: are senior officers of a company aware that its human moderators are allowing this type of content to be distributed? Who receives notification when content is flagged as child sexual abuse material on the platform, and if it is senior officers do they act expediently to have it removed? What constitutes expedient removal? To what extent are senior officers of the company involved in content moderation decisions or decisions regarding advertising placement? Are senior officers at Pornhub aware that the platform is running "fuck your family" advertisements at the beginning of incest-themed videos that depict the sexual assault of (step)children by their (step)fathers? Is this intentional, and if so, would this constitute evidence that they know that their platform hosts content that promotes sex with children and that there is an intention to benefit from this content?[117]

Moving beyond the offences related to the non-consensual distribution of intimate images and so-called child pornography, it would be a mistake to rely heavily on criminal law as the primary tool for responding to the harmful aspects of mainstream porn. This is true for several reasons. First, the focus of criminal law is necessarily reactive and individual, not pro-active and systemic. As a consequence, its remedies are typically individualized and punitive, not structural. This makes it ill equipped to address systemic challenges and harms. Generally, when we think about the relationship between criminal law, social and cultural norms, and the platformization of porn, framings like the one suggested in chapter 6 are probably somewhat more productive. How ought legal actors, police, and courts to understand their roles in light of the social role of porn today? What is the relationship between porn on the platform and the application of the doctrine of consent? What does porn literacy mean for judges called upon to adjudicate consensual rough sex defences, or for those in education, healthcare, or social work who encounter allegations of sexual assault that closely mirror the sexual scripts reflected in mainstream porn?

Second, criminal law responses to social problems and harms inevitably disproportionately criminalize men marginalized on the basis of race, poverty, and Indigeneity.[118] While this is only a concern regarding criminal liability for individual users, not criminal liability for privileged and powerful corporate actors, for the former it remains a salient factor.

Third, in terms of criminal liability for platforms, the multinational character of large platforms may present feasibility challenges with respect to the investigation of criminal offences and the enforcement of Canadian criminal law against some mainstream porn-streaming platforms. For example, the RCMP justified its failure to investigate MindGeek following the *New York Times* scandal, in part, because the company keeps its servers in foreign jurisdictions, limiting the efficacy of Canadian search warrants.[119] It may well be that the RCMP lacks the resources, inclination, or competence to conduct this type of complex, cross-border criminal investigation of a multinational porn company with a complex corporate structure. To be clear, there was no jurisdictional challenge to applying Canadian criminal law in this case. MindGeek's head offices are in Montreal, there was no suggestion it was being criminally prosecuted elsewhere for this conduct, and the harmful consequences of allegedly distributing child sexual abuse material, or non-consensual images of Canadian girls or women, were occurring in Canada. The jurisdictional nexus to prosecute the company in Canada – a real and substantial connection – was clearly made out.[120] But the RCMP's disinclination, for whatever reason, to investigate and/or charge the former owners of MindGeek is a separate question.

That said, pragmatically, for platforms that are operating in Canada and certainly for those that are not knowingly distributing content that violates the *Criminal Code*, it will likely be more effective for criminal law enforcement to work with them to identify, and retain evidence regarding, users who are distributing child sexual abuse material and non-consensually distributed images. The new owners of MindGeek appear to have taken this approach to child sexual abuse material on its platforms.[121] (It is not clear whether the company has adopted this approach with respect to non-consensually distributed images of adults. According to the 2024 report released by Canada's privacy commissioner, the company had not provided any evidence to the commissioner of MindGeek having *ever* referred an uploader of non-consensual content of adults to law enforcement.)[122]

In addition, criminal law is not oriented to ameliorating and mitigating the harms caused to specific, individual victims. In particular, the track record of the criminal justice system and law enforcement regarding the protection of women and children from gender-based harm is very poor.[123] In some cases there may be more to be gained for victims through governments working with platforms to encourage them to take down unlawful content expeditiously, preserve evidence, and report the content, than through attempting to prosecute them criminally. In others, the use of victim-centred civil statutes not bogged down with the procedural requirements of criminal law, and designed to offer what many victims want most, fast removal and destruction of the content, will often be preferable to those most adversely impacted by harmful content. This leads us to consideration of civil law responses to porn on the platform.

Civil Liability and Remedies as a Response to Unlawful Porn on the Platform

Several Canadian provinces have adopted legislation to provide civil remedies for the non-consensual distribution of intimate images (which by definition would also include child sexual abuse material).[124] The most promising laws follow the recommendations offered by Hilary Young and Emily Laidlaw, and adopted by the Uniform Law Conference of Canada as the *Uniform Non-consensual Disclosure of Intimate Images Act* (2021).[125] This is a model civil liability statute with two aims: (1) to create fast and accessible take-down, destruction, and de-indexing orders for victims of non-consensual distribution of intimate images; and (2) to create compensation remedies, without unduly compromising freedom of expression.[126]

Crucial aspects of this model legislation include allowing victims to fast track the removal of content through a declaratory remedy without the need to prove that it was intentionally distributed without their consent; laying the burden of proving that the complainant did not have a reasonable expectation of privacy in the intimate image on the respondent; having the law apply to content that was originally created consensually; making these remedies available to an individual person, even if she is not recognizable in the intimate image (provided she can establish that it is her); and having it apply to altered images or synthetic media, which would include deepfake porn.[127]

The model law creates what is called a strict liability tort for distributing or threatening to distribute intimate images. Under this strict liability tort, the complainant does not need to prove that she suffered harm, or prove fault on the part of the respondent. The respondent, typically the person who the complainant alleges uploaded the image, bears the onus of proving that he had consent to distribute the image. The court can order both the user who uploaded the image and the platform to make every reasonable effort to make the image unavailable to others and to have the image de-indexed from any search engines.[128] The aim is to give victims the ability to have non-consensual content removed easily and quickly without the cost and time involved in pursuing a conventional legal process.

The model statute also creates a second, fault-based tort under which a victim can bring a more traditional legal claim seeking compensatory, aggravated, and punitive damages. Under this tort a user, or respondent, is not liable if they can prove that they did not intend to distribute the image, or that they honestly and reasonably believed that they had consent to distribute the image at the time, and to the extent, that it was distributed. A complainant could potentially pursue both types of torts: an expedited application to have the images quickly taken down under the strict liability tort, and then a follow-up action claiming damages.[129]

One of the significant advantages of this model law is that it does not require victims to rely as heavily on platforms to adjudicate their claims that the images of them were uploaded without their consent. As Young and Laidlaw note, "intermediaries do not always take down content alleged to be unlawful … [but] a court order provides clarity that the content is un-lawful and can instruct that content should be taken down by third party providers."[130] Provinces that have not yet adopted civil statutes to address the issue of non-consensual distribution of intimate images should base their laws on this model statute.[131] Provinces that have enacted protection of intimate image laws would do well to revisit their legislation in light of the recommendations provided by Young and Laidlaw, and reflected in the *Uniform Non-consensual Disclosure of Intimate Images Act* (2021).

In addition to the individual users who post this content, what liability ought to be imposed against platforms that host non-consensually produced and/or distributed content? To understand the Canadian legal context re-garding platform liability, it is necessary to appreciate the American context. Again, section 230 of the United States' *Communications Decency Act* creates almost complete immunity from civil liability for platform intermediaries for the content posted by their users.[132] While there have been some recent suggestions and efforts to shift this approach in the United States,[133] it re-mains true that in America, platforms are largely not liable for the content posted by their users.[134] The justification for offering intermediaries this im-munity is articulated as a concern with protecting freedom of speech and avoiding the censorship that platforms may engage in if they were broadly subject to liability for the content of their users. The American reluctance or refusal to hold platforms liable looms in the background for Canadian lawmakers. There is even concern that Canada has made treaty commitments to immunize platforms from civil liability for the wrongful conduct of users in Canada (and Mexico) in a manner similar to what occurs in the United States.[135] A better approach than immunizing platforms from civil liability, one that balances freedom of expression and protection of the dignity and privacy interests of victims would hold platforms liable for failing to take all possible reasonable measures to prevent the non-consensual distribution of intimate images. For porn-streaming platforms, assessing what is reasonable must be done in light of the risk of non-consensual distribution of intimate images that these platforms create.

The model statute advanced by Laidlaw and Young, and adopted by the Uniform Law Conference, provides that no application or claim for liability can be brought against a platform if it has taken reasonable steps to address unlawful distribution of intimate images in the use of its services. The model statute does not identify what constitutes reasonable steps. Jurisdictions that have followed the recommendations of the Uniform Law Conference, such as Prince Edward Island and British Columbia, have adopted this provision.[136] Prince Edward Island's legislation, for example, stipulates that "[n]o application or claim may be brought against an internet intermediary if the internet intermediary has taken reasonable steps to address unlawful distribution of intimate images in the use of its services."[137] British Columbia's act includes the same provision.[138]

On one hand, these provisions do indirectly impose liability on platforms by stipulating that the failure to take reasonable steps to prevent the non-consensual distribution of intimate images disqualifies their eligibility for the immunity otherwise available under the statute. That said, the model statute does broadly exempt platforms from liability provided they can meet this reasonableness standard. This departure from the American approach, depending on how reasonable steps are interpreted, is similar to the approach taken in the European Union and in Quebec.[139] Platforms in the EU receive a qualified immunity or safe harbour from liability for the speech of their users: the law imposes obligations on the platform to respond expeditiously if they have knowledge of unlawful content, and imposes liability if they fail to meet those obligations. Quebec takes a similar approach.[140]

How would the model statute apply to mainstream porn-streaming platforms? In developing their analysis, Young and Laidlaw were in the main contemplating other types of platforms.[141] They concede that "it may be justifiable for intermediaries to be [directly] liable in narrow circumstances where their contribution to the harm is more direct and egregious."[142] It is not clear that they would endorse an exception to immunity broad enough to categorically include mainstream porn-streaming platforms. The example that they give is of platforms that either encourage the posting of non-consensual intimate images or that primarily host such content.[143] Some mainstream porn-streaming platforms could perhaps, in some instances, be accused of encouraging the posting of non-consensual intimate images, but likely not of primarily hosting such content. Assuming that most porn-streaming platforms will be treated like other Internet intermediaries under these statutes, it is critical that courts appreciate that the "reasonable steps" required of a platform dedicated to hosting user-uploaded porn videos, before it could avail itself of the immunity for liability provided for under the Act, must be more extensive and onerous than what would be reasonable for a platform that prohibits pornography. In other words, courts must be attentive to how the objective element of the reasonable steps requirement is applied. What is reasonable in these circumstances?

Consider the example of Pornhub and the massive spike in non-consensual distribution of intimate images that occurred concurrent to its COVID-19 lockdown promotion, discussed in chapter 3. In spring 2020, Pornhub provided its "models" with a larger proportion of video sales during the month of April (100 per cent of video sales minus a 15 per cent "processing fee").[144] Presumably this created a financial incentive to encourage people to upload videos. The same week that Pornhub announced its offer, traffic to the British government's Revenge Porn Helpline nearly doubled.[145] It is not possible to know whether the increase in non-consensual distribution of intimate images was in any way connected to Pornhub's offer. But it is true that Pornhub not only created a platform for this non-consensual activity and enabled users to distribute this content globally, it also financially incentivized users to upload intimate images by offering them a larger proportion of the advertising revenue for the month of April. It is also true that it is porn-streaming platforms – not email, group messaging apps, or other social media – that serve as the most common venue for the non-consensual distribution of intimate images.[146] The risk of non-consensual disclosure of intimate images is heightened in this context and the reasonable steps required should be as well.

But there is more to this analysis. At the time it made this offer – that is, before Pornhub adopted its new trust and safety protocols in response to the *New York Times* scandal – the company could have pointed to a multitude of steps it had taken to prevent this type of abuse: its Non-consensual Content Policy, which strictly prohibited this type of content; its content removal request form and process; its human moderators; and its PhotoDNA technology, which the company said was intended to prevent the re-uploading of flagged content. Indeed, in a 2018 article published in the feminist law journal *Canadian Journal of Women in the Law*, Andrea Slane and Ganaele Langlois distinguished Pornhub from platforms that they indicated were not taking adequate steps to verify the consent of everyone appearing in the videos uploaded to their sites, and applauded Pornhub for the protocols it relied upon at the time (which were far less rigorous than what the platform requires today) to verify that the content uploaded to its platform was consensual.[147] In other words, Pornhub could have pointed to the many steps it was taking, and feminist academics *were* pointing to the steps Pornhub was taking relative to other platforms, to prevent non-consensual distribution of intimate images at the very time the company was reportedly ignoring the repeated take-down requests of rape victims, and as discussed next, allegedly profiting off of millions of views of hundreds of non-consensual videos on its GirlsDoPorn channel. The question is this: what constitutes reasonable steps in the face of a promotion that might have encouraged, or at least risked encouraging, the distribution of non-consensual videos in the first place? As the *New York Times* scandal and the GirlsDoPorn example discussed next demonstrate, a porn-streaming platform may well be able to point to a seemingly proficient set of protocols, more than what other types of platforms have in place, to prevent non-consensual content, while simultaneously failing to act reasonably (or ethically or humanely).

GirlsDoPorn victimized, according to some reports,[148] over 100 women by coercing them to perform in pornography videos, promising them that the videos would never be shared online or distributed in the United States, and then uploading them to online platforms, including Pornhub.[149] In fact, Pornhub had a formal partnership with GirlsDoPorn – including a subscription-based GirlsDoPorn channel. In a lawsuit brought by fifty of the women victimized as part of the GirlsDoPorn scheme, the complainants' legal counsel asserted that as of 2019 the videos hosted on Pornhub's subscription-based GirlsDoPorn channel had 700,000 subscribers and had been viewed 700,000,000 times.[150] Hundreds of other versions of the videos were allegedly hosted on other MindGeek platforms.[151] MindGeek eventually settled with these plaintiffs.[152]

In her investigative journalism subsequent to the GirlsDoPorn lawsuit brought by several of the women victimized, Samantha Cole reported that Pornhub's supposedly cutting-edge PhotoDNA technology (which it said it relied upon to prevent the re-uploading of non-consensually distributed content) was easily circumvented by modestly editing and then re-uploading versions of the same content, and that it was still possible at the time of her investigation to find countless GirlsDoPorn videos on the platform with minor modifications to one's search terms. Years later, hundreds of versions of the videos reportedly remained viewable on platforms, especially Pornhub.[153] As outlined in chapter 1, numerous girls and women have accused Pornhub of ignoring their repeated requests to have non-consensual content removed until they finally retained lawyers, or initiated lawsuits against the company.[154]

The intention of the model legislation advanced by Laidlaw and Young is explicitly remedial. The aim is to provide victims with the ability to have non-consensual content removed, destroyed, and de-indexed as quickly as possible. Its secondary objective is to provide victims with compensation, and to perhaps deter users from engaging in this unlawful activity. Unduly protecting porn-streaming platforms from lawsuits, by failing to adequately contextualize the notion of reasonable steps, will undermine these objectives. What is reasonable in an industry that financially incentivizes users to distribute intimate images, and in which Internet intermediaries base their business models not just on attention economics and volume of traffic and correspondingly volume of content, like many platforms, but on attention economics related to intimate image content? In other words, how does the concept of reasonable steps work for companies that may incentivize, even if unintentionally, and profit from this type of content?[155]

Again, reasonable steps have to be considered contextually and in light of Internet intermediaries whose primary business involves financially incentivizing user-generated intimate images and revenue generation through advertising. Given the risks these platforms create regarding the distribution of non-consensual intimate images, and given that their own financial incentives may run contrary to aggressively eliminating this content, the reasonable steps required of this type of commercial entity should be onerous. They should include, for instance, a verification system that requires proof of identity of everyone appearing in the video through the provision of government-issued identification, as well as concrete punitive and preventative measures to restrict future access to any user found to have knowingly uploaded non-consensual content. Identity verification could be provided to a third-party company, given that content producers may be hesitant to provide this type of information to a pornography company. This would not be foolproof, and some sex workers have understandable concerns about providing their identification to anyone. But it does seem reasonable and the trade-offs acceptable, assuming mechanisms are in place to ensure a secure process for the provision of government-issued identification.

For porn-streaming platforms that do not rely on the attention economics of this business model, such as those that do not provide free porn, accept user-generated content from non-professionals, or base their revenue on advertising, the reasonable steps requirement may not be as onerous. These platforms may not be creating the same degree of risk as those that incentivize user-generated videos and rely on advertising revenue (and thus volume of traffic). That said, even for these platforms a properly calibrated reasonable-steps analysis would still appreciate that what is "reasonable" in terms of preventative measures for a porn-streaming platform will be more extensive than what would be considered reasonable for a site that prohibits pornography (accepting that any platform that accepts user-generated content is posing a risk and should be required to take reasonable steps to prevent and respond expeditiously to this harmful activity or face liability).

Laidlaw and Young recommend that the fault element for this tort be an honest and objective standard, the onus of which would lie on the respondent to prove. Respondent platforms that take steps to meaningfully verify consent, and that honestly and objectively believed that they had explicit direct consent to distribute the intimate image from everyone appearing in it, would not be found liable.

Properly applied, this type of law would encourage platforms to evolve their responses to take-down requests from individual victims, like the women victimized by GirlsDoPorn. Presumably, as soon as they received the first request to remove an intimate image because it contained non-consensual content, a platform would no longer be able to assert that they honestly and objectively believed that they had consent to distribute the image. This would encourage platforms to treat take-down requests from individual victims with the same expediency and seriousness as they treat requests that come from lawyers, law enforcement, or "trusted flaggers," such as organizations that target the sexual exploitation of children. A platform would not be able to avail itself of the immunity clause in this type of law unless it responded expeditiously, regardless of who made the request. As a result, take-down requests based on an assertion that the content was distributed without consent would be more likely to result in immediate removal and de-indexing by the platform.[156] This would mean that in some cases victims would not have to undertake the emotionally distressing process of retaining a lawyer, or having an application drafted, to have the content immediately removed and de-indexed. In the context of sexually explicit material alleged to be distributed without consent, at least on porn-streaming platforms, individual take-down requests should be treated with a high degree of expediency and seriousness, approximating the response given to requests from "trusted flaggers." As noted, this has not always been the case.[157]

This raises the specter of collateral censorship. Again, one of the justifications for granting Internet intermediaries immunity from liability for the content they host is based on concerns that imposing liability for third-party speech will encourage platforms to apply content moderation too broadly so as to include material that is not unlawful, or that they will be too liberal in responding to take-down requests, thus unduly impacting free speech. This is also a freedom of expression concern.[158] These laws do place limits on freedom of expression, but ones that would be justifiable if properly calibrated based on the degree of risk the platform poses. Given the important objective of the law in this instance – protecting the privacy, equality, and dignity interests of victims of non-consensual distribution of intimate images – laws that motivate these types of platforms in particular, to err on the side of vigilance, and expediency and responsiveness regarding take-down requests based on assertions of lack of consent by the women and girls appearing in sexually explicit content, are likely to be deemed justifiable by Canadian courts. Moreover, while the data on this is limited, some experience with imposing stricter regimes on Internet intermediaries in other jurisdictions, such as Germany, suggests that a tidal wave of illegitimate take-down requests may be unlikely, and that platforms generally do not over-block content when legal expectations to respond expeditiously to requests to take down unlawful content are imposed.[159]

If it is enacted in its current form, Bill C-63 would also create an expedited take-down process for sexually explicit content distributed without consent. The process would be administered by a newly created Digital Safety Commission of Canada and complainants would be supported through a digital safety ombudsperson. The *Online Harms Act* would place a duty on platforms to make inaccessible any content they have reasonable grounds to suspect was communicated without consent, or that is flagged by a user as communicated without consent, within twenty-four hours (subject to a process of reconsideration). Platforms could be held liable for failing to meet this duty and potential financial penalties would be severe. At the time of writing, the bill was at first reading. It is too early to speculate on whether it will be enacted and if so, what shape it might ultimately take.

British Columbia's newly launched Intimate Images Protection Service and the ability of victims to apply online for an intimate image protection order from the province's Civil Resolution Tribunal (CRT), rather than requiring them to pursue one in court, makes British Columbia the national leader in this context. Once a person has applied online to obtain a take-down order (in addition, if they choose, to damages of less than $5,000), a CRT case manager is assigned to them and will contact them to assist them with obtaining the order.[160] In addition, the Intimate Images Protection Service provides emotional support, and information and support regarding legal options, including pursuing the expedited application process at the CRT; the service will also communicate take-down orders to platforms and individual perpetrators on behalf of victims once they have been obtained.[161] Absent a federal regime, similar to what is contemplated under Bill C-63, other provinces should put in place an administrative system and set of supports akin to what has been set up to address this problem in British Columbia. Moreover, some of the supports provided for under British Columbia's regime would not, and due to our constitutional division of powers could not, be established under the federal government's legislation. In this regard, other provinces in Canada should follow British Columbia's lead.

This chapter addressed legal responses to unlawful porn on the platform. Chapter 8 considers what to do about the platformization of porn generally, beyond the issue of content that is unlawful.

CHAPTER 8

What to Do about Lawful Porn on the Platform?

We can't code our way out of social issues.
– Samantha Cole, *How Sex Changed the Internet and the Internet Changed Sex*[1]

The World Health Organization defines sexual health as requiring "a positive and respectful approach to sexuality and sexual relationships, as well as the possibility of having pleasurable and safe sexual experiences, free of coercion, discrimination and violence."[2] While there is a good deal that will be contested when we use adjectives like "positive" and "respectful" to describe sex and sexuality, these do resonate as necessary components to our sexual health, or to use the conceptual framing I prefer: sexual integrity.[3] That said, and as explained in chapter 6, the preservation and promotion of sexual integrity requires not only freedom *from* coercion, discrimination, and violence, but also the capacity and freedom *to* explore identity, seek pleasure in new or different ways, and find joy. Related to this, and as highlighted at the end of chapter 5, the costs of harmful sexual norms, while most acute for those subjected to sexual violence, are nevertheless borne by everyone in a community. This is why the World Health Organization's definition of sexual health includes the statement "[f]or sexual health to be attained and maintained, the sexual rights of all persons must be respected, protected and fulfilled."[4] Certainly, a rights framework is part of the puzzle, in terms of our law and social policy engagements in response to porn, and sexual rights secured through law, as explored in chapter 7. It is unlikely, though, that a rights framework can do all of the work necessary to adapt our legal and social practices and responses to the rise of mainstream porn-streaming platforms.

When we think about issues of sexuality, of desire and pleasure, and of sexual violence – whether this be in the context of porn or otherwise – we need to understand sexual integrity as a shared good, as a relational interest. At a minimum, this suggests that the concept of individual rights to liberty, expression, equality, and privacy will be insufficient to address the systemic and structural interests at issue. Concepts of liberty, such as freedom of expression, human rights to equality, and the notion of individual legal entitlements to, for instance, privacy and property, are necessary aspects of our response to the platformization of porn, but so too are considerations regarding education, media accountability, and corporate responsibility. The consumption, production, and distribution of porn, as a consequence of its platformization, have become widely engaged in social practices. Addressing mainstream porn's potential harms demands the same degree of nuance, calibration, and multiplicity as does social and legal policy with respect to other forms of social media, and other complex, widely engaged in social practices more generally.

Broadly speaking, and this is where chapter 1 began, to say that porn on the platform demands this type of response has at least three implications: (1) we have to accept porn, which means accepting both that there appears to be an incredible human demand to consume porn, *and* that like any other widely engaged in social practice, this one impacts society, sometimes in ways that are harmful; (2) we have to talk about porn, which means both changes to the ways in which the media and academics often discuss porn, and consultation and reliance on the expertise and knowledge of those most impacted when we devise law and policy responses to pornography; and (3) we have to hold mainstream porn-streaming platforms accountable for, and responsible to respond to, porn on the platform that is lawful but that platforms themselves have identified as harmful.

These three implications regarding mainstream porn on the platform should, in turn, inform our analysis and responses to issues such as whether or how to prevent children or young people from being confronted with or accessing pornography; how to augment the possibility for porn to serve, rather than diminish, sexual integrity; and whether and how to impose legal obligations regarding content moderation (beyond those with respect to unlawful porn, such as child sexual abuse material and non-consensual content) on porn-streaming platforms. This is the focus of this final chapter of *Mainstreaming Porn*.

Tracking these three implications, the first part of chapter 8 identifies several drawbacks and pitfalls of adopting age-verification legislation as a response to the platformization of porn. Part two takes up the issue of porn literacy, advocating for pedagogical rather than technological responses to mainstream porn's potential harms and benefits. The final section offers recommendations aimed at encouraging or requiring mainstream porn-streaming platforms to enforce their own community standards regarding content moderation.

To summarize, chapter 8 recommends:

- that age-verification legislation to block access to porn platforms for those under the age of eighteen be rejected;
- that public and formal educational curricula be modernized, in collaboration with educators, researchers, and other knowledge holders, to include genuine porn literacy education to be delivered by those best qualified do so and targeted at all of those who would benefit from it (which is an audience much broader than kids and youth);
- that the federal government's legislative approach to online safety require porn-streaming platforms to assess and mitigate the risks that their services pose not only to children, but also to women specifically; and
- that the federal government's online safety legislation specifically contemplate the use of law to require mainstream porn-streaming platforms to comply with their own terms of service and community standards.

Age-Verification Legislation Does Not Work and Compromises the Expressive Rights of Children and Youth

In an article commenting on the March 2023 acquisition of MindGeek by newly formed venture capitalist firm Ethical Capital Partners (ECP), Ottawa lawyer Alexandra Kirschbaum stated, "We cannot be a society that does not talk about something that is almost as present as air."[5] Perhaps the most important part of what it means to "talk about porn" is to talk with and to those who are targeted by, or most likely to be impacted by, a particular legal regime or policy effort aimed at ameliorating mainstream porn's harmful impacts. Legislative or policy-based efforts to regulate or respond to a social activity, practice, or phenomenon are likely to be of limited value, and risk causing additional harms, if we fail to consult with and rely on the knowledge and experience of their central beneficiaries or targets. This is particularly true with respect to laws aimed at a social practice that is as ubiquitous as the consumption of mainstream pornography has become due to its platformization. A key question that should animate legislative and policy-based efforts to respond to the potential harms of mainstream porn-streaming platforms is the following: have the politicians, educators, lawmakers, and/or policymakers who designed a particular strategy consulted sufficiently with, and adequately relied upon, the perspectives and knowledge of those who will be most impacted?

Consider the example of age-verification laws. One approach to the platformization of porn that has gained traction in several jurisdictions around the world, including France, Germany, the United Kingdom, some American states, and now Canada, is to adopt age-verification legislation in an effort to prevent access to porn-streaming platforms by those under a certain age – typically those under age eighteen.

There are different ways to approach age-verification laws: through the provision of some form of formal identification (typically government ID, or information from a financial institution); self-declaration (which is used now by most social media sites and is largely considered almost completely ineffective); social profiling based on what a user has posted online in the past (which is considered unreliable and depends on what a user has posted on the platform, and thus would not be as applicable to free porn-streaming platforms, which typically receive more visits from "tourists," who are unable to post material themselves, than from "residents" with accounts);[6] and estimation based on an analysis of biometric data (which also has reliability issues, and, even more than the provision of formal identification, brings with it significant privacy concerns).[7]

In the context of porn-streaming platforms, it is the first option, the provision of some form of identification, that is most frequently contemplated. Typically, what is envisaged is the provision of identification to a third-party entity (either online or otherwise) in order to mitigate both the risk of serious privacy breaches related to the collection and linking of personal identification and consumption information by porn companies, and the risk that platforms would cross-reference the data gathered through age identification mechanisms with user practices on their sites, and then employ it for their own commercial purposes.[8]

The United Kingdom was one of the first democracies to pass legislation to limit access in this manner to otherwise lawful porn.[9] However, implementation of this law met with technical difficulties, primarily related to privacy concerns regarding how companies would prevent data leaks of the personal information that users were to provide to verify their ages.[10] There were also concerns that the law would give an unfair market advantage to MindGeek, which owns AgeID, the software that likely would have served as one of the main age-verification providers in Britain.[11] The law was never enforced, and was eventually repealed by a broader *Online Safety Act* that includes a section imposing age-verification requirements on commercial porn sites.[12]

Some American states are contemplating, or in the case of Louisiana[13] and Utah[14] have passed, age-verification legislation. Utah's law requires users to provide government identification every time they access a site on which a substantial portion of its content is pornography. Utah does not have an approved digitized government service to perform this function.[15] The response by Pornhub to Utah's law was to immediately disable access to the site for the entire state in order to protest the law on the basis that it is impossible for the company to comply with it, and problematic to require verification every time a user accesses a site.[16] A constitutional challenge under the First Amendment to the *Bill of Rights* was brought shortly after Utah's law was passed.[17] Pornhub appears to have complied with Louisiana's new law, which also requires government identification but for which a third-party verification provider associated with an approved government process is available.[18]

Canada is also contemplating age-verification legislation. Bill S-210, *An Act to Restrict Young Persons' Online Access to Sexually Explicit Material,* was introduced in the Canadian Senate, and at the time of writing was working its way through the House of Commons.[19] Bill S-210 would make it an offence to make sexually explicit material available to a person under the age of eighteen for commercial purposes. The law would permit the government to obtain a court order requiring Internet service providers to prevent access to sexually explicit materials by young persons if a platform refused to comply.

Privacy and Internet law experts have suggested that, in addition to concerns regarding the privacy interests of adults who provide personal information either to the platform or a third-party provider in order to verify their age, Bill S-210 is too broad in terms of its impact on freedom of expression. Professor Michael Geist argues that it is likely to result in blocking websites not intended to be blocked by the law, and to require age verification not simply for porn-streaming platforms like Pornhub, YouPorn, and xHamster, but also for platforms like Twitter, Reddit, and Snapchat.[20] He suggests that the proposed law could even require age verification to use Google, blocking the ability of children in school to conduct Internet searches.[21] This would severely limit the rights of children in Canada to freedom of expression. The impact of an age-verification law has to be assessed in light of the reality that "the digital world is not optional for most children. It is where they access education, health services and entertainment, build and maintain their relationships, and engage in civic and social activities."[22]

France introduced legislation in 2020 that requires porn-streaming platforms to employ age-verification mechanisms limiting access to their sites to those over the age of eighteen.[23] The law empowers the French government to obtain a court order blocking access in France to websites that do not comply.[24] At the time of writing, MindGeek was challenging the constitutionality of the law on the basis that it will not be effective due to the widespread use of virtual private networks (VPNS),[25] that it is not possible to comply with the law due to a lack of technical ability in France,[26] and that parental controls (which under a new French law have become the default setting on devices)[27] are sufficient to keep children safe online.[28] In 2022, France's data protection regulator published a report concluding that there were not currently any available age-verification mechanisms in France that were both effective and sufficiently protective of people's privacy.[29] Germany has also imposed age-verification requirements on major platforms.[30] As in France, Germany's efforts initially met with resistance from some large porn-streaming platforms.[31] While Pornhub refused to comply in France, in Germany, where MindGeek's AgeID verification software is being used across its platforms, the company appears to be complying with the law.[32]

One of the constituents likely to be most impacted by this type of legislative intervention is individual content creators. As Danielle Blunt, cofounder of Hacking/Hustling, a New York–based sex worker collective, observes, "sex workers are often living at the intersection of multiple marginalized identities, making them particularly susceptible to violence from poorly designed technology."[33] Blunt argues that "sex workers are experts of their own experiences and experts in how technology impacts their lives."[34] This would be equally true of their expertise pertaining to the impact on them of laws responding to technology and sex work. Have lawmakers consulted with, and adequately incorporated the knowledge and perspectives of, performers and other content creators, about the implications of age-verification laws for their work and safety?

One issue that content creators raise concerning age-restriction laws involves the implications of such regimes for smaller porn sites with modest profit margins.[35] Age verification is likely to be done by third-party entities rather than porn sites themselves, given the privacy concerns many are likely to have with providing porn companies with the personal information necessary to verify age.[36] Depending on how age-verification systems are designed, this could mean requiring sites to pay to verify each of their users. Feminist porn producer Pandora Blake argues that:

> websites providing niche content such as queer, fetish and feminist pornographies bring diversity to the adult industry, empower performers, subvert stereotypes and disrupt the homogeneity of mainstream porn. Age verification will put many such sites out of business, while the behemoths of commercial porn (which are far more likely to be stumbled across by under-18s) benefit from economies of scale that will permit them to survive. This will discriminate against people with marginalized sexualities, and will stifle diversity of representation.[37]

The disparate economic impact of such laws on smaller, queer, and feminist porn producers, relative to large mainstream platforms, is compounded by the reality that companies like MindGeek have created their own age-verification software to market to other commercial porn companies. (Granted, MindGeek has said it will offer its AgeID software for free to independent porn producers.[38] This may mitigate the disparate economic impact of these regimes, depending on MindGeek's criteria in terms of who is eligible to receive the software for free, and whether this offer comes to fruition.) Depending on the reach of age-verification legislation, there is a risk that individual sex workers will be further socially and/or economically marginalized through what is sometimes called the "deplatforming of sex."[39] This refers to the "trend of banning, shadowbanning and demonetizing sexual content on social media."[40] If age-verification laws apply to websites beyond those dedicated specifically to pornography, sex workers may find their ability to participate in the digital world severely compromised. This has already occurred in some countries. For instance, adult content creators report having their Twitter accounts blocked by the company in Germany in response to the country's age-verification requirements regarding sexually explicit material online.[41] Twitter does not have an age-verification system and so instead it has simply imposed a nationwide block on these users' accounts, which obviously has broader adverse implications for the freedom of expression interests of users who are already more at risk of having their voices marginalized.

Similarly, Blake observes that independent sex workers who advertise their services online could be captured by age-verification laws.[42] She notes that the clients of these workers may be deterred from accessing their websites due to a reluctance to provide the personal informational necessary to verify their age. As a result, some sex workers may find it necessary to turn to, or return to, less rewarding,[43] or more dangerous or exploitative, forms of work to maintain their income, such as street-based sex work or work that is mediated through an agent or pimp.[44]

The adverse impacts of deplatforming are disproportionately experienced by marginalized sex workers, not powerful corporate platform companies. Paasonen, Jarrett, and Light quote feminist porn producer Erika Lust: "sex bloggers and smaller, independent companies – like feminist, body-positive, and fetish sites – which rely on social media to attract traffic will struggle, while inherently misogynistic mainstream sites can afford to weather the storm."[45]

Legislative and social policy–based interventions regarding any aspect of the porn industry should not be pursued without substantive and ongoing consultation with, and contribution and involvement from, a sufficiently representative cohort of those who earn their income, or a portion of their income, from appearing in pornography. In part, this is what it means to "talk about porn" at a law and policy level.

What else does it mean to say that legislative and social policy efforts must be guided by consultation with those who are targeted by, and/or most likely to be impacted by, a particular strategy aimed at ameliorating mainstream porn's potential harm? In the context of debates about age verification regimes it means co-opting the "save the children" rhetoric and reconceiving it as a social and ethical responsibility to actually talk with children and adolescents, in age-appropriate ways, about porn.

In addition to performers, individual content creators, and sex workers, the other cohort or segment of society most likely to be impacted by age-verification laws are young people interested in consuming (and producing) sexually explicit material. Indeed, other than children exposed to porn, this segment of society is presumably the main target of such legislative efforts. Have those who are designing these laws adequately relied upon the knowledge and perspectives of adolescents regarding their relationships to porn, and their views regarding this type of legislation, its bearing on them, and how or whether it will impact their access to pornography or porn-consumption practices, or those of their friends and siblings? As Professor Simone van der Hof argues, "[i]t is essential to involve children and parents when designing and developing age verification methods because they are best placed to indicate their experiences, expectations and concerns."[46] While I would add the term "youth," or "adolescents," and not conflate it with the term "children," I agree that it is essential that they be involved, and that their knowledge be relied upon, in making determinations regarding the feasibility (in terms of the efficacy) and advisability (in terms of the impact on their expressive rights) of age-verification laws.

Take the issue of efficacy. Consultation with youth reveals that adolescents with even modest technology skills seeking to visit a website that requires age verification will likely know how to download a VPN (or Tor browser) that could be used to hide one's IP address, such that one appears to be in a country without age-verification laws, thus allowing access to the site.[47] A 2020 New Zealand survey of adolescents on the necessity and efficacy of legislative efforts to regulate Internet pornography, conducted by Neil Thurman and Fabian Obster, revealed that 46 per cent of sixteen- and seventeen-year-olds had used a VPN or Tor browser and another 23 per cent knew how these mechanisms functioned.[48]

Even younger teenagers, who have perhaps not learned about VPNs specifically but who are interested in accessing websites with age-verification requirements, may know to do a Google search seeking instructions. A Google search conducted on 10 April 2023 using the phrase "how to access blocked porn sites" yielded numerous results, including articles on the first page of search results with titles such as, "Want Porn? Prove Your Age (or Get a VPN),"[49] "Best VPN to Avoid the UK's Porn Age Verification,"[50] and "How to Access and Watch Pornhub If It's Blocked in Your Country [Tutorial]."[51]

It is true that age-verification mechanisms are in use on websites for other types of activities typically restricted to adults, such as gambling and the purchase of alcohol or cannabis. However, successfully accessing and using a website for the purposes of gambling, or one that sells alcohol or cannabis, comes with additional barriers, such as paying for and arranging for the delivery of goods, that mean age verification mechanisms are not as easily overcome by VPNs in these contexts. This is not true of porn-streaming platforms. Unless the companies that own these platforms decide to impose age-verification requirements, globally, regardless of jurisdiction,[52] VPNs are likely to have a far greater negative impact on the efficacy of these legislative efforts than would be the case with respect to age verification in other contexts, like alcohol sales or gambling.

The likelihood of major platforms like Pornhub, xHamster, or YouPorn voluntarily imposing age verification globally, in order to address the efficacy challenges posed by VPNs and Tor browsers seems extremely low given the response of these platforms to the imposition of age-verification laws to date. As noted, in some countries, such as France, when age-verification laws have been passed, the response of platforms like Pornhub and xHamster has been to refuse to comply.[53]

The business model of mainstream porn-streaming platforms that are reliant on advertising revenue turns on volume of traffic; genuine implementation of any system that effectively limits the number of visitors to their sites, whether those visitors are children, adolescents, or adults, is presumably adverse to the financial interests of these companies. Whatever legislative or policy interventions might be contemplated as a response to the possible harms of mainstream porn, relying on platforms operating in an attention economy to voluntarily implement measures that significantly reduce traffic to their sites would be foolhardy. Indeed, recall that one of Mind-Geek's arguments against France's age-verification law, and justification for refusing to comply with it, was that the law is ineffective because of the way in which it could be circumvented by a reliance on VPNs.[54] This is a problem MindGeek could seemingly fix for purposes of its own platforms if it applied age verification to all of its sites globally.

The results of studies attempting to determine whether children and adolescents are inadvertently exposed to pornography online, or whether they actively seek out such content are conflicting. Some research indicates that for the majority of children, first exposure occurs when they accidently find porn while online or are involuntarily exposed to it, typically by a friend or older family member, such as a sibling.[55] Other studies suggest that, at least by a certain age, many youth have actively sought it out online.[56] Similarly, there are conflicting statistics on the proportion of teenagers who consume porn regularly, and at what age. However, it is reasonably clear that, by age sixteen or seventeen, a majority of adolescent men have watched porn online and that a significant proportion of them are regular consumers.[57] These youth are not stumbling upon this content inadvertently. This empirical reality is significant for the purposes of understanding the limited efficacy of age-verification legislation.

As already explained, online sexually explicit material is not limited to porn-streaming platforms. It can be found on social media platforms like Twitter, Facebook, and Instagram, and subsections of websites like Reddit are dedicated to sharing pornography. This raises a separate efficacy challenge with respect to age-verification laws, in terms of whether efforts to regulate or limit access to mainstream porn-streaming platforms will have much impact if children and adolescents are just as likely to view it elsewhere online – as well as a freedom of expression concern in terms of the extent to which we are willing to impede the online freedom of children and adolescents, and to censor Internet content generally.[58]

It is important to take guidance from the knowledge and experience of those most likely to be impacted. The study conducted by Thurman and Obster revealed that while 80.5 per cent of sixteen- and seventeen-year-old teenagers in the United Kingdom had seen sexually explicit porn videos or pictures, more of them had been initially exposed to it on search engines (51 per cent) and other types of social media (63 per cent), than on porn-streaming platforms (47 per cent).[59] That said, porn is much more *frequently* viewed by this cohort on porn-streaming platforms than on social media, search engines, or YouTube.[60] Porn-streaming platforms were by far the most frequently used source of porn by the sixteen- and seventeen-year-olds in their study – with an average use of two hours and eighteen minutes per month.[61] Research from New Zealand similarly shows that adolescents seeking porn online turn to porn-streaming platforms more frequently than other social media or online sources.[62] What these various studies suggest when considered as a whole is that, for the cohort of people under the age of eighteen who are frequenting porn-streaming platforms, an age-verification law applied to commercially driven porn-streaming platforms would likely be useless.

Age-verification barriers are more likely to be more effective at preventing children and teenagers from accidently stumbling across free porn on the Internet than at preventing access to determined teenagers who actively seek out porn online. Locking down parts of the Internet is very unlikely to work for this latter cohort. Consider the following anecdote. Journalist Samantha Cole documents that "[a]s a teenager in the late nineties, Fabian Thylmann was perusing CompuServe's porn forums when he had the idea that would forever change the adult industry."[63] The purpose of the CompuServe forums he was exploring was to allow users to exchange porn site login information. As Cole explains:

> Thylmann was still too young to subscribe to those sites, which usually required a credit card as proof of being legal age ... but he was old enough to start learning the trade from the pirated side of things. In a 2019 interview, he called this practice of finding and sharing logins for paywalled sites "a sport."[64]

Fabian Thylmann was the founder of the company Manwin, the name of which was later changed to MindGeek. His world-changing idea, of course, was a data-driven porn-streaming platform in which the content itself was free. The inspiration for Pornhub was sparked by the workarounds, such as online forums to share login information, developed by a motivated young Thylmann, to deal with the age-verification requirements of that era. That is to say, if Cole's historical account of Thylmann's teenage capers is accurate, the genesis for the idea for Pornhub was born of efforts to prevent adolescents from accessing online porn.

Canada's proposed age-verification legislation originated in the Senate. The average age of senators in the Canadian Senate is sixty-three.[65] It may be that a cohort of lawmakers from this demographic, even with experts and research guiding them, is not well positioned to design a technology-based system that will keep adolescent men, for example, from accessing digital spaces that are intriguing or appealing to them. Indeed, as Pornhub's origin story suggests, sometimes such approaches can have the opposite effect.

But efficacy should not be our only concern with these age-verification laws. In a 2016 study in the United Kingdom, young people were surveyed about their views regarding age-verification laws.[66] In some focus groups, youth asked why the law would allow them to consent to sex at age sixteen but not permit them to legally access (lawful) pornography.[67]

There are some additional potential downsides, for youth, presented by age-verification legislation. Some VPNS, particularly free ones (which are presumably the ones most likely to be downloaded by children and adolescents seeking to evade an age-verification requirement), also pose privacy and security risks.[68] In addition, some have argued that creating barriers to free mainstream platforms like Pornhub might incline some youth to move towards platforms with even more problematic content, such as what might be found using a Tor browser, which permits one to access the so-called dark web.[69]

Accepting that age-verification requirements are unlikely to prevent young people who are seeking access to dedicated porn-streaming platforms from doing so, and have other potential failings related to privacy protections and expressive rights, what should be done regarding the accidental exposure of children to sexually explicit content online? The likely answer may be reliance on the types of parental device controls and browser filters already available.[70] These mechanisms, and there are a variety of options, can be used to prevent young children from accidently stumbling upon online porn on social media, search engines, and porn-streaming platforms.[71] These tools do not pose the same privacy issues, freedom of expression concerns (at least for adults), and threats to the livelihoods and safety of sex workers and other performers that age-restriction laws pose.

It is true that relying on parental controls/safe-search mechanisms typically requires relying on parents/guardians or other family members to deploy these mechanisms, and that research indicates the uptake of such software is modest.[72] Moreover, it matters not only whether parents use these mechanisms, but *how* they use them and for what age group. Are they being used proportionate to the nature and level of risk relevant to the child's age? Are they being used in a manner that respects children's rights?

In addition, there is an argument to be had about whether safe-search mechanisms construct sex as inherently dangerous, thus differentiating it from other explicit online materials that children may be inadvertently exposed to, such as homophobic or racist violence. Is this the best way to deal with the issue? But ultimately, for parents and guardians who seek to address the reality of sexually explicit content online by attempting to prevent young children from being accidently exposed to it, these tools are already available without imposing age-verification laws.

What about children who are old enough to work their way around safe-search mechanisms? Kids who can undermine parental controls and safe-search filters will also know how to use VPNs. Unsurprisingly, research suggests that parental control software works better for preventing children from accessing pornography online than it does with respect to adolescents.[73]

By the time young people are old enough to circumvent parental controls such as search-blocking software, they will presumably also know how to use a VPN. In other words, absent global buy-in by platforms, age-verification legislation is unlikely to serve as an effective backup when children or youth age out of the protection offered by the parental control/safe-search options already available.

One further concern with age verification as a strategy, let alone a primary strategy, for responding to the potential harms caused to children by mainstream porn-streaming platforms is that it risks leaving parents and educators with the erroneous assumption that they do not need to talk about, and prepare young people for, both the sexually explicit materials that they will inevitably confront (and/or seek out) online, and the ways in which the ubiquity of porn on the platform is impacting the sexual landscape and the social interactions and relationships in which children and adolescents engage.

Harmful sexual behaviour is a human problem that demands, first and foremost, human responses and strategies. Trying to protect young people from the potential harms of consuming porn (or too much pornography or certain types of pornography) by attempting to simply lockdown, or lock them out of, parts of the Internet is akin to trying to protect children and youth from exploitative and non-consensual sex by telling them not to talk to strangers or not to have sex. It might be effective at the margins, or for some it might be temporarily effective, but it is not an appropriate strategy to support the development and maintenance of sexual integrity, understood as both an individual capacity to experience the good of sex and a relational interest in which sexuality is a feature of human flourishing rather than oppression. And it *does* construct sex as inherently harmful. As Paasonen, Jarrett, and Light argue in *#NSFW: Sex, Humor, and Risk in Social Media*, "conflating safety with the filtering of sexual content both builds on and bolsters an understanding of sex and sexuality as inherently risky, potentially harmful, and best hidden away and left unmentioned."[74]

Relying on (age-verification) technology, rather than pedagogy, is likely to leave children and adolescents with less capacity and knowledge to identify and competently mitigate the potential harms arising from some porn – such as harmful sexual scripts (including inadequate representations of consent) and misogynistic and racist norms (including those that hold in place sex- and race-based structures of sex, gender, and race-based oppression). Protecting children and adolescents from the potential harms of consuming pornography (or too much or some types of porn) requires talking to them about porn – and about the good and bad of sex, about consent and desire and sexual pleasure and bodies, as well as about power and misogyny and racism and rape, and about the potential benefits of porn.

Porn Literacy (And for Whom ...?)

In conducting research for her book on the sexual lives of young men in America, *Boys and Sex*, Peggy Orenstein conducted a set of in-depth interviews with adolescent boys and men between the ages of sixteen and twenty-two.[75] Porn was one of the topics frequently raised. Orenstein included a discussion with one of her interview subjects, Mason, who had spent a good portion of his teenage years circumventing the various parental controls and safe-search blocks his parents had placed on the household devices in an unsuccessful effort to prevent him from accessing porn online. By the time he reached university, Mason was questioning whether his relationship with porn was serving him well. He described an interaction he had had with his father after his father caught him watching porn on his school laptop when he was in high school. The extent of his father's conversation with him was: "You shouldn't be watching that ... It's bad for you."[76] Mason told Orenstein, "I kind of wish ... there was an opportunity to have that conversation with me. Maybe if he had said, 'This will skew the way you view women. It's not real. And it's not going to help you get a girl, it's only going to keep you from interacting with girls in a healthy manner.' But my parents were too fearful to actually deal with any of it."[77]

Parents are sometimes reluctant to have or uncomfortable with having these conversations, but research that asks young people about their views indicates that most of them want adults, whether that be family members or educators, to talk with them about sex and sexuality, including about porn.[78] Adolescent boys and men like Mason would be better served by frank, non-judgmental, concrete discussions about porn and its potential harms and benefits than by (inevitably unsuccessful) efforts to restrict their access to parts of the Internet. They would benefit from learning that there are other types of porn, including porn that presents more gender diversity and diverse representations of sexual pleasure, than what is available on free porn-streaming platforms – even if most of this porn is not free and thus less likely to be available to them at their age. Asking them to think about whether the porn they consume depicts the affirmative, contemporaneous, communicative standard of consent required under Canadian law, and if it does, how they might learn from that, could be a useful way to talk to young men about consent. Suggesting that the representations of sexuality in mainstream porn may teach them some of the mechanics of different types of sexual activities to explore, but that it may not provide them with sufficient knowledge on how they might provide sexual pleasure to, or instigate orgasms for, the girls or women they are engaging with sexually "in real life," seems productive. Explaining that some of the porn they may be consuming on tube sites is likely distributed without the consent of those appearing in it, and exploring with them how that aligns with their values, would be useful. Talking to them about the fact that looking only at mainstream porn is, as Shira Tarrant puts it, "the sex equivalent of eating all our meals at McDonalds," whereas moving away from those mainstream tube sites "could really expand our definitions of sexuality, sexual pleasure, and sexual desire," would be productive.[79] But telling kids like Mason, "You shouldn't be watching that ... It's bad for you," provides them with no information, no invitation for follow-up discussion, and no guidance on how to consume porn ethically – on how to access its benefits, rather than perpetuate its harms.

The young women engaging in sexual activity with the Masons of today's sexual landscape (and consuming the content on sites like Pornhub and xHamster) would also benefit greatly from such conversations. In her follow-up to *Boys and Sex*, Orenstein talked to high school– and university-aged girls and women in America. The girls and young women interviewed in *Girls and Sex* made comments such as:

- "I watch porn because I am a virgin and I want to figure out how sex works."[80]
- "Especially with my first boyfriend. He had no experience. He thought it would happen like in porn, that I'd be ready a lot faster and he could just, you know, *pound*."[81]
- "I remember sort of hating it ... I wanted to please him, but it felt sometimes like we couldn't have a normal conversation because he was so distracted by wanting to have sex. And I couldn't really think of a *reason* to refuse ... Sometimes I felt like I was just a receptacle for his hormones."[82]
- "They think they're supposed to do this hammer-in-and-out thing

and that's what girls like ... They don't realize, 'Dude, that does *not feel good.*' It's all they know. It's what they see. If you're just hooking up with someone, like a one-time thing or whatever, you just *pretend* it feels good."[83]

Teenage girls and adolescent women deserve the benefit of detailed and concrete conversations that, if they are not aroused by or interested in engaging in some of the acts they see depicted in mainstream porn, will support and enhance their capacity to communicate their disinterest or displeasure to sexual partners who *are* interested in engaging in such acts. And conversely, they deserve support in building their capacity to communicate their desires regarding the sexual activities that they are interested in exploring. Assuming young women know that the female performers in the videos on mainstream porn platforms who respond with orgasmic delight to everything that is done to them might also be *pretending it feels good*, some, or a lot, of the time, it would be helpful to have discussions with them about why some (or a lot) of mainstream porn represents sexuality this way, and how they relate to this in their sexual experiences.

While these would be more productive ways for parents to respond to the platformization of porn than trying to lock their teenagers out of parts of the Internet, there are some parents we do *not* want talking to their children about porn. Fathers and stepfathers making the types of comments examined in chapter 5 would fall into that category. More generally, there are some pedagogical interventions, less likely to occur in the parental or familial domain, that have or should become an increasing point of focus in more formal forms of education.

One clear point of consensus among the youth interviewed in the 2016 study from the United Kingdom, referenced earlier in this chapter, was their need and desire for better, and more, "sex education" about porn: "a strong view that was voiced across both genders and all age groups was related to open discussion on online pornography in all schools, religious and secular."[84] In a 2021 survey of over 1,200 young people in Australia between the ages of fifteen and twenty-nine (90 per cent of whom had at some point watched porn intentionally), 87 per cent supported some form of school-based sex education focusing on pornography.[85] Comments from interview participants in favour of education on porn emphasized the need for this education to focus on consent and to be sex positive. Young people told their interviewers:

- "Discussions should be about the differences between porn and sex in reality. [They should] come coupled with talks about consent and communication between partners."[86]
- "I hope they are sex positive and if people over the age of 18 want to access porn, their demand for feminist or female friendly porn should be encouraged."[87]

Numerous other studies in several countries have produced the same results. Adolescents and young adults consistently identify (1) a need for more information and education regarding pornography; (2) the need for media literacy related to porn (including, one would hope, the ability to critically assess content in order to understand its potential negative influences, but also its potential beneficial influences); and (3) an insufficiency in relation to both of these matters in the education that they are receiving.[88]

Irish sex educator and researcher Kate Dawson observed a similar trend among the fourteen- to sixteen-year-old youth she works with: "[Increasingly] a lot of their anonymous questions are related to porn and the types of bodies and sex acts that feature within it, yet the majority appear extremely embarrassed when it comes to discussing porn."[89] Dawson argues that "porn literacy education at secondary school level could reduce the stigma around porn engagement, highlight the differences between porn sex and 'real' sex, and promote critical thinking skills which could have far-reaching positive effects, not only in young people's sexual lives."[90] In fact, building the capacity for critical thinking (in order to improve our engagements with porn) needs to extend well beyond our engagements with porn.

One of the challenges is that there is no settled view of what porn literacy, a phrase coined by Tarrant around the time porn-streaming platforms emerged,[91] entails, nor on what its objectives should be.[92] Porn literacy education often has been,[93] but does not have to be, a pedantic exercise that constructs youth as sexually innocent, simplistic, and unsophisticated media consumers. While it is often deployed in a reductionist manner aimed at conveying information about the harms of porn, in an effort to deter youth from consuming it,[94] the concept has the capacity, if broadly understood, to include not only knowledge, understanding, and self-awareness, but critical engagement skills and competencies. As summarized by Dawson, porn literacy could include the "capacity to understand pornography production, challenge perceived pornography realism, ethically consume pornography, critically appraise pornography, challenge negative outcomes of pornography engagement, and facilitate positive sexual experiences with pornography use."[95]

Research comparing the content of mainstream porn to that of feminist pornography suggests that the latter is less likely to focus on depictions of women that are degrading and objectifying, and more likely to depict the genuine sexual agency, empowerment, and pleasure of everyone involved.[96] Porn that meets these criteria has the potential to teach people about sexual pleasure generally, about the physiology and aesthetic of bodies that are different from theirs and of those dominantly represented to them in mainstream media, about their own sexual pleasure and that of others, about consent and sexual health, and about a diversity of sexual practices, gender performances, and preferences.[97] While that might not sound particularly spicy, widespread advances in these forms of knowledge would undoubtedly promote our collective sexual integrity, and in doing so produce a community of sexual actors with the capacity for all sorts of spicy sex. Unfortunately, as explained in chapter 2, the homogenizing impact of the data-driven manner in which mainstream porn today is produced means that this type of content is increasingly unlikely to emerge on the landing pages of, and top search results for users on, mainstream platforms like Pornhub and xHamster.

To borrow from Clarissa Smith, a genuine form of porn literacy would "approach pornography as a complex media form" that youth are likely to engage with in a multiplicity of ways, rather than act as a rhetorical device invoked to mask what is really a "public health message" intended solely to inoculate youth from the dangers of porn.[98] As Paul Byron aptly states it, "[i]f porn literacy education only serves to deter young people from porn use, then it is not guided by a concern for literacy."[99] To be effective, Kath Albury notes, this type of intervention likely must intersect with debates, knowledge, and discussion "around young people's sexual practices, sexual self-representation and sexual knowledge" more broadly.[100] In other words, "it is unlikely that education programmes which focus exclusively on pornography will effect significant change."[101] This makes sense. It is also true of pedagogical interventions regarding consent, and respect for the sexual integrity of others. Building our capacity as a community to benefit from, rather than perpetuate harm through, the production and consumption of sexually explicit material (and sexual activity more generally) demands integrating these lessons and values throughout our pedagogy and daily practices more generally.

   As is the case with any other form of media and online activity, young people need education to develop a "critical understanding of" their online activities.[102] Smith suggests that education in this context might include asking questions like:

> What sparks pleasure, what sparks excitement in viewing, what sparks disgust, or boredom … [Y]oung people could be invited to think about the contexts of sexual representation … They could be encouraged to explore how pornography is defined, represented and debated in public spaces, and by whom? What kinds of regulation are promoted and who might benefit from that, who might not?[103]

She observes that "[p]orn literacy requires understanding how pornography relates to mainstream culture, gender and sexual politics, recognising industry practices, histories, aesthetics, performance styles are neither unitary nor transparent."[104]

   There are some challenges related to porn literacy as a response to the platformization of porn. As already noted, there is not a clear consensus on the aims and objectives of porn literacy education, and to date it has often been used in an effort simply to deter young people from accessing online porn.[105] Moreover, porn screenings are unlikely to be added to public school curriculums anytime soon, and the physical and psychological health and safety risks to students, staff, and teachers that doing so would pose, in addition to the professional competency requirements it would demand, means that this is for the best. But this raises a practical challenge: how is porn literacy education to be taught in schools?

   One way to mitigate this challenge is to include young people in the design and development of curricula, learning objectives, and materials in this context. Young people have knowledge and experience to contribute to the development of these educational interventions. Again, law and policy responses aimed at addressing the platformization of porn should be developed in coordination with, consultation with, and contribution from those most likely to be impacted by them. Moreover, it would be foolish for educators or policymakers to start from the assumption that adolescents are porn illiterate.[106] As Byron notes, "[i]nviting young people's contributions to our discussions of porn literacy will give us insight into their many strategies for using porn in ways that feel better for them."[107]

Some researchers and educators are pursuing this strategy. Dawson is involved in a project to design an evidence-based program in Ireland in which young people have been invited "to participate in the research process, to generate and analyze their own data, so that the outcomes truly reflect their needs."[108] According to her, data from this project thus far suggests that "the key areas of interest for porn researchers and other adults, like self-exploration, body image and sexual communication, are also at the forefront of young people's thoughts and concerns related to online porn."[109] Similar empirical projects are being pursued in other parts of the world.[110]

Next, when we invoke the concept of porn literacy, we have to consider for whom these interventions are required. The answer is that it is not only young people. Byron draws on research which suggests that one of the main challenges may be encouraging or enabling educators to approach the subject from a perspective that is not motivated solely by deterrence.[111] Incorporating porn literacy into the curriculum of secondary school education would first require building the competency and literacy of some educators. It would require not only building substantive competency in (porn) media literacy but, for some educators, a normative shift in orientation sufficient to open them to the possibility that porn is not a monolithic medium, that it comes in many forms, and can be engaged with in a multiplicity of ways, some of which are positive for some people – including for some youth. It may also require educators, and/or the politicians who interfere with public school sex education curriculums, to shift their views more generally. Unfortunately, without these changes, we may not want public schools to take on the task of developing and delivering porn literacy education.

In light of porn's prominent social role, other types of professionals also require pedagogical interventions, in addition to teachers. For instance, porn literacy at a community level requires building knowledge and competence among healthcare providers and social service providers. Consider, for example, family physicians consulted by concerned parents seeking assistance on how to respond to their children's porn consumption. Think of young patients seeking guidance from healthcare providers on how to engage with pornography. Postsecondary curriculums in professional schools should be updated to provide students with competency on how to offer this type of care in ways that are non-judgmental, avoid shaming, and are informed and patient or client centred.

Similarly, as demonstrated in chapter 6, judges require a form of porn literacy regarding the heightened significance of the subjective, contemporaneous, affirmative, and communicative definition of consent. Porn literacy for judges also means an understanding of the ways in which the implications of the platformization of mainstream porn, as outlined in chapter 4, contribute to today's sexual landscape. This includes self-awareness concerning how this reality may inform their own social assumptions and biases in terms of credibility assessments in the context of sexual assault prosecutions. Porn literacy for judges should involve the type of pedagogical interventions contemplated by Professor Ummni Khan: that is to say, interventions which distinguish between heteronormative media narratives about the relationship between sexual violence, BDSM, and queer sexual identities, and practices and empirical realties concerning harmful sexual behaviour.[112] The same is true for other actors in the legal system, such as crown attorneys and police.

Parents and guardians already have the tools to keep young children from accidental exposure to sexually explicit images and videos. Frankly, this should not be our main concern. Youth who are yoking their masturbatory and arousal patterns, their sexual education and self-esteem, or their understandings of porn, consent, gender performance, sexual pleasure, and desire to what they seek out, view on, or produce for platforms like Pornhub and xHamster without education on how to critically engage with, and understand, the porn that they are consuming (and/or producing) should be much more our concern.

"Keeping our children safe from porn" is powerful political rhetoric that spawns a nonpartisan project for politicians of every stripe. Less palatable, and sure to be more partisan and divisive, is convincing voters that we need to change school curricula to incorporate lessons on porn literacy (including curriculum content that is developed in consultation with, and with contribution from, sex workers/content producers and youth) and spend resources to develop public education and other supports that assist educators in providing education about porn, sex, misogyny, heteronormativity, consent, desire, and pleasure.

All of this said, for young people and adults alike, porn literacy education will only take us so far. As explained in chapters 3 and 4, social meaning and norms derived from cultural scripts, including those sourced in porn, help to constitute our understandings of our sexual behaviours and our interpretations of others' sexual behaviours. The iterative, complex, and constant set of interactions and interpretations that occur on porn-streaming platforms inform porn's social role today, including its relationship to the promotion, violation, and diminishment of sexual integrity. This is true not only of the types of unlawful porn examined in chapter 7, but also of some porn which is not prohibited by criminal, human rights, or civil legislation.

Moderating the Content of Lawful Porn on the Platform

In her 2023 piece, Alexandra Kirschbaum noted that while it is important, of course, to deal with major issues such as child pornography, the non-consensual distribution of intimate images, and human trafficking, it would be a "massive mistake" to think that the conversation about porn starts and ends there.[113] Focusing almost exclusively on unlawful content is a problem because it obscures other significant challenges concerning mainstream porn-streaming platforms: the piracy of content created by professional content creators, porn performers, and sex workers, and the associated loss of income for them; what to do about the readily available content on streaming platforms that is not unlawful, but is arguably harmful and clearly violates platforms' own community standards or terms of service; the reality that the dominance of monopolistic, multinational corporate porn platforms are likely to result in increasingly homogenized, White, able-bodied, male-dominated, algorithmically determined sexual scripts; the problem of mainstream porn that supports and reifies the same norms that underpin constructions of female sexuality and women's pleasure as acquiescent, subordinate, and secondary; and the eroticization in mainstream porn of the sexual assault of unconscious women and the grooming patterns prevalent in intra-family sexualized violence.

Given its dominance of the digital porn market globally, Pornhub again serves as an illuminating example. Framing the issue too narrowly on "unlawful content" provides companies like Ethical Capital Partners (ECP) with precisely the public relations campaign that the company appears to have pursued upon purchasing MindGeek, the owner of Pornhub. ECP's post-purchase communications strategy revealed two consistent, and interrelated, themes: (1) MindGeek is a tech company that has developed cutting-edge, highly sophisticated, world-leading IT technology that will identify, fingerprint, and eliminate child sexual abuse material and non-consensually produced and/or distributed content; and (2) the perception that Mind-

Geek platforms monetize child rape and human trafficking, rather than sex-positive adult entertainment, reflects a public misunderstanding that ECP has set out to rectify.[114]

The statistics from entities such as the National Center for Missing and Exploited Children, tech companies themselves, and law enforcement, will likely turn out to broadly support these two contentions (with the exception of the sex positivity aspect of the latter assertion).[115] Facebook and Twitter have been found to have exponentially more child sexual abuse material on their sites than Pornhub.[116] ECP will likely be able to show that its platforms do now host less child sexual abuse material than other major platforms.[117] Pornhub's verification requirements for uploading videos were improved in 2020. Its verification protocols may be further strengthened in response to online safety laws in jurisdictions like Canada and the United Kingdom. While it has yet to do so, at least according to Canada's privacy commissioner, the company may, in the future, also be able to demonstrate that its platforms host less intimate content distributed without the consent of those appearing in it than other platforms.

To be clear, these are positive developments with respect to the world's largest free porn-streaming platform. However, there is a risk that once ECP has established these two claims, public criticism of the company's problematic aspects will subside, the censure of credit card companies will lift, and the attention of law and policymakers will shift. Focus on how to ensure that content producers are appropriately compensated and do not have their intellectual property stolen by corporate porn platforms with cannibalistic business practices, as has been alleged,[118] will not endure. Public debate and legislative consideration regarding the norm-setting implications for our communities of an increasingly homogenized, data-driven, corporate, monopolistic porn industry[119] will not continue. Journalists will persist in providing trivial reports on Pornhub's year-in-review trends and foot fetishes among women in certain cities, rather than judiciously examining what it means to allow algorithms to determine for large swathes of our communities what they masturbate to before going to work, or after attending school. And the media will continue to publish uncritical articles connecting the popularity of television series like *Game of Thrones* to the explosion in consumption of incest-themed porn, while ignoring the fact that a prominent subset of this genre eroticises not simply the taboo of incest but the sexual assault of (step)daughters, (step)sons, and (step)sisters by their (step)-fathers and (step)brothers.

Take the issue of content moderation. When we talk about the potential harms related to mainstream pornography, we cannot speak only about child sexual abuse material, videos of non-consensual sexual activity, the non-consensual distribution of intimate images, and hate porn. Some sexually explicit content, while not unlawful, is still harmful. Law and policy responses to porn on the platform must also seek to mitigate the harms of some lawful porn. This suggests moderating content that does not violate criminal or human rights laws and that is produced and distributed consensually. But the issue of content moderation regarding lawful pornography is a thorny one. It raises important concerns regarding the rights to privacy, freedom of expression, and sexual liberty and equality, as well as major issues related to feasibility.

How to sort lawful but harmful porn from innocuous content, as well as the criteria by which to make such delineations, is deeply contested. So-called anti-porn feminists or religiously motivated abolitionists might argue that we ought not to tolerate and accept any porn. On the other side of the debate are folks who would perhaps draw the line at any consensually made content, regardless of what it depicts. But consent, like any doctrine, has its conceptual limits. It cannot do all of the work asked of it in this context. That a particular depiction or sexual practice is a fetish or arousing for some, and is produced by and targeted at consenting adults, may be necessary, but are not always sufficient, criteria for tolerance and acceptance.

If we accept the implications of the platformization of porn advanced in chapters 2 and 3, and the relationship that these implications bear to our sexual scripts – the socially acquired aspects of our sexualities – then there are critical distinctions to be drawn, for instance, between vampire porn and so-called intoxication porn, between incest-themed porn that eroticizes the fact patterns of intra-family sexualized violence and unicorn porn, and between s/m porn and misogynistic, rough sex porn. Legal approaches to content moderation regarding lawful but harmful porn, in the context of mainstream porn-streaming platforms, ought to be informed by this reality.

A partial solution, one which will likely satisfy neither end of this polemic divide, is that we start by targeting the content that mainstream porn platforms themselves have prohibited under their content moderation policies. Much of the pornography I have identified as problematic and potentially harmful in the preceding chapters, lawful and otherwise, contravenes the content moderation policies adopted by mainstream platforms like Pornhub and xHamster. Unfortunately, these platforms often seem not to comply with, or require their users to comply with, the prohibitions and rules articulated in their own community standards, and other content-based rules. Indeed, one of the most challenging factors regarding content moderation and mainstream porn-streaming platforms is the contradiction between what mainstream porn platforms say they prohibit on their sites and some of the content that, in fact, appears on these platforms.

One way to frame an examination of the considerations that lawmakers, and those advising them, ought to take into account vis-à-vis porn-streaming platforms, is to ask two questions: (1) What would porn on the platform look like if the content on mainstream porn-streaming platforms was consistent with the content moderation and community standards policies adopted by porn platforms, and (2) How can law be used to encourage or require porn platforms to follow and uphold their self-selected content standards?

What Would Porn on the Platform Look like If Platforms Followed Their Own Content Policies?

Again, Pornhub serves as a useful example. In part, this is because the platform's content policies are robust. In terms of the rules themselves, other mainstream porn-streaming platforms would do well to follow Pornhub's lead. Pornhub's terms of service stipulate that all content must comply with its Child Sexual Abuse Material Policy and its Non-consensual Content Policy.[120] The platform also publishes a Violent Content Policy that prohibits "any content that depicts activity or behaviour posing a real threat or likelihood of causing serious physical injury or death," and a Community Guidelines document and a statement of Core Values, both of which further outline content that is prohibited on Pornhub.[121] The company emphasizes that all content on the site is reviewed by human moderators and that any content that fails to meet the rules articulated in these policies is removed.[122] What are some of these rules?

Pornhub's Community Guidelines stipulate that any "actual, simulated or animated content" that "depicts, promotes or advocates" for illegal conduct of any kind, depicts children, depicts non-consensual acts or hate speech, "depicts, role-plays or implies incest," or "encourages conduct that would be considered a criminal offence" is prohibited.[123] Pornhub's statement of Core Values defines consent as "the express, voluntary, and non-coerced agreement or willingness to engage in a specific sexual activity."[124]

The platform's Non-consensual Content Policy stipulates that "[c]ontent featuring or promoting non-consensual acts, real or simulated, is ... prohibited."[125] This policy also prohibits content, including "fictional, simulated or animated," that "features or depicts" sexual assault.[126]

To raise the question again, having canvassed the company's rules: what would it look like if Pornhub were to actually do what it says it is doing in terms of content moderation?

Pornhub's policies prohibit nearly every type of problematic content identified in this book. What would porn on the platform look like if the company actually refused to platform what it purports to disallow on what the platform's parent company, ECP, describes as its "safe, responsible, sex positive" adult entertainment site?[127] The "wake up pornography" discussed in chapter 3, videos such as "Best Friend Fell Asleep"[128] and "Teen Woke Up with Big Cock in Her Big Pussy,"[129] which depict men penetrating women and adolescent girls who initially appear to be unconscious or asleep, would not be distributed on the platform.[130] These are depictions of sexual assault; these videos violate the platform's Non-consensual Content Policy, which prohibits real, fictional, or simulated depictions of sexual assault. These videos also violate Pornhub's Community Guidelines, which prohibit depictions, actual or simulated, of non-consensual acts or acts that would be considered a criminal offence.

There would be no videos that depict men sneaking into the bedrooms of performers depicted as sleeping children and adolescents – their (step)sons and (step)daughters – and engaging in sexual activity with them. So, too, with respect to the "wake-up (step)sister" genre of incest-themed porn. Indeed, the entire subset of incest-themed porn examined in chapter 5 that depicts intra-family sexualized violence would be gone. In addition, all videos on the platform that do away with the pretence of adding "step" in front of either "father," "daughter," "son," or "sister" would be removed, whether they parallel or eroticize the fact patterns in intra-family sexualized violence, given that Pornhub purports to ban incestuous role-playing altogether.

Were Pornhub to follow its own Non-consensual Content Policy and community standards, it would stop running advertisements that encourage users, through animated porn, to buy videogames that will purportedly allow them to experience what it really feels like to "lock the door and fuck [their] step-sisters."[131] Certainly the platform would stop running these advertisements at the beginning of videos that depict intra-family sexualized violence, as discussed in chapter 1.[132] But, were it to follow its own policy prohibiting the promotion of any illegal activity, Pornhub would presumably stop running these types of advertisements altogether.

The synthetic porn that co-opts the images of celebrity women, discussed in chapter 3, would also be removed. Instead of simply ceasing to celebrate in its annual year-in-review reports the degree to which its community of users is producing and consuming this content, like it did up until 2020, Pornhub would actually stop distributing porn videos appropriating the images of celebrities like Ariana Grande, Miley Cyrus, and Jennifer Lopez. Obviously, any non-consensual deepfake porn involving non-celebrities, made known to the platform, would be removed.

Were Pornhub to do what its new owner, ECP, says it will do in terms of centring the experience, knowledge, and rights of content providers – including, to use ECP's words, responding to the "financial discrimination" they face – the company would not only better protect the intellectual property rights of content producers, but would compensate them for the economic losses they have sustained to date, as a result of MindGeek's business model.[133]

Were the new owner of MindGeek to bring to reality what ECP purports is "MindGeek's *absolute* commitment to safe, responsible sex-positive free expression,"[134] the company would ensure that Pornhub does not create, enable, or promote for its users conceptual links between women and terms such as "disgusting," "stupid," and "dumb blonde."[135] Were Pornhub to uphold its hate speech policy, the platform would stop accepting and linking tags such as "Stupid Cunt," "Dumb Bitch," and "Cum Dumpster," or allowing users to use these terms to search for videos. Nor would the platform continue to approve videos with misogynistic, discriminatory titles like "Throat from Stupid Ugly Cunt. She Almost Good at It Too,"[136] "Stupid Blonde Fucks Her Sister's Boyfriend in Anal,"[137] and "Brainless Cunt Laughing and Waddling Naked for Live Webcam,"[138] let alone accept such titles and then connect them with each other as "related" concepts through search terms or tags like "Stupid Cunt."[139] It would remove metadata with this type of content from the platform, following which its explicit matrix of misogyny and racism would somewhat diminish. Were Pornhub to do what says it does under its hate speech policy, the hate porn on the platform would be substantially reduced.

Similarly, were ECP to honour its publicly articulated commitment to safe, responsible, sex-positive free expression, it would insist that Pornhub and other MindGeek platforms not approve, distribute, curate, and categorize at least some of the content that elides the distinction between BDSM porn with carefully negotiated, robust articulations of consent, and depictions of so-called rough sex, with inadequate or non-existent representations of consent.

What I am proposing is far from a perfect solution, nor one that will satisfy everyone. It does not speak to feminisms that reject pornography wholesale. It would not eliminate all content in mainstream porn likely to impact our sexual scripts adversely. It would do nothing to respond to the distribution of harmful content on platforms that do not have such policies. Moreover, there is a risk that if mainstream porn-streaming platforms like Pornhub began to enforce their content moderation policies in a more meaningful way, beyond child sexual abuse material (and the non-consensual distribution of intimate images), they would do so in a manner that targets racialized or otherwise marginalized folks, and non-normative and queer sexualities, while maintaining heteronormative representations that are hateful or otherwise violate their content policies. As Ari Ezra Waldman writes, too often when applied to sexual expression, content moderation has been marshalled as a social force to maintain and reify social media as a "straight space" free from queerness.[140]

However, while strategies to respond to the harmful aspects of porn on the platform will be unlikely to address all aspects of the problem, removing some of the most problematic, but lawful, content in mainstream porn would be a positive development. Take the example of incest-themed porn. Eliminating such content from mainstream tube sites would not eradicate it from the Internet, but if the incredible global rise of its popularity was fed by search engine optimizers, algorithms, and an unbeatable price tag – free – as it reportedly was,[141] its popularity is sure to diminish rapidly if it is put behind a paywall or requires a Tor browser to find it on the dark web.

If platforms like Pornhub did what they say they do in terms of content moderation, it would mean that adolescent porn users, the majority of whom consume porn on porn-streaming platforms,[142] would likely not be watching incest-themed videos that eroticize the sexual assault of (step)-sisters by their (step)brothers; hate porn in which women classified as "stupid sluts" and "dumb bitches" are being "wrecked," "railed," and "destroyed"; and videos that represent adolescent girls and women as thrilled to discover themselves being penetrated in the anus and vagina upon waking up from sleep or after passing out. Take the latter example: the perpetration of sexual assault against sleeping, incapacitated, or otherwise unconscious girls and women is a common fact pattern in sexual assaults perpetrated by accused adolescents and young men. To be clear, there seem to be as many empirical studies indicating neither a causal nor correlative connection between porn consumption and sexually violent behaviour as there are studies indicating a relationship.[143] But given how similar the fact patterns in sexual assault cases involving accused adolescents and young men are to these narratives, and the commonality of such cases, entrenching sexual scripts in which adolescent men are met with such affirming responses when they penetrate unconscious or sleeping girls and women cannot possibly serve them or our sexual integrity as a community.

In considering what to do about porn on the platform, in addition to properly tailored civil, criminal, and human rights laws to deal with unlawful porn, we should turn to law to encourage or require porn-streaming platforms to follow and uphold the community standards that they themselves have set.

How Can Law Be Used to Encourage or Require Porn Platforms to Follow and Uphold Their Community Standards?

In developing a legislative framework aimed at addressing online safety, which at the time of writing had culminated in Bill C-63 (the *Online Harms Act*), the Government of Canada constituted an expert working group that conducted a set of workshops from which emerged some key takeaways regarding the shape that Canada's regulatory framework ought to assume. The overarching orientation of these experts' recommendations involved a risk-based approach anchored in the imposition on platforms of a duty to act responsibly to reduce risk and protect human rights.[144] This duty to act responsibly is reflected in Bill C-63 in the form of a duty to mitigate the risk that users will be exposed to harmful content, a duty to protect children, and a duty to make content that sexually victimizes children or revictimizes survivors inaccessible. Harmful content, in terms of pornography, is defined in Bill C-63 as content that is communicated without consent or content that sexually victimizes a child or revictimizes a survivor. The problem with this proposed legislation, as it pertains to pornography, is that its focus is too narrow. The content moderation it imposes would only address child sexual abuse material, fictional depictions of sexual activity with children, and the non-consensual distribution of intimate images. With the exception of intimate content distributed without consent, this law would provide little, if any, response to the specific harms posed to women by the platformization of porn.[145]

The working group did identify the need to impose a special duty to protect children, given their inherent vulnerability, and stressed that "online services must be obligated to assess and mitigate any risk that their services pose to children specifically."[146] This emphasis on specificity is important. However, given the prevalence of gender-based violence, intimate partner violence, and sexualized violence in Canada, and given that all three are overwhelmingly disproportionately perpetrated by men against women, the same observations the expert working group made about children pertain to the specificity of women's vulnerability.

The government's regulatory framework should recognize, and when necessary treat distinctly, platforms that pose unique risks. Given the vulnerability of women to both online harms[147] and mainstream porn's contributions to our sexual scripts and the norms that underpin them, free porn-streaming platforms pose unique risks to women. This does not mean replicating the kind of disproportionate interferences with freedom of expression that Emily Laidlaw highlights in her work regarding the United Kingdom's experience with creating lists of banished sites.[148] It means that, just as platforms ought to be required to respond to the particular risks that their services pose to children specifically (as they would be under the federal government's proposed law), commercial porn-streaming platforms – given the nature of their businesses – should be required to assess and mitigate the risks that their services pose to women specifically. While the bill includes a requirement that platforms provide information in their digital safety plans about content, other than "harmful content," that they moderated on the basis that it posed "a risk of significant psychological or physical harm," there is no duty to actually assess or mitigate that risk, nor any requirement to respond to the unique harms their businesses pose for women.[149]

But what if Canada's approach to online safety did impose a duty to protect women on porn-streaming platforms? It is worth considering how some of the expert working group's general takeaways might be operationalized in specific ways to encourage or require free porn-streaming platforms to obey and uphold their own community standards and terms of service, in order to comply with a duty to protect women.

The working group emphasized an iterative process in which a legal regime's transparency and reporting requirements would promote a form of "safety by design."[150] The idea is that the data and information a platform is required to provide through transparency and accountability measures would foster a more proactive and preventative approach to online harm with respect to new features and affordances the platform might design. While safety by design has most definitely not been the approach taken in the context of free porn-streaming platforms, one might imagine its potential benefit, at least theoretically. For instance, as synthetic media and technology-generated porn, in particular, become ever present, the need to ensure that content moderation is not exclusively focused on non-consensual content, and the non-consensual distribution of content, is even more critical. Porn-streaming platforms presumably accept that it is not only the production but also the depiction of content that can be harmful, which is why community standards policies prohibit certain types of depictions. Removing human performers from the production of some or most content creation will not solve content issues. The expert working group also emphasized the need for the legislative framework to be technology neutral, rather than contingent on today's technology and thus at risk of becoming obsolete. This too seems to be applicable as virtual reality, synthetic media, and artificial intelligence take further hold in the porn industry.

The European Union has also taken a risk-based approach to content moderation on large platforms. The EU's new *Digital Services Act* imposes upon very large platforms a duty to put in place "reasonable, proportionate and effective mitigation measures, tailored to the specific systemic risks" posed by the platform's operation.[151] Included in the list of systemic risks is the adverse effects on preventing discrimination under the *Charter of Fundamental Rights of the European Union*.[152] When conducting this risk assessment, these platforms are required to take into account how their content moderation systems, recommender systems, and systems for selecting and displaying advertisements influence the risk of prohibited discrimination, including through content that is incompatible with their terms and conditions.

How might such a law, adapted to take into account the recommendations of Canada's expert working group, apply to a company like Pornhub in light of human rights and equality protections under Canadian law?

Under such a law Pornhub would be required in its transparency report, or "digital safety plan" as it is referred to in the government's current bill, to assess and respond to risks to the equality and human rights of adolescent girls or women posed by the advertisements, metadata and content on its platform. For instance, the law would require Pornhub to assess and implement measures to mitigate the risk to women of running advertisements such as "This hole has only one task: to make you cum"[153] and "In these games you will fuck more bitches than you ever saw in porn"[154] at the beginning of videos with titles that degrade and dehumanize women. Pornhub would be required, in its digital safety plan, to assess and mitigate the risk to the human rights of women posed by the decisions of its human moderators to approve videos with titles such as "Father in Law Tricks Stupid Bitch into Cheating Sex"[155] or "College Student Takes Out Finals Frustration on Hot Dumb Slut."[156] In other words, a duty to protect women, modelled on the EU law, would require the platform to reconsider its maintenance of, and reliance on, metadata which wraps some of its users in a fascia of intersecting misogynistic and racist hatred.

What other steps might Pornhub be required to take to mitigate the risks that such advertisements and content pose to the equality rights of women and girls in Canada? Given the disproportionately gendered nature of sexualized violence, the farcical nature of this question raises some issues regarding the potential efficacy of this proposed safety by design, transparency, and accountability approach to online harms, at least in the context of mainstream porn-streaming platforms. At a minimum, it suggests that this approach would need to be bolstered by clear standards on what constitutes a breach of the duty to protect women. One clear breach of this duty to mitigate risk to women, in the context of porn-streaming platforms, would involve knowingly making accessible content that breaches a platform's own policies with respect to "lawful pornography." In the context of a regulatory regime (as opposed to, for example, the criminal law context) a platform like Pornhub can presumably be said to "know" all of the content it makes available, given that all of its content is approved by human moderators.

Last, the contours of a duty to protect women must be informed by the nature of a platform's business. Content regulation, as Katrin Tiidenberg argues, has to be specific, not general. Tiidenberg explains that making it general because we are too embarrassed to talk about sex leaves the door open to the reification of heteronormativity and the further marginalization of already vulnerable communities.[157] According to Tiidenberg, speaking in reference to American sex trafficking laws, "[a]s we saw with the shifts in content moderation following SESTA/FOSTA, it is the original creative con-

tent, self-expression and some people's livelihood and safety that fall between the cracks when regulation fails to be specific."[158] Waldman makes
a related observation regarding the censorship of queer folks on social
media.[159] To draw on some of his examples, a law that encourages platforms
to take down the accounts of drag queens but leave up those of white sup-
remacists, or write algorithms that flag the images of shirtless trans men but
not those of cisgender men, is a failure.[160]

The steps necessary to meet the duty to mitigate the systemic risks posed
to the equality rights of women will be different for Pornhub than they
would be for Snapchat or YouTube. To offer an example, free porn-streaming
platforms, given the nature of their business, would likely all be required to
adopt stricter uploader verification than a platform dedicated to vacation
rentals or the dissemination of music. The duty to act responsibly and to
protect the human rights of women (and children, and vulnerable minorities) would presumably require different, and likely more demanding, training and supervision of content moderators for Pornhub than for Amazon
– it would also, presumably, require different supports for the former company's content moderators.

The requirement of digital safety plans or transparency reports and
other accountability measures regarding breaches of a platform's own policies might be most effective in incentivizing a company like Pornhub to
better uphold its community standards, given that its new ownership appears invested in shifting its public reputation. One wonders whether such
an approach would work as well with other free porn-streaming platforms.
Nevertheless, legislative mechanisms that result in MindGeek ensuring
that its platforms, including Pornhub, comply with and uphold their own
content moderation policies and commitments, would constitute meaningful improvement.

One further point regarding the design of online safety legislation must
be made: the same recommendation regarding age-verification legislation
applies to the development of legislation aimed at platform governance and
online safety, and to legal interventions regarding porn-streaming platforms
more broadly. The knowledge, experience, and expertise of content producers should be included in the design and drafting of the aspects of this
framework that will be relevant to porn platforms and that will impact content producers, porn performers, and sex workers generally. As legislative
efforts in other jurisdictions have demonstrated, failure to consult with, and

incorporate the knowledge of, these stakeholders will result in their further marginalization, and financial discrimination against them.[161]

The presence and promotion of misogynistic and racist videos and metadata on a platform like Pornhub reflects a choice. The platform and its community of users have the facility to reject this content..Consider Pornhub's approach to the treatment of non-human animals. Pornhub has an animal welfare policy that prohibits "all forms of animal abuse and cruelty, whether physical or psychological."[162] The platform "does not allow any visual or written content involving animal abuse," or the "sexual exploitation of animals," or any content that "advocates for the sexual exploitation of animals, including as the object of sexual interest."[163] The policy applies to all "non-human animals."[164]

The first video on the page of search results using the search term "cat," on 17 June 2023, was entitled "Pussy Gets Soaked by Her First Toy."[165] It is a nine-minute video of a cat discovering and drinking from a water fountain. None of the videos on the first two pages of search results using any of the following search terms – "pet," "dog," "sheep," "cat," "bestiality," and "animal" – produced a single title that framed the video as one that would violate Pornhub's animal welfare policy.

The first video using the search term "dog" was titled "Playing with My Dogs, It's Not Sexual You Degenerates."[166] It is a six-minute video of a young woman playing with her two dogs. Among the many user comments on the video, the first few included: "'Playing with my dogs. It's not sexual,' Fuck I hope not," "Don't even think about it. The possibility of it should be ignored in our minds," and "Can I like the video again for the title alone?"[167] Another user commented, "I wonder how disappointed the sickos are when they saw this?"[168] Comments from these and other users demonstrate a clear maintenance of the normative boundary set by Pornhub's animal welfare policy: the abuse and mistreatment of animals, which for these users includes sexual activity with them, is not acceptable, nor will it be tolerated in this platform community.

It would appear, then, that the problem – in terms of following and upholding the content rules reflected in Pornhub's Community Guidelines, Core Values, and Non-consensual Content Policy – is one of willingness, not capacity.

It is clear that Pornhub has the technological ability, and its community of users the social infrastructure, to establish and rigorously maintain content norms. We should require mainstream porn-streaming platforms to comply with and uphold the normative commitments they have established and the boundaries they have drawn with respect to women and girls as effectively as they do when it comes to cats and dogs.

Canada's online harms law should be designed in a way that requires – not only asks, but *requires* – porn-streaming platforms to assess and mitigate the unique risks they pose not only to children but also to women (including, specifically, women who belong to racialized communities, and communities marginalized on the basis of ableism, gender identity, and poverty) as well as the risks they pose to our shared interest in sexual integrity more broadly. The lack of willingness on the part of porn-streaming platforms to do so voluntarily appears to require this type of legislative intervention.

Conclusion

In 2023, an Ottawa man was convicted of sexually assaulting two women, with whom he had had ostensibly consensual sexual interactions, because he had surreptitiously videoed the sexual interactions and posted these videos, "complete with degrading titles," on Pornhub.[169] This is thought to be the first Canadian case in which someone has been convicted of sexual assault for this form of violation of another person's sexual integrity. The trial judge, Ontario Court Justice Ann Alder, found that these women's consent was vitiated by fraud because they did not know that they were being recorded, would not have had sex with the accused had they known, and suffered significant emotional and psychological harm as a consequence of him having created and distributed these recordings on Pornhub.[170]

In sentencing the accused, Jacob Rockburn, Justice Alder rightly observed that: "It is impossible with today's technology to consider the risk of deprivation in the form of serious psychological harm from surreptitiously recording as separate and distinct from the risk of distribution of those recordings."[171]

Mainstream porn-streaming platforms are part of our sexual landscape. We must pay attention to the relationship between the platformization of porn and the protection and promotion of sexual integrity. This requires acclimating our social, legal, and pedagogical institutions and practices to this aspect of our social environment. Justice Alder's recognition in *R v*

Rockburn that it is no longer possible to distinguish between the risk of psychological harm imposed by recording someone having sex without their consent and distributing that recording, given our technological context, is an example of the type of acclimatization required.

The *Rockburn* decision generated public attention when it was released in August 2023.[172] Commenting on the case, ECP's vice-president of compliance, Solomon Friedman, told the media that the videos were uploaded to the site before the platform had improved its uploader verification system.[173] According to the article, Friedman added that Pornhub no longer allows users to search for videos using the term "hidden camera" – which Rockburn had used to tag the videos when he uploaded them.[174] A search on Pornhub conducted on the day Friedman made this public statement confirmed that the term "hidden camera" yielded no videos. However, users could still search for videos using the term "hidden," which did yield videos on the day Friedman made this statement to the media, with titles on the first page of search results such as "Dragged a Sexy Classmate into Bed and Filmed Sex on a Hidden Phone" and "Secret Video Cheating Wife Fucked Her Husband's Best Friend."[175] Pornhub also still permitted the use of search terms like "secret voyeur," "real amateur hidden," and "spy," all of which produced videos with titles that suggest depictions of sex caught on hidden cameras, and/or videos that depict the surreptitious recording of sexual activity.[176]

I am not suggesting that the individuals appearing in these videos did not consent to their recording and/or distribution, as occurred in *Rockburn*. But when Friedman made these comments, Pornhub remained rife with videos that *depict* "hidden camera sexual activity" – that *depict* the same violation of sexual integrity for which Rockburn was convicted. This is content that Friedman's comments to the media could easily be understood to suggest is no longer tolerated on ECP's platform. It is content that violates Pornhub's Community Guidelines and Non-consensual Content Policy, both of which prohibit depictions, real or simulated, of the surreptitious recording of sexual activity.[177]

On the same day in August 2023 that Friedman made these public comments on behalf of ECP, about the hidden camera content on Pornhub, the company announced that it was rebranding MindGeek because of "the need for a fresh start and a renewed commitment to innovation, diverse and inclusive adult content, and trust and safety."[178] Going forward, MindGeek will be called Aylo. According to its press release, ECP believes the name Aylo "truly represents them and allows the company to re-focus its efforts to lead by example, through transparency and public engagement."[179] Trust, safety, and transparency ... ECP tells us.

In addition to acclimating our social and legal systems and policies, attending to the relationship between the platformization of porn and the protection and promotion of sexual integrity will require us to interrogate much more carefully what highly monopolistic, corporate porn companies tell us about porn on the platform. As is the case with Google, Facebook, and Apple, we will have to decide for ourselves which parts of their messages and branding are misleading, obfuscating, or simply not true.

• • •

Sex should not be mean. This is not a claim based on some problematic distinction between supposedly "healthy sex" (read: monogamous, straight, heteronormative sex) and "unhealthy sex" (read: queer, kinky, commodified, promiscuous sex), or an assumption that there exists "a proper purpose for sex."[180] Sex, and porn in particular, are divisive topics with limited terrain for normative agreement. We will not find consensus, for example, on whether it is acceptably feminist for sex to be about danger, temporary loss of self, or the assertion of power over another. We may not find consensus, even, on whether sex can be about – simply, only – having fun. People, of course, have all kinds of sex (straight, kinky, vanilla, s/m, and queer), for all kinds of reasons (fun, lust, boredom, money, desire, love, social or political power, procreation, and curiosity) and in all kinds of ways (alone, partnered, in groups, and mediated through technology). But sex should not be mean.

Whatever one thinks about the costs, harms, and benefits of pornography, they are not shared equally between men and women. Representations of sex in mainstream porn that are mean, that weaponize sex against women and girls, that represent it as a tactic to be deployed against unconscious women or unsuspecting "daughters" when their mothers are not home, that are captured and distributed without the consent of the women and girls appearing in them, or that characterize women as useless "crackheads" whose only purpose is to "suck cock," contribute to our sexual norms – to our social understandings of sex and gender, and of what is hot and what is not – in ways that do not promote sexual integrity and human flourishing.

Indeed, these cultural and social contributions to our sexual scripts cause harm, and have real costs to all of us, particularly to women and girls. Mainstream porn-streaming platforms should be held more responsible for preventing these harms and for bearing their costs when they fail in this regard. About this, everyone should agree.

Notes

CHAPTER ONE

1 See Eran Shor and Kimberley Seida, "'Harder and Harder'? Is Mainstream Pornography Becoming Increasingly Violent and Do Viewers Prefer Violent Content?," *Journal of Sex Research* 51, no. 1 (2019): 16–28 (noting the common narrative among some feminists that porn continues to become "harder and harder" but finding it has not become more "hardcore" over the period they studied). But see Gail Dines, "Not Your Father's Playboy," *Counterpunch*, 17 May 2010, https://www.counterpunch.org/2010/05/17/not-your-father-s-playboy.

2 This is an intractable debate. See, for example, Gail Dines, *Pornland: How Porn Has Hijacked our Sexuality* (Boston: Beacon Press, 2010) (claiming the content of pornography continues to become more extreme); Eran Shor and Kimberly Seida, *Aggression in Pornography: Myths and Realities* (London and New York: Routledge, 2021) (claiming the content of pornography has not gotten more extreme).

3 For a description of the "golden era" of porn, see Shira Tarrant, *The Pornography Industry: What Everyone Needs to Know* (Oxford: Oxford University Press, 2016), 22.

4 Kal Raustiala and Christopher Sprigman, "The Second Digital Disruption: Streaming and the Dawn of Data-Driven Creativity," *New York University Law Review* 94, no. 6 (2019): 1563.

5 See, for example, Qayyah Moynihan, "Internet Users Access Porn Sites More than Twitter, Wikipedia and Netflix," *Business Insider*, 30 September

2018, www.businessinsider.com/internet-users-access-porn-more-than-twitter-wikipedia-and-netflix-2018-9; Jessica Clement, "Most Popular Websites Worldwide as of June 2021, by Total Visits," Statista, 7 September 2021, www.statista.com/statistics/1201880/most-visited-websites-worldwide.

6   See, for example, "2019 Year in Review," Pornhub, 22 December 2019, www.pornhub.com/insights/2019-year-in-review; "2020 Super Bowl 54," Pornhub, 3 February 2020, www.pornhub.com/insights/2020-super-bowl-54; "Canada's Traffic During Roger's Internet Outage," Pornhub, 11 July 2022, https://www.pornhub.com/insights/canadas-traffic-during-rogers-internet-outage.

7   Raustiala and Sprigman, "Second Digital Disruption," 1592.

8   See, for example, José van Dijck, Thomas Poell, and Martijn de Waal, *The Platform Society: Public Values in a Connective World* (New York: Oxford University Press, 2018), 2, 4; David Nieborg and Thomas Poell, "The Platformization of Cultural Production: Theorizing the Contingent Cultural Commodity," *New Media and Society* 20, no. 11 (2018): 4275; Tarleton Gillespie, "Platforms Are Not Intermediaries," *Georgetown Law Technology Review* 2, no. 2 (2018): 199.

9   Van Dijck, Poell, and de Waal, *Platform Society*, 2.

10 Ibid.

11 Fiona Vera-Gray, Clare McGlynn, Ibad Kureshi, and Kate Butterby, "Sexual Violence as a Sexual Script in Mainstream Online Pornography," *British Journal of Criminology* 61, no. 5 (2021): 1243 (drawing sexual script theory and cultural criminology together in consideration of pornography's relationship to sexual violence).

12 Amia Srinivasan, *The Right to Sex: Feminism in the Twenty-First Century* (New York: Farrar, Straus and Giroux, 2021), 67.

13 "It's Not a Pussy Its My Asshole" (video), Pornhub, accessed 24 June 2023 (11,500,000 views, 75 per cent approval rating). See also xHamster, "That's the Wrong Hole You Son of a Bitch" (video), accessed 19 November 2023 (248,775 views, 98 per cent approval rating).

14 "Skinny Bitch Asks for Slower but the Man Fucks Her Ass Even Harder" (video), Pornhub, accessed 24 June 2023 (415,000 views, 83 per cent approval rating).

15 "Wrong Hole! She Tries to Escape While I Fuck Her Ass!" (video), Pornhub, accessed 16 November 2023 (791,000 views, 75 per cent approval rating). There is a second layer of deception or opaqueness operating with respect to some of these videos. The actual content of some such videos, such as

"Wrong Hole," which explicitly label the video one of non-consensual anal penetration, are in fact depictions of seemingly consensual sex in which both participants are represented as engaged, aroused, and orgasmic. In other words, these videos are marketed/misrepresented as sexual assault by their titles, despite depicting what appears to be consensual sexual activity. Other videos depict acts that would constitute sexual assault.

16 "Snuck Condom Off and Accidently Rammed It up Her Ass" (video), Pornhub, accessed 8 March 2023 (2,900,000 views, 64 per cent approval rating). See also "Creampie Surprise. I Tricked My Stepsister, Took Off the Condom and Filled Her Pussy Full of Cum" (video), Pornhub, accessed 20 November 2023 (516,000 views, 92 per cent approval rating).

17 "Oops I Take Off the Condom and Fuck Her Ass" (video), xHamster, accessed 4 May 2023. See also "He Takes the Condom off and Puts it in My Ass by Surprise and Cums Twice" (video), xHamster, accessed 7 March 2023 (157,771 views, 99 per cent approval rating).

18 "Real Surprise Painful Anal with Anal Cream Pie for Amateur Teen" (video), Pornhub, accessed 24 June 2023 (4,400,000 views, 83 per cent approval rating).

19 "*** sneak ***" (video), xHamster, accessed 20 November 2023 (1,916,586 views, 98 per cent approval rating). Note: the title of this video has been modified to make it less searchable online because it is not clear to me whether it captures an actual sexual assault or depicts a fictional sexual assault. I do not include the full titles of videos if I am uncertain in this regard.

20 "WTF! That's the Wrong Hole, Stop Fucking My Ass It Hurts!" (video), Pornhub, accessed 27 June 2023 (928,000 views, 76 per cent approval rating).

21 "Wrong Hole Compilation. Painal – Not for the Faint Hearted" (video), Pornhub, accessed 19 November 2023 (3,300,000 views, 79 per cent approval rating.

22 Testimony of Feras Antoon, House of Commons, Standing Committee on Access to Information, Privacy and Ethics, *Evidence*, 43-2, No. 19 (5 February 2021): 1.

23 Ibid., 3.

24 Testimony of David Tassillo, House of Commons, Standing Committee on Access to Information, Privacy and Ethics, *Evidence*, 43-2, No. 19 (5 February 2021): 3.

25 Ibid., 3.

26 "Non-consensual Content Policy," Pornhub, accessed 30 March 2023,

https://help.pornhub.com/hc/en-us/articles/4419871787027-Non-Consen
sual-Content-Policy.

27 Ibid.

28 Vera-Gray et al., "Sexual Violence as a Sexual Script," 1255.

29 Catharine A MacKinnon, *Only Words* (Cambridge, MA: Harvard University Press, 1993).

30 Ibid., 15.

31 Pornhub, accessed 15 June 2023, www.pornhub.com.

32 Tarrant, *Pornography Industry*, 37.

33 Ibid., 31.

34 Vera-Gray et al., "Sexual Violence as a Sexual Script," 1249

35 Van Dijck, Poell, and de Waal, *Platform Society*.

36 Feona Attwood and Clarissa Smith, "Emotional Truths and Thrilling Sideshows: The Resurgence of Antiporn Feminism," in *The Feminist Porn Book: The Politics of Producing Pleasure*, eds Tristan Taormino et al. (New York: Feminist Press at CUNY, 2013), 48.

37 Hill and Knowlton Strategies, "Sarah Bain," https://hkstrategies.ca/en/authors/sarah-bain.

38 Sarah Bain, LinkedIn, https://ca.linkedin.com/in/sarah-bain-mba-a32a8750.

39 "ECP Announces Acquisition of MindGeek, Parent Company of Pornhub," Ethical Capital Partners, 16 March 2023, https://www.ethicalcapitalpartners.com/news/ecp-announces-acquisition-of-mindgeek%2C-parent-company-of-pornhub.

40 Maiya Keidan and Isla Binnie, "Canadian Buyer Aims to Improve PornHub Owner's Reputation," 17 March 2023, *Financial Post*, https://financialpost.com/pmn/business-pmn/canadian-buyer-aims-to-improve-pornhub-owners-reputation.

41 Vanmala Subramaniam, "MindGeek Owner Stymies Multiple Bids by Investors to Buy Firm," *Globe and Mail*, 28 September 2021, https://www.theglobeandmail.com/business/article-mindgeek-owner-stymies-multiple-bids-by-investors-to-buy-firm.

42 Testimony of Feras Antoon, *Evidence*, 2.

43 "Family Simulator Porn Games," Pornhub, accessed 4 April 2023. As noted in the text, these types of advertisements also run before other kinds of videos on Pornhub. My point is about the irresponsibility of running them before incest-themed videos, and in particular incest-themed vidoes that eroticize intra-family sexualized violence.

44 Ibid.

45 "Teen (18+) Stepsis Tricked into Sex. She Just Wanted a Massage" (video), Pornhub, accessed 4 April 2023 (127,000 views, 89 per cent approval rating).

46 "Fuck My Teen Stepsis Pussy While Her Mom Is Not Home" (video), Pornhub, accessed 3 April 2023 (1,900 views, 74 per cent approval rating).

47 Ibid.

48 "The Stepdaughter Was Tired of the Dick, but the Stepfather Did Not Stop Fucking Her" (video), Pornhub, accessed 6 April 2023 (1,000,000 views, 87 per cent approval rating).

49 "Step Sister with Perfect Ass Woke Up When I Fucked Her" (video), Pornhub, accessed 3 April 2023 (804,000 views, 84 per cent approval rating). The video depicts a woman who is asleep for the first part of the video, including while digital penetration occurred. This is a clear depiction of sexual assault. After a period of time, she is depicted as awakening and becoming an active participant in the sexual acts.

50 Ibid.

51 "Waking Up Step-Daughter with a Cock inside Her" (video), Pornhub, accessed 31 May 2023 (317,000 views, 86 per cent approval rating).

52 For example, it is clear across legal jurisdictions that people who are asleep or unconscious cannot consent. Similarly, some jurisdictions recognize a criminal offence of sexual exploitation in circumstances involving substantial power differentials between vulnerable young people and adults in relationships of power (such as the relationship between a [step]father and a teenage [step]daughter).

53 "Stepdaughter Was Tired," Pornhub.

54 "Fuck My Teen Stepsis," Pornhub.

55 "Teen (18+) Stepsis," Pornhub.

56 "Step Sister with Perfect Ass," Pornhub.

57 "Waking Up Step-Daughter," Pornhub.

58 *Criminal Code*, RSC 1985, c C-46, s. 273.1(2)(a.1); *R v JA*, 2011 SCC 28.

59 "Non-consensual Content Policy," Pornhub. Pornhub's policy, as explained in chapter 3, stipulates that in videos in which a performer is asleep or depicted as asleep when the sexual activity commences, they must "awake" within a reasonable period of time. The policy does not indicate what constitutes a reasonable period of time. Regardless, under Canadian law (and that of many other jurisdictions) one cannot consent to sexual activity occurring while one is asleep or unconscious.

60 "Stepdaughter Was Tired," Pornhub.

61 Samantha Cole, "I Tried not to Cum While Playing the Adult Games Advertised on Pornhub," *Vice*, 10 February 2020, https://www.vice.com/en/article/wxeja5/i-tried-not-to-cum-while-playing-the-adult-games-advertised-on-pornhub. Cole examined some of the earlier videogame advertisements on Pornhub and reported that they were neither free nor appeared to offer what the initial advertisement promised.

62 "Family Simulator Porn Games," Pornhub.

63 "Step Sister with Perfect Ass," Pornhub.

64 See, for example, UK Office for National Statistics, *Child Sexual Abuse in England and Wales: Year Ending March 2019*, by Meghan Elkin (2020), 21, table 12a, www.ons.gov.uk/peoplepopulationandcommunity/crimeandjustice/articles/childsexualabuseinenglandandwales/yearendingmarch2019 (in the United Kingdom, nearly 40 per cent of women who were sexually abused by age sixteen were abused by family members); Janine Benedet and Isabel Grant, "Breaking the Silence on Father-Daughter Sexual Abuse of Adolescent Girls: A Case Law Study," *Canadian Journal of Women and the Law* 32, no. 2 (2020): 240 (finding that in almost half of all reported cases the accused was a male family member of the complainant, and in more than 25 per cent of sexual assault prosecutions in which the complainant was a teenage girl, the accused was the girl's biological, adoptive, step, or foster father); Peter Yates, "Sibling Sexual Abuse: Why Don't We Talk about It?," *Journal of Clinical Nursing* 26, nos. 15–16 (2016): 2482; Bonnie E Carlson, Katherine Maciol, and Joanne Schneider, "Sibling Incest: Reports from Forty-One Survivors," *Journal of Child Sexual Abuse* 15, no. 4 (2006): 22 (citing several studies indicating that brother-initiated incest towards sisters is the most common form of sibling incest); Peter Yates and Stuart Allardyce, "Sibling Sexual Abuse: A Knowledge and Practice Overview," Centre of Expertise on Child Sexual Abuse, January 2021, 18, https://www.csacentre.org.uk/app/uploads/2023/09/Sibling-sexual-abuse-report.pdf.

65 Sarah Bain. "ECP Announces Acquisition," Ethical Capital Partners.

66 Fady Monsour. "Ethical Capital Partners Undertaking Stakeholder Consultations," Ethical Capital Partners, 27 April 2023, https://www.ethicalcapital-partners.com/news/ethical-capital-partners-undertaking-stakeholder-consultations (emphasis added).

67 "This Stupid Whores Only Good for One Thing" (video), Pornhub, accessed 1 June 2023 (8,300 views, 93 per cent approval rating).

68 "Slutty Step-Daughter is a Cum Dumpster" (video), Pornhub, accessed 6 December 2023 (285,000 views, 91 per cent approval rating). In this video

the female performer writes "slut" on her body and "cum dumpster" (with tally beside it) on her buttocks.

69 "Dumb Black Bitch Squirts" (video), Pornhub, accessed 26 June 2023 (450 views, 91 per cent approval rating).

70 "Dumb Girl Begs to Suck Your Dick and Get Fucked," Pornhub, accessed 27 June 2023 (8,500 views, 92 per cent approval rating).

71 "This Hole Has Only One Task" advertisement, playing in front of the video "Dumb Girl Begs," ibid.

72 "Fuck More Bitches" (video advertisement), Pornhub, accessed 7 May 2023.

73 Fady Monsour. "Ethical Capital Partners Undertaking," Ethical Capital Partners.

74 See *Saskatchewan (Human Rights Commission) v Whatcott* 2013 scc 11 (for the constitutionally sound definition of hate speech under Canadian human rights law).

75 Fady Monsour. "Ethical Capital Partners Undertaking," Ethical Capital Partners.

76 Joe Lofaro, "MindGeek's New Owner Vows 'Public and Transparent Ownership' after Pornhub Controversy," ctv News, 17 March 2023, https://montreal.ctvnews.ca/mindgeek-s-new-owner-vows-public-and-transparent-ownership-after-pornhub-controversy-1.6318238.

77 "ecp Announces Acquisition," Ethical Capital Partners.

78 Testimony of Llyod Richardson, House of Commons, Standing Committee on Access to Information, Privacy and Ethics, *Evidence*, 43-2, No. 21 (22 February 2021), 9.

79 "Investigation into Aylo (formerly MindGeek)'s Compliance with pipeda," pipeda Findings # 2024-001, 29 February 2024, para. 74, https://www.priv.gc.ca/en/opc-actions-and-decisions/investigations/investigations-into-businesses/2024/pipeda-2024-001.

80 Ibid.

81 Ibid.

82 Mark Gollom, "Can Pornhub Evolve? A National Security Expert, Body Builder and Porn Researchers Are Going to Try," cbc, 23 April 2023, https://www.cbc.ca/news/canada/porn-hub-advisory-board-1.6814347.

83 Andrew Duffy, "Solomon Friedman Is on a Mission to Save PornHub," *Ottawa Citizen*, 3 April 2023, https://ottawacitizen.com/feature/solomon-friedman-is-on-a-mission-to-save-pornhub.

84 Ibid.

85 Ibid. In her initial coverage of this purge, Samantha Cole reported that the

original volume was unclear: something between 6.3 million and 8.8 million. Samantha Cole, "Pornhub Just Purged All Un-Verified Content from the Platform," *Vice*, 14 December 2020, https://www.vice.com/en/article/jgqjjy/pornhub-suspended-all-unverified-videos-content.

86 See, for example, Testimony of Serena Fleites, House of Commons, Standing Committee on Access to Information, Privacy and Ethics, *Evidence*, 43-2, No. 18 (1 February 2021), 1–2, 6–11; Testimony of John Clark, House of Commons, Standing Committee on Access to Information, Privacy and Ethics, *Evidence*, 43-2, No. 21 (22 February 2021), 4–5; Nicholas Kristof, "The Children of Pornhub," *New York Times*, 6 December 2020, www.nytimes.com/2020/12/04/opinion/sunday/pornhub-rape-trafficking.html (documenting the failure of Pornhub to adequately respond when someone requests that content be removed); Samantha Cole and Emanuel Maiberg, "Pornhub Doesn't Care," *Vice*, 6 February 2020, https://www.vice.com/en/article/9393zp/how-pornhub-moderation-works-girls-do-porn.

87 Russell Brandom, "Pornhub Limits Uploads and Disables Downloads After New York Times Exposé," *Verge*, 8 December 2020, http://www.theverge.com/2020/12/8/22164031/pornhub-upload-limit-blocked-download-nyt-kristof-child-abuse (reporting on the timeline of Pornhub's policy changes and the *New York Times* article).

88 Suzanne Hillinger, dir., *Money Shot: The Pornhub Story* (Netflix, 2023), documentary.

89 See, for example, Kristof, "Children of Pornhub"; *Serena Fleites et al. v MindGeek SARL et al.* (2021), 617 F Supp 3d 1146 (Statement of Claim); Joe Lofara, "Pornhub Owner Settles Lawsuit with 50 Women, including Four Canadians," CTV News, 20 October 2021, https://montreal.ctvnews.ca/pornhub-owner-settles-lawsuit-with-50-women-including-four-canadians-1.5630651.

90 Kristof, "Children of Pornhub."

91 Testimony of David Tassillo, *Evidence*, 6:

David Tassillo: For the re-uploading process, when a piece of content is taken down by either one of those paths, we now automatically create a digital fingerprint of it, so when someone attempts to re-upload the content, it will get blocked at the upload phase.
Marie-Hélène Gaudreau: Was it like that before your new procedures? According to testimony we have heard, the content clearly reappeared.
David Tassillo: The software was always available. In early 2020, I believe, we made the process automatic so that it was automatically added

to the database, but the end-user always had the ability to use it. We decided it's one thing we shouldn't ask the enduser to use, so we added it automatically.

92 Lofaro, "MindGeek's New Owner."

93 Cole and Maiberg, "Pornhub Doesn't Care."

94 Kristof, "Children of Pornhub."

95 Cole and Maiberg, "Pornhub Doesn't Care."

96 Duffy, "Solomon Friedman."

97 Ibid.

98 See, for example, Duffy, ibid.; Vanmala Subramaniam and Jo Castaldo, "Pornhub Owner MindGeek Acquired by Ottawa-Based Equity Firm," *Globe and Mail*, 16 March 2023, https://www.theglobeandmail.com/busi ness/article-pornhub-mindgeek-acquisition-ethical-capital-partners.

99 Solomon Friedman, "After Ghomeshi Case, Is More Legal Advice Really What Victims Need?," *Ottawa Sun*, 25 March 2016, https://ottawasun.com/ 2016/03/25/friedman-after-ghomeshi-case-is-more-legal-advice-really- what-victims-need.

100 Ibid. (italics in the original).

101 Solomon Friedman, "The Numbers Contradict Ghomeshi Case Rhetoric," *Ottawa Sun*, 7 February 2016, http://www.ottawasun.com/2016/02/07/fried man-the-numbers-contradict-ghomeshi-case-rhetoric; *R v T(J)*, 2015 ONSC 3866, para. 5 [*T(J)*]. In fact, the numbers contradict Friedman. In this article, in which he falsely asserts that "almost half of sexual assault charges result in convictions" and contests the claim that "three-quarters of all such claims are ultimately dismissed," he refers to Statistics Canada data from 2013 to 2014. But he fails to distinguish between all post-charge attrition and conviction rates at trial. According to Statistics Canada, between 2009 and 2014, only 49 per cent of cases in which sexual assault incidents resulted in a charge being laid proceeded to court, of which just over half resulted in a conviction. In other words, the number is closer to 21 per cent, not the 45 per cent he asserted. Friedman left this substantial stage of attrition out of his narrative. He also compared sexual assault statistics with statistics for physical assault, arguing they were similar. In fact, according to Statistics Canada, during the time period Friedman relied upon, "when compared with physical assault, [sexual assaults] were far more prone to dropping out of the justice system between police and court; while three-quarters (75%) of physical assaults proceeded to court after being charged by police, only half (49%) of sexual assaults did." While conviction rates for

these offences at trial are comparable, overall attrition for sexual assault is substantially higher: indeed, approximately three-quarters of such charges do not result in conviction. Statistics Canada, "From Arrest to Conviction: Court Outcomes of Police-Reported Sexual Assaults in Canada," 26 October 2017, https://www150.statcan.gc.ca/n1/en/daily-quotidien/171026/dq171026b-eng.pdf.

102 Duffy, "Solomon Friedman."

103 Reader's comments responding to Alexandra Kirschbaum, "Pornography Is Almost as Present as Air and We Need to Talk About It," *Ottawa Citizen*, 3 April 2023, https://ottawacitizen.com/opinion/kirschbaum-porn-is-as-present-as-air-and-we-need-to-talk-about-it.

104 Ibid.

105 See, for example, Rosemary Radford Reuther, "Sexism and Misogyny in the Christian Tradition: Liberating Alternatives," *Buddhist-Christian Studies* 34, no. 1 (2014): 83.

106 See, for example, Sharon Cook, "Do Not… Do Anything That You Cannot Unblushingly Tell Your Mother: Gender and Social Purity in Canada," *Social History* 30, no. 60 (1997): 215; Anya Jabour, "Prostitution Politics and Feminist Activism in Modern America," *Journal of Women's History* 25, no. 3 (2013): 141.

107 See, for example, Lykke de la Cour, "Eugenics, Race and Canada's First-Wave Feminists: Dis/Abling the Debates," *Atlantis: Critical Studies in Gender, Culture and Social Justice* 38, no. 2 (2017): 176, 182; Jabour, "Prostitution Politics."

108 Feona Attwood and Clarissa Smith, "Emotional Truths and Thrilling Sideshows: The Resurgence of Antiporn Feminism" in *The Feminist Porn Book: The Politics of Producing Pleasure*, eds Tristan Taormino et al. (New York: Feminist Press at CUNY, 2013), 44.

109 See, for example, Tarpley Hitt, "Inside Exodus Cry: The Shady Evangelical Organization With Trump Ties Waging War on PornHub," *Daily Beast*, 2 November 2020, https://www.thedailybeast.com/inside-exodus-cry-the-shady-evangelical-group-with-trump-ties-waging-war-on-pornhub; Samantha Cole, "How a Petition to Shutdown Pornhub got Two Million Signatures," *Vice*, 1 September 2020, https://www.vice.com/en/article/wxqy4z/petition-shut-down-pornhub-trafficking-hub-earn-it.

110 See, for example, Allison Smith, "Collateral Damage in the War on Sex Trafficking," *Bloomberg News*, 24 March 2023, https://www.bnnbloomberg.ca/collateral-damage-in-the-war-on-sex-trafficking-1.1899880.

111 Robert Heynen and Emily van der Meulen, "Anti-trafficking Saviors: Celebrity, Slavery, and Branded Activism," *Crime, Media, Culture* 18, no. 2 (2022): 316–17. See also Cole, "Petition to Shutdown Pornhub."

112 For a wonderful essay on the "porn wars" or "feminist sex wars," see Betty Dodson, "Porn Wars" in *The Feminist Porn Book: The Politics of Producing Pleasure*, eds Tristan Taormino et al. (New York: Feminist Press at CUNY, 2013), 23.

113 See, for example, Danielle Blunt and Zahra Stardust, "Automating Whorephobia: Sex, Technology and the Violence of Deplatforming," *Porn Studies* 8, no. 4 (2021): 350; Smith, "Collateral Damage." The issue of discriminatory deplatforming is examined in chapter 8.

114 Marleen Klaassen and Jochen Peter, "Gender (In)equality in Internet Pornography: A Content Analysis of Popular Pornographic Internet Videos," *Journal of Sex Research* 52, no. 7 (2015): 727 (showing a strong focus on sex acts and orgasm in which men rather than women are depicted as gaining sexual pleasure in mainstream porn); Eran Shor, "Age, Aggression, and Pleasure in Popular Online Pornographic Videos," *Violence Against Women* 25, no. 8 (2019): 1027–32 (showing that popular mainstream porn videos on Pornhub portray aggression and degradation towards women as pleasure-producing for women).

115 See, for example, Eran Shor and Golshan Golriz, "Gender, Race, and Aggression in Mainstream Pornography," *Archives of Sexual Behavior* 48, no. 3 (2019): 745 (finding that 43 per cent of videos in their sample included depictions of aggression, which they broke down as gagging [24.4%], forceful vaginal penetration [20.4%], spanking [13.4%], and rough handling [12.8%]; and finding that there were significant differences in rates of aggression depending on the race of those depicted, with much higher rates of aggression against Latina [51.9%] and Asian [75%] women); Yaser Mirzaei, Somayyeh Zare, and Todd Morrison, "Hijab Pornography: A Content Analysis of Internet Pornographic Videos," *Violence Against Women* 28, no. 6–7 (2021): 1420 (showing the prevalence of discriminatory stereotypes and a disproportionate degree of aggression towards Muslim women reflected in so-called "hijab porn" on mainstream porn-streaming platforms); Klaassen and Peter, "Gender (In)equality," 727 (asserting that when violence or dominance is depicted in mainstream porn it is significantly more likely to be male perpetrated against females than female perpetrated against males).

116 Niki Fritz and Bryant Paul, "From Orgasms to Spanking: A Content Analysis of the Agentic and Objectifying Sexual Scripts in Feminist, for Women,

and Mainstream Pornography," *Sex Roles* 77, no. 9–10 (2017): 639 (finding that feminist porn was substantially less likely to include cum shots, genital focus, gaping, and aggression).

117 Ibid., 641.

118 Constance Penley et al., "Introduction: The Politics of Producing Pleasure," in *The Feminist Porn Book: The Politics of Producing Pleasure*, eds Tristan Taormino et al. (New York: Feminist Press at CUNY, 2013), 15.

119 See, for example, Alan McKee, "The Objectification of Women in Mainstream Pornographic Videos in Australia," *Journal of Sex Research* 42, no. 4 (2005): 285 (finding aggression in less than 2 per cent of videos in a 2005 study); Ana J. Bridges et al., "Aggression and Sexual Behavior in Best-Selling Pornography Videos: A Content Analysis Update," *Violence Against Women* 16, no. 10 (2010): 1065 (finding aggression in over 88 per cent of mainstream porn videos).

120 Shor and Seida, *Aggression in Pornography*, 65 (finding that 39.8 percent of Pornhub videos included visible acts of aggression, with spanking, hair pulling, forceful vaginal penetration, and gagging being the most common). Vera-Gray et al., "Sexual Violence as a Sexual Script," 1243 (finding that one in eight titles shown to first-time users on the landing pages of mainstream porn-streaming platforms describe sexual violence). Niki Fritz and Paul Bryant, "A Descriptive Analysis of the Types, Targets, and Relative Frequency of Aggression in Mainstream Pornography," *Archives of Sexual Behavior* 49, no. 8 (2020): 3041 (finding that 45 per cent of Pornhub scenes and 35 per cent of scenes on XVideos included acts such as spanking, gagging, slapping, and hair pulling).

121 Tarleton Gillespie, *Custodians of the Internet: Platforms, Content Moderation, and the Hidden Decisions That Shape Social Media* (New Haven: Yale University Press, 2018).

122 Ibid.

CHAPTER TWO

1 This includes home video technology, video rental markets, and the commercialization of the Internet – developments that have radically changed mass media in general. See, for example, Samantha Cole, *How Sex Changed the Internet and the Internet Changed Sex: An Unexpected History* (New York: Workman Publishing, 2022); Peter Alilunas, *Smutty Little Movies: The Creation and Regulation of Adult Video* (Oakland: University of California Press, 2016), 42; Peter Johnson, "Pornography Drives Technology: Why Not to Censor the Internet," *Federal Communications Law Journal* 49 (1996): 217.

2 Shira Tarrant, *The Pornography Industry: What Everyone Needs to Know* (Oxford: Oxford University Press, 2016), 11–27; Heather Berg, *Porn Work: Sex, Labor and Late Capitalism* (Chapel Hill: University of North Carolina Press, 2021).

3 Susanna Paasonen, Kylie Jarrett, and Ben Light, *#NSFW: Sex, Humor, and Risk in Social Media* (Cambridge, MA: MIT Press, 2019), 45.

4 Tarrant, *Pornography Industry*, 22.

5 In 1972 the film *Deep Throat* was released. It was the first pornographic movie to be widely shown in mainstream theatres across North America. See Tarrant, *Pornography Industry*.

6 See, for example, Carolyn Bronstein, "Clashing at Barnard's Gates: Understanding the Origins of the Pornography Problem in the Modern American Women's Movement," in *New Views on Pornography: Sexuality, Politics and the Law*, eds Lynn Comella and Shira Tarrant (Santa Barbara: Praeger, 2015), 63 (noting the increase in the American context due to increasing recognition by courts that pornography should receive free speech protections under the First Amendment), and 72 (noting that by 1987 there were over 100 million adult videos rented per year in the United States). See also Tarrant, *Pornography Industry*, 22.

7 Tarrant, *Pornography Industry*, 23.

8 Ibid.

9 Ibid.

10 Susanna Paasonen, *Carnal Resonance: Affect and Online Pornography* (Cambridge, MA: MIT Press, 2011), 36.

11 Tarrant, *Pornography Industry*, 24.

12 Ibid., 15–27; Kal Raustiala and Christopher Sprigman, "The Second Digital Disruption: Streaming and the Dawn of Data-Driven Creativity," *NYU Law Review* 94 (2019): 1563 (explaining that the dominant business model in mainstream porn shifted to address the type of piracy presented by online streaming).

13 See Berg, *Porn Work*, 14. I am grateful to Jane Bailey for drawing my attention to the utility of relying on Lessig's thinking on the regulatory impact of law, norms, and technological (including Internet) architecture: Lawrence Lessig, "The New Chicago School," *Journal of Legal Studies* 27 (1998): 661.

14 See Tarleton Gillespie, *Custodians of the Internet: Platforms, Content Moderation, and the Hidden Decisions That Shape Social Media* (New Haven: Yale University Press, 2018). Gillespie defines platforms as "online sites and services that (a) host, organize, and circulate users' shared content or social interactions for them, (b) without having produced or commissioned

(the bulk) of that content, (c) built on an infrastructure, beneath that circulation of information, for processing data for customer service, advertising and profit" (Gillespie, *Custodians of the Internet*, 18).

15 See, for example, Aleksandra Diana Dwulit and Piotr Rzymski, "Prevalence, Patterns and Self-Perceived Effects of Pornography Consumption in Polish University Students: A Cross-Sectional Study," *International Journal of Environmental Research and Public Health* 16, no. 10 (2019): 1861 (showing that among Polish postsecondary students, streaming platforms were by far the most common way to access pornography); Tarrant, *Pornography Industry*, 24. In a 2016 interview, Tarrant suggested that there were estimates of as much as $2 billion of stolen porn from the adult entertainment industry each year: Joe Pinsker, "The Hidden Economics of Porn," *Atlantic*, 2016, www.theatlantic.com/business/archive/2016/04/pornography-industry-economics-tarrant/476580.

16 Raustiala and Sprigman, "Second Digital Disruption," 1563.

17 In noting the "ubiquitous and instantaneous" access to pornography facilitated by the Internet, Amia Srinivasan adds that this is only true in half of the world. A large proportion of the world's population does not have access to high-speed Internet. See Amia Srinivasan, *The Right to Sex: Feminism in the Twenty-First Century* (New York: Farrar, Straus, and Giroux, 2021), 198n15.

18 Cameron Wong, Yo-Der Song, and Aniket Mahanti, "YouTube of Porn: Longitudinal Measurement, Analysis, and Characterization of a Large Porn Streaming Service," *Social Network Analysis and Mining* 10, no. 62 (2020): 1.

19 "2019 Year in Review," Pornhub, 22 December 2019, www.pornhub.com/insights/2019-year-in-review.

20 Ibid.

21 Qayyah Moynihan, "Internet Users Access Porn Sites More than Twitter, Wikipedia and Netflix," Business Insider, 30 September 2018, www.businessinsider.com/internet-users-access-porn-more-than-twitter-wikipedia-and-netflix-2018-9.

22 Ibid. According to this source, Amazon is the fourth most visited site and Pornhub the sixth most visited site.

23 Testimony of Feras Antoon, House of Commons, Standing Committee on Access to Information, Privacy and Ethics, *Evidence*, 43-2, No. 19 (5 February 2021), 1.

24 Sheelah Kolhatkar, "The Fight to Hold Pornhub Accountable," *New Yorker*, 13 June 2022, www.newyorker.com/magazine/2022/06/20/the-fight-to-hold-pornhub-accountable.

25 "2019 xHamster Year-End Report" (blog), xHamster, 9 December 2019, xhamster.com/blog/posts/9715646.

26 Jessica Clement, "Most Popular Websites Worldwide as of June 2021, by Total Visits," Statista, 7 September 2021, www.statista.com/statistics/1201880/most-visited-websites-worldwide.

27 Mark Regnerus, David Gordon, and Joseph Price, "Documenting Pornography Use in America: A Comparative Analysis of Methodological Approaches," *Journal of Sex Research* 53, no. 7 (2016): 873.

28 Ingrid Solano, Nicholas Eaton, and K. Daniel O'Leary, "Pornography Consumption, Modality and Function in a Large Internet Sample," *Journal of Sex Research* 57, no. 1 (2020): 92 (this included not only streaming free videos online but also written pornography and photos). See also Jason S. Carroll et al., "Generation xxx: Pornography Acceptance and Use Among Emerging Adults," *Journal of Adolescent Research* 23, no. 1 (2008): 6 (finding that 87 per cent of college age men consume pornography).

29 Testimony of Feras Antoon, *Evidence*, 1.

30 Paasonen, Jarrett, and Light, *#nsfw*, 55.

31 Anne M. Coughlin, "Representing the Forbidden," *California Law Review* 90, no. 6 (2002): 2144 (exploring the way in which consumption of pornography remains unspeakable).

32 Rowland Atkinson and Thomas Rodgers, "Pleasure Zones and Murder Boxes: Online Pornography and Violent Video Games as Zones of Cultural Exception," *British Journal of Criminology* 56, no. 6 (2015): 1298.

33 India Thusi, "Reality Porn," *New York University Law Review* 96, no. 3 (2021): 748. For a discussion of how social media intervenes in public spaces generally, see Jose van Dijck and Thomas Poell, "Social Media and the Transformation of Public Space," *Social Media and Society* 1, no. 2 (2015): 1.

34 Thusi, "Reality Porn," 748.

35 Paasonen, *Carnal Resonance*, 76.

36 Wong, Song, and Mahanti, "YouTube of Porn," 2.

37 Testimony of Feras Antoon, *Evidence*, 1. See also "Pornhub Comments," Pornhub, 5 July 2014, www.pornhub.com/insights/pornhub-comments.

38 "Pornhub Community," Pornhub, accessed 30 September 2021, www.pornhub.com.

39 See, for example, Pornhub, accessed 30 September 2021, www.pornhub.com/signup. The same is true of many other porn-streaming platforms, such as xHamster, RedTube, and YouPorn.

40 Ibid.

41 See Thusi, "Reality Porn" (for a discussion of the sharing of material with

an interactive, online audience, such as on websites like OnlyFans). See
also Alyson Kreuger, "Virtual Reality Gets Naughty," *New York Times*, 28
October 2017, www.nytimes.com/2017/10/28/style/virtual-reality-porn.html
(for an examination of the proliferation of virtual reality porn on Pornhub
and other porn-streaming platforms).

42 This change happened after the company received significant criticism following an exposé in the *New York Times*. See Nicholas Kristof, "An Uplifting
Update, on the Terrible World of Pornhub," *New York Times*, 9 December
2020, www.nytimes.com/2020/12/09/opinion/pornhub-news-child-
abuse.html.

43 "2019 Year in Review," Pornhub.

44 Ibid.

45 "Pornhub Comments," Pornhub.

46 Gareth Tyson et al., *Are People Really Social on Porn 2.0?* Proceedings of
the Ninth International AAAI Conference on Web and Social Media (Palo
Alto: AAAI Press, 2015), 438 (in their study of 563,000 profiles on Pornhub,
75 per cent were male identified).

47 Dana Rotman and Jennifer Preece, "The 'WeTube' in YouTube: Creating an
Online Community Through Video Sharing," *International Journal of Web
Based Communities* 6, no. 3 (2010): 320.

48 Che-Wei Liu, Guodong (Gordon) Gao, and Ritu Agarwal, "Unraveling the
'Social' in Social Norms: The Conditioning Effect of User Connectivity,"
Information Systems Research 30, no. 4 (2019): 1272 (empirical study demonstrating that people with a high level of connectivity in a virtual community are more susceptible to its social-norm messages); Gregor Petric and
Andraz Petrovcic, "Elements of the Management of Norms and Their
Effects on the Sense of Virtual Community," *Online Information Review* 38,
no. 3 (2014): 436 (examining how decisions of managers of online communities, about a community's norms, impact the sense of virtual community).

49 Atkinson and Rodgers, "Pleasure Zones," 1299.

50 Gillespie, *Custodians*, 17; Nick Srnicek, *Platform Capitalism* (Cambridge,
UK: Polity Press, 2017), 22–46 (discussing this reliance on user interaction
by platforms generally).

51 Tarrant notes that "'[s]tag' – meaning 'men only' – referred to the all-male
homosocial groups who watched these films together" (Tarrant, *Pornography Industry*, 20); John Gagnon and William Simon, *Sexual Conduct: The
Social Sources of Human Sexuality* (Chicago: Aldine Publishing Company,

1973), 265–6; Tarrant, *Pornography Industry*, 22; See Cole, *How Sex Changed*, 11 (observing that many BBS system operators devoted their online worlds to porn).

52 Pornhub measures the number of visits to its site each year in the billions, while the number of comments and messages number in the millions ("2019 Year in Review," Pornhub). See also Rotman and Preece, "'WeTube' in YouTube," 325.

53 Rotman and Preece, "'WeTube' in YouTube," 325.

54 "2019 Year in Review," Pornhub; "2021 Year in Review," Pornhub, 14 December 2021, www.pornhub.com/insights/yir-2021.

55 Tyson et al., *Are People Really Social*, 441.

56 Pornhub, for example, permitted unverified users to upload videos until 2020, when it came under public scrutiny for hosting countless videos of child sexual abuse and rape. This practice meant that once a video had been posted to the platform, including one that was filmed without the consent of the subject(s) of the video, even if the original was ultimately removed following a complaint, it could be (and frequently was) re-uploaded over and over again. See, for example, Testimony of Feras Antoon, *Evidence* (distinguishing between this approach and 2021, by which time they had stopped permitting unverified users from uploading content: "Today, only professional studios and verified users and creators, whose personal identity and date of birth have been confirmed by MindGeek, may upload content").

57 Whether users on porn-streaming platforms exercise this power frequently or appropriately, and whether companies adequately respond when they do, is a separate question. See Nicholas Kristof, "The Children of Pornhub," *New York Times*, 6 December 2020, www.nytimes.com/2020/12/04/opinion/sunday/pornhub-rape-trafficking.html (documenting the failure of Pornhub to adequately respond when someone requests that content be removed; see the follow-up article at Kristof, "An Uplifting Update").

58 Tarleton Gillespie, "Platforms Are Not Intermediaries," *Georgetown Law Technology Review* 2, no. 2 (2018): 201. Gillespie argues that platforms should conceive of users not only as customers and data providers, but as an important part of their labour force.

59 Carlisle George and Jackie Scerri, "Web 2.0 and User-Generated Content: Legal Challenges in the New Frontier," *Journal of Information, Law and Technology* 2 (2007): 1.

60 Gillespie, *Custodians*, 5.

61 "2018 Year in Review," Pornhub, 11 December 2018, www.pornhub.com/insights/2018-year-in-review.

62 "2019 Year in Review," Pornhub.

63 Wong, Song, and Mahanti, "YouTube of Porn," 3 (studying xHamster).

64 Ibid., 5.

65 Ibid., 6.

66 Tarrant, *Pornography Industry*, 50 (suggesting they are paid substantially less). Berg, *Porn Work*, 14 (noting that as performer pools have grown, rates have decreased).

67 See, for example, David Auerbach, "Vampire Porn: MindGeek Is a Cautionary Tale of Consolidating Production and Distribution in a Single, Monopolistic Owner," *Slate*, 23 October 2014, https://slate.com/technology/2014/10/mindgeek-porn-monopoly-its-dominance-is-a-cautionary-tale-for-other-industries.html.

68 Ibid.

69 Auerbach, "Vampire Porn"; Berg, *Porn Work*, 96; Tarrant, *Pornography Industry*, 49–68.

70 Berg, *Porn Work*, 102.

71 Tarrant, *Pornography Industry*, 55. For an in-depth examination of the camming industry, see Angela Jones, *Camming: Money, Power and Pleasure in the Sex Work Industry* (New York: New York University Press, 2019). For a critique of webcamming, see Catharine A. MacKinnon, "OnlyFans Is Not a Safe Platform for 'Sex Work.' It's a Pimp," *New York Times*, 6 September 2021, www.nytimes.com/2021/09/06/opinion/onlyfans-sex-work-safety.html.

72 Berg, *Porn Work*, 102.

73 Ibid.

74 "Social Media Automation," Pornhub, accessed 8 June 2023, https://help.pornhub.com/hc/en-us/articles/4419866229395-Social-Media-Automation.

75 Peggy Orenstein, *Boys and Sex: Young Men on Hookups, Love, Porn, Consent, and Navigating the New Masculinity* (New York: Harper Collins, 2020), 43.

76 Srinivasan, *Right to Sex*, 65.

77 "2019 Year in Review," Pornhub.

78 Kreuger, "Virtual Reality" (citing Pornhub's claim in 2017 that it receives 500,000 views of virtual reality porn per day – an increase of 275 per cent since it was introduced to the site in 2016); David Ewalt, "The First Real Boom in Virtual Reality? It's Pornography," *Wall Street Journal*, 11 July 2018,

www.wsj.com/articles/the-first-real-boom-in-virtual-reality-its-pornog
raphy-1531320180 (reporting on the expansive growth of virtual reality
pornography).

79 Thusi, "Reality Porn," 772.

80 Ibid.

81 "2018 Year in Review," Pornhub. The company suggests the same is true for
the categories "Hentai" and "Tattooed Women."

82 Ibid.

83 See also Arne Dekker et al., "VR Porn as 'Empathy Machine'? Perception of
Self and Others in Virtual Reality Pornography," *Journal of Sex Research* 58,
no. 3 (2021): 273 (finding that men felt more connected with the actors in
virtual porn and that virtual reality porn seems to elicit the illusion of a
sexually intimate experience more powerfully than two-dimensional porn).

84 Kreuger, "Virtual Reality."

85 Raustiala and Sprigman, "Second Digital Disruption," 1555.

86 Tarrant, *Pornography Industry*, 166–7 (noting that "the majority of pornography currently features heteronormative, phallocentric and often-racist
material").

87 Tarrant, ibid., 72; Srinivasan, *Right to Sex*, 67.

88 Raustiala and Sprigman, "Second Digital Disruption," 1558. For them this is
actually the second digital disruption.

89 Ibid.

90 Ibid., 1587. See also Gillespie, *Custodians*, 15.

91 Jose van Dijck, Thomas Poell, and Martijn de Waal, *The Platform Society:
Public Values in a Connective World* (New York: Oxford University Press,
2018), 33–4.

92 Raustiala and Sprigman, "Second Digital Disruption," 1587; Gillespie, "Platforms," 202.

93 Raustiala and Sprigman, "Second Digital Disruption," 1593. See Wong,
Song, and Mahanti, "YouTube of Porn," 4 (reporting that 80 per cent of videos on xHamster are less than thirteen minutes long). See Gareth Tyson et
al., *Demystifying Porn 2.0: A Look into a Major Adult Video Streaming Website*, Proceedings of the 2013 Conference on Internet Measurement Conference (ACM Digital Library, 2013), 417–26 (making similar findings regarding
YouPorn); Raymond Yu et al., *Comparative Analysis of Adult Video Streaming Services: Characteristics and Workload*, Proceedings of the 2019 Network
Traffic Measurement and Analysis Conference (IEEE, 2019), 49–56 (making
similar findings regarding Pornhub). In both the YouPorn and Pornhub

studies the most frequent length of a video was between five and seven
minutes (see Wong, Song, and Mahanti, "YouTube of Porn," 4).

94   Ilir Rama et al., "The Platformization of Gender and Sexual Identities:
An Algorithmic Analysis of Pornhub," *Porn Studies* 10, no. 2 (2023): 154;
Raustiala and Sprigman, "Second Digital Disruption," 1593; Gillespie,
"Platforms," 210.

95   Srinivasan, *Right to Sex*, 68.

96   "t," Pornhub, search conducted 12 November 2021, www.pornhub.com.

97   "Step," xHamster, search conducted 12 November 2021, www.xhamster.
com/search/step.

98   Gillespie, *Custodians*, 186.

99   Raustiala and Sprigman, "Second Digital Disruption," 1559.

100 Ibid., 1560n14.

101 Ibid., 1559. For a discussion of vertical integration in platform companies
generally, see Friso Bostoen, "Online Platforms and Vertical Integration:
The Return of Margin Squeeze?," *Journal of Antitrust Enforcement* 6, no. 3
(2017): 355; Jose van Dijck, "Seeing the Forest for the Trees: Visualizing
Platformization and its Governance," *New Media and Society* 23, no. 9
(2021): 2808.

102 Auerbach, "Vampire Porn." See Orenstein, *Boys and Sex*, 43 (noting that
MindGeek owns several pornography production studios, including
Brazzers, Digital Playground, and Reality Kings).

103 Orlando Crowcroft, "Pornhub: How 'The YouTube of Sex' Changed the
Porn World – and How It May Still Destroy It," *International Business
Times*, 23 April 2016, https://www.ibtimes.co.uk/Pornhub-how-youtube-
sex-changed-porn-world-how-it-may-stilldestroy-it-1554844.

104 Raustiala and Sprigman, "Second Digital Disruption," 1572.

105 Ibid., 1599.

106 Ibid., 1592; Tarrant, *Pornography Industry*, 36 (noting that with MindGeek
subsidiaries, like Brazzers, which is one of the larger companies, decisions
such as who to cast are made by the company rather than individual
producers).

107 Raustiala and Sprigman, "Second Digital Disruption," 1592.

108 Rama et al., "Platformization of Gender," 156.

109 Ibid., 11.

110 Cole, *How Sex Changed*, 163.

111 "How to Succeed Model Guide," Pornhub, accessed 4 March 2022, https://
www.pornhub.com.

112 David Nieborg and Thomas Poell, "The Platformization of Cultural Pro-
     duction: Theorizing the Contingent Cultural Commodity," *New Media and
     Society* 20, no. 11 (2018): 4277 (examining the ways in which cultural pro-
     duction, which would include the production of pornographic videos
     [although the authors do not discuss pornography], are becoming increas-
     ingly "platform dependant").
113 Ibid., 4279.
114 Ibid., 4280.
115 Rishabh Mehrotra and Prasanta Bhattacharya, *Characterizing and Predict-
     ing Supply-Side Engagement on Video Sharing Platforms Using a Hawkes
     Process Model*, Proceedings of the ACM SIGIR International Conference
     on Theory of Information Retrieval (ACM: 2017), 163.
116 Ibid.
117 Ibid., 164.
118 Ibid., 163.
119 Ibid.
120 Wong, Song, and Mahanti, "YouTube of Porn," 6.
121 Atkinson and Rodgers, "Pleasure Zones," 1298. See also Tarrant, *Pornog-
     raphy Industry*, 167.
122 Stacy Gorman, Elizabeth Monk-Turner, and Jennifer Fish, "Free Adult In-
     ternet Web Sites: How Prevalent are Degrading Acts?," *Gender Issues* 27,
     no2. 3–4 (2010): 136. See also Niki Fritz et al., "A Descriptive Analysis of the
     Types, Targets, and Relative Frequency of Aggression in Mainstream Por-
     nography," *Archives of Sexual Behaviour* 49, no. 8 (2020): 3041 (finding that
     women were the targets in 97 per cent of the videos that included acts of
     aggression on both Pornhub and XVideos (such videos constituted 45 per
     cent of their sample). See also Yaser Mirzaei, Somayyeh Zare, and Todd G.
     Morrison, "Hijab Pornography: A Content Analysis of Internet Porno-
     graphic Videos," *Violence Against Women* 28, nos. 6–7 (2021):1420.
123 Gorman, Monk-Turner, and Fish, "Free Adult Internet," 138.
124 Ibid., 139 (finding that this occurred in 45 per cent of the videos in their
     sample).
125 Eran Shor, "Age, Aggression, and Pleasure in Popular Online Pornographic
     Videos," *Violence Against Women* 25, no. 8 (2019): 1026 (finding that this oc-
     curred in 45 per cent of the videos involving adult women in his sample).
126 Ibid.
127 Sarah A. Vannier, Anna B. Currie, and Lucia F. O'Sullivan, "Schoolgirls and
     Soccer Moms: A Content Analysis of Free 'Teen' and 'MILF' Online Pornog-
     raphy," *Journal of Sex Research* 51, no. 3 (2014): 263.

128 Ibid., 261.

129 "Pornhub Model Payment Program: How to Succeed," Pornhub, accessed
     3 April 2022, https://www.pornhub.com/partners/models.

130 Ibid.

131 For a discussion of the ways in which YouTube has fed antifeminist and
     misogynist sentiment online, see Laura Bates, *Men Who Hate Women: From
     Incels to Pickup Artists – The Truth About Extreme Misogyny and How it
     Hurts Us All* (Naperville: SourceBook, 2020).

132 "The Pornhub PlayBook: How to Make Money with Pornhub," Pornhub,
     accessed 4 April 2022, https://www.pornhub.com/partners/cpp.

133 These titles were taken from a study of the content of videos found on
     Pornhub conducted by Eran Shor and Kimberley Seida, "'Harder and
     Harder'? Is Mainstream Pornography Becoming Increasingly Violent and
     Do Viewers Prefer Violent Content?," *Journal of Sex Research* 56, no. 1
     (2019): 24. To be clear, this study was not claiming that titles or content
     have become more "hardcore." In fact, these researchers found that users
     were more likely to prefer videos that did not depict non-consensual ag-
     gression and in which both parties were depicted as experiencing pleasure.
     They did not find that titles are increasingly suggesting aggression. That
     said, the most recent and comprehensive study of video titles on main-
     stream porn platforms found that one in eight titles implied or referenced
     some form of sexual violence: Fiona Vera-Gray et al., "Sexual Violence as a
     Sexual Script in Mainstream Online Pornography," *British Journal of Crimi-
     nology* 61, no. 5 (2021): 1243 (examining tens of thousands of video titles
     on major mainstream porn-streaming platforms).

134 Whitney Strub, "From Porno Chic to Porn Bleak: Representing the Urban
     Crisis in American 1970s Pornography," in *Porno Chic and the American Sex
     Wars: American Sexual Representation in the 1970s*, eds Carolyn Bronstein
     and Whitney Strub (Amherst and Boston: University of Massachusetts
     Press, 2016), 27.

135 Cynthia Khoo, "Deplatforming Misogyny: Report on Platform Liability for
     Technology-Facilitated Gender-Based Violence," *Womens Legal Education
     and Action Fund* (2021), 55, https://www.leaf.ca/publication/deplatforming-
     misogyny.

136 Vera-Gray et al., "Sexual Violence," 133.

137 "Trans Teen Slut Anal Fucked by Police Officer" (video), Pornhub, accessed
     23 November 2023 (3,000,000 views, 89 per cent approval rating).

138 "Little Slut Wanted to Leave but Was Fucked in Clothes" (video), Pornhub, accessed 23 November 2023 (2,000,000 views, 89 per cent approval rating).

139 See, for example, Bonnie Ruberg, "Doing It for Free: Digital Labour and the Fantasy of Amateur Online Pornography," *Porn Studies* 3, no. 2 (2016): 154 (challenging the utopic narrative that online amateur porn uploaded for free has democratized the pornography industry). See Srnicek, *Platform Capitalism*, 27 (examining the "rhetoric of democratizing communication" advanced in relation to platforms generally).

140 Bronstein, "Clashing at Barnard's Gates," 71–2; Berg, *Porn Work*, 16–17.

141 Thusi, "Reality Porn," 774.

142 See Ana J. Bridges et al., "Aggression and Sexual Behaviour in Best-Selling Pornography Videos: A Content Analysis Update," *Violence Against Women* 16, no. 10 (2010): 1080 (finding that in the vast majority of videos, female performers demonstrated a willingness to have aggressive acts imposed upon them; they either responded to aggression against them with expressions of enjoyment or did not respond at all); Shor, "Age, Aggression, and Pleasure," 1027 (in which a similar finding is made regarding videos involving teens: 90 per cent of the teenage women in videos containing visible aggression displayed pleasure). See also Henry Talbot et al., "Breaking Down Porn: A Classification Office Analysis of Commonly Viewed Pornography in NZ," Office of Film and Literature Classification, 2019, 7, researchspace.auckland.ac.nz/bitstream/handle/2292/49408/Breaking-Down-Porn.pdf. The Government of New Zealand's Classification Office found that 43 per cent of the most popular Pornhub videos in that country were categorized by Pornhub as "step fantasy" – videos that depict sex between stepsiblings or between stepparents and stepchildren.

143 Srinivasan, *Right to Sex*, 67.

144 Ibid.

145 Ibid.

146 Ruberg, "Doing It for Free," 150.

147 Auerbach, "Vampire Porn."

148 "MindGeek Company Profile," The Best Porn, www.thebestporn.com/review_company.html, cited in Margaret MacDonald, "Desire for Data: Pornhub and the Platformization of a Culture Industry" (master's thesis, Concordia University, 2019), spectrum.library.concordia.ca/id/eprint/986147.

149 Srnicek, *Platform Capitalism*, 24.

150 Ibid., 24–5. See also van Dijck, Poell, and de Waal, *Platform Society*, 15–16 (making a similar observation).

151 Cole, *How Sex Changed*, 162.

152 Ibid., 162.

153 Raustiala and Sprigman, "Second Digital Disruption," 1558.

154 Laura McVey, Lauren Gurrieri, and Meagan Tyler, "The Structural Oppression of Women by Markets: The Continuum of Sexual Violence and the Online Pornography Market," *Journal of Online Marketing Management* 37, nos. 1–2 (2020): 56 (finding that over 80 per cent of online porn is consumed on mobile devices). See "2019 Year in Review," Pornhub (reporting that 83.7% of Pornhub's content is viewed on phones and tablets).

155 See Annie Smith et al., "Balance and Connection in BC: The Health and Well-Being of Our Youth," McCreary Centre Society, 2019, 8, www.mcs.bc. ca/pdf/balance_and_connection.pdf (finding that "twelve percent of youth with a phone used their device on their most recent school day to watch pornography"). See also Jennifer Feinberg, "Crusade to Prevent Kids from Accessing Internet Porn Pitched in Chilliwack," *Chilliwack Progress*, 8 May 2019, www.theprogress.com/news/child-proofing-porn-crusade-could-begin-in-chilliwack.

156 McVey, Gurrieri, and Tyler, "Structural Oppression of Women," 56.

157 Martin Downing et al., "Sexually Explicit Media Use by Sexual Identity: A Comparative Analysis of Gay, Bisexual, and Heterosexual Men in the United States," *Archives of Sexual Behavior* 46, no. 6 (2017): 1769.

158 Tarrant, *Pornography Industry*, 76.

159 See, for example, Emily F. Rothman et al., "'Without Porn … I Wouldn't Know Half the Things I Know Now': A Qualitative Study of Pornography Use among a Sample of Urban, Low-Income, Black and Hispanic Youth," *Journal of Sex Research* 52, no. 7 (2015): 739 (finding that youth report frequently watching pornography at school on desktop computers and smartphones during school hours).

160 Jennifer O'Connell, "It's Not Illegal to Watch Porn on Public Transport. But Is It Wrong?," *Irish Times*, 3 October 2018, www.irishtimes.com/culture/tv-radio-web/it-s-not-illegal-to-watch-porn-on-public-transport-but-is-it-wrong-1.3650059 (describing her experience, and the experience a colleague shared, of encountering a man watching pornography on the train and discussing her disinclination to complain or raise it with the viewer). One of the subjects in Rothman et al.'s study indicated that "it is not unusual for

friends to share such sex videos in a casual manner, even in public places like a subway car" ("Without Porn," 741).

161 Siobhann Tighe, "Is It OK to Watch Porn in Public?," BBC, 16 January 2017, www.bbc.com/news/magazine-38611265; O'Connell, "It's Not Illegal"; Rhiannon Lucy Cosslett, "Watching Porn in Public Is Not OK. It's Harassment," *Guardian*, 16 January 2017, www.theguardian.com/commentis free/2017/jan/16/watching-porn-bus-public-harassment-education.

162 See, for example, Tighe, "Is It OK" (recounting an experience of sitting beside someone on a London bus who was watching porn on his phone, and similar experiences of others on public transport and in airports); Lauren O'Neil, "People Keep Watching Porn on the TTC," BlogTO, 12 September 2019, www.blogto.com/city/2019/09/people-watching-porn-ttc (documenting numerous experiences of people encountering someone watching porn on public transit in Toronto, Canada); Cosslett, "Watching Porn in Public" (discussing the prevalence of men watching porn in public spaces in the United Kingdom); Douglas Johnston, "Public Viewing of Porn Perverse, but Legal," *Free Press*, 8 April 2013, www.winnipegfreepress.com/opinion/ analysis/public-viewing-of-porn-perverse-but-legal-201884481.html (discussing complaints in Windsor, Ontario, about a man watching porn on public transit and the fact that it is likely legal to do so under Canada's *Criminal Code*).

163 See, for example, Jack Doyle, "Ministers Plan to Ban Watching Porn on Buses on Mobile Phones and Tablets amid Crackdown on Sexual Harassment," *Daily Mail*, 7 May 2019, www.dailymail.co.uk/news/article-7003991/Ministers-plan-ban-watching-porn-buses-mobile-phones.html (discussing a proposed law to ban porn consumption in public spaces).

164 See, for example, "Library Use Guidelines: Code of Conduct and Internet Use," Brampton Public Library, January 2018, 3, bramptonlibrary.ca/ images/PDFs/PoliciesJune2018/BRD—-15-Library-Use-Guidelines—- Code-of-Conduct-and-Internet-Use.pdf (which permits patrons to view pornography on the library's computers but stipulates that staff can ask them to stop if children are in the vicinity or if the content is disturbing others); David Mathews, "You Can Watch Porn at Chicago Libraries, but That Doesn't Mean You Should," *DNAinfo*, 24 January 2017, www.dnainfo. com/chicago/20170124/downtown/public-library-pornography-allowed-first-amendment-harold-washington-library (discussing the library's position that absent a complaint they cannot stop people from viewing adult pornography on the library's computers).

165 See, for example, "New York Public Library General Policies and Rules,"
     New York Public Library, December 2019, https://www.nypl.org/help/
     about-nypl/legal-notices/policies-and-rules#General%20Policies%20and
     %20Rules (which prohibits consumption of child sexual abuse material
     (child pornography) but by implication does not preclude consumption
     of adult porn on its public computer terminals).

166 See, for example, Mathew Kupfer, "Ottawa Public Library Changes Porn
     Policy Following Controversy," cbc, 20 September 2017, www.cbc.ca/news/
     canada/ottawa/ottawa-public-library-porn-policy-1.4297814. Following
     complaints by patrons that they were being exposed involuntarily to porn
     being viewed by other visitors to the library, the Ottawa Public Library
     changed its policy so that, now, if it receives a complaint of someone
     openly viewing porn in the library they will be asked to turn it off. See
     also "Porn Can Be Viewed on Public Computers at Regina Libraries," cbc,
     5 June 2015, www.cbc.ca/news/canada/saskatchewan/porn-can-be-viewed-
     on-public-computers-at-regina-libraries-1.3102646.

167 Matt Ritchel, "He's Watching That, in Public? Pornography Takes Next
     Seat," *New York Times*, 21 July 2012, www.nytimes.com/2012/07/21/us/tab
     lets-and-phones-lead-to-more-pornography-in-public.html.

168 Kaleigh Rogers, "Why Librarians Are Defending Your Right to Watch Porn
     at the Library," *Vice*, 11 December 2014, www.vice.com/en/article/wnj4ey/
     why-librarians-defend-the-right-to-watch-porn-at-the-library (discussing
     a Chicago-area library with an adults-only computer lab).

169 McVey, Gurrieri, and Tyler, "Structural Oppression of Women," 56 (high-
     lighting the increased consumption of pornography in public spaces and
     characterizing it as a form of public sexual harassment. They argue that
     viewing porn in public sexualizes public spaces, removes women's choice
     as to whether they will be exposed to porn, or particular types of porn,
     and creates a climate of public fear for women in public spaces).

170 Ron Dicker, "Pornhub Times Square Billboard Meets Stiff Opposition,
     Comes Down," *HuffPost*, 9 October 2014, www.huffpost.com/entry/porn
     hub-billboard-times-square_n_5955824; Sadaf Ashan, "Pornhub Creates
     $25,000 Scholarship to Give One Lucky Student a Very Happy Ending,"
     National Post, 4 September 2015, nationalpost.com/entertainment/porn
     hub-created-a-25000-scholarship-to-give-one-lucky-student-a-very-
     happy-ending; Testimony of Feras Antoon, *Evidence*, 13 (the assertion was
     put to former ceo of MindGeek Feras Antoon by Member of Parliament

Han Dong that its approximate revenue was $460 million); Spencer Buell, "Pornhub Says It Will Plow Snow in Boston for Free," *Boston Magazine*, 13 March 2017, www.bostonmagazine.com/news/2017/03/13/pornhub-snow-plow-boston; "xHamster Launches Live-Cam Pride Fundraiser!" xHamster, 26 June 2020, xhamster.com/blog/posts/9989895.

CHAPTER THREE

1   Jose van Dijck, Thomas Poell, and Martijn de Waal, *The Platform Society: Public Values in a Connective World* (New York: Oxford University Press, 2018), 2, 4.

2   Ibid.

3   For feminist work that has considered this development, see, for example, Bernadette Barton, *The Pornification of America: How Raunch Culture is Ruining our Society* (New York: NYU Press, 2021); Amia Srinivasan, *The Right to Sex: Feminism in the Twenty-First Century* (New York: Farrar, Straus and Giroux, 2021), 198n15; Danielle Blunt et al., "Deplatforming Sex: A Roundtable Conversation," *Porn Studies* 8, no. 4 (2021): 420.

4   Van Dijck, Poell, and de Waal, *The Platform Society*.

5   David Nieborg and Thomas Poell, "The Platformization of Cultural Production: Theorizing the Contingent Cultural Commodity," *New Media and Society* 20, no. 11 (2018): 4275; Shoshanna Zuboff, *The Age of Surveillance Capitalism: The Fight for a Human Future at the New Frontier of Power* (New York: Public Affairs, 2019); Tarleton Gillespie, "Platforms Are Not Intermediaries," *Georgetown Law Technology Review* 2, no. 2 (2018): 201; van Dijck, Poell, and de Waal, *Platform Society*.

6   Van Dijck, Poell, and de Waal, *Platform Society*, 169n18. Van Dijck, Poell, and de Waal distinguish between what they call *infrastructure* platforms (platforms, primarily the "Big Five" – Apple, Facebook, Microsoft, Google, and Amazon – which control how online data is managed, processed, and stored through functions such as search engines, cloud computing, advertising networks, pay systems, and geospatial navigation systems) and *sectoral* platforms (which serve a particular sector like news, transportation, or food) (*Platform Society*, 12–13). They assert that "virtually all platforms outside the Big Five constellation are dependent on the ecosystem's infrastructural information services" (*Platform Society*, 15).

7   Ibid., 2.

8   Nieborg and Poell, "Platformization of Cultural Production," 4276.

9   Danielle Keats Citron and Helen Norton, "Intermediaries and Hate Speech: Fostering Digital Citizenship for Our Information Age," *Boston University Law Review* 91, no. 4 (2011): 1435.

10 Ibid., 1438.

11 An important exception to this is the work of Katrin Tiidenberg, "Sex, Power and Platform Governance," *Porn Studies* 8, no. 4 (2021): 381–93, which is referenced later in this chapter and discussed in chapters 7 and 8.

12 Van Dijck, Poell, and de Waal, *Platform Society*, 11.

13 Ibid., 11.

14 Ilir Rama et al., "The Platformization of Gender and Sexual Identities: An Algorithmic Analysis of Pornhub," *Porn Studies* 10, no. 2 (2023): 154.

15 Ibid., 165.

16 Ibid., 165.

17 Ibid., 165.

18 Ibid.

19 Ibid., 165.

20 Tarleton Gillespie, *Custodians of the Internet: Platforms, Content Moderation, and the Hidden Decisions That Shape Social Media* (New Haven: Yale University Press, 2018), 205.

21 Gillespie, "Platforms," 202.

22 Ibid.; van Dijck, Poell, and de Waal, *Platform Society*, 9–10.

23 Gillespie, "Platforms," 207.

24 Ibid., 210–11.

25 Ibid., 199.

26 Van Dijck, Poell, and de Waal, *Platform Society*, 34.

27 Ibid.

28 Vindu Goel, "Facebook Tinkers with Users' Emotions in News Feed Experiment, Stirring Outcry," *New York Times*, 29 June 2014, https://www.nytimes.com/2014/06/30/technology/facebook-tinkers-with-users-emotions-in-news-feed-experiment-stirring-outcry.html. I am grateful to Suzie Dunn for drawing this example to my attention.

29 Van Dijck, Poell, and de Waal, *Platform Society*, 34–5.

30 See van Dijck, Poell, and de Waal, *Platform Society* (the authors dedicate chapters of their book to the platformization of news, urban transport, healthcare, and education; they do not include a chapter on the platformization of sex or pornography). See also Nieborg and Poell, "Platformization of Cultural Production" (focusing their examination on news and gaming platforms and making no mention of pornography); Nick Srnicek, *Plat-*

form Capitalism (Cambridge, UK: Polity Press, 2017) (the same is true of Srnicek's consideration of the transformation of the economy in *Platform Capitalism*); see also Citron and Norton's consideration of intermediaries and hate speech (Citron and Norton, "Intermediaries"). While Gillespie does address the issue of pornography in his work, he treats it as a problem that major platforms must contend with, rather than the raison d'être of some of the largest, most popular platforms in the world (see Gillespie, "Platforms"; and Gillespie, *Custodians*). While many of the significant, general works on platformization do not seem to consider porn-streaming platforms, there are scholars who have specifically examined the relationship between pornography and the Internet, including streaming platforms. See, for example, Feona Attwood, ed., *Porn.com: Making Sense of Online Pornography* (New York: Peter Lang, 2010); Katrin Tiidenberg, "Sex, Power and Platform Governance," *Porn Studies* 8, no. 4 (2021): 381; Emily van der Nagel, "Competing Platform Imaginaries of NSFW Content Creation on OnlyFans," *Porn Studies* 8, no. 4 (2021): 394. See also Cynthia Khoo, "Deplatforming Misogyny: Report on Platform Liability for Technology-Facilitated Gender-Based Violence," LEAF, 2021, 55, https://www.leaf.ca/publication/deplatforming-misogyny.

31 Van Dijck, Poell, and de Waal, *Platform Society*, 149.

32 Gillespie, *Custodians*, 208.

33 Van Dijck, Poell, and de Waal, *Platform Society*, 23.

34 Ibid., 23.

35 Ibid., 23.

36 Testimony of Feras Antoon, House of Commons, Standing Committee on Access to Information, Privacy and Ethics, *Evidence*, 43-2, No. 19 (5 February 2021), 1.

37 See "Meta Investor Relations FAQ," Meta, investor.fb.com/resources/default.aspx. (Note that Facebook's parent company is now called Meta, which includes several other social media platforms owned by CEO Mark Zuckerberg. They all share the same articulated mission.)

38 See, for example, "Pornhub Offers Free Pornhub Premium to Users Worldwide for 30 Days during COVID-19 Pandemic," Pornhub, 24 March 2020, accessed 20 December 2022, www.pornhub.com/press/show?id=1951; "Pornhub stands in solidarity against racism and social injustice. If you are able, we encourage you to give to organizations like @bailproject @Black VisionsMN @MNFreedomFund @splcenter @NAACP," Pornhub, Twitter, 31 May 2020 at 00:06, twitter.com/pornhub/status/1266929094329016325.

39 See, for example, "xHamster.com Declares Brock Turner Rule" (blog post), xHamster, 10 June 2016, xhamster.com/blog/posts/544905.

40 Testimony of Feras Antoon, *Evidence*, 1.

41 Fiona Vera-Gray et al., "Sexual Violence as a Sexual Script in Mainstream Online Pornography," *British Journal of Criminology* 61, no. 5 (2021): 1255.

42 "Non-consensual Content Policy," Pornhub, accessed 30 March 2023, help.pornhub.com/hc/en-us/articles/4419871787027.

43 "Community Guidelines," Pornhub, accessed 31 May 2023, https://help.pornhub.com/hc/en-us/articles/4419900587155-Community-Guidelines.

44 See, for example, "2020 Transparency Report," Pornhub, accessed 8 June 2023, https://help.pornhub.com/hc/en-us/articles/4419860718483-2020-Transparency-Report.

45 "Non-consensual Content Policy," Pornhub.

46 Ibid.

47 See, for example, *Sexual Offences Act* (UK), 2003, s. 75(2)(d); *Sexual Offences (Northern Ireland) Order* (NI), 2008 SI 2008/1769, s. 9(2)(d); *Sexual Offences (Scotland) Act* (Scot), 2009, ASP 9 s. 14(2); *Crimes Act* (Vic), 1958/6231, s. 36(1)(d); *Crimes Act* (NSW), 1900/40, s. 61HJ(d); *Criminal Law Consolidation Act* (SA), 1935, version; 28.8.2022, s. 46(3)(b).

48 See, for example, *R v Bree*, [2007] EWCA Crim 804, para. 24: "Section 75(2)(d) repeats well established common law principles, and acknowledges plain good sense, that, if the Complainant is unconscious as a result of her voluntary consumption of alcohol, the starting point is to presume that she is not consenting to intercourse"; *GW v R*, [2019] HCJAC 23: "it is axiomatic that, if the law provides that a person is incapable, whilst asleep or unconscious, of consenting to any conduct, there can never be a reasonable belief of consent in such circumstances … Section 14 is equally clear in its statement that a person cannot consent to conduct whilst she is asleep or unconscious. This too is unambiguous. It means what it says. A sleeping person is not capable of consenting"; *R v JA*, 2011 SCC 28.

49 "Step Sis Gets Woke Up" (video), Pornhub, accessed 3 April 2023 (148,000 views, 91 per cent approval rating). The video depicted a woman asleep on a bed in a darkened room. Filmed from a "point of view" angle, the woman is depicted as being asleep for the first part of the video (which appears to be fictional) while sexual acts are performed on her – a clear portrayal of non-consensual sexual touching. She then "awakes" and begins to participate enthusiastically in the sexual activity.

50 "Teen Woke Up" (video), Pornhub, accessed 3 April 2023 (407,000 views,

87 per cent approval rating). Filmed from a "point of view" angle, the video, which appears to be fictional, is of a woman "asleep" in a darkened bedroom. The woman is depicted as asleep on her stomach for the first part of the video while sexual acts are performed on her from behind, including vaginal penetration. This is a depiction of rape. After several minutes she begins to moan and participate in the penetration by thrusting her hips.

51 "Accidently Woke Up My Step Sister With My Dick" (video), Pornhub, accessed 20 November 2023 (264,000 views, 94 per cent approval rating). Filmed from the point of view of the male participant, the video (which appears to be fictional) depicts a male lying in bed beside a female who is depicted as asleep. After masturbating briefly, he pulls the covers off of her, exposing her buttocks and begins to penetrate her while she remains "asleep."

52 For legal research examining this issue, see, for example, Janine Benedet, "The Sexual Assault of Intoxicated Women," *Canadian Journal of Women and the Law* 22, no. 2 (2010): 435; Elaine Craig, "Sexual Assault and Intoxication: Defining (In)Capacity to Consent," *Canadian Bar Review* 98, no. 1 (2020): 70. See also "Step Sis Gets Woke Up" (video), Pornhub (as noted from note 63 on, a search of the platform xHamster using the term "wake up" yielded hundreds of videos).

53 "xHamster Turner Statement," xHamster.

54 See *People v Turner* (8 August 2018), California No. H043709 (Cal Ct App) (appealing the decision of a jury to convict Turner of three felonies).

55 See, for example, Liam Stack, "Light Sentence for Brock Turner in Stanford Rape Case Draws Outrage," *New York Times*, 6 June 2016, www.nytimes.com/2016/06/07/us/outrage-in-stanford-rape-case-over-dueling-statements-of-victim-and-attackers-father.html.

56 "xHamster Turner Statement," xHamster.

57 Ibid.

58 Ibid.

59 Ibid.

60 It is not clear that the pop-up message promised by xHamster, given its potential to shame users and the limited access most people have to a professional psychologist, would have had a beneficial effect.

61 *People v Turner*.

62 "Unconscious" (video), xHamster, search conducted 15 December 2021; "Rape" (video), xHamster, search conducted 15 December 2021.

63 "Wake Up" (video), xHamster, search conducted 15 December 2021.

64 "Wake Up Sis" (video), xHamster, accessed 6 January 2022 (4,100,000 views, 100 per cent approval rating).

65 Ibid.

66 "Her Wake Up Call" (video), xHamster, accessed 20 September 2022 (467,135 views, 98 per cent approval rating).

67 Ibid.

68 Ibid.

69 To be equally clear, under Canadian law people who do initiate "sleepy sex" with a spouse take the risk that they are exposing themselves to criminal liability. In *R v JA* (see note 48) the dissent raised the concern that precluding the capacity for advance consent to sexual touching while incapacitated might inadvertently criminalize the sleepy caress of a cohabitating spouse. This has not proven to be an issue in Canada post-*JA* and certainly not one that outweighs the risks to women posed by men who prey on them while intoxicated or otherwise incapacitated.

70 "Terms & Conditions / User Agreement," xHamster, accessed 23 November 2023, xhamster.com/info/terms.

71 "Her Wake Up Call," xHamster.

72 See, for example, Lori E. Shaw, "Title IX, Sexual Assault, and the Issue of Effective Consent: Blurred Lines – When Should Yes Mean No," *Indiana Law Journal* 91, no. 4 (2016): 1363; Bryan Birtles, "On Sexual Consent in Canada: The Balance Between Protecting and Respecting Sexual Autonomy," *Western Journal of Legal Studies* 10, no. 2 (2020): 1.

73 "Her Wake Up Call," xHamster.

74 Ibid.

75 Ibid.

76 "Wake Up Sis," xHamster.

77 Ibid. (accessed 20 September 2022).

78 Ibid.

79 Testimony of Feras Antoon, *Evidence*, 11.

80 Angela C. Davis et al., "What Behaviors Do Young Heterosexual Australians See in Pornography? A Cross-Sectional Study," *Journal of Sex Research* 55, no. 3 (2018): 315.

81 Vera-Gray et al., "Sexual Violence," 1254–5. See also Davis et al., "What Behaviors Do," 317 (it is not clear whether there was a distinction made between fictional and real in this study).

82 See, for example, Nicholas Kristof, "The Children of Pornhub," *New York*

Times, 6 December 2020, www.nytimes.com/2020/12/04/opinion/sunday/
pornhub-rape-trafficking.html; Ashley Belanger, "Popular Porn Site Must
Delete All Amateur Videos Posted without Consent," *Ars Technica*, 12 April
2023, https://arstechnica.com/tech-policy/2023/04/popular-porn-site-must-
delete-all-amateur-videos-posted-without-consent.

83   *Serena Fleites et al. v MindGeek SARL et al.* (2021), 617 F Supp 3d 1146 (Statement of Claim), para. 230.

84   Ibid., para. 323.

85   Ibid., para. 230.

86   Ibid., para. 231.

87   United States Department of Justice, Press Release, CAS21-0614-Garcia,
"Twenty Year Sentence in GirlsDoPorn Sex Trafficking Conspiracy," US
Department of Justice, 14 June 2021, https://www.justice.gov/usao-sdca/
pr/twenty-year-sentence-girlsdoporn-sex-trafficking-conspiracy.

88   Samantha Cole and Emanuel Maiberg, "Pornhub Doesn't Care," *Vice*, 6
February 2020, https://www.vice.com/en/article/9393zp/how-pornhub-
moderation-works-girls-do-porn; *Doe v Mindgeek USA Inc*, 558 F Supp (3d)
828 (Cal Dist Ct 2021), para. 111 (Statement of Claim) submitted by Brian
M Holm, https://www.documentcloud.org/documents/20425190-mind
geekjanedoes1-40; Samantha Cole and Emanuel Maiberg, "How Pornhub
Enables Doxing and Harassment," *Vice*, 16 July 2019, https://www.vice.
com/en/article/mb8zjn/pornhub-doxing-and-harassment-girls-do-
porn-lawsuit.

89   Cass Sunstein coined the term "norm entrepreneur" in "Social Norms and
Social Roles," *Columbia Law Review* 96, no. 4 (1996): 909, to describe those
who take advantage of the fragility (manipulability?) of our social condition – a fragility caused by our reliance on social norms and their suscepti-
bility to norm cascades and norm bandwagons – to pursue change.
Entrepreneurship does not always result in positive change.

90   "Pornhub Offers Free Pornhub Premium," Pornhub (see note 38).

91   Hannah Price, "Coronavirus: 'Revenge Porn' Surge Hits Helpline," BBC,
25 April 2020, www.bbc.com/news/stories-52413994.

92   Ibid.

93   Suzie Dunn, Tracy Vaillancourt, and Heather Brittain, "Supporting Safer
Digital Spaces," Centre for International Governance Innovation, 8 June
2023, 23, https://www.cigionline.org/publications/supporting-safer-digital-
spaces.

94   Pornhub has become somewhat known for these types of publicity strategies.

In 2019 the platform launched a campaign to raise awareness around de-
clining bee populations and raise money for bee conservation. See Curtis
Silver, "Pornhub's Beesexual Campaign Buzzes with Beerotica to Help Save
the Bees," *Forbes*, 16 April 2019, www.forbes.com/sites/curtissilver/2019/
04/16/pornhub-beesexual. See also "Beesexual," Pornhub, www.pornhub.
com/cares/beesexual. In 2017 Pornhub announced that it would use a fleet
of Pornhub trucks to plow snow in Boston during and following a major
snowstorm – promising to help anyone who wanted to "get plowed." See
Spencer Buell, "Pornhub Says It Will Plow Snow in Boston for Free," *Boston
Magazine*, 13 March 2017, www.bostonmagazine.com/news/2017/03/13/
pornhub-snow-plow-boston.

95   "Pornhub Offers Free Pornhub Premium," Pornhub.

96   Price, "Coronavirus."

97   See, for example, Asia A. Eaton et al., "Nonconsensual Porn as a Form of
Intimate Partner Violence: Using the Power and Control Wheel to Understand Nonconsensual Porn Perpetration in Intimate Relationships,"
Trauma, Violence and Abuse 22, no. 5 (2021): 1140 (demonstrating that the
non-consensual distribution of intimate images in the context of intimate
relationships is commonly perpetrated through relational abuse tactics,
including most commonly emotional abuse, coercion and threats, and
denial/blame and minimization); Asia A. Eaton and Clare McGlynn, "The
Psychology of Nonconsensual Porn: Understanding and Addressing a
Growing Form of Sexual Violence," *Policy Insights from Behavioral and
Brain Sciences* 7, no. 2 (2020): 192 (reviewing the psychology literature on
non-consensual distribution of intimate images and the finding that the
non-consensual distribution of intimate images is often perpetrated in
the context of current or former intimate partner relationships).

98   Nick Stripe, "Domestic Abuse During the Coronavirus (COVID-19) Pandemic, England and Wales: November 2020," Office for National Statistics,
25 November 2020, www.ons.gov.uk/peoplepopulationandcommunity/cri
meandjustice/articles/domesticabuseduringthecoronaviruscovid19pande
micenglandandwales/november2020 (noting an increase in calls received by
London police and increased demand for services from victims of intimate
partner violence); Jeffrey Kluger, "Domestic Violence Is a Pandemic Within
the COVID-19 Pandemic," *Time*, 3 February 2021, time.com/5928539/do
mestic-violence-covid-19 (discussing the ways in which the COVID-19 pandemic has exacerbated domestic violence during the pandemic); Nicole

Thomson, "Reports of Domestic, Intimate Partner Violence Continue to Rise During Pandemic," CBC, 15 February 2021, www.cbc.ca/news/canada/toronto/domestic-intimate-partner-violence-up-in-pandemic-1.5914344 (noting that in Canada, seventeen police forces across the country reported that calls related to "domestic disturbances" rose by 12 per cent between March and June 2020).

99 See, for example, Anthony Morgan and Hayley Boxall, "Social Isolation, Time Spent at Home, Financial Stress and Domestic Violence during the COVID-19 Pandemic," *Trends and Issues in Crime and Justice* 609 (2020): 1 (concluding "that the pandemic was associated with an increased risk of violence against women in current cohabiting relationships, most likely from a combination of economic stress and social isolation"); Louis-Phillippe Béland et al., "Determinants of Family Stress and Domestic Violence: Lessons from the COVID-19 Outbreak," *Canadian Public Policy* 47, no. 3 (2021): 454 (finding that the "inability to meet financial obligations and concerns about maintaining social ties during Covid-19 [were] significantly related to concerns about family stress and domestic violence"); Mathew P. Crayne, "The Traumatic Impact of Job Loss and Job Search in the Aftermath of COVID-19," *Psychological Trauma: Theory Research Practice and Policy* 12, no. 1 (2020): 180 (documenting the stress caused by job loss during the pandemic).

100 Eaton and McGlynn, "Psychology," 192 (reviewing psychological literature on the social, emotional, physical, and economic trauma some victims of non-consensual distribution of intimate images experience) (see note 97).

101 Testimony of Serena Fleites, House of Commons, Standing Committee on Access to Information, Privacy and Ethics, *Evidence*, 43-2, No. 18 (1 February 2021); Testimony of John Clark, House of Commons, Standing Committee on Access to Information, Privacy and Ethics, *Evidence*, 43-2, No. 21 (22 February 2021). Convened in response to Kristof, "The Children of Pornhub."

102 Testimony of Serena Fleites, *Evidence*, 2.

103 "Our Commitment to Trust and Safety," Pornhub, accessed 3 April 2023, help.pornhub.com/hc/en-us/categories/360002934613; Russell Brandom, "Pornhub Limits Uploads and Disables Downloads after New York Times Exposé," *Verge*, 8 December 2020, www.theverge.com/2020/12/8/22164031/pornhub-upload-limit-blocked-download-nyt-kristof-child-abuse (reporting on the timeline of Pornhub's policy changes and the *New York Times* article).

104 Samantha Cole, "Pornhub Just Purged All Un-verified Content from the
     Platform," *Vice*, 14 December 2020, https://www.vice.com/en/article/jgqjjy/
     pornhub-suspended-all-unverified-videos-content.

105 Testimony of Michael Bowe, House of Commons, Standing Committee on
     Access to Information, Privacy and Ethics, *Evidence*, 43-2, No. 18 (1 Febru-
     ary 2021), 3.

106 Ibid.

107 Ibid.

108 "Pornhub stands in solidarity," Pornhub (see note 38).

109 "Black Lives Matter" (video), Pornhub, search conducted 7 January 2022.

110 "Black Lives Matter Pornhub," Google, search conducted 14 December 2021.

111 "Sexy Cotton Picking Field Slave Gets Fucked for Freedom" (video), Porn-
     hub, accessed 16 May 2022, (17,200 views, 74 per cent approval rating).

112 "Thick White Girl Getting Stuffed with BBC Black Lives Matter!" (video),
     Pornhub, accessed 16 May 2022 (2,100 views, 84 per cent approval rating).

113 Ibid.

114 Carolyn West and Stephany Powell, "Confronting Racism in the Pornog-
     raphy Industry," *Newsweek*, 17 June 2021, www.newsweek.com/confronting-
     racism-pornography-industry-opinion-1601228 (noting the long-standing
     anti-Black racism in pornography).

115 Heather Berg, *Porn Work: Sex, Labor and Late Capitalism* (Chapel Hill: Uni-
     versity of North Carolina Press, 2021), 114, 117; Shira Tarrant, *The Pornog-
     raphy Industry: What Everyone Needs to Know* (Oxford: Oxford University
     Press, 2016), 98; Mireille Miller-Young, *A Taste for Brown Sugar: Black
     Women in Pornography* (Durham: Duke University Press, 2015) (examining
     the representation of Black women in sexually explicit material as well as
     an examination of the challenges faced by Black women in the porn indus-
     try). See also Niki Fritz et al., "Worse than Objects: The Depiction of Black
     Women and Men and Their Sexual Relationship in Pornography," *Gender
     Issues* 38, no 1 (2020): 100.

116 Jennifer C. Nash, "Strange Bedfellows: Black Feminism and Antipornog-
     raphy Feminism," in *New Views on Pornography: Sexuality, Politics and the
     Law*, eds Lynn Comella and Shira Tarrant (Santa Barbara: Praeger, 2015),
     100.

117 Ibid.

118 Ibid., 101.

119 See Jennifer Nash, *The Black Body in Ecstasy: Reading Race, Reading
     Pornography* (Durham: Duke University Press, 2014).

120 Nash, "Strange Bedfellows."

121 See, for example, Patricia Hill Collins, "Pornography and Black Women's Bodies," in *Making Violence Sexy: Feminist Views on Pornography*, ed. Diana E. Russell (New York: Teachers College Press, 1993), 98.

122 Miller-Young, *A Taste*.

123 Angela Jones, *Camming: Money, Power and Pleasure in the Sex Work Industry* (New York: NYU Press, 2020), 193.

124 Berg, *Porn Work*, 57–8.

125 Mireille Miller-Young, "Race and the Politics of Agency in Porn: A Conversation with Black BBW Performer Betty Blac," in *New Views on Pornography: Sexuality, Politics and the Law*, eds Lynn Comella and Shira Tarrant (Santa Barbara: Praeger, 2015), 362.

126 Berg, *Porn Work*, 53.

127 Ibid.

128 Ibid., 55.

129 Ibid., 32, 116.

130 Miller-Young, "Race and Politics of Agency," 360–2.

131 "Ebony," Pornhub, search conducted 15 December 2021.

132 "2021 Year in Review," Pornhub, 14 December 2021, www.pornhub.com /insights/yir-2021.

133 West and Powell, "Confronting Racism."

134 "Hate Speech Policy," Pornhub, accessed 3 April 2023, https://help.porn hub.com/hc/en-us/articles/14512634908819-Hate-Speech-Policy.

135 Ibid.

136 Samantha Cole, *How Sex Changed the Internet and the Internet Changed Sex: An Unexpected History* (New York: Workman Publishing, 2022).

137 Henry Ajder et al., "The State of Deepfakes: Landscape, Threats, and Impact," *Deeptrace*, September 2019, https://regmedia.co.uk/2019/10/08/deep fake_report.pdf. For a discussion of the use of this technology to perpetrate gender-based harm, see Suzie Dunn, "Identity Manipulation: Responding to Advances in Artificial Intelligence and Robotics" (paper delivered at We-Robot Ottawa, 4 April 2020), 10 [unpublished], https://digitalcommons.

138 See, for example, Noelle Martin, "Online Predators Spread Fake Porn of Me. Here's How I Fought Back," TED Talk, 13 February 2020, https://www.ted. com/talks/noelle_martin_online_predators_spread_fake_porn_of_me_her e_s_how_i_fought_back; Karen Hao, "Deepfake Porn Is Ruining Women's Lives: Now the Law May Finally Ban It," *MIT Technology Review*, 12 February 2021, https://www.technologyreview.com/2021/02/12/1018222/deepfake-

revenge-porn-coming-ban. See, generally, Danielle Keats Citron and Mary Anne Franks, "Criminalizing Revenge Porn," *Wake Forest Law Review* 49, no. 2 (2014): 345; Danielle Citron, *Hate Crimes in Cyberspace* (Cambridge, MA: Harvard University Press, 2014).

139   Canadian Press, "Weeks after Posting Haunting YouTube Video on Her Years of Torment at Classmates' Hands, 15-Year-Old BC Girl Commits Suicide," *National Post*, 12 October 2012, https://nationalpost.com/news/canada/amanda-todd-suicide-2012; "RCMP Probes Online Links to Teen's Suicide," CBC News, 12 October 2012, http://www.cbc.ca/news/canada/british-columbia/rcmp-probes-online-links-to-teen-s-suicide-1.1141477; "Rape, Bullying Led to NS Teen's Death, Says Mom," CBC News, 12 April 2013, https://www.cbc.ca/news/canada/nova-scotia/rape-bullying-led-to-n-s-teen-s-death-says-mom-1.1370780.

140   Alexa Dodge, "Deleting Digital Harm: A Review of Nova Scotia's Cyber-Scan Unit," VAW Learning Network, August 2021, 4, 26, https://www.vawlearningnetwork.ca/docs/CyberScan-Report.pdf (finding that while many victims did not want to seek civil or criminal legal recourse, the thing of utmost importance to them was to have the content removed from online expeditiously). See Hilary Young and Emily Laidlaw, "Creating a Revenge Porn Tort for Canada," *Supreme Court Law Review* 96, no. 2 (2020): 147.

141   See Rana Ayyub, "I Was the Victim of a Deepfake Porn Plot Intended to Silence Me," *Huffington Post*, 21 November 2018), https://www.huffingtonpost.co.uk/entry/deepfakeporn_uk_5bf2c126e4b0f32bd58ba316.

142   Dunn, "Identity Manipulation," 10.

143   Jane Bailey et al., "AI and Technology-Facilitated Violence and Abuse," in *Artificial Intelligence and the Law in Canada* (Toronto: LexisNexis Canada, 2021). See also Cynthia Khoo, "Deplatforming Misogyny," LEAF, 2021, 35, https://www.leaf.ca/publication/deplatforming-misogyny (observing that the type of misogyny reflected in technology-facilitated gender-based violence generally is also more likely to be racist, ableist, and homophobic).

144   Samantha Cole, "Pornhub Is Banning AI-Generated Fake Porn Videos, Says They're Nonconsensual," *Vice*, 6 February 2018, https://www.vice.com/en/article/zmwvdw/pornhub-bans-deepfakes; Alex Hern, "Deepfake Face-Swap Porn Videos Banned by Pornhub and Twitter," *Guardian*, 7 February 2018, https://www.theguardian.com/technology/2018/feb/07/twitter-pornhub-ban-deepfake-ai-face-swap-porn-videos-celebrities-gfycat-reddit.

145   Cole, "Pornhub Is Banning."

146   Ibid.

147 Ibid.

148 Ibid.

149 "2019 Year in Review," Pornhub, 11 December 2019, www.pornhub.com/insights/2019-year-in-review.

150 Ibid.

151 Ibid.

152 Sarah Bain, "ECP Announces Acquisition of MindGeek, Parent Company of Pornhub," Cision, 16 March 2023, https://www.newswire.ca/news-releases/ecp-announces-acquisition-of-mindgeek-parent-company-of-pornhub-842182865.html.

153 Ibid.

154 See Jess Klein, "For Better and for Worse: The 'Playboy Magazine' of the '70s Helped Shape the America of Today," *Outline*, 29 July 2018, theoutline.com/post/5600/for-better-and-for-worse-the-playboy-of-the-70s-helped-shape-the-america-of-today.

155 See Elizabeth Fraterrigo, *Playboy and the Making of the Good Life in Modern America* (Oxford: Oxford University Press, 2009), 4, 11.

156 Klein, "For Better and for Worse."

157 Elizabeth Fraterrigo, "Taking Stock of Playboy Legacy as Hugh Hefner Tries to Buy Back Rest of Company," *Washington Post*, 18 July 2010, www.washingtonpost.com/wp-dyn/content/article/2010/07/16/AR2010071602718.html.

158 See "2019 Year in Review," Pornhub. Pornhub did not release an annual report for 2020 – the year in which the *New York Times* exposé was published. In its 2021 "Year in Review" the company did not include the number of total visits for the year (see "2021 Year in Review," Pornhub). This was the first annual report not to include this data.

159 Van Dijck, Poell, and de Waal, *Platform Society*, 50 (observing that Facebook has "repeatedly emphasized that its prime objective is to connect users with posts from their friends and family"). See also Mike Isaac, "Facebook Overhauls News Feed to Focus on What Friends and Family Share," *New York Times*, 11 January 2018, www.nytimes.com/2018/01/11/technology/facebook-news-feed.html; Tarleton Gillespie, "The Politics of 'Platforms,'" *New Media and Society* 12, no. 3 (2010): 348; Testimony of Feras Antoon, *Evidence*, 1.

160 Gillespie, "Platforms," 205.

161 The Dick Cavett Show, "Hugh Hefner Clashes With Feminists" (video), YouTube, 28 February 2020, 00h:08m:00s, www.youtube.com/watch?v=5BXALFRMpCw.

162 Klein, "For Better."

163 Testimony of David Tassillo, House of Commons, Standing Committee on Access to Information, Privacy and Ethics, *Evidence*, 43-2, No. 19 (5 February 2021), 10.

164 "Terms and Conditions," xHamster.

165 Susanna Paasonen, Kylie Jarrett, and Ben Light, #NSFW: *Sex, Humor, and Risk in Social Media* (Cambridge, MA: MIT Press, 2019), 55.

166 See, for example, Mary Ann Watson and Randyl D. Smith, "Positive Porn: Educational, Medical, and Clinical Uses," *American Journal of Sexuality Education* 7, no. 2 (2012): 127; Emily F. Rothman et al., "'Without Porn … I Wouldn't Know Half the Things I Know Now': A Qualitative Study of Pornography Use among a Sample of Urban, Low-Income, Black and Hispanic Youth," *Journal of Sex Research* 52, no. 7 (2015): 736; Emily F. Rothman and Avanti Adhia, "Adolescent Pornography Use and Dating Violence among a Sample of Primarily Black and Hispanic, Urban-Residing, Underage Youth," *Behavioural Sciences* 6, no. 1 (2015): 1. For journalistic support for this claim, see Peggy Orenstein, *Girls and Sex: Navigating the Complicated New Landscape* (New York: Harper Collins, 2016), 46.

167 Srinivasan, *Right to Sex*, 44.

168 Ibid.

169 Rothman et al., "'Without Porn,'" 740.

170 Ibid.

171 See, for example, Vlad Burtăverde et al., "Why Do People Watch Porn? An Evolutionary Perspective on the Reasons for Pornography Consumption," *Evolutionary Psychology* 19, no. 2 (2021): 10 (finding that reasons commonly included sexual gratification, and social motivations such as acceptance among one's peer group). See Rothman et al., "'Without Porn,'" 740.

172 Curtis Silver, "Pornhub 2017 Year in Review Insights Report Reveals Statistical Proof We Love Porn," *Forbes*, 9 January 2018, www.forbes.com/sites/curtissilver/2018/01/09/pornhub-2017-year-in-review-insights-report-reveals-statistical-proof-we-love-porn; Justine Kirkland, "Pornhub's 2019 Insights Show That When the Going Gets Tough, People Watch Porn," *Esquire*, 19 February 2019, www.esquire.com/lifestyle/sex/a26409934/porn-trends-government-shutdown-winter; Zachary Zane, "Pornhub Just Dropped Some VERY Interesting Stats About Women's Porn Habits," *Men's Health*, 11 December 2019, www.menshealth.com/sex-women/a30171574/pornhub-year-in-review-2019.

173 Cincinnati City Beat Staff, "Pornhub's 2019 Year-in-Review Reveals Ohio

Women Are Way into Feet Porn," *Cleveland Scene*, 16 December 2019, www.clevescene.com/news/pornhubs-2019-year-in-review-reveals-ohio-women-are-way-into-feet-porn-31963547.

174   Harrison Abott, "Pornhub Reveals Gen Z, Millennials and Boomers' Search Behaviour in 2021 Review," *Newsweek*, 14 December 2021, www.newsweek.com/pornhub-year-review-gen-z-millennials-boomers-1658787.

175   Jane Bailey made a similar observation regarding the online interaction, including mutual affirmation for the "rightness" of what they were doing, among a community of offenders created virtually in the context of child pornography consumers, in "Confronting Collective Harm: Technology's Transformative Impact on Child Pornography," *University of New Brunswick Law Journal* 56 (2007): 96.

176   Van Dijck, Poell, and de Waal, *Platform Society*, 4–5.

CHAPTER FOUR

1   See Fiona Vera-Gray et al., "Sexual Violence as a Sexual Script in Mainstream Online Pornography," *British Journal of Criminology* 61, no. 5 (2021): 1243 (drawing sexual script theory and cultural criminology together in consideration of pornography's relationship to sexual violence).

2   John Gagnon and William Simon, *Sexual Conduct: The Social Sources of Human Sexuality* (Chicago: Aldine Publishing Company, 1973), 261.

3   See Susan Bordo, "Feminism, Foucault and the Politics of the Body," in *Up Against Foucault: Explorations of Some Tensions Between Foucault and Feminism*, ed. Caroline Ramazanoglu (London and New York: Routledge, 1993), 185 (discussing feminist contributions to theoretical thinking on the relationship between power, discourse, and constructions of the body historically). See also Carole S. Vance, "Social Construction Theory: Problems in the History of Sexuality," in *Homosexuality, Which Homosexuality?* Dennis Altman et al. (Amsterdam and London: An Dekker/Schorer and GMP Publishers, 1989), 13; Michel Foucault, *The History of Sexuality*, vol. 1 (London: Allen Lane, 1979).

4   Gagnon and Simon, *Sexual Conduct*, 262; See also Nicola Gavey, *Just Sex? The Cultural Scaffolding of Rape*, 2nd ed. (New York: Routledge, 2018), 75–96 (provides a helpful overview of the key theoretical claims poststructuralists make, in chapter 3 of her book).

5   Vera-Gray et al., "Sexual Violence," 1244.

6   Michael W. Wiederman, "Sexual Script Theory: Past, Present and Future," in *Handbook of the Sociology of Sexualities*, eds John DeLamater and Re-

becca F. Plante (Switzerland: Springer, 2015), 7, citing William Simon, *Post-modern Sexualities* (London: Routledge, 1996). See also William Simon and John Gagnon, "Sexual Scripts," *Society* 22, no. 1 (1984): 53.

7   Wiederman, "Sexual Script Theory," 7.

8   Ibid., 8.

9   "Thinking Sex: Notes for a Radical Theory of the Politics of Sexuality," in *Culture, Society, and Sexuality*, eds Peter Aggleton and Richard Parker (London and New York: Routledge, 1998), 149.

10 Vera-Gray et al., "Sexual Violence," 1244.

11 Ibid., 1244.

12 For research that relies on sexual script theory and individual sexual behaviours, see, for example, Dan J. Miller, Kerry Anne Mcbain, and Peter T.F. Raggat, "An Experimental Investigation Into Pornography's Effect on Men's Perceptions of the Likelihood of Women Engaging in Porn-Like Sex," *Psychology of Popular Media Culture* 8, no. 4 (2019): 365; Scott R. Braithwaite et al., "Is Pornography Consumption Associated with Condom Use and Intoxication During Hookups?," *Culture, Health and Sexuality* 17, no. 10 (2015): 1155; Meagan J. Brem et al., "Problematic Pornography Use and Physical and Sexual Intimate Partner Violence Perpetration Among Men in Batterer Intervention Programs," *Journal of Interpersonal Violence* 36, nos. 11–12 (2021): 6085; Debby Herbenick et al., "Diverse Sexual Behaviours and Pornography Use: Findings from a Nationally Representative Probability Survey of Americans Aged 18 to 60 Years," *Journal of Sexual Medicine* 17, no. 4 (2020): 623.

13 Vera-Gray et al., "Sexual Violence," 1244.

14 Ibid.

15 Ibid.

16 Ibid. See also Fiona Vera-Gray, "The Authority of Pornography," in Adele Bardazzi and Alberica Bazzoni, eds, *Gender and Authority across Disciplines, Space and Time* (Cham: Palgrave Macmillan, 2020), 291.

17 Vera-Gray et al., "Sexual Violence," 1244.

18 Ibid., 1244.

19 José van Dijck, Thomas Poell, and Martijn de Waal, *The Platform Society: Public Values in a Connective World* (New York: Oxford University Press, 2018), 24.

20 Ibid., 34.

21 Ibid.

22 Ibid., 11.

23 Ibid., 2.

24 Ibid., 24.

25 Ibid., 5.

26 Ibid., 11.

27 Tarleton Gillespie, "Platforms Are Not Intermediaries," *Georgetown Law Technology Review* 2, no. 2 (2018): 198.

28 Ibid., 210–11.

29 Catharine A. MacKinnon, *Only Words* (Cambridge, MA: Harvard University Press, 1993), 15.

30 Catharine A. MacKinnon, "OnlyFans Is Not a Safe Platform for 'Sex Work.' It's a Pimp," *New York Times*, 6 September 2021, www.nytimes.com/2021/09/06/opinion/onlyfans-sex-work-safety.html.

31 MacKinnon, *Only Words*; Catharine A. MacKinnon, *Toward A Feminist Theory of the State* (Cambridge, MA: Harvard University Press, 1989), 204.

32 Amia Srinivasan, *The Right to Sex: Feminism in the Twenty-First Century* (New York: Farrar, Straus and Giroux, 2021), 42.

33 Ibid., 39–40: "But what if the true significance of the perspective of anti-porn feminists lay not in what they were paying attention to but when? What if they weren't hysterical, but prescient?"

34 Ibid., 42.

35 Ibid. (discussing Ronald Dworkin's critique of *Only Words*).

36 Ronald Dworkin, "Women and Pornography," book review of *Only Words* by Catharine A. MacKinnon, *New York Review of Books*, 21 October 1993, www.nybooks.com/articles/1993/10/21/women-and-pornography.

37 Srinivasan, *Right to Sex*, 42.

38 See Eran Shor and Kimberly Seida, *Aggression in Pornography: Myths and Realities* (London and New York: Routledge, 2021), 12; Phil Lord, "Pornhub: Opening the Floodgates?," *Houston Law Review, Off the Record* 11, no. 2 (2020): 54 (asserting that Pornhub receives more visitors every day than Amazon).

39 Evangelos Tziallas, "Pornophilia: Porn Gifs, Fandom, Circuitries," *Porn Studies* 3, no. 3 (2016): 311.

40 MacKinnon, *Only Words*, 15.

41 Ibid., 21.

42 Ibid.

43 Ibid., 17.

44 Carlin Romano, "Between the Motion and the Act," book review of *Only Words* by Catharine A. MacKinnon, *Nation* 25, no. 6 (1993): 563.

45 Ibid.

46 George F. Will, "Pornography Scare," *Washington Post*, 28 October 1993, www.washingtonpost.com/archive/opinions/1993/10/28/pornography-scare/01851eba-3587-4692-87f7-71b04d5d9df8.

47 Richard Posner, "Obsession," book review of *Only Words* by Catharine A. MacKinnon, *New Republic* 209, no. 16 (1993): 36, 31.

48 Dworkin, "Women and Pornography."

49 Calvin Woodard, "Speak No Evil," book review of *Only Words* by Catharine A. MacKinnon, *New York Times*, 2 January 1994, www.nytimes.com/1994/01/02/books/speak-no-evil.html; Posner, "Obsession"; Romano, "Between the Motion."

50 Mim Udovitch, "Imagine That," *Village Voice* 39, no. 4 (1994): 19, cited in David Dinielli, book review of *Only Words* by Catharine A. MacKinnon, *Michigan Law Review* 92, no. 6 (1994): 1943n10.

51 MacKinnon rejected this concern on the basis that there are many examples of words that are treated as acts in law and thus not subject to the protections of the First Amendment: for example, "I do" and "not guilty" are treated (in law) as the institutions and practices they constitute, rather than expressions of the ideas they embody, she argued (see MacKinnon, *Only Words*, 12–13). She noted other legal contexts in which the words constitute the act: "help wanted – male," "whites only," or "fuck me or you're fired" are treated in law as more than their meaning; uttering them constitutes acts of discrimination (MacKinnon, *Only Words*, 13–14). She also rejected the absolutist position on freedom of speech adopted by defenders of pornography as itself an articulation of gender inequality because of the manner in which porn silences women.

52 See, for example, Kate Manne, *Down Girl: The Logic of Misogyny* (New York: Oxford University Press, 2018), 163.

53 See, for example, Lyn Harrison and Debbie Ollis, "Young People, Pleasure, and the Normalization of Pornography: Sexual Health and Well-Being in a Time of Proliferation?," in *Handbook of Children and Youth Studies*, eds Johanna Wyn and Helen Cahill (Singapore: Springer, 2015), 155 (suggesting the average age of exposure [either voluntary or accidental] to online pornography in the United States is eleven years); An-Sing Chen et al., "Exposure to Internet Pornography among Taiwanese Adolescents," *Social Behaviour and Personality* 41, no. 1 (2013): 157 (finding that 71 per cent of Taiwanese adolescents were exposed); Mathias Weber, Oliver Quiring, and Gregor Daschmann, "Peers, Parents, and Pornography: Exploring Adoles-

cents' Exposure to Sexually Explicit Material and its Developmental Correlates," *Sexuality and Culture* 16, no. 4 (2012): 417 (finding that 93 per cent of
adolescent boys and 52 per cent of adolescent girls had watched pornography). See also Peter Jochen and Patti M. Valkenburg, "Adolescents and
Pornography: A Review of 20 Years of Research," *Journal of Sex Research* 53,
nos. 4–5 (2016): 509 (meta-study which identified significant range in findings regarding the prevalence of pornography consumption by adolescents). See, for example, David Loftus, *Watching Sex: How Men Really
Respond to Pornography* (New York: Thunders Mouth Press, 2002), 246–50.

54 "Terms & Conditions / User Agreement," xHamster, accessed 23 November
2023, xhamster.com/info/terms.

55 To be clear, MacKinnon did not propose that all pornography should be
censored. The so-called Dworkin–MacKinnon Porn Ordinances targeted
pornography that was degrading to women. MacKinnon drew a distinction
between pornography, which she defined as the sexually explicit subordination of women and erotica (sexually explicit materials premised on equality). See Catharine A. MacKinnon, *Feminism Unmodified: Discourses on Life
and Law* (Cambridge, MA: Harvard University Press, 1987), 176. See also
Robin Morgan, *Going Too Far: The Personal Chronicle of a Feminist*, 1st ed.
(New York: Vintage Books USA, 1978), 169.

56 See Carolyn Bronstein, "Clashing at Barnard's Gates: Understanding the
Origins of the Pornography Problem in the Modern American Women's
Movement," in *New Views on Pornography: Sexuality, Politics and the Law*,
eds Lynn Comella and Shira Tarrant (Santa Barbara: Praeger, 2015), 57
(examining the schism in the American feminist movement that crystalized
around the time of New York City's Barnard College annual Feminist Conference in 1982); Mireille Miller-Young, "Race and the Politics of Agency in
Porn: A Conversation with Black BBW Performer Betty Blac," in *New Views
on Pornography: Sexuality, Politics and the Law*, eds Lynn Comella and Shira
Tarrant (Santa Barbara: Praeger, 2015), 359 (for a brief history of events
leading up to the Barnard Conference); Alice Echols, "Retrospective:
Tangled Up in Pleasure and Danger," *Journal of Women in Culture and Society* 42, no. 1 (2016): 11; Elizabeth Wilson, "The Context of 'Between Pleasure and Danger': The Barnard Conference on Sexuality," *Feminist Review*
13, no. 1 (1983): 35. Wilson describes the clash between American feminists
over the issue of pornography – particularly between anti-porn scholars
who were largely excluded and others – that erupted/cohered at the time of
the conference, contrasting it to some extent with feminist movements in

Britain at the time. She goes on to describe some of the themes around women's sexual pleasure that were explored. Arguably, many of the questions and themes raised – particularly regarding heterosexual women's pleasure – remain central issues of dispute among feminists today.

57 See generally Patricia Hill Collins, *Black Feminist Thought: Knowledge, Consciousness and the Politics of Empowerment* (Boston: Unwin Hyman, 1990); Patricia J. Williams, *The Alchemy of Race and Rights* (Cambridge, Mass: Harvard University Press, 1991).

58 See, for example, Susan Stryker, "Stray Thoughts on Transgender Feminism and the Barnard Conference on Women," *Communication Review* 11, no. 3 (2008): 217 (documenting the exclusion of trans women from the women's movement in the 1970s and the opportunities that were opened up for their inclusion as a consequence of the porn debates).

59 MacKinnon, *Only Words*, 21.

60 Antoine Mazieres et al., "Deep Tags: Toward a Quantitative Analysis of Online Pornography," *Porn Studies* 1, nos. 1–2 (2014): 82 (discussing the popularity of platforms that "enable direct interaction between pornographic actors and viewers"); Heather Berg, *Porn Work: Sex, Labor, and Late Capitalism* (Chapel Hill: University of North Carolina Press, 2021), 102; Shira Tarrant, *The Pornography Industry: What Everyone Needs to Know* (New York: Oxford University Press, 2016), 54; Emily van der Nagel, "Competing Platform Imaginaries of NSFW Content Creation on OnlyFans," *Porn Studies* 8, no. 4 (2021): 397. See also Kavita I. Nayar, "Working It: The Professionalization of Amateurism in Digital Adult Entertainment," *Feminist Media Studies* 17, no. 3 (2017): 473 (discussing, in part, the way in which some women who engage in camming develop ongoing relationships with users as part of their strategy to earn income).

61 Angela Jones, *Camming: Money, Power and Pleasure in the Sex Work Industry* (New York: New York University Press, 2020), 41.

62 Ibid.

63 Van der Nagel, "Competing Platform Imaginaries," 395–6.

64 Berg, *Porn Work*, 14–15, 97. See also Susanna Paasonen, Kylie Jarrett, and Ben Light, *#NSFW: Sex, Humor, and Risk in Social Media* (Cambridge, MA: MIT Press, 2019), 58.

65 Mireille Miller-Young, "Race and the Politics of Agency in Porn: A Conversation with Black BBW Performer Betty Blac," in *New Views on Pornography: Sexuality, Politics and the Law*, eds Lynn Comella and Shira Tarrant (Santa Barbara: Praeger, 2015), 361 (noting that porn does not pay as well as it did in earlier eras).

66 See van der Nagel, "Competing Platform Imaginaries," 395 (noting that the practices of camming and producing pornographic content for the platform OnlyFans overlap).

67 The sexual interactions made possible by webcam technology, and camming platforms, makes untenable the distinction that was sometimes drawn by lawmakers between "live sex shows" (which were prohibited) and pornographic films (which were not prohibited). For a discussion distinguishing between the latter two by the United Kingdom's 1970s Committee on Obscenity and Film Censorship, chaired by Bernard Williams, see *Obscenity and Film Censorship: An Abridgement of the Williams Report*, quoted in Frances Ferguson, "Pornography: The Theory," *Spring Critical Inquiry* 21, no. 3 (1995): 684–5.

68 Jones, *Camming*.

69 Henry Jenkins, Sam Ford, and Joshua Green, *Spreadable Media: Creating Value and Meaning in a Networked Culture* (New York: NYU Press, 2013), 2 (the term was originally coined by Henry Jenkins in 1992 to describe so-called fan communities, but has been expanded since then to include different types of groups and to capture the ways in which networked communities today shape and reshape media (Jones, *Camming*).

70 See Joseph Brennan, "Microporn in the Digital Media Age: Fantasy Out of Context," *Porn Studies* 5, no. 2 (2018): 152. See also Aster Gilbert, "Sissy Remixed: Trans* Porno Remix and Constructing the Trans* Subject," *Transgender Studies Quarterly* 7, no. 2 (2020): 222.

71 Brennan, "Microporn," 152.

72 Katrin Tiidenberg and Emily van der Nagel, *Sex and Social Media* (Bingley, UK: Emerald Publishing, 2020), 92.

73 Brennan, "Microporn," 152. A gif is a short (usually only a few seconds), moving image taken from a longer video file that continuously loops.

74 Helen Hester, Bethan Jones, and Sarah Taylor-Harman, "Giffing a Fuck: Non-Narrative Pleasures in Participatory Porn Cultures and Female Fandom," *Porn Studies* 2, no. 4 (2015): 361. While the authors suggest that user-generated (micro)porn in the form of gifs might offer users the potential to undermine the dominant paradigms in mainstream pornography, they concede that "the space remains dominated by white, able-bodied, heterosexual and cis-gendered bodies" and that 56 per cent of the gifs in their modest quantitative sample were of the same three acts: male-to-female oral, anal, and vaginal penetration (Brennan, "Microporn," 361, 360).

75 "Pornhub Gifs," Pornhub, accessed 27 November 2023, www.pornhub.com/gifs.

76 Berg, *Porn Work*, 95–125.

77 Brennan, "Microporn," 152.

78 Ibid., 152–3. Brennan distinguishes the original video by describing it as commercial and by describing the site it was originally posted on as a commercial website. This is somewhat misleading. While it is true that he is discussing what happens when the excerpt is posted on a free tube site, these free streaming platforms – or "tube sites" – are very much commercial enterprises.

79 Ibid. The term "bareback" refers to the practice of anal sex without a condom. It is typically used in reference to men barebacking other men. For a general examination of bareback culture, see Tim Dean, *Unlimited Intimacy: Reflections on the Subculture of Barebacking* (Chicago: University of Chicago Press, 2009).

80 Gonzo porn refers to a style of pornography, or form of filming, which is typically low budget, without a narrative or plot, graphic, and often made with the use of handheld cameras to create the point-of-view perspective. It is often represented through reliance on the "real sex with real people" discourse, and while it may have originally been associated with amateur porn, professional studios today also produce a great deal of pornography that could be described as gonzo porn. See, generally, Enrico Biasin and Federico Zecca, "Introduction: Inside Gonzo Porn," *Porn Studies* 3, no. 4 (2016): 332; Renato Stella, "The Amateur Roots of Gonzo Pornography," *Porn Studies* 3, no. 4 (2016): 351; Robert Jensen, "Just a John? Pornography and Men's Choices," in *Gender, Sex, and Politics: In the Streets and Between the Sheets in the 21st Century*, ed. Shira Tarrant (New York: Routledge, 2016), 74.

81 Brennan, "Microporn," 154.

82 Ibid., 153.

83 See, for example, Sebastian Meineck and Yannah Alfering, "We Went Undercover in xHamster's Unpaid Content Moderation Team," *Vice*, www.vice.com/en/article/akdzdp/inside-xhamsters-unpaid-content-moderation-team (examining the presence of illegal content on xHamster, including non-consensual voyeur videos). See also Joseph Cox, "Pornhub Is Hosting Illegal Upskirt Videos," *Vice*, 13 June 2018, www.vice.com/en/article/pavv47/pornhub-hosting-illegal-upskirt-videos. The upload verification system adopted by Pornhub in 2021, and discussed in chapter 7, pre-

sumably prevents users from uploading actual hidden camera/upskirting videos to this platform. However, as noted in chapter 8, the fictional depiction of surreptitiously recorded nudity and sexual activity remains readily available on Pornhub.

84 Martin Amis, "Rough Trade," *Guardian*, 17 March 2001, https://www.the guardian.com/books/2001/mar/17/society.martinamis1.

85 Ibid.

86 Ibid.

87 *Serena Fleites et al. v MindGeek SARL et al.* (2021), 617 F Supp 3d 1146 (Statement of Claim, para. 181).

88 Susanna Paasonen, *Carnal Resonance: Affect and Online Pornography* (Cambridge, MA: MIT Press, 2011), 84. See also Shira Tarrant, "Pornography and Pedagogy: Teaching Media Literacy," in *New Views on Pornography: Sexuality, Politics and the Law*, eds Lynn Comella and Shira Tarrant (Santa Barbara: Praeger, 2015), 426 (discussing the distinction between amateur and professional content in the context of porn as pedagogy).

89 Aidan McGlynn, "Blurred Lines: How Fictional Is Pornography?," *Philosophy Compass* 16, no. 4 (2021): 1. See also Paasonen, *Carnal Resonance*, 85.

90 McGlynn, "Blurred Lines," 2.

91 Ibid.

92 Ibid.

93 Ibid.

94 On the issue of genuine female pleasure, mainstream heterosexual porn produced and/or commissioned by large corporations can perhaps be distinguished from that produced by feminist porn producers. See Emily E. Crutcher, "'She's Totally Faking It!': The Politics of Authentic Female Pleasure in Pornography," in *New Views on Pornography: Sexuality, Politics and the Law*, eds Lynn Comella and Shira Tarrant (Santa Barbara: Praeger, 2015), 319. On the difficulty of coding for female orgasm in content-based porn research, see Michaela Lebedíková, "How Much Screaming Is an Orgasm: The Problem with Coding Female Climax," *Porn Studies* 9, no. 2 (2022): 208.

95 For an examination of the cultural anxiety surrounding the realness of female orgasm in porn and generally, see Hannah Frith, "Visualising the 'Real' and the 'Fake': Emotion Work and the Representation of Orgasm in Pornography and Everyday Sexual Interactions," *Journal of Gender Studies* 24, no. 4 (2015): 386.

96 MacKinnon, *Only Words*, 27.

97   See, for example, MacKinnon, *Feminism Unmodified*, 125–214.

98   Alyson Krueger, "Virtual Reality Gets Naughty," *New York Times*, 28 October 2017, www.nytimes.com/2017/10/28/style/virtual-reality-porn.html.

99   India Thusi, "Reality Porn," *New York University Law Review* 96, no. 3 (2021): 772–3.

100 MacKinnon, *Only Words*, 17.

101 "2019 Year in Review," Pornhub, 11 December 2019, www.pornhub.com/insights/2019-year-in-review.

102 Thusi, "Reality Porn," 772–4.

103 Gilad Yadin, "Virtual Reality Exceptionalism," *Vanderbilt Journal of Entertainment and Technology Law* 20 (2018): 865. See also Mel Slater, "Immersion and the Illusion of Presence in Virtual Reality," *British Journal of Psychology* 109, no. 3 (2018): 432.

104 Christine Clarridge and Jennifer Sullivan, "Porn-Star Stalker: Pierce County Man Gets 4-Month Sentence," *Seattle Times*, 27 January 2011, https://www.seattletimes.com/seattle-news/porn-star-stalker-pierce-county-man-gets-4-month-sentence; "*Serena Fleites et al. v MindGeek*," paras 337, 341, 347, 359, 375, 394, 457.

105 See, for example, "*Serena Fleites et al. v MindGeek*."

106 Suzie Dunn, "Technology Facilitated Gender Based Violence: An Overview," Centre for International Governance Innovation: Supporting a Safer Internet Paper No. 1 (2020), 14, https://www.cigionline.org/publications/technology-facilitated-gender-based-violence-overview.

107 Bonnie Ruberg, "Doing It for Free: Digital Labour and the Fantasy of Amateur Online Pornography," *Porn Studies* 3, no. 2 (2016): 147 (discussing the rise in unpaid amateur porn production uploaded to tube sites); Russel Goldman, "Do It Yourself! Amateur Porn Stars Make Bank," *ABC News*, 22 January 2008), abcnews.go.com/Business/SmallBiz/story?id=4151592&page=1.

108 Berg, *Porn Work*, 66 (suggesting that a rise in amateur pornography began in the 1980s).

109 Ibid.

110 Brandon Arroyo, "From Flow to Float: Moving through Porn Tube Sites," *Porn Studies* 3, no. 3 (2016): 309. It is worth noting that the community that Arroyo describes is not a fantasy simply because it exists online, nor is the sense of belonging that this community might foster among users imaginary because their connections with one another are mediated through technology.

111   Ibid.

112   Rishabh Mehrotra and Prasanta Bhattacharya, *Characterizing and Predicting Supply-Side Engagement on Video Sharing Platforms Using a Hawkes Process Model:* Proceedings of the ACM SIGIR International Conference on Theory of Information Retrieval (ACM: 2017), 163.

113   Web 2.0 refers to a set of technological advances that facilitated the ability of users to publish and share content and establish social networks online.

114   Gillespie, "Platforms Are Not Intermediaries," 199–200.

115   Van Dijck, Poell, and de Waal, *Platform Society*, 11.

116   Vera-Gray et al., "Sexual Violence," 1246; Safiya U. Noble, *Algorithms of Oppression: How Search Engines Reinforce Racism* (New York: New York University Press, 2018).

117   Noble, *Algorithms of Oppression*, 140.

118   Ariadna Matamoros-Fernández, "Platformed Racism: The Mediation and Circulation of an Australian Race-Based Controversy on Twitter, Facebook and YouTube," *Information, Communication and Society* 20, no. 3 (2017): 930.

119   See, for example, Tom Simonite, "AI Is the Future – But Where Are the Women?," *Wired*, 17 August 2018, https://www.wired.com/story/artificial-in telligence-researchers-gender-imbalance (reporting that only 12 per cent of computer learning researchers were women and that at Google only 21 per cent of technical roles were filled by women); Cade Metz, "Who Is Making Sure the AI Machines Aren't Racist?," *New York Times*, 15 March 2021, https://www.nytimes.com/2021/03/15/technology/artificial-intelligence-google-bias.html (examining the racism embedded in facial recognition AI); Kate Crawford, "Artificial Intelligence's White Guy Problem," *New York Times*, 25 June 2016, https://www.nytimes.com/2016/06/26/opinion/sunday/artificial-intelligences-white-guy-problem.html (documenting racism and sexism in the way machine learning algorithms were classifying users for purposes of running ads, sorting pictures for camera software, and profiling neighbourhoods).

120   Van Dijck, Poell, and de Waal, *Platform Society*, 33.

121   Ibid., 41: "algorithmic personalization builds on signals of both the individual user as well as larger user aggregates."

122   Ibid., 33.

123   See, for example, "2019 Year in Review," Pornhub.

124   Van Dijck, Poell, and de Waal, *Platform Society*, 40.

125   Luke O'Neil, "Incest Is the Fastest Growing Trend in Porn. Wait, What?," *Esquire*, 28 February 2018, www.esquire.com/lifestyle/sex/a18194469/incest-

porn-trend. See also Jenny Kutner, "Why Do Millennials Love Faux-Incest Porn So Much?," *MIC*, 10 February 2016, www.mic.com/articles/134715/why -do-millennials-love-faux-incest-porn-so-much.

126 "My Step-Father Loves to Fuck Me without Protection" (video), xHamster, accessed 2 June 2022 (71,202 views, 99 per cent approval rating).

127 "Step Father Porn Videos," xHamster, accessed 15 January 2022.

128 "xHamster Signup," xHamster, accessed 15 January 2022, xhamster.com/ signup.

129 "xHamster Signup," xHamster, accessed 8 April 2022; 12 September 2022, xhamster.com/signup.

130 "My Step-Father," xHamster.

131 Ibid.

132 Eran Shor, "Age, Aggression, and Pleasure in Popular Online Pornographic Videos," *Violence Against Women* 25, no. 8 (2019): 1029.

133 Vera-Gray et al., "Sexual Violence," 1248.

134 Ibid.

135 Angela Davis et al., "What Behaviors Do Young Heterosexual Australians See in Pornography? A Cross-Sectional Study," *Journal of Sex Research* 55, no. 3 (2018): 310. Granted, it is not clear in this study whether the subjects were being asked only about content they identified as recordings of actual sexual assaults or all depictions of sexual assault.

136 See Shen-yi Liao and Sara Protasi, "The Fictional Character of Pornography," in *Pornographic Art and the Aesthetics of Pornography*, ed. Hans Maes (New York: Palgrave MacMillan, 2013), 109.

137 "My Step-Father," xHamster.

138 See Gavey, *Just Sex?* This is an example of Gavey's notion of the cultural scaffolding of rape: a script of female resistance "as a faux front that masks [a woman's] real underlying desires" (22).

139 Recall that one of the comments in response to the micro-porn examined by Brennan was by a user who claimed to have "done something similar'" (Brennan, "Microporn," 154).

140 See, for example, "step father daughter," xHamster, search conducted 11 December 2021 (comments on seven xHamster videos on the first page of search results under the categories "step father daughter") at note 142.

141 "Wake Up Sis" (video), xHamster, accessed 2 March 2019 (5,175,278 views, 100 per cent approval rating).

142 See "step father daughter," search, xHamster.

143 Rebecca Inez Saunders, "The Pornographic Paratexts of Pornhub," in

Examining Paratextual Theory and Its Applications in Digital Culture, eds Nadine Desrochers and Daniel Apollon (IGI Global: 2014), 243. Thank you to Ummni Khan for drawing my attention to this article.

144 Ibid., 245.

145 Ibid., 245.

146 Van Dijck, Poell, and de Waal, *Platform Society*, 11. For a discussion of the way in which porn-streaming platforms do this, see Kal Raustiala and Christopher Sprigman, "The Second Digital Disruption: Streaming and the Dawn of Data-Driven Creativity," *New York University Law Review* 94 (2019): 1555.

147 See, for example, Shoshanna Zuboff, *The Age of Surveillance Capitalism: The Fight for a Human Future at the New Frontier of Power* (New York: Public Affairs, 2019); Valerie Steeves, "Terra Cognita: Surveillance of Young People's Favorite Websites," in *Surveillance Futures: Social and Ethical Implications of New Technologies for Children and Young People*, eds Emeline Taylor and Tonya Rooney (London and New York: Routledge, 2017), 174. I am grateful to Jane Bailey for emphasizing this point to me.

148 Clarissa Smith and Feona Attwood, "Emotional Truths and Thrilling Sideshows," in *The Feminist Porn Book: The Politics of Producing Pleasure*, eds Tristan Taormino et al. (New York: Feminist Press at CUNY, 2013), 48.

CHAPTER FIVE

1 Isabel Kohn, "Will the Fauxcest Bubble Ever Burst?," *Mel Magazine*, 2021, www.melmagazine.com/en-us/story/fauxcest-porn-incest-tube-stepsibling-pornhub (comment by professional porn performer Tasha Reign explaining that she believes incest-themed pornography is important because it normalizes people's fantasies about incest).

2 Henry Talbot et al., "Breaking Down Porn: A Classification Office Analysis of Commonly Viewed Pornography in NZ," New Zealand Classification Office, 2019, 14, www.classificationoffice.govt.nz/media/documents/Breaking_Down_Porn.pdf (reporting that 43 per cent of the most popular Pornhub videos in New Zealand in 2019 involved depictions of sex between stepsiblings or stepparents and stepchildren; according to the report it was clear in these videos that the performers were not actually related).

3 Ibid., 7.

4 "2021 Year in Review," Pornhub, 14 December 2021, www.pornhub.com/insights/yir-2021; "2019 Year in Review," Pornhub, 11 December 2019, www.pornhub.com/insights/2019-year-in-review; "2018 Year in Review,"

Pornhub, 11 December 2018, www.pornhub.com/insights/2018-year-in-review; "2017 Year in Review," Pornhub, 9 January 2018, www.pornhub.com/insights/2017-year-in-review; "2016 Year in Review," Pornhub, 4 January 2017, www.pornhub.com/insights/2016-year-in-review; "2015 Year in Review," Pornhub, 6 January 2016, www.pornhub.com/insights/pornhub-2015-year-in-review.

5 "Year in Review 2017," Pornhub.

6 "Recently Trending Terms," Pornhub, 30 June 2022, https://help.pornhub.com/hc/en-us/articles/4419883702035-Recently-Trending-Terms.

7 Jon Millward, "Deep Inside: A Study of 10,000 Porn Stars and their Careers" (blog), 14 February 2013, jonmillward.com/blog/studies/deep-inside-a-study-of-10000-porn-stars.

8 Antoine Mazières et al., "Deep Tags: Toward a Quantitative Analysis of Online Pornography," *Porn Studies* 1, nos 1–2 (2014): 85.

9 See, for example, Jenny Kutner, "Why Do Millennials Love Faux-Incest Porn So Much?," *MIC*, 10 February 2016, www.mic.com/articles/134715/why-do-millennials-love-faux-incest-porn-so-much; Gareth May, "Why Is Incest Porn So Popular?," *Vice*, 25 February 2015, www.vice.com/en/article/8gdz8k/why-is-incest-porn-so-popular-332; Luke O'Neil, "Incest Is the Fastest Growing Trend in Porn. Wait, What?," *Esquire*, 28 February 2018, www.esquire.com/lifestyle/sex/a18194469/incest-porn-trend. But see the 1970s porno-chic-era film *Mona: The Virgin Nymph*, which depicted a young woman traipsing through Los Angles fellating men at will while remaining a so-called virgin until marriage, which included a flashback scene to her childhood in which her father sexually assaults her by penetrating her mouth with his penis. See Whitney Strub, "From Porno Chic to Porn Bleak: Representing the Urban Crisis in American 1970s Pornography," in *Porno Chic and the American Sex Wars: American Sexual Representation in the 1970s*, eds Carolyn Bronstein and Whitney Strub (Amherst and Boston: University of Massachusetts Press, 2016), 34.

10 Fiona Vera-Gray et al., "Sexual Violence as a Sexual Script in Mainstream Online Pornography," *British Journal of Criminology* 61, no. 5 (2021): 1249 (finding that one in eight titles on platforms like Pornhub, xHamster, and xTube depict sexual violence and that sexual activities between family members is the most common form of sexual violence depicted on the landing pages of these sites).

11 O'Neil, "Incest Is the Fastest." (Interview with Bree Mills.)

12 Ibid.

13   Ibid.

14   Ibid.

15   Kutner, "Why Do Millennials."

16   Ibid.

17   Ibid.

18   Search of *Porn Studies* journal, conducted on 27 July 2022.

19   See, for example, Kyler R. Rasmussen, Daniel Millar, and Jeremy Trenchuk, "Relationships and Infidelity in Pornography: An Analysis of Pornography Streaming Websites," *Sexuality and Culture* 23, no. 2 (2019): 571.

20   See, for example, Zeynep Yenisey, "'Incest Porn' Is on the Rise, and These Are the Reasons Why," *Maxim*, 2 March 2018, www.maxim.com/maxim-man /why-is-incest-porn-so-popular-2018-3; May, "Why Is Incest"; O'Neil, "Incest Is the Fastest"; Kutner, "Why Do Millennials"; Tracy Clark-Flory, "Can a Woman Get Away with Making Fucked Up Faux-Incest Porn like No Man Could?," *Jezebel*, 4 October 2018, jezebel.com/can-a-woman-get-away-with-making-fucked-up-faux-incest-1828968461; Kohn, "Will the Fauxcest."

21   Vanessa Brown, "Faux-cest Is the Hottest New Thing in Porn – and Women Love It," *New York Post*, 13 June 2016, www.nypost.com/2016/06/13/faux-cest-is-the-hottest-new-thing-in-porn-and-women-love-it.

22   Clark-Flory, "Can a Woman."

23   See, for example, Yenisey, "'Incest Porn'"; May, "Why Is Incest."

24   See May, "Why Is Incest" ("there has long been a market for 'incest' scenes in porn – 'daddy–daughter' scenarios, for example, acted out between two perfect strangers for the titillation of masturbators who want to go a bit … darker. But that audience has – in certain areas of the US, at least – grown"). See also O'Neil, "Incest Is the Fastest."

25   O'Neil, "Incest Is the Fastest."

26   Ibid.

27   May, "Why Is Incest."

28   Virginia C. Andrews, *Flowers in the Attic* (New York: Simon and Schuster, 1979).

29   Elizabeth Kulze, "America's Incest Obsession: 'Flowers in the Attic' Is Back, as Are the Memories," *Vocativ*, 16 January 2014, www.vocativ.com/under world/sex/americas-incest-obsession-flowers-attic-back-memories/ index.html.

30   Kutner, "Why Do Millennials."

31   Sadaf Ahsan, "Is Game of Thrones to Blame for the Rise in Incest-Themed Pornography and Desensitizing the Taboo?," *National Post*, 16 June 2016,

nationalpost.com/entertainment/television/is-game-of-thrones-to-blame-for-the-rise-in-incest-themed-pornography-and-desensitizing-the-taboo; Vanessa Brown, "Is Game of Thrones Desensitizing Us to Fictional Incest Pornography and Driving our Interest in Faux-cest?," News.com.au, 11 June 2016, www.news.com.au/lifestyle/relationships/sex/is-game-of-thrones-desensitising-us-to-fictional-incest-pornography-and-driving-our-interest-in-fauxcest/news-story/ea793f6cd8034e70180e75edce957802; Clark-Flory, "Can a Woman."

32 David Levesley, "An Investigation into the Incest in Game of Thrones," GQ *Magazine*, 8 April 2019, www.gq-magazine.co.uk/article/game-of-thrones-family-tree.

33 Dave Itzkoff, "For 'Game of Thrones,' Rising Unease Over Rape's Recurring Role," *New York Times*, 3 May 2014, www.nytimes.com/2014/05/03/arts/television/for-game-of-thrones-rising-unease-over-rapes-recurring-role.html.

34 Lucie Ogrodnik, "Child and Youth Victims of Police-reported Violent Crime, 2008," Statistics Canada, 2010, 12–14, https://www150.statcan.gc.ca/n1/en/pub/85f0033m/85f0033m2010023-eng.pdf?st=SjXxMjs3 (reporting that rates of sexual victimization peak between ages thirteen and fifteen).

35 Howard N. Snyder, "Sexual Assault of Young Children as Reported to Law Enforcement: Victim, Incident, and Offender Characteristics," National Center for Juvenile Justice, July 2000, 2–4, bjs.ojp.gov/content/pub/pdf/saycrle.pdf. See also Sharon G. Smith et al., "The National Intimate Partner and Sexual Violence Survey: 2015 Data Brief – Updated Release," National Center for Injury Prevention and Control, and Centers for Disease Control and Prevention, 2018, 4, www.cdc.gov/violenceprevention/pdf/2015data-brief508.pdf (reporting that, among female victims, 43 per cent of rape and attempted rape victims were under age eighteen [30 per cent between the ages of eleven and seventeen, and 13 per cent under the age of ten]).

36 See, for example, Shanta R. Dube et al., "Long-Term Consequences of Childhood Sexual Abuse by Gender of Victim," *American Journal of Preventive Medicine* 28, no. 5 (2005): 430 (finding 25 per cent of adult women report having experienced child sexual abuse); David Finkelhor et al., "The Lifetime Prevalence of Child Sexual Abuse and Sexual Assault Assessed in Late Adolescence," *Journal of Adolescent Health* 55, no. 3 (2014): 331 (finding 26 per cent of seventeen-year-old girls report experiencing sexual assault).

37 Meghan Elkin, "Child Sexual Abuse in England and Wales: Year Ending March 2019," Office for National Statistics, 2020, 21, table 12a, www.ons.gov.

uk/peoplepopulationandcommunity/crimeandjustice/articles/childsexual
abuseinenglandandwales/yearendingmarch2019. In the United Kingdom
nearly 40 per cent of women who were sexually abused by age sixteen were
abused by family members.

38 See, for example, John Briere and Diana M. Elliott, "Prevalence and Psychological Sequelae of Self-Reported Childhood Physical and Sexual Abuse
in a General Population Sample of Men and Women," *Child Abuse and
Neglect* 27, no. 10 (2003): 1210 (finding that in 46.8 per cent of cases the
perpetrator was a family member).

39 See, for example, Elkin, "Child Sexual Abuse," 12 (finding that 37 per cent of
sexual assaults against children occurred in their home); Protect Children,
"Survivors' Survey Full Report 2017," Canadian Centre for Child Sexual
Abuse, 2017, 15, www.protectchildren.ca/pdfs/C3P_SurvivorsSurveyFull
Report2017.pdf (finding that 70 per cent of child sexual abuse material
["child pornography"] was produced in the child's home).

40 See, for example, Scott D. Easton et al., "The Effect of Childhood Sexual
Abuse on Psychosexual Functioning During Adulthood," *Journal of Family
Violence* 26, no. 1 (2011): 46 (finding that victims of incestuous child sexual
abuse are more likely than victims of non-incestuous sexual abuse to
experience problems with psychosexual functioning).See Ateret Gewirtz-
Meydan and David Finkelhor, "Sexual Abuse and Assault in a Large National Sample of Children and Adolescents," *Child Maltreatment* 25, no. 2
(2020): 204 (reporting that survivors of childhood sexual abuse perpetrated
by a family member were 2.6 times more likely to report having alcohol use
disorder and two times more likely to report substance use disorders than
survivors who were assaulted by a non–family member).

41 Janine Benedet and Isabel Grant, "Breaking the Silence on Father–Daughter
Sexual Abuse of Adolescent Girls: A Case Law Study," *Canadian Journal of
Women and the Law* 32, no. 2 (2020): 240.

42 Ibid., 242. See also Protect Children, "Survivors' Survey," 28, 30–31 (finding
that in cases of child sexual abuse recorded for purposes of producing pornography, over 80 per cent of perpetrators were family members, with 42
per cent of single offenders being biological fathers or (step)fathers, and
where there were multiple perpetrators 38 per cent were biological fathers
of the victims).

43 Peter Yates, "Sibling Sexual Abuse: Why Don't We Talk About It?," *Journal
of Clinical Nursing* 26, nos 15–16 (2016): 2482; Bonnie E. Carlson, Katherine
Maciol, and Joanne Schneider, "Sibling Incest: Reports from Forty-One

Survivors," *Journal of Child Sexual Abuse* 15, no. 4 (2006): 22 (citing several studies indicating that brother-initiated incest towards sisters is the most common form); Peter Yates and Stuart Allardyce, "Sibling Sexual Abuse: A Knowledge and Practice Overview," Centre of Expertise on Child Sexual Abuse, January 2021, 18, https://www.csacentre.org.uk/app/uploads/2023/09/Sibling-sexual-abuse-report.pdf.

44 Inês C Relva, Otília M. Fernandes, and Madalena Alarcao, "Dyadic Types of Sibling Sexual Coercion," *Journal of Family Violence* 32, no. 6 (2017): 580.

45 Carlson, Maciol, and Schneider, "Sibling Incest," 21–2.

46 See, for example, Kutner, "Why Do Millennials"; May, "Why Is Incest."

47 See, for example, Rosaleen McElvaney, "Disclosure of Child Sexual Abuse: Delays, Non-Disclosure and Partial Disclosure – What the Research Tells Us and Implications for Practice," *Child Abuse Review* 24 (2015): 161, citing Irit Hershkowitz, Omer Lanes, and Michael E. Lamb, "Exploring the Disclosure of Child Sexual Abuse with Alleged Victims and Their Parents," *Child Abuse and Neglect* 31 (2007): 111; Steven M. Kogan, "Disclosing Unwanted Sexual Experiences: Results from a National Sample of Adolescent Women," *Child Abuse and Neglect* 28 (2004): 148; Benedet and Grant, "Breaking the Silence," 249; Patricia Phelan, "Incest and Its Meaning: The Perceptions of Fathers and Daughters," *Child Abuse and Neglect* 19, no. 1 (1995): 19; Kamala London et al., "Disclosure of Child Sexual Abuse: What Does the Research Tell Us about the Ways That Children Tell?," *Psychology, Public Policy, and Law* 11, no. 1 (2005): 194 (reporting that the majority of children do not disclose child sexual abuse during childhood).

48 See, for example, Margaret W. Ballantine, "Sibling Incest Dynamics: Therapeutic Themes and Clinical Challenges," *Clinical Social Work Journal* 40 (2012): 57 (finding that sibling sexual abuse is rarely disclosed); Yates and Allardyce, "Sibling Sexual Abuse," 20 (noting low rates of disclosure); Carlson, Maciol, and Schneider, "Sibling Incest," 20 (noting that less is known about rates of sibling sexual abuse but that some studies suggest it is more common even than adult–child incest); David Finkelhor, "Sex Among Siblings: A Survey on Prevalence, Variety, and Effects," *Archives of Sexual Behavior* 9, no. 3 (1980): 174.

49 Kohn, "Will the Fauxcest."

50 Talbot, "Breaking Down Porn," 5.

51 Ibid., 7.

52 Ibid.

53   Search of *Porn Studies* journal, conducted on 27 July 2022. Of the thirty-five articles that mentioned incest (see note 18), none address topics such as incest-themed porn that eroticizes the sexual assault of sisters and daughters by their family members.

54   See, for example, Ana J. Bridges et al., "Aggression and Sexual Behavior in Best-Selling Pornography Videos: A Content Analysis Update," *Violence Against Women* 16, no. 10 (2010): 1065; Alan McKee, "Methodological Issues in Defining Aggression for Content Analyses of Sexually Explicit Material," *Archives of Sexual Behavior* 44, no. 1 (2015): 81; Alan McKee "The Objectification of Women in Mainstream Pornographic Videos in Australia," *Journal of Sex Research* 42, no. 4 (2005): 277. These articles by Bridges et al. and McKee are two of the most cited works on the definition of aggression in content analysis of pornography. Bridges et al. relied on a definition of aggression that did not turn on the absence of consent; surprisingly they did not discuss incest-themed porn in their definition. McKee relied on a definition of aggression that did turn on the presence of consent. Less surprisingly, he did not include reference to incest as part of his definition. See also Eran Shor, "Age, Aggression, and Pleasure in Popular Online Pornographic Videos," *Violence Against Women* 25, no. 8 (2018): 1018.

55   Vera-Gray et al., "Sexual Violence," 1244.

56   Ibid., 1249.

57   "Year in Review 2017," Pornhub; Talbot, "Breaking Down Porn."

58   "Truth or Dare with Hot Step Sister" (video), Pornhub, accessed 5 April 2022 (5,600,000 views, 84 per cent approval rating).

59   See, for example, Ibid.

60   "My Little Step Sister Let's Me Do Everything" (video), Pornhub, accessed 10 May 2023 (92,800 views, 80 per cent approval rating); "Step-Father Demands Me to Fuck My Step-Sister … in Front of Him" (video), Pornhub, accessed 31 May 2023 (4,500,000 views, 86 per cent approval rating); "Accidently Woke Up My Step Sister with My Dick" (video), Pornhub, accessed 31 May 2023 (125,000 views, 93 per cent approval rating).

61   See, for example, "Step-Sister Gets Woken Up by a Hard Cock" (video), Pornhub, accessed 5 April 2022 (7,500,000 views, 76 per cent approval rating); "Step Sister Woke Up When She Felt a Dick" (video), xHamster, accessed 5 April 2022 (1056 views, 100 per cent approval rating); "Step Sister with a Perfect Ass Woke Up When I Fucked Her" (video), Pornhub, accessed 5 April 2022 (671,000 views, 83 per cent approval rating).

62 Ibid.

63 See, for example, notes 60, 61, 66, and 67 for views and approval ratings on videos.

64 "My Little Step Sister," Pornhub.

65 Ibid.

66 "Step Sister" (video), xHamster, accessed 5 April 2022 (6,254,887 views, 99 per cent approval rating).

67 "Stepbro Surprises Stepsis with Cock in Her Mouth" (video), Pornhub, accessed 5 April 2022 (38,700 views, 85 per cent approval rating).

68 Ibid.

69 See, for example, *Sexual Offences Act 2003* (UK), s. 75(2)(d) [*Sexual Offences Act UK*]; *Criminal Code*, RSC 1985, c C-46, s. 273.1(2)(a.1) [*Criminal Code*]; *Criminal Law (Sexual Offences and Related Matters) Amendment Act*, 2007 (South Africa), No. 32 of 2007, s. 1(3)(d)(ii); *New York Penal Law* § 130.05(3)(d) [*Penal Code New York*]; *California (Penal Code)* § 261(4) [*Penal Code California*].

70 "Waking Up Stepdaughter with a Cock Inside Her" (video), Pornhub, accessed 5 April 2022 (18,000 views, 89 per cent approval rating); "Ahh Ahh Don't Scream! Stepdaughter Gets Fucked by Her Stepdad While She Was Taking a Nap" (video), Pornhub, accessed 1 December 2023 (779,000 views, 82 per cent approval rating) (depicting a male performer who enters the room of a sleeping young woman and touches her buttocks and genital area while she is asleep; when she "awakens" he puts his hand over her mouth and tells her not to scream and promises he will be quick and that she will "enjoy it"; when she nods, indicating she will not scream, he removes his hand from her mouth and they engage in sexual activity); "Daddy Dominates Stepdaughter While She Is Resting" (video), xHamster, accessed 5 April 2022 (1,100,000 views, 99 per cent approval rating).

71 That said, there are videos on these platforms depicting brothers and step-brothers engaging in sexual acts with female subjects who are represented as children. See, for example, "Fuck My Teen Stepsister Pussy When Her Mom Is Not at Home" (video), Pornhub, accessed 5 April 2022 (1,600 views, 75 per cent approval rating) (depicts a male penetrating a young-looking teenage girl in childish pyjamas clutching a teddy bear).

72 See, for example, "Barely Legal Step Daughter Gets Surprised before School: Had to Wake Her Up with My Cock" (video), Pornhub, accessed 1 December 2023 (408,000 views, 88 per cent approval rating). The title of this video signals that the "daughter" is over the age of consent, albeit

"barely." However, the female performer in this video is shown in a childish bedroom with stuffed animals on the bed, wearing pigtails and knee-high socks. Moreover, the video begins with the male performer initiating sexual acts on her while she is depicted as asleep – also a sexual assault.

73 "Daughter Creampied by Stepfather in Her Bedroom" (video), xHamster, accessed 28 March 2022 (803,440 views, 99 per cent approval rating). "Creampie" is a colloquial term used to describe the act of ejaculating into a vagina during vaginal penetration. See Alex Manley, "Everything You Need to Know About Creampies," *Askmen*, 10 March 2022, www.askmen. com/sex/sex_tips/everything-you-need-to-know-about-creampies.html.

74 "Daughter Creampied," xHamster. The female performer in this video appears to be a teenage girl or young woman who is intentionally represented through costume and props as a young child.

75 Ibid., 06m:45s.

76 Ibid.

77 "Stepfather Gets Stepdaughter Pregnant with Accidental Creampie" (video), xHamster, accessed 5 April 2022 (306,783 views, 99 per cent approval rating).

78 Ibid.

79 Ibid.

80 "Giving Step-Daddy Her Virginity for Step-Father's Day – What More Could a Man Ask For?" (video), Pornhub, accessed 1 December 2023 (333,000 views, 90 per cent approval rating).

81 As noted in chapter 1, gay porn is not examined this book. So-called gay-cest porn is included in this section because intra-family child sexual abuse is not unique to girl-identified children. Boys are also victimized by family members, and the "gay-cest porn" described here raises the same types of issues as the father–daughter porn.

82 "Young Twink Step Son Morning Family Fuck Step Dad" (video), xHamster, accessed 21 June 2023 (38,557 views; 99 per cent approval rating).

83 "My Step-Father Usually Fucks Me Before Bed" (video), xHamster, accessed 21 June 2023 (175,053 views, 97 per cent approval rating).

84 Ibid.

85 "My Step-Father Usually Fucks me Before Bed" (video), Pornhub, accessed 21 June 2023 (1,000,000 views, 85 per cent approval rating).

86 "Father and Son Re-connect with Buttplug and Breeding" (video), Pornhub, accessed 21 June 2023 (483,000 views, 92 per cent approval rating).

87 *Sexual Offences Act UK*, s. 9; *Sexual Offences (Northern Ireland) Order 2008*

(NI), SI 2008/1769, s. 16; *Sexual Offences (Scotland) Act* 2009 (Scot), ASP 9, s. 28; *Criminal Code*, s. 150.1(1)–(2.2).

88 *Penal Code New York*, § 130.05, cl 3(a).

89 *Penal Code California*, § 261.5.

90 See, for example, *Sexual Offences Act* UK, ss 16, 25; *Criminal Code*, s. 153(2). In Canada a young person is defined, for the purposes of Canada's prohibition on sexual exploitation, as someone between the ages of sixteen and eighteen.

91 *Criminal Code*, s. 155 (distinguishing for purposes of sanction between those over and under sixteen); *Sexual Offences Act* UK, ss 25–26, 64–65 (note that these latter provisions include adoptive parents).

92 *Criminal Code*.

93 *R v Beattie* (2005), 75 OR (3d) 117, para. 23, [2005] OJ No 1302 (CA), leave to appeal to SCC refused, [2005] SCCA No 319.

94 Ibid., para. 24.

95 Bill C-63, *Online Harms Act*, 1st sess, 44th Parl, 2024, s. 2.

96 Ibid.

97 Ibid., s. 7.

98 "I Take Advantage of My 18 Year Old Step-Daughter" (video), xHamster, accessed 5 April 2022 (97,558 views, 99 per cent approval rating).

99 "Step-Daughter Horrified by Step-Daddy's Monster Cock" (video), xHamster, accessed 5 April 2022 (3,209 views, 95 per cent approval rating); "Stepdaughter Horrified by Stepdaddy's Monster Cock" (video), Pornhub, accessed 13 April 2023 (416,000 views, 93 per cent approval rating).

100 "Step-father Tricks Step-Daughter into Perverted Photo Shoot and First Facial" (video), xHamster, accessed 6 March 2022 (3,180 views, 100 per cent approval rating). The term "facial" appears to mean a man ejaculating on the face of someone.

101 "Step-daughter Fucked in the Ass" (video), xHamster, accessed 5 April 2022 (3,400,000 views, 99 per cent approval rating).

102 "Dad Manipulates Step-Daughter into Sex" (video), Pornhub, accessed 5 April 2022 (8,900,000 views, 78 per cent approval rating).

103 Theodore P. Cross and Thaddeus Schmitt, "Forensic Medical Results and Law Enforcement Actions Following Sexual Assault: A Comparison of Child, Adolescent and Adult Cases," *Child Abuse and Neglect* 93 (2019): 103 (finding that there was no significant difference between the types of acts, the degree of injuries, and the nature of injuries as between adolescent and adult victims of sexualized violence).

104 Benedet and Grant, "Breaking the Silence," 253.

105 "Daddy Forces Stepdaughter ***" (video), xHamster, accessed 4 March 2022 (1,100,000 views, 99 per cent approval rating). I have redacted a portion of the title of this video to make it unsearchable because it was not clear to me whether it was a fictional depiction of sexual assault or a video of an actual rape.

106 Ibid.

107 "Stepdad Fucks and *** His Crying Daughter ***" (video), xHamster, accessed 28 July 2022 (2,244,353 views, 99 per cent approval rating). I have redacted portions of the title of this video to make it unsearchable because it is not clear to me whether it was fictional or a video of an actual rape.

108 Ibid.

109 "Year in Review 2021," Pornhub; "Year in Review 2019," Pornhub; "Year in Review 2018," Pornhub; "Year in Review 2017," Pornhub.

110 "Sexy Step Mom Turned On after Catching Her Step Son Sniffing on Her Panties" (video), Pornhub, accessed 5 April 2022 (91,000 views, 92 per cent approval rating).

111 "Mommy Gives In and Gives Up the Pussy" (video), xHamster, accessed 5 April 2022 (394,4100 views, 99 per cent approval rating).

112 "He Couldn't Help Himself and Started Hitting on Mother" (video), xHamster, accessed 5 April 2022 (1,400,000 views, 99 per cent approval rating).

113 "Extra Thick Stepmom Emily Addison Fucks Horny Stepson to Make Him Keep Her Sinful Secrets" (video), Pornhub, accessed 5 April 2022 (19,100,000 views, 87 per cent approval rating).

114 "Moms Teach Sex – Step Mom Says 'You Dreaming About Your Step Moms Big Titties Again?'" (video), Pornhub, accessed 5 April 2022 (16,200,000 views, 90 per cent approval rating).

115 Ibid.

116 Sophie Augarde and Michelle Rydon-Grange, "Female Perpetrators of Child Sexual Abuse: A Review of the Clinical and Empirical Literature – A 20-Year Update," *Aggression and Violent Behaviour* 62 (2022): 1. In reviewing the empirical studies on the prevalence of female-perpetrated sexual abuse of children, of which there are not a plethora, the authors found that the vast majority of child sexual abuse is perpetrated by men and that the victims of female-perpetrated child sexual abuse are more likely to be girls rather than boys.

117 Niki Fritz and Bryant Paul, "From Orgasms to Spanking: A Content Analy-

sis of the Agentic and Objectifying Sexual Scripts in Feminist, for Women, and Mainstream Pornography," *Sex Roles* 77, nos 9–10 (2017): 647–9. The authors found in a content analysis of 300 porn videos that mainstream porn, and "for women porn" offered on mainstream sites, was significantly more likely to depict women as objects and significantly less likely to depict their sexual agency than either queer or feminist porn.

118   Benedet and Grant, "Breaking the Silence," 242.

119   Protect Children, "Survivors' Survey" (see note 39).

120   Ibid., 34.

121   See, for example, Benedet and Grant, "Breaking the Silence," 251–2.

122   Protect Children, "Survivors' Survey," 35–6.

123   Ibid., 36–7.

124   Phelan, "Incest and Its Meaning."

125   Ibid., 10.

126   "Step-Dad Fucks Stepdaughter While Mom Is Away at Work" (video), Pornhub, accessed 4 March 2022 (2,000,000 views, 79 per cent approval rating).

127   "Alone with My Slut Teen Daughter" (video), xHamster, accessed 26 June 2023 (1,245,907 views, 99 per cent approval rating).

128   "Daddy Fucks Stepdaughter Everytime Mommy Leaves" (video), Pornhub, accessed 26 June 2023 (28,500,000 views, 70 per cent approval rating).

129   "Step Sister Fucks with Step Daddy, Mom at Work!!!" (video), Pornhub, accessed 26 June 2023 (201,000 views, 78 per cent approval rating).

130   Snyder, "Sexual Assault."

131   "Year in Review 2017," Pornhub.

132   "My Step Sister Suck My Cock While My Parents Aren't Home" (video), Pornhub, accessed 26 June 2023 (7,400,000 views, 78 per cent approval rating).

133   "Stepbrother and Step-Sister Home Alone" (video), Pornhub, accessed 5 April 2022 (3,400,000 views, 86 per cent approval rating).

134   "Fucked My Step Sis While Parents Are Not Home" (video), Pornhub, accessed 5 April 2022 (591,000 views, 97 per cent approval rating).

135   To be clear, this framing of heterosexuality is not a desirable one. Constructing men as always and only responsible for initiating sexual activity and women as the reluctant, and potentially passive, recipients of these advances contributes to rape culture, distorted legal and social understandings of consent, and ineffective sexual communications between men and women. See, for example, Jaclyn Friedman and Jessica Valenti, eds, *Yes*

Means Yes! Visions of Female Sexual Power and a World without Rape (Berkeley: Seal Press, 2008).

136 Adam Cotter and Pascale Beaupré, "Police-Reported Sexual Offences Against Children and Youth in Canada, 2012," Statistics Canada, Catalogue No. 85-002-X (Ottawa: Statistics Canada, 2014), 14. According to Statistics Canada, 74 per cent of sexual assaults against children occur in private residents.

137 Protect Children, "Survivors' Survey," 36.

138 Phelan, "Incest and Its Meaning," 11, 15–16.

139 Ibid., 9.

140 Ibid., 11–12.

141 "Father Sneaks into Daughter's Bedroom and Touches Her Pussy" (video), xHamster, accessed 5 April 2022 (857,162 views, 99 per cent approval rating).

142 "Daughter Snuggles with Step-Father in Bed and Gets Fucked" (video), xHamster, accessed 5 April 2022 (322,414 views, 99 per cent approval rating).

143 "Waking Up Stepdaughter," Pornhub (see note 70).

144 "Scared Stepdaughter Gets Fucked While Wife Sleeps" (video), Pornhub, accessed 5 April 2022 (65,800,000 views, 69 per cent approval rating).

145 "My Little Stepsister," Pornhub; "Daughter Creampied," xHamster (see note 73); "Stepfather Gets Stepdaughter Pregnant," xHamster (see note 77).

146 Phelan, "Incest and Its Meaning," 15–16; Benedet and Grant, "Breaking the Silence," 253 (finding that in 24.4 per cent of cases involving fathers or stepfathers, their daughters were asleep or intoxicated when the abuse occurred).

147 *R v RC*, 2021 ONCA 419 at para. 20.

148 *R. v CG*, 2019 ONSC 6173 at para. 5.

149 *State v L—*, *** So (3d) 463, 1 (La Ct App 2022) (style of cause and citation redacted to ensure complainant's anonymity).

150 *R v G—*, 2021 ABCA ***, para. 6 (style of cause and citation redacted to ensure complainant's anonymity).

151 See, for example, Gewirtz-Meydan and Finkelhor, "Sex Abuse," 211 (citing studies indicating that one of the main harms of child sexual abuse is the shame and stigma it instils in victims).

152 Finkelhor, "Sex Among Siblings," 180: "Not a single child who had been involved in sex with a much older sibling confided it to anyone … the pain of secrecy was added to whatever unpleasantness the experience itself

involved." See, generally, Dafna Tener, "The Secret of Intrafamilial Child Sexual Abuse: Who Keeps It and How?," *Journal of Child Sexual Abuse* 27, no. 1 (2018): 1; Samantha Craven, Sarah Brown, and Elizabeth Gilchrist, "Sexual Grooming of Children: Review of Literature and Theoretical Considerations," *Journal of Sexual Aggression* 12, no. 3 (2006): 295.

153 See, for example, "Daughter Creampied," xHamster.

154 See, for example, "Stepfather Gets Stepdaughter Pregnant," xHamster.

155 "Father Punishes Daughter" (video), xHamster, accessed 26 June 2023 (518,294 views, 99 per cent views). See also, "Scared Stepdaughter," Pornhub; "Step-Daughter Horrified," xHamster.

156 Benedet and Grant, "Breaking the Silence," 253–4.

157 "Stepdad Caughts [*sic*] Stepdaughter Naked and Cums All over Her" (video), Pornhub, accessed 5 April 2022 (704,000 views, 89 per cent approval rating).

158 "Naughty Stepdaughter Ep. 6: Caught by Stepdad Making a Video for My Boyfriend" (video), Pornhub, accessed 5 April 2022 (2,400,000 views, 84 per cent approval rating).

159 "Step Daddy Caught Me Playing with My Pussy and Fucked Me Hard (*** ***)" (video), Pornhub, accessed 5 April 2022 (1,400,000 views, 92 per cent approval rating).

160 "Stepdad Gives Me a Sex Education Lesson" (video), xHamster, accessed 5 April 2022 (1,600,000 views, 98 per cent approval rating).

161 "Step Dad Pays 18 Year Old Step Daughter Money for Intimate Intimacy – Homemade Porn" (video), Pornhub, accessed 5 April 2022 (181,000 views, 75 per cent approval rating). In this video the female subject is wearing little girl pyjamas and is depicted as being under the age of consent.

162 Ibid.

163 "Stepdaughter Submits to Humiliating Punishment" (video), xHamster, accessed 5 April 2022 (128,679 views, 99 per cent approval rating). This video depicts a teenage girl being spanked and forced to perform oral sex on her "father" as punishment for dressing "like a slut" and missing her curfew.

164 Mary I. Benedict et al., "Types and Frequency of Child Maltreatment by Family Foster Care Providers in an Urban Population," *Child Abuse and Neglect* 18, no. 7 (1994): 581 (finding that sexual abuse was reported to have occurred in 2.3 per cent of foster families, compared to 0.5 per cent of non-foster families); Georgina F. Hobbs and Christopher J. Hobbs, "Abuse of Children in Foster and Residential Care," *Child Abuse and Neglect* 23, no. 12 (1999): 1239 (children in foster care were seven to eight times more likely to

be assessed by a pediatrician for physical and sexual abuse); Sarah A. Font, "Child Protection Investigations in Out-of-Home Care: Perpetrators, Victims, and Contexts," *Child Maltreatment* 20, no. 4 (2015): 252.

165 Ibid.

166 Benedet and Grant, "Breaking the Silence," 261.

167 "Skinny Teen Fucked by Her Controlling Foster Parents" (video), Pornhub, accessed 5 April 2022 (859,000 views, 87 per cent approval rating); "My Foster Daughter Wanted Some Dick before the Social Workers Came for a House Visit" (video), Pornhub, accessed 5 April 2022 (23,300 views, 62 per cent approval rating).

168 Tracy Clark-Flory, "Can a Woman Get Away with Making Fucked Up Faux-Incest Porn Like No Man Could?," *Jezebel*, 4 October 2018, jezebel.com/can-a-woman-get-away-with-making-fucked-up-faux-incest-1828968461.

169 Ibid.

170 Ibid.

171 Ibid.

172 "Daughter Creampied," xHamster.

173 Ibid.

174 "Stepfather Gets Stepdaughter Pregnant," xHamster.

175 "Father Sneaks into Daughter's Bedroom," xHamster.

176 "Daddy Forces Stepdaughter," xHamster.

177 "Horny Stepdad Fucked His Stepdaughter" (video), Pornhub, accessed 4 March 2022 (665,000 views, 81 per cent).

178 See, for example, "step father daughter," search, xHamster (see note 140).

179 "Wake Up Sis," xHamster.

180 "Daddy Forces Stepdaughter," xHamster.

181 Protect Children, "Survivors' Survey," 370 (see note 39).

182 Tracy Clark-Flory, "Can a Woman."

183 Phelan, "Incest and Its Meaning," 14–15.

184 Benedet and Grant, "Breaking the Silence," 253.

185 Phelan, "Incest and Its Meaning," 21.

186 Ibid.

187 "Stepfather Gets Stepdaughter Pregnant," xHamster; "Barbie Doll Blonde Is Feeding on Cock" (video), xHamster, accessed 5 April 2022 (1,200,000 views, 99 per cent approval rating) (depicts a woman dressed as an infant with a teddy bear and pacifier who wakes up crying, at which point a male subject depicted as her [step]father enters the bedroom, feeds her a bottle, burps her, and then engages in sexual acts upon her, to which she expresses

sexual pleasure); "A Game With My Step-Daughter Finished in Masturbation" (videos), Pornhub, accessed 5 April 2022 (148,000 views, 87 per cent approval rating) (depicts a young teenage girl, in Hello Kitty baby doll pyjamas, playing music on her phone, and involves playful tickling by male hand, which leads to tickling and light playful wrestling on her bed and then sexual acts, including mutual masturbation).

188   I borrow this phrase from Kim Brooks, who borrowed it from Jane Farrow.

189   See, for example, Briere and Elliott, "Prevalence and Psychological Sequelae," 1207 (noting numerous studies finding that child sexual abuse was associated with a set of harms including low self-esteem, anxiety, depression, anger and aggression, post-traumatic stress, dissociation, substance abuse, and sexual difficulties); Dube et al., "Long-Term Consequences," 433–4 (finding a two-fold increase in suicidality, increased risk of addictions and of marrying a spouse with addictions, and increased likelihood of marital and family problems); Mireille Cyr et al., "Intrafamilial Sexual Abuse: Brother–Sister Incest Does Not Differ from Father–Daughter and Step-father–Stepdaughter Incest," *Child Abuse and Neglect* 26 (2002): 968 (finding that the psychosocial harms caused by sibling sexual assault paralleled those caused by father or stepfather sexual assault).

190   A search on Pornhub using the terms "adult baby diaper lover" and "AB/DL diaper" produced no videos on the first two pages of search results with titles suggesting intra-family sexualized violence or any of the narratives critiqued in this chapter. None of the titles included words such as "(step)-father," "(step)brother," or "daughter." For an examination of AB/DL porn, see, for example, Elisa Cuter, "The Shock Value of Infantilism: AB/DL Practices in Porn, Documentaries and Public Perception," *Porn Studies* (2022).

191   Susanna Paasonen, *Carnal Resonance: Affect and Online Pornography* (Cambridge, MA: MIT Press, 2011).

192   Benedet and Grant, "Breaking the Silence," 266.

193   Ibid.

194   Kara Shead, "Responding to Historical Child Sexual Abuse: A Prosecution Perspective on Current Challenges and Future Directions," *Current Issues in Criminal Justice* 26 (2014): 56.

195   Benedet and Grant, "Breaking the Silence," 266.

196   Kulze, "America's Incest Obsession."

197   Note that in their study, Vera-Gray et al. found more videos suggesting biological family members ("Sexual Violence," 1294).

198   Clark-Flory, "Can a Woman."

199 Ibid. See, for example, John Verdeschi, "Protecting Our Network, Protecting You: Preventing Illegal Adult Content on Our Network" (blog), Mastercard, 14 April 2021, www.mastercard.com/news/perspectives/2021/pro tecting-our-network-protecting-you-preventing-illegal-adult-content-on-our-network (blog post by the vice-president at Mastercard announcing stricter content controls required by the company to ensure that Mastercard is not used for payments on sites with "illegal content"; a lot turns on what constitutes illegal content for the purposes of this policy); see also Nelson Eshe, "Visa and Mastercard to Investigate Financial Ties to Pornhub," *New York Times*, 7 December 2020, https://www.nytimes.com/2020/12/07/business/visa-mastercard-pornhub.html. Mastercard banned the use of its services on Pornhub following allegations in the *New York Times* regarding videos on the site that included people who had not consented (either to the sexual activity or to having the videos posted – including videos of girls under the age of consent).

200 Benedet and Grant, "Breaking the Silence," 250. The authors state that their results showed this pattern, and cite Diana E.H. Russell, "The Prevalence and Seriousness of Incestuous Abuse: Stepfathers vs. Biological Fathers," *Child Abuse and Neglect* 8 (1984): 15.

201 Jane M. Rudd and Sharon Herzberger, "Brother–Sister Incest – Father–Daughter Incest: A Comparison of Characteristics and Consequences," *Child Abuse and Neglect* 23, no. 9 (1999): 926. The survivors in their study belonged to incest support or treatment groups.

202 Protect Children, "Survivors' Survey," 270.

203 Rudd and Herzberger, "Brother–Sister Incest," 922.

204 Phelan, "Incest and Its Meaning," 19.

205 Benedet and Grant, "Breaking the Silence," 253.

206 Phelan, "Incest and Its Meaning," 22.

207 Ibid., 10, 22.

208 Ibid., 11.

209 Ibid., 12.

210 Rudd and Herzberger, "Brother–Sister Incest," 923–4.

211 Ibid., 924.

212 Ibid.

213 Ibid., 921.

214 Protect Children, "Survivors' Survey," 157.

215 Ibid.

216 Ibid., 156.

217 Phelan, "Incest and Its Meaning," 10.

218 Ibid., 11.

219 Ibid., 12. Victims of sexual abuse sometimes have the same physiological response to sexual touching that occurs during consensual sexual contact; this is not a sign of enjoyment, or arousal.

220 Ibid.

221 Ibid., 13.

222 Linda Williams and David Finkelhor, "The Characteristics of Incestuous Fathers," US, Department of Health and Human Services (NCJ No 141116) (Washington, DC: US Government Printing Office, 1992), 33.

223 Ibid., 38–9.

224 Benedet and Grant, "Breaking the Silence," 255.

225 Ibid.

226 Phelan, "Incest and Its Meaning," 15–16.

227 Ibid., 15.

228 Ibid.

229 Ibid.

230 Ibid.

231 Protect Children, "Survivors' Survey," 53.

232 Ibid., 52–4.

233 See, for example, Bridges et al., "Aggression and Sexual Behavior," 1065 (finding that the targets of aggression in adult pornography most often responded with pleasure or neutrally to the aggression); Shor, "Age, Aggression, and Pleasure," 1018 (finding that female performers, and in particular teenage performers, were more likely to be depicted as responding to aggression with expressions of pleasure). See also Eran Shor and Kimberly Seida "'Harder and Harder'? Is Mainstream Pornography Becoming Increasingly Violent and Do Viewers Prefer Violent Content?," *Journal of Sex Research* 56, no. 1 (2019): 16 (finding that videos containing explicit aggression received less views and lower ratings; note that like other researchers they do not use a definition that explicitly addresses incest); Marleen J.E. Klaassen and Jochen Peter, "Gender (In)equality in Internet Pornography: A Content Analysis of Popular Pornographic Internet Videos," *Journal of Sex Research* 52, no. 7 (2015): 721 (finding that men were more often depicted as dominant and women submissive, but that depictions of non-consensual sex were rare).

234 Nicola Gavey, *Just Sex: The Cultural Scaffolding of Rape* (New York: Routledge, 2005).

235 Aidan McGlynn, "Blurred Lines: How Fictional Is Pornography?," *Philosophy Compass* 16, no. 4 (2021): 2.

CHAPTER SIX

1 *R v MM*, 2017 ABPC 268, para. 5; *R v AE* (29 November 2018), Calgary 161500723Q1 (AB KB) (trial transcript of 29 November 2018 PM, 55:15) (testimony of AE).

2 See Cheryl Hanna, "Sex Is Not a Sport: Consent and Violence in Criminal Law," *Boston College Law Review* 42, no. 2 (2001): 243; Margot D. Weiss, "Mainstreaming Kink: The Politics of BDSM Representation in US Popular Media," *Journal of Homosexuality* 50, nos 2–3 (2006): 103; Theodore Bennett, "A Fine Line between Pleasure and Pain: Would Decriminalising BDSM Permit Non-consensual Abuse?," *Liverpool Law Review* 42 (2021): 180.

3 See Ashley Brown, Edward D. Barker, and Qazi Rahman, "A Systematic Scoping Review of the Prevalence, Etiological, Psychological, and Interpersonal Factors Associated with BDSM," *Journal of Sex Research* 57, no. 6 (2020): 783; Cara Dunkley and Lori Brotto, "The Role of Consent in the Context of BDSM," *Sexual Abuse* 32, no. 6 (2020): 659–60; Violette Coppens et al., "A Survey on BDSM-related Activities: BDSM Experience Correlates with Age of First Exposure, Interest Profile, and Role Identity," *Journal of Sex Research* 57, no. 1 (2020): 129 (citing several recent studies). Maneesha Deckha summarizes descriptions of sadomasochism as follows: "While s/M has varied meanings to its practitioners and eludes precise definition, it is generally associated with the giving and receiving of pain to incite sexual pleasure in a role-play/relationship mediated by power." See Maneesha Deckha, "Pain, Pleasure, and Consenting Women: Exploring the Feminist Response to s/M and Its Legal Regulation in Canada through Jelinek's *The Piano Teacher*," *Harvard Journal of Law and Gender* 30 (2007): 429–30.

4 See Elizabeth Sheehy, Isabel Grant, and Lise Gotell, "Resurrecting 'She Asked For It': The Rough Sex Defence in Canada," *Alberta Law Review* 60, no. 3 (2023): 652. Their research summarizes multiple studies involving high self-reported rates of slapping (59 per cent), biting (59 per cent), gagging (34 per cent), spitting (20 per cent), etc. during sex, among American and British men and women.

5 Based on a search of Canadian cases on the database CanLII, conducted 3 April 2021, more than 80 per cent of reported cases involving the terms "rough sex" and "sexual assault" occurred after 2010. Of the thirty-one reported cases that include the terms "sexual assault" and "BDSM," only one

occurred prior to 2010 (*R v Price*, 2004 BCPC 103 [CanLII]). It did not involve a rough sex or consensual sadomasochism (s/m) defence to sexual assault. There are no reported cases prior to 2010 in which an accused relied
on consensual "sadomasochism" as a defence to sexual assault. There is one
case – *R v RDW*, 2006 BCPC 300 (CanLII) – in which an accused pleaded
guilty to the lesser included offence of assault but relied on the argument
that the incident involved consensual s/m at sentencing. See also Sheehy,
Grant, and Gotell, "Resurrecting," 653.

6 Ibid.

7 I found only two reported cases in Canada prior to 2000 that raised the
prospect of a "rough sex defence": *R v Welch*, [1995] OJ No 2859, 25 OR
(3d) 665; *R v RKJ*, [1998] NBJ No 483 (QL), 207 NBR (2d) 24. It is not clear
whether the accused in *RKJ* relied on the couple's supposed history of
consensual rough sex as a defence. The accused in *Welch* did rely on the
so-called rough sex defence.

8 See Hannah Bows and Jonathan Herring, "Getting Away with Murder?
A Review of the 'Rough Sex Defence,'" *Journal of Criminal Law* 84, no. 6
(2020): 526.

9 Much of the dispute regarding the content of mainstream porn seems to
centre around the proportion of pornography that contains aggression
and/or whether aggression is the proper measure of what some researchers
identify as problematic porn – as opposed to objectification, violence, or
degradation and dehumanization. See, for example, Alan McKee, "Methodological Issues in Defining Aggression for Content Analyses of Sexually
Explicit Material," *Archives of Sexual Behavior* 44, no. 1 (2015): 81 (asserting
that the focus on aggression in content analysis of pornography is a research tradition). Estimates range from between less than 2 per cent to over
88 per cent – suggesting a significant lack of clarity, or agreement, among
researchers on what is meant by the terms and/or discrepancies in the types
of material analyzed. See Alan McKee, "The Objectification of Women in
Mainstream Pornographic Videos in Australia," *Journal of Sex Research* 42,
no. 4 (2005): 285 (finding violence in less than 2 per cent of mainstream videos in Australia – videos were identified as aggressive if they included acts
intended to cause harm that were met with resistance. Done in 2005, before
the 2007 introduction of porn-streaming platforms, this research may not
be particularly reflective of mainstream porn content today). See, for
example, Ana J. Bridges et al., "Aggression and Sexual Behavior in Best-S
elling Pornography Videos: A Content Analysis Update," *Violence Against*

Women 16, no. 10 (2010): 1065 (finding aggression in over 88 per cent of mainstream porn videos).

10   McKee, "Objectification of Women," 283.

11   Bridges et al., "Aggression and Sexual Behavior," 1073, for example, coded videos on the issue of consent based on whether the "target [of the act] expresse[d] pleasure or respond[ed] neutrally" or whether they "express[ed] displeasure."

12   See, for example, "That's the Wrong Hole You Son of a Bitch" (video), xHamster, accessed 19 November 2023 (248,775 views, 98 per cent approval rating); "He Takes the Condom Off and Puts It in My Ass by Surprise and Cums Twice" (video), xHamster, accessed 7 March 2023 (157,771 views, 99 per cent approval rating); "Oops Wrong Hole, Sorry!! Accidental and Painful Anal with My Innocent 18 Year Old Stepsister" (video), Pornhub, accessed 7 March 2023; "Wrong Hole. Unexpected and Really Painful Anal" (video), xHamster, accessed 19 November 2023 (2,954,255 views, 95 per cent approval rating); "Creampie Surprise. I Tricked My Stepsister, Took Off the Condom and Filled Her Pussy Full of Cum" (video), Pornhub, accessed 20 November 2023 (516,000 views, 92 per cent approval rating); "Snuck Condom Off and Accidently Rammed It up Her Ass" (video), Pornhub, accessed 8 March 2023 (2,900,000 views, 64 per cent approval rating).

13   See Eran Shor, "Age, Aggression and Pleasure in Popular Online Pornographic Videos," *Violence Against Women* 25, no. 8 (2019): 1030; Shelley Walker et al., "'It's Always Just There in Your Face': Young People's Views on Porn," *Sexual Health* 12, no. 3 (2015): 201 (finding that in 49 per cent of the sample, female actors displayed eagerness or willingness to comply with whatever was asked of them no matter how violent or aggressive); Bridges et al., "Aggression and Sexual Behavior," 1065 (finding that the targets of aggression were overwhelmingly female, and most often showed pleasure or responded neutrally to the aggression).

14   Eran Shor and Kimberly Seida, *Aggression in Pornography: Myths and Realities* (London and New York: Routledge, 2021), 31; Eran Shor and Kimberley Seida, "'Harder and Harder'? Is Mainstream Pornography Becoming Increasingly Violent and Do Viewers Prefer Violent Content?," *Journal of Sex Research* 56, no. 1 (2020): 24 (finding that users prefer videos that do not include depictions of non-consensual aggression).

15   In their study, Shor and Seida found that 39.8 per cent of Pornhub videos included visible acts of aggression, with spanking, hair pulling, forceful vaginal penetration, and gagging being the most common (although they

found that only 12.9 per cent of the most popular videos on Pornhub included acts they coded as visible aggression). Shor and Seida, *Aggression in Pornography*, 65.

16 Niki Fritz and Paul Bryant, "A Descriptive Analysis of the Types, Targets, and Relative Frequency of Aggression in Mainstream Pornography," *Archives of Sexual Behavior* 49, no. 8 (2020): 3041, 3047.

17 Shor, "Age, Aggression and Pleasure," 1029.

18 Ibid., 1025–6.

19 Sheehy, Grant, and Gotell, "Resurrecting," 665.

20 Over a five-year period between 1996 and 2000 there were fifty-one reported decisions in Canada involving adult complainants who alleged non-consensual anal penetration. During the five-year period between 2016 and 2020, there were 157 reported decisions involving allegations of non-consensual anal penetration, suggesting a 207.8 per cent increase. In 1996 there were seven reported cases and in 2021 there were twenty-six, representing a 271.4 per cent increase (CanLII search of all reported cases involving charges of sexual assault, conducted in 2021, using the search terms "sodomy," "anal sex," "anal intercourse," and "anal penetration").

21 Over a five-year period between 1996 and 2000 there were forty-six reported decisions in Canada involving adult complainants who alleged sexual assault involving acts of strangulation. During the five-year period between 2016 and 2020, there were 141 reported decisions involving adult complainants who alleged sexual assault involving acts of strangulation, suggesting a 206.5 per cent increase. In 1996 there were nine cases and in 2021 there were twenty-five cases (CanLII search of all reported cases involving charges of sexual assault, conducted in 2021, using the search terms "choke," "strangle," and "suffocate"). See Karen Busby, "Every Breath You Take: Erotic Asphyxiation, Vengeful Wives, and Other Enduring Myths in Spousal Sexual Assault Prosecutions," *Canadian Journal of Women and the Law* 24, no. 2 (2012): 338. Busby's study discusses the distinction between strangulation (which involves applying external pressure to the trachea to impede blood and oxygen flow to the brain and is more dangerous) and choking (which involves an obstruction inside the throat caused by a foreign object or substance).

22 Over a five-year period between 1996 and 2000 there were two reported decisions in Canada involving adult complainants who alleged sexual assault involving acts of urination. During the five-year period between 2016 and 2020, there were six reported decisions involving adult complainants

who alleged sexual assault involving acts of urination (CanLII search of all reported cases involving charges of sexual assault, conducted in 2021, using the search term "urinate"). It should be noted that in both date ranges these are small numbers. Over a five-year period between 1996 and 2000 there were two reported Canadian decisions involving adult complainants who alleged sexual assault involving acts of spitting. During the five-year period between 2016 and 2020, there were seven reported decisions involving adult complainants who alleged sexual assault involving acts of spitting (CanLII search of all reported cases involving charges of sexual assault, conducted in 2021, using the search terms "spit," "spat," and "spitting"). It should be noted that in both date ranges these are small numbers.

23 Only two reported cases prior to 2000 raised the prospect of a "rough sex defence": see *R v Welch* and *R v RKJ*. It is not clear whether the accused in *RKJ* relied on the couple's supposed history of consensual rough sex as a defence. The accused in *Welch* did rely on the "rough sex defence."

24 In the thirty years between 1996 and 2015 there were two reported "stealthing" cases, whereas in the five-year period between 2016 and 2020 there were twelve reported cases. (CanLII search conducted in 2021 of all reported cases involving charges of sexual assault, using search terms related to "took off" and "removed" in relation to "condom.")

25 *R v Kirkpatrick*, 2022 SCC 33, para. 2.

26 Ibid, para. 12.

27 See, for example, "BBC Scotland/Radio 5 Live, Rough Sex Survey with Men – 14th February 2020," Savanta ComRes, 2020, comresglobal.com/wp-content/uploads/2020/03/Final-5Live-Mens-Poll-Tables-140220-2c0d4h9.pdf. In this survey, 53 per cent of men reported biting, 24 per cent spitting on, 34 per cent gagging or blocking a partner's mouth with a body part or item, 35 per cent choking (or more properly called strangling), and 55 per cent slapping a sexual partner.

28 See, for example, "BBC 5 Live, Women's Poll – 21st November 2019," Savanta ComRes, 2019, https://savanta.com/wp-content/uploads/2022/12/Final-BBC-5-Live-Tables_211119cdh.pdf. In this survey, 38 per cent of women reported experiencing gagging, slapping, biting spitting, strangling, or hair pulling incidents during sex that were unwanted.

29 This remains a contested issue. Social scientists for decades have produced competing empirical studies on whether the consumption of pornography causes, or correlates with, individual sexual aggression or violence. For more recent empirical work supporting the connection, see, for example,

Paul J. Wright, Robert S. Tokunaga, and Ashley Kraus, "A Meta-Analysis of
Pornography Consumption and Actual Acts of Sexual Aggression in General Population Studies," *Journal of Communications* 66 (2016): 196 (meta-
analysis indicating people who consume pornography more frequently are
more likely to be sexually aggressive, and in particular more likely to be
verbally aggressive); Neil Malamuth, "Adding Fuel to the Fire? Does Exposure to Non-consenting Adult or to Child Pornography Increase Risk of
Sexual Aggression?," *Aggression and Violent Behavior* 41 (2018): 87 (finding
exposure to non-consenting pornography may add to sexual aggression for
men who have a pre-disposition); Gert Martin Hald, Neil Malamuth, and
Carlin Yuen, "Pornography and Attitudes Supporting Violence Against
Women: Revisiting the Relationship in Nonexperimental Studies," *Aggressive Behaviour* 36, no. 1 (2010): 18 (meta-analysis finding positive association
between porn consumption and attitudes supporting violence against
women). For studies disproving the connection, see Gabe Hatch et al.,
"Does Pornography Consumption Lead to Intimate Partner Violence Perpetration? Little Evidence for Temporal Precedence," *Canadian Journal of
Human Sexuality* 29, no. 3 (2020): 293 (finding that porn use does not predict intimate partner violence); Christopher J. Ferguson and Richard D.
Hartley, "Pornography and Sexual Aggression: Can Meta-Analysis Find a
Link?," *Trauma, Violence and Abuse* 23, no. 1 (2022): 283 (meta-analysis finding no evidence that non-violent porn consumption is associated with
sexual aggression and weak evidence that consumption of violent porn is
correlated with aggression).

30 Alexa Dodge, "The Digital Witness: The Role of Digital Evidence in Criminal Justice Responses to Sexual Violence," *Feminist Theory* 19, no. 3 (2018):
303. See, for example, *R v Percy*, 2019 NSPC 12; *R v MM*; *R v PO*, 2021 ABQB
318; *R v Gairdner*, 2017 BCCA 425 at para. 2 (as cited in Sheehy, Grant, and
Gotell, "Resurrecting 'She Asked for It,'" 672).

31 For an examination of this tension, see Monica Pa, "Beyond the Pleasure
Principle: The Criminalization of Consensual Sadomasochistic Sex," *Texas
Journal of Women and the Law* 11, no. 1 (2001): 51; Lise Gotell, "Governing
Heterosexuality through Specific Consent: Interrogating the Governmental
Effects of *R. v. J.A.*," *Canadian Journal of Women and the Law* 24, no. 2
(2012): 359; Sharon Cowan, "Criminalizing SM: Disavowing the Erotic,
Instantiating Violence," in *The Structures of the Criminal Law*, eds Antony
Duff et al. (Oxford: Oxford University Press, 2011), 59; Ummni Khan,
Vicarious Kinks: S/M in the Socio-Legal Imaginary (Toronto: University of

Toronto Press, 2014); Vera Bergelson, "The Right to Be Hurt: Testing the Boundaries of Consent," *George Washington Law Review* 75 (2007): 165; Nils-Hennes Stear, "Sadomasochim as Make-Believe," *Hypatia* 24, no. 2 (2009): 21; Deckha, "Pain, Pleasure, and Consenting"; Hanna, "Sex Is Not a Sport." For an argument that society's paradoxical relationship to sex (sexual exceptionalism and sex negativity) results in legal regulation that undervalues sexual autonomy, see Ummni Khan, "Hot for Kink, Bothered by the Law: BDSM and the Right to Autonomy," Canadian Bar Association, 8 August 2016, www.cba-alberta.org/Publications-Resources/Resources/Law-Matters/Law-Matters-Summer-2016-Issue/Hot-for-Kink,-Bothered-by-the-Law-BDSM-and-the-Rig.

32 Katherine Franke, "Theorizing Yes: An Essay on Feminism, Law and Desire," *Columbia Law Review* 101, no. 1 (2001): 182.

33 Ibid., 183.

34 I have examined the failings of a strict good sex/bad sex dichotomy elsewhere. See Elaine Craig, *Troubling Sex: Towards a Legal Theory of Sexual Integrity* (Vancouver: UBC Press, 2012).

35 Franke would arguably agree with this proposition: "It may be that the best we can aspire to, as feminist *legal* theorists, is a set of legal analyses, frames, and supports that erect the enabling conditions for sexual pleasure" (Franke, "Theorizing Yes," 208).

36 In *R v Jobidon*, [1991] 2 SCR 714, 128 NR 321 [*R v Jobidon*], the court held that one cannot consent to the infliction of bodily injury arising from a socially undesirable activity such as a fist fight. The same approach was used in *R v Welch*, in which the accused claimed to have engaged in consensual s/M. In *R v Paice*, 2005 SCC 22, the Supreme Court of Canada clarified that the rule in *Jobidon* stipulated that consent to a fist fight would be vitiated in circumstances in which the accused intended to, and did, cause bodily harm. In *R v Quashie*, [2005] OJ No 2694, 198 CCC (3d) 337, the Court of Appeal for Ontario confirmed that consent is only vitiated if the accused both causes, and subjectively intended to cause, bodily harm. In *R v Barton* (2024) ABCA 34 (CanLII), para. 218, the Court of Appeal of Alberta rejected the court's approach in *Quashie*, concluding that consent will be vitiated if the accused caused significant bodily harm that was objectively foreseeable.

37 Sheehy, Grant and Gotell, "Resurrecting," 666.

38 Franke, "Theorizing Yes."

39 See Busby, "Every Breath." See also, Jennifer Koshan, "The Judicial Treatment of Marital Rape in Canada: A Post-Criminalisation Case Study," in

The Right to Say No: Marital Rape and Law Reform in Canada, Ghana, Kenya and Malawi, eds Melanie Randall, Jennifer Koshan and Patricia Nyaundi (Oxford: Hart Publishing, 2017), 257; Melanie Randall, "Sexual Assault Law, Credibility, and 'Ideal Victims': Consent, Resistance, and Victim Blaming," *Canadian Journal of Women and the Law* 22 (2010): 397.

40   *R v Barton*, ABCA, 2024, para. 218.

41   Ibid.

42   Malachi Willis et al., "Sexual Consent Communication in Best-Selling Pornography Films: A Content Analysis," *Journal of Sex Research* 57, no. 1 (2020): 59. Willis found that in 25 per cent of best-selling videos the sexual behaviour had started before the professional edit. In other words, there was no depiction of consent. This sample was of twenty-minute segments from fifty best-selling videos. It is likely that the percentage of content on mainstream platforms that cuts directly to sexual activity without any depiction of consent is much higher than 25 per cent, given the much shorter, gonzo-style nature of the videos, relative to the videotapes she was studying.

43   Shor and Seida, *Aggression in Pornography*, 19, citing David A. Makin and Amber L. Morczek, "X Views and Counting: Interest in Rape-Oriented Pornography as Gendered Microaggression," *Journal of Interpersonal Violence* 31, no. 12 (2016): 2131. This is not to imply that Pornhub has drawn a distinction between rough sex and S/M or BDSM in categorizing the content on its platform. Based on the results on the first two pages of search results it was not obvious that this is the case. It may be a coincidence that the first video I described was in the "Rough Sex" category on Pornhub and the second in the "Bondage" category.

44   Shor and Seida *Aggression in Pornography*, 19.

45   Busby, "Every Breath," 346.

46   See, for example, "Blonde Riding BBC Anal Gape" (video), Pornhub, accessed 26 March 2023 (2,300,000 views, 89 per cent approval rating); "Her Limit: Try Not to Cum Compilation Part 2. Rough Fuck and Hard Anal" (video), Pornhub, accessed 26 March 2023 (8,500,000 views, 87 per cent approval rating) (which is a nearly thirty-minute compilation of scenes of very rough penetration in which the sexual acts commence before the video begins).

47   "Busty Teen Step-Sister Skylar Vox Gets Pussy Pounded by Frustrated Step-Brother" (video), Pornhub, accessed 2 April 2023 (224,000 views, 88 per cent approval rating).

48   Ibid.

49 "Daddy Makes Petite Newcomer Lilli Chanel's Pussy Squirt" (video), Porn-
    hub, accessed 2 April 2023 (1,500,000 views, 87 per cent approval rating).
    This video had been posted for two months as of 19 April 2022. It had, at
    that point, received 215,000 views and an 89 per cent approval rating. Com-
    ments on the video included: "what a good girl" and "yea fuck her right
    smash into her hole."

50 Ben Zimmer, "'Casting Couch': The Origins of a Pernicious Hollywood
    Cliché," *Atlantic*, 16 October 2017, www.theatlantic.com/entertainment/
    archive/2017/10/casting-couch-the-origins-of-a-pernicious-hollywood-
    cliche/543000.

51 Jodi Kantor and Megan Twohey, "Harvey Weinstein Paid Off Sexual Har-
    assment Accusers for Decades," *New York Times*, 5 October 2017, www.ny
    times.com/2017/10/05/us/harvey-weinstein-harassment-allegations.html.

52 Sarah Polley, "The Men You Meet Making Movies," *New York Times*, 14
    October 2017, www.nytimes.com/2017/10/14/opinion/sunday/harvey-wein
    stein-sarah-polley.html.

53 "Daddy Makes Petite Newcomer," Pornhub.

54 "Diviyne Does Vegas Mayhem Extreme in Las Vegas Bondage Assisted
    Masturbation" (video), Pornhub, accessed 2 April 2023 (74,800 views, 79 per
    cent approval rating).

55 Ibid.

56 See, for example, Shor, "Age, Aggression, and Pleasure," 1031 (content analy-
    sis demonstrating that female performers, and in particular teenage female
    performers, are likely to respond to acts of aggression with pleasure, solid-
    ifying the association between violence and pain on one hand and pleasure
    on the other); Walker et al., "It's Always," 201 (finding in 49 per cent of
    videos, female actors displayed eagerness or willingness to comply with
    whatever was asked of them no matter how violent or aggressive). See
    also Bridges et al., "Aggression and Sexual Behavior," 9.

57 In analyzing the *actus reus*, "the focus is placed squarely on the complain-
    ant's state of mind, and the accused's perception of that state of mind is
    irrelevant": *R v Barton*, 2019 SCC 33, para. 89. See also *R v Ewanchuk*, [1999]
    1 SCR 330, para. 26, 169 DLR (4th) 193.

58 See "Daddy Makes Petite Newcomer," Pornhub; "Diviyne Does Vegas May-
    hem," Pornhub; *R v Hunter*, 2019 NSSC 369; *R v AE*, 2021 ABCA 172.

59 *R v Hunter*; *R v AE* ABCA.

60 *R v Hunter*, para. 6.

61 Ibid., para. 8.

62 Ibid., para. 181.

63 Ibid., para. 82.

64 *R v Hunter* (audio file, trial transcript: testimony of accused, 26 September 2019), 14h:37m:01s.

65 Ibid.

66 *R v Hunter* (audio file, trial transcript: testimony of complainant, 25 September 2019), 11h:28m:35s.

67 Ibid., 11h:33m:02s–27s. A.G. stated in her testimony: "Eventually he then instructed me to lay on the bed with my head over the edge of the bed because he wanted to perform oral sex, but this time when I did that he would be in complete control and I was again hesitant but I did lay on the bed with my head over the edge."

68 Ibid., 11h:33m:31s.

69 *R v Hunter* (audio file, trial transcript: testimony of S.D., 26 September 2019), 11h:16m:00s–26s.

70 Ibid., 11h:06m:30s–09m:40s.

71 *R v Hunter* (audio file, trial transcript: testimony of accused, 26 September 2019), 11h:36m:03s, 11h:36m:28s.

72 Ibid., 11h:36m:06s.

73 Ibid., 11h:36m:35s.

74 Ibid., 11h:39m:58s.

75 Ibid., 14h:18m:13s.

76 Ibid., 14h:21m:00s (the Crown put this to him during cross-examination).

77 Ibid., 14h:21m:28s–57s: "Q: So, Ms. G's eyes may in fact have been watering as she was gagging. A: That's correct. Q: There may have been tears coming from her eyes. A: Yes. Q: And you're not a mind-reader. A: That's correct. Q: You don't know for sure why there may have been tears from her eyes. You were simply guessing it was because she was gagging and not because she was upset or in distress. A: That's a fair assessment."

78 *R v Hunter*, para. 161.

79 Ibid., para. 156.

80 Ibid., para. 157.

81 Ibid.

82 It is not that evidence of the accused's observations of the complainant's conduct or (lack of) communication is irrelevant to the trier of fact's assessment of her state of mind at the time of the incident under this legal definition. Such evidence is relevant if it is probative of her state of mind

at the time. What is not relevant for this aspect of the analysis is his state of mind at the time the act occurred. *R v Ewanchuk*, para. 29 ("While the complainant's testimony is the only source of direct evidence as to her state of mind, credibility must still be assessed by the trial judge, or jury, in light of all the evidence. It is open to the accused to claim that the complainant's words and actions, before and during the incident, raise a reasonable doubt against her assertion that she, in her mind, did not want the sexual touching to take place"). See also Lisa Dufraimont, "Myth, Inference and Evidence in Sexual Assault Trials," *Queen's Law Journal* 44, no. 2 (2019): 316.

83 The trial judge in *R v Ewanchuk*, who was overturned by the scc, concluded that the complainant's conduct (her failure to resist) could be objectively construed as consent to Ewanchuk's sexual touching, despite accepting her evidence that it was fear-based and that she did not in fact want the sexual touching to occur. *R v Ewanchuk*, para. 16.

84 Some research suggests that Latina and Asian women, in particular, are disproportionately featured in videos that include these types of acts. See, for example, Eran Shor and Golshan Golriz, "Gender, Race and Aggression in Mainstream Pornography," *Archives of Sexual Behavior* 48 (2019): 745. Shor and Golriz found, contrary to their hypothesis, that in their sample, Black women performers were not, relative to White performers, subjected to more of these types of acts. Earlier research, on nondigital forms of pornography, did find that Black women performers were overrepresented in porn that depicted rough sex as I have characterized it here. Further content-based research is needed to determine whether other patterns of societal marginalization are also replicated in rough-sex porn.

85 *R v Hunter*, para. 42 (in reference to the first instances of oral penetration – which she characterized as consensual – before she took the position on the bed), para. 43 (in reference to the oral penetration while she was lying on the bed – which she testified was non-consensual).

86 *R v Barton*, scc, para. 89; *R v Ewanchuk*, para. 26.

87 *R v Hunter* (audio file, trial transcript: testimony of complainant, 25 September 2019), 11h:34m:00s, 12h:15:12s.

88 *R v Hunter*, para. 16. The Crown prosecutor introduced photographs A.G. took after the incident that showed some bruising on her breast.

89 *R v Hunter* (audio file, trial transcript: testimony of complainant, 25 September 2019), 11h:39m:14s.

90 Ibid., 15h:44m:23s–45m:07s. The evidence of the length of time between when the complainant told him to stop and when he ejaculated and then

removed his penis was inconsistent. The complainant initially indicated that it was one to two minutes but later agreed that the period of time was short. S.D. told the police that there was a delay between A.G. telling him to stop and the accused actually stopping. *R v Hunter* (audio file, trial transcript: testimony of S.D., 26 September 2019), 10h:09m:05s–10m:53s; *R v Hunter*, para. 76. At trial, she testified that it was a matter of seconds, agreeing on cross-examination that it was approximately ten seconds; *R v Hunter*, para. 77. The trial judge rejected the Crown's suggestion that Hunter ignored the complainant's direction for him to stop, instead ceasing only after he had ejaculated.

91   *R v Hunter*, para. 175.

92   Justice Duncan's conclusion that "breast pinching" (which is not the term A.G. used to describe the incident) is within the scope of BDSM activities was not probative of A.G.'s state of mind at the time her breast was, according to her, squeezed "incredibly hard" by the accused. Consent must be determined in relation to specific sexual acts, not a scope of activities: *R v JA*, 2011 SCC 28, para. 33. The next part of this chapter examines this particular aspect of the reasoning in *Hunter*. There was no evidence, expert or otherwise, that "breast pinching" was "within the scope of BDSM activities." Justice Duncan appears to have taken judicial notice of this "fact." More significantly, there was no evidence from either the complainant or the accused that the complainant had agreed to breast pinching. Justice Duncan found that the parties had not communicated about which sexual acts they would engage in as part of the "threesome."

93   Ibid.

94   Busby, "Every Breath."

95   *R v Barton*, SCC, para. 91 (quoting Justice L'Heureux-Dubé's decision in *R v Park*, [1995] 2 SCR 836, para. 44, 169 AR 241).

96   *R v Goldfinch*, [2019] 3 SCR 3, para. 44.

97   *R v Barton*, SCC, para. 91.

98   Ibid. (emphasis in original).

99   Ibid., para. 92 (emphasis added).

100 Ibid.

101 *R v Hunter*, para. 176 (emphasis added). Of note, it was not the first time a choking action was attempted. The accused repeatedly choked the complainant with his penis prior to placing his hand around her throat. Moreover, the appropriate word to use to describe this latter aspect of the

allegation is strangulation or partial strangulation, not choking. Although pushing his penis that far down her throat did involve choking, partially constricting her breathing by placing his hand around her throat was an act of strangulation, not choking. See Busby, "Every Breath," 338.

102 *R v Hunter*, para. 179.

103 *R v Hunter*, para. 181.

104 *R v Hunter* (audio file, trial transcript: testimony of complainant, 25 September 2019), 11h:22m:24s. When asked by the Crown what the purpose of the meeting was, A.G. responded: "The purpose was for a um like a threesome almost, so in a – so it was um, like a dominant–submissive kind of relationship."

105 *R v Hunter*, para. 150.

106 *Ibid.*, para. 181.

107 See *R v Hunter* (audio file, trial transcript: testimony of complainant, 25 September 2019), 14h:23m:12s–46s.

108 See *R v Hunter*, para. 88.

109 Ibid., para. 28.

110 Ibid., para. 173.

111 *R v Hunter*, para. 181.

112 Ibid., 181.

113 *R v Hunter* (audio file, trial transcript: testimony of S.D., 26 September 2019).

114 Dunkley and Brotto, "Role of Consent," 673.

115 Deckha, "Pain, Pleasure, and Consenting," 438.

116 See *R v Barton*, scc, para. 99. "A belief that the complainant gave broad advance consent to sexual activity of an undefined scope will afford the accused no defence, as that belief is premised on a mistake of law, not fact." (*R v Barton*, scc, para. 99, citing *R v JA*.)

117 *R v Hunter*, para. 181; *R v Hunter* (audio file, trial transcript: testimony of accused, 26 September 2019), 11h:30s (while the complainant had previously communicated with the accused through a form of text messaging, and there was some suggestion she had previously met him, he was relatively unknown to her; indeed, as noted, she did not even know his real name at the time of the incident). See Lise Gotell, "Rethinking Affirmative Consent in Canadian Sexual Assault Law: Neoliberal Sexual Subjects and Risky Women," *Akron Law Review* 41, no. 4 (2008): 865.

118 *R v Hunter*, para. 181. See Elizabeth Sheehy, Isabel Grant, and Lise Gotell,

"The Misogyny of the So-Called Rough Sex Defence," *Policy Options*, 31 January 2020, policyoptions.irpp.org/magazines/january-2020/the-misogyny-of-the-so-called-rough-sex-defence.

119   See *R v Hunter* (audio file, trial transcript: testimony of complainant, 25 September 2019), 11h:23m:17s–26s.

120   See *R v Hunter* (audio file, trial transcript: testimony of accused, 26 September 2019), 11h:29m:59s–30m:30s.

121   See Gotell, "Rethinking Affirmative Consent."

122   I have written about the allocation of sexual risk generally in previous work. See, for example, Elaine Craig, "Capacity to Consent to Sexual Risk," *New Criminal Law Review* 17, no. 1 (2014): 103.

123   The complainant testified that all of the sexual activity was non-consensual. She admitted on cross-examination that she did perform consensual oral sex on T.F., who she had a long-standing crush on, after the main incident. Directly prior to the commencement of the sexual touching, while in the basement of the youth with the three accused, the complainant sent a series of text messages to her friend suggesting that she was contemplating a consensual sexual encounter with the three men. The complainant deleted this exchange on her phone before going to the police (*R v AE* [22 November 2018], Calgary 161500723Q1 [AB KB] [trial transcript: testimony of the complainant, 22 November 2018, at 60:31–61:6]). The complainant admitted during cross-examination that she was considering having sexual activity with the men but asserted again that "regardless [she] did not consent to what they did to [her]" (*R v AE* [trial transcript: testimony of complainant, 22 November 2018], 64:8). See Meghan Grant, "Judge Sentences 'Sexually Immature' Offender to 3 Years in Prison for Violent Group Sex," CBC News, 30 July 2019, www.cbc.ca/news/canada/calgary/AE-group-sex-assault-weapon-sentence-1.5230532.

124   *R v AE* (29 November 2018), Calgary 161500723Q1 (AB KB) (trial transcript: testimony of complainant, 29 November 2018, 60:31–44:30).

125   *R v MM*, para. 5.

126   *R v AE* ABCA, para. 36 (see note 58).

127   *R v MM*, para. 59.

128   Ibid., para. 57.

129   Ibid.

130   In his decision to overturn the acquittals, Justice Martin of the Court of Appeal of Alberta noted that Justice Brooker's failure to give legal recognition to the complainant's clear withdrawal of consent by crying out "no" on

the videotape (before the toothbrush was introduced) was fatal to his reasoning (*R v AE* ABCA, para. 40); while the evidence suggested T.F. did not know that she was being penetrated with the toothbrush and he was not involved in this act, he was penetrating her mouth with his penis at the time it occurred. When she cried out in pain, he ordered her to "spread her legs" and "keep sucking," and then continued penetrating her mouth with his penis (*R v AE* ABCA, paras 155, 167). Justice Brooker concluded that "telling her to spread her legs is, in my view, at best, equivocal" (Ibid., para. 167). It is difficult if not impossible to conjure up what might be equivocal about T.F.'s order. In addition to the other acts of violence he engaged in and the sexual acts he had already engaged in after she had clearly withdrawn consent, regardless of what he knew about the toothbrush, T.F. should have been convicted of sexual assault for ordering her to spread her legs in response to her resistance and expression of pain and then continuing to penetrate her mouth with his penis. In overturning T.F.'s acquittal, Justice Pentelechuk found he should have been convicted of sexual assault on this basis (Ibid., para. 167).

131 *R v AE* (10 April 2019), Calgary 161500723Q1 (AB KB) (trial transcript: trial decision, 10 April 2019, 17:03).

132 *R v MM*, paras 59, 57.

133 In substituting a conviction for Justice Brooker's decision to acquit A.E. and T.F., Justice Peter Martin of the Court of Appeal of Alberta stated: "With respect, the trial judge erred in law by assuming that since the complainant had initiated the sex and asked that it be rough, she was consenting to all that followed. His apparent reliance on broad advance consent was misplaced. He failed to consider whether the complainant consented to all that occurred at the time it occurred" (*R v AE* ABCA, para. 99).

134 "Daddy Makes Petite Newcomer," Pornhub; "Diviyne Does Vegas Mayhem," Pornhub.

135 *R v AE* (trial transcript: trial decision, 10 April 2019, 11:14, 14:23).

136 *R v AE* ABCA, paras 9, 36, 37.

137 *R v AE* (trial transcript: trial decision, 10 April 2019, 9:14).

138 "Celebrating the Retirement of the Honourable Justice Scott Brooker," Court of King's Bench of Alberta, 5 June 2020, www.albertacourts.ca/kb/resources/announcements/celebrating-the-retirement-of-the-honourable-justice-scott-brooker.

139 *R v AE* ABCA (all three members of the panel wrote decisions in this appeal and all three overturned the acquittal, but for somewhat different reasons).

140 Ibid., para. 36.

141 *R v AE* (trial transcript: trial decision, 10 April 2019, 14:27).

142 *R v AE* ABCA, para. 154.

143 *R v MM*, para. 58.

144 To be clear, her evidence was that she did not consent to any of this activity and that she agreed with them at times throughout the incident because if she did not do so they would hit her very hard in the head (*R v AE*, [trial transcript: trial decision, 10 April 2019, 5:28]); *R v AE* (trial transcript: testimony of A.E., 29 November 2018, 41:00–42:00m).

145 During the Crown's cross-examination of T.F., she showed him video of him laughing during this part of the assault. Despite repeatedly showing him the video of himself laughing, he refused to concede that he was laughing, admitting only that he had a smirk on his face (*R v AE* [28 November 2018], Calgary 161500723Q1 [AB KB] [trial transcript: testimony of T.F., 28 November 2018 AM, 22:00]).

146 Ibid., 20:32.

147 Recall from chapter 1 that Pornhub only limited video uploads to verified users *after* a December 2020 *New York Times* article exposing the horrifying stories of girls and women who struggled to have videos of themselves being sexually assaulted and raped removed from the site, and after the platform's payment processors, Visa and Mastercard, cut ties in response to public outcry following the *New York Times* article: Nicholas Kristof, "The Children of Pornhub," *New York Times*, 6 December 2020, ww.nytimes.com/2020/12/04/opinion/sunday/pornhub-rape-trafficking.html (documenting the failure of Pornhub to adequately respond when someone requests that content be removed); Russell Brandom, "Pornhub Limits Uploads and Disables Downloads after New York Times Exposé," *Verge*, 8 December 2020, www.theverge.com/2020/12/8/22164031/pornhub-upload-limit-blocked-download-nyt-kristof-child-abuse (reporting on the timeline of Pornhub's policy changes and the *New York Times* article). In October 2021, MindGeek settled a lawsuit with fifty women who sued it and a company called "GirlsDoPorn" who they allege posted videos of them on sites like Pornhub without their consent, including some videos that captured non-consensual sexual acts: Joe Lofaro, "Pornhub Owner Settles Lawsuit with 50 Women, including Four Canadians," CTV News, 20 October 2021, https://montreal.ctvnews.ca/pornhub-owner-settles-lawsuit-with-50-women-including-four-canadians-1.5630651.

148 *R v AE* (trial transcript: trial decision, 10 April 2019, 7:32).

149 *R v AE* ABCA, para. 37.

150 *R v AE* (trial transcript: testimony of A.E., 29 November 2018, 18:00).

151 Ibid., 21:41.

152 Ibid., 58; *R v AE* ABCA, para. 169; *R v AE* (trial transcript: testimony of T.F., 28 November 2018, 18:15, 18:12).

153 *R v AE* (trial transcript: testimony of A.E., 29 November 2018 AM, 8:00).

154 *R v AE* (27 November 2018), Calgary 161500723Q1 (AB KB) (trial transcript: testimony of T.F., 27 November 2018 PM) at 24:4–24:9.

155 *R v AE* CA, para. 169.

156 *R v AE* (trial transcript: testimony of T.F., 27 November 2018 PM, 22:34) (emphasis added).

157 *R v AE* (trial transcript: testimony of A.E., 29 November 2018 AM, 59:00).

158 Ibid., 22.

159 *R v AE* (trial transcript: trial decision, 10 April 2019, 11:14).

160 *R v AE* (trial transcript: testimony of A.E., 29 November 2018 AM, 43:17).

161 *R v AE* (trial transcript: testimony of T.F., 28 November 2018 AM, 18:12).

162 Ibid., 19:5.

163 Ibid., 19:7–12

164 *R v MM*, para. 57.

165 "Daddy Makes Petite Newcomer," Pornhub.

166 Ibid.

167 *R v AE* (trial transcript: testimony of T.F., 28 November 2018 AM, 12:32).

168 *R v AE* (trial transcript: testimony of A.E., 29 November 2018 PM, 43:24).

169 *R v AE* (trial transcript: trial decision, 10 April 2019, 9:50).

170 *R v AE* (trial transcript: testimony of A.E., 29 November 2018, 55:15) (emphasis added).

171 Ibid.

172 *R v MM*, para. 43.

173 *R v AE* (trial transcript: testimony of A.E., 29 November 2018 PM, 46:00).

174 Ibid., 43:31.

175 *R v AE* (trial transcript: testimony of T.F., 28 November 2018 AM, 19:5).

176 *R v MM*, para. 9.

177 Ibid., para. 20.

178 Ibid., para. 62.

179 "My Stepbrother and I Destroy a Teen with Our Huge Cocks While My Friend Films It on His iPhone" (video), Pornhub, accessed 16 April 2023 (1,400,000 views, 84 per cent approval rating); "Tiny 18 Year Old Teen Gets Wrecked by Muscular Stud" (video), Pornhub, accessed 16 April 2023

(14,400 views, 78 per cent approval rating); "18 Year Old College Slut Getting Railed from Behind" (video), Pornhub, accessed 16 April 2023 (20,100 views, 97 per cent approval rating) (this video had been posted for one month at the time of writing and had been viewed 12,600 times, with a 100 per cent approval rating) (emphases added).

180 *R v AE* (trial transcript: testimony of T.F., 28 November 2018 AM, 12:00).

181 *R v AE* (trial transcript: testimony of A.E., 29 November 2018 PM, 55:17) (emphasis added).

182 Franke, "Theorizing Yes," 206; *R v Hunter*, 2019 NSSC 369; *R v AE* ABCA.

183 Shor and Golriz, "Gender, Race and Aggression."

184 See *R v Barton* ABCA 2024, in which the court unanimously concluded that, given the gendered nature of the rough sex defence, consent to sexual touching will be vitiated if the sexual touching was intentional and it caused significant bodily harm that was objectively foreseeable. See also Elizabeth Sheehy, Isabel Grant, and Lise Gotell, "Resurrecting 'She Asked for It': The Rough Sex Defence in Canada," *Alberta Law Review* 60, no. 3 (2023): 651.

185 See, for example, *R v Ewanchuk*, paras 26, 45 (in which the majority of the Supreme Court of Canada adopted the definition of consent articulated by Justice Claire L'Heureux-Dubé in *R v Park*, [1995] 2 SCR 836). Justice L'Heureux-Dubé was widely known to be a feminist (see Constance Backhouse, *Claire L'Heureux-Dubé: A Life* [Vancouver: UBC Press, 2017]) and regularly relied on the work of feminist academics in her decisions (see, for example, *R v Ewanchuk*, paras 68, 82).

186 See, for example, *R v Barton*, SCC.

CHAPTER SEVEN

1 Pornhub, "Terms of Service," accessed April 2022, https://www.pornhub.com/information/terms.

2 Tarleton Gillespie, *Custodians of the Internet: Platforms, Content Moderation, and the Hidden Decisions That Shape Social Media* (New Haven: Yale University Press, 2018), 7 (explaining how platforms construct themselves as mere conduits in an effort to avoid criticism and responsibility).

3 *R v Butler*, [1992] 1 SCR 452, para. 49, 89 DLR (4th) 449.

4 Ibid., para. 49

5 Ibid., para. 60.

6 "Swallowing Bitch" (video), Pornhub, accessed 26 May 2023.

7 "Slutty Black Serving Group of 5 BBC" (video), Pornhub, accessed 26 May 2023.

8 "Nasty ʙʙᴡ Slut Gangbanged in Bowling Alley" (video), Pornhub, accessed 26 May 2023 (542,000 views, 92 per cent approval rating).

9 "Hardcore Slut Takes It Rough" (video), Pornhub, accessed 26 May 2023 (15,600,000 views, 84 per cent approval rating).

10 "Slapped, Facialed Then Pissed on … Dumb Slut" (video), xHamster, accessed 27 June 2023 (213,122 views, 98 per cent approval rating).

11 "Dumb Piss Slut Gets Pissed On" (video), xHamster, accessed 27 June 2023 (26,636 views, 99 per cent approval rating).

12 "Dumb Black Bitches" (video), xHamster, accessed 27 June 2023 (156,585 views, 92 per cent approval rating).

13 "Dumb Slut Needed to Learn Her Place. On Her Knees Sucking Dick" (video), xHamster, accessed 7 June 2023 (11,241 views, 92 per cent approval rating).

14 "Dumb Bitch Gettin Fucked Real Good" (video), Pornhub, accessed 20 November 2023 (137,000 views, 87 per cent approval rating).

15 "Dumb Bitch!!! Get's Facefucked for Lying" (video), Pornhub, accessed 7 June 2023 (96,000 views, 90 per cent approval rating).

16 Ibid.

17 For a discussion and rejection of this stereotype, see Gina Rippon, *The Gendered Brain: The New Neuroscience That Shatters the Myth of the Female Brain* (London: Bodley Head, 2019).

18 Diane Felmlee, Paulina Inara Rodis, and Amy Zhang, "Sexist Slurs: Reinforcing Feminine Stereotypes Online," *Sex Roles* 83, nos 1–2 (2020): 25.

19 *R v Butler*, para. 49.

20 In their study of videos on Pornhub, Shor and Seida found that approximately 25 per cent of the most popular videos involved ejaculating on the (typically female) performer's face, more than half of videos that included Latina performers involved visible aggression, and three-quarters of videos with Asian women performers included acts of aggression such as hitting, choking, and slapping. One-third of these depictions of aggression against Asian women were of non-consensual acts. Eran Shor and Kimberley Seida, *Aggression in Pornography: Myths and Realities* (New York: Routledge, 2020), 67, 111.

21 *Little Sisters Book and Art Emporium v Canada (Minister of Justice)*, [2000] 2 ꜱᴄʀ 1120, [2000] ꜱᴄᴊ No. 66 [*Little Sisters v Canada*]. See, generally, Brenda Cossman et al., *Bad Attitude(s) on Trial: Pornography, Feminism and the Butler Decision* (Toronto: University of Toronto Press, 1997). When it is used outside of this context today it is mostly a charge laid in cases

involving extremely violent content – like *R v Marek*, 2016 ABQB 18 (Can-LII) (which involved a depiction of the murder and dismemberment of a human victim) – or cases involving child pornography – like *R v JC*, 2013 BCPC 237 (CanLII) (which involved the depiction of a naked, distressed toddler who was strapped to a board and defecated on by a naked adult male). See also *R v Danylak*, 2012 ABCA 179 (CanLII) (in which the accused sent an obscene message to a young person). See also Janine Benedet, "The Paper Tigress: Canadian Obscenity Laws 20 Years After R v Butler," *Canadian Bar Review* 93, no. 1 (2015): 1 (documenting the very modest application of the obscenity provisions post-*Butler* to mainstream, heterosexual porn).

22 *R v Butler*, para. 59.

23 *R v Ronish*, 1993 CanLII 17013, para. 58, 15 OR (3d) 549 (Ont CA). Two other Ontario cases, *R v Hawkins* and *R v Jorgensen*, were also heard by the Court of Appeal at the same time. For an examination of the court's reasoning in this appeal, see, for example, Benedet, "Paper Tigress," 18.

24 "Dumb Slut" (video), xHamster (11,241 views, 92 per cent approval rating).

25 "Nothing but a Useless, Toothless Cum Dumpster Slut Sucking Dick on the Porch" (video), Pornhub, accessed 31 May 2023 (45,600 views, 88 per cent approval rating).

26 Testimony of Feras Antoon, House of Commons, Standing Committee on Access to Information, Privacy and Ethics, *Evidence*, 43-2, No. 19 (5 February 2021), 3. Pornhub maintains that its human moderators approve every upload, and so presumably that means that every one of the titles on its platforms is also approved by its employees.

27 "Nothing but a Useless," Pornhub.

28 "Katrin Tiidenberg, "Sex, Power, and Platform Governance," *Porn Studies* 8, no. 4 (2021): 388.

29 Lise Gotell, "Inverting Image and Reality: *R v Sharpe* and the Moral Panic around Child Pornography," *Constitutional Forum* 12, no. 1 (2001): 12.

30 *Little Sisters v Canada* (accepting that this weaponization was committed by administrative arms of the state such as censor boards and custom officials, rather than by criminal law enforcement).

31 *Alberta Human Rights Act*, RSA 2000, c A-25.5, s. 3; *British Columbia Human Rights Code*, RSBS 1996, c 210, s. 7(1); *Saskatchewan Human Rights Code*, SS 2018, c S-24.2, s. 14(1).

32 *Canadian Human Rights Act*, RSC 1985, c H-6, s. 13, as repealed by *An Act to amend the Canadian Human Rights Act (protecting freedom)*, SC 2013, c 37.

33 Bill C-36, *An Act to amend the Criminal Code and the Canadian Human Rights Act and to make related amendments to another act (hate propaganda, hate crimes and hate speech)*, 2nd Sess, 43rd Parl, 2021 (first reading 23 June 2021). This bill died when Parliament was dissolved.

34 Bill C-63, *Online Harms Act*, 1st sess, 44th Parl, 2024, s. 2.

35 *Criminal Code*, RSC 1985 c C-46, s. 319(2); *R v Sears*, [2019] OJ No. 1005, 2019 ONCJ 104. This appears to be the only reported case in which the provision has been used to prosecute someone for willfully promoting hatred against women. Sears and St Germaine published an online magazine that, in addition to hateful speech against Jewish people, represented women as irrational, unworthy of the vote, liars, and men's chattel, and which called on men to shut down vile women.

36 *R v Buzzanga and Durocher* (1979), 101 DLR (3d) 488, paras 25–26, 25 OR No (2d) 705.

37 Emily Laidlaw advances a human rights framework for holding platform intermediaries responsible in *Regulating Speech in Cyberspace: Gatekeepers, Human Rights and Corporate Responsibility* (Cambridge, MA: Cambridge University Press, 2015). While her focus in this book is on non-state–based governance models, and Internet service providers and search engines in particular, one of her central insights is instructive in this context: regulating "cyber speech" in a manner that is sufficiently protective of freedom of expression through a human rights framework requires a proportionate and transparent approach, with sufficient state oversight. This is true of both state governance and non-state–based corporate responsibility approaches to the regulation of the Internet (including platform intermediaries).

38 See Jane Bailey, "Twenty Years Later *Taylor* Still Has It Right: How the *Canadian Human Rights Act*'s Hate Speech Provision Continues to Contribute to Equality," *Supreme Court Law Review* 50 (2d) (2010): 35 (advocating for a broad-based ameliorative and remedial equality approach to online hate speech, which would be more attainable under human rights legislation, such as the former section 13 of the *Canadian Human Rights Act* than through a criminal law prohibition).

39 For a discussion of the international human rights law context, see, for example, Jane Bailey, "Private Regulation and Public Policy: Toward Effective Restriction of Internet Hate Propaganda," *McGill Law Journal* 49, no. 1 (2004): 59.

40 See *Family Caring Society of Canada v Canada (Attorney General)*, [2021]

FCJ No. 104 (QL); Gwen Brodsky, Shelagh Day, and Frances Kelly, "The Authority of Human Rights Tribunals to Grant Systemic Remedies," *Canadian Journal Human Rights* 6, no. 1 (2017): 1.

41 Brodsky, Day, and Kelly, *Authority of Human Rights*, 4.

42 Ibid., 45.

43 Ibid., 13.

44 *Saskatchewan (Human Rights Commission) v Whatcott*, 2013 SCC 11 [*Saskatchewan v Whatcott*].

45 Ibid., para. 132; *R v Keegstra*, [1990] 3 SCR 697, [1990] SCJ No. 131 (QL); *Canada (Human Rights Commission) v Taylor*, [1990] 3 SCR 892, [1990] SCJ No. 129.

46 *Saskatchewan v Whatcott*, para. 132.

47 Ibid., para. 133, citing *Thomson Newspapers Co v Canada (Attorney General)*, [1998] 1 SCR 877 at 116, [1998] SCJ No. 44.

48 Ibid., para. 41.

49 Ibid., para. 43.

50 Ibid., para. 43.

51 Ibid., para. 43.

52 Ibid., para. 45.

53 Testimony of Feras Antoon, *Evidence*, 1.

54 "Dumb Bitch Gettin Fucked," Pornhub.

55 "Stupid Slut Used" (video), Pornhub, accessed 26 June 2023 (257,000 views, 87 per cent approval rate).

56 "2 Stupid Sluts Getting Their Faces Fucked by 1 Guy While He Slaps Them Around" (video), Pornhub, accessed 26 June 2023 (360,000 views, 84 per cent approval rating).

57 "Two Stupid Sluts Degrading Themselves" (video), Pornhub, accessed 26 June 2023 (45,900 views, 83 per cent approval rating).

58 Ibid.

59 "Desperate for Money Cum Dumpster College Teens Fucked" (video), Pornhub, accessed 26 June 2023 (2,000,000 views, 88 per cent approval rating).

60 "Slutty Step Daughter Is a Cum Dumpster" (video), Pornhub, accessed 26 June 2023 (234,000 views, 91 per cent approval rating).

61 "This Stupid Whores Only Good for 1 Thing" (video), Pornhub, accessed 1 June 2023 (8,300 views, 93 per cent approval rating).

62 "Nothing but a Useless," Pornhub.

63 Ibid.

64 "Crack Whore Fresh from Jail. She'll Run the Streets. In a Few Months, She'll Be Strung Out and Skinny" (video), Pornhub, accessed 26 June 2023 (27,100 views, 90 per cent approval rating).

65 "Crackhead Shows Up to Suck and Fuck for More Money" (video), Pornhub, accessed 26 June 2023 (58,200 views, 83 per cent approval rating).

66 Ibid.

67 "Strung Out Crack Slut Fucks While Boyfriend Has to Wait Outside" (video), Pornhub, accessed 26 June 2023 (82,800 views, 88 per cent approval rating).

68 "Homeless Skank Sucks and Fucks Me in My Bathroom" (video), Pornhub, accessed 26 June 2023 (52,200 views, 80 per cent approval rating).

69 "Crackhead Slut Expertly Sucks My Cock. Best Blowjob of My Life" (video), Pornhub, accessed 26 June 2023 (25,400 views, 93 per cent approval rating).

70 *Saskatchewan v Whatcott*.

71 Ibid., para. 57.

72 Ibid., para. 127.

73 Ibid., para. 82.

74 Marie Wolfe, "Online Harms Bill Proposed Changes Risk Silencing Free Speech, Experts," *Globe and Mail*, 27 February 2024, accessed 19 March 2024, https://www.theglobeandmail.com/politics/article-online-harms-bills-proposed-changes-risk-silencing-free-speech-experts.

75 Pornhub, "dumb bitch" (search conducted 15 June 2023); Pornhub, "stupid cunt" (search conducted 15 June 2023); Pornhub, "cum dumpster "(search conducted 15 June 2023). At the bottom of each of these searches, Pornhub offers videos that are "related." For example, a search of "stupid cunt" produces, from Pornhub, a section of "Searches related to Stupid Cunt" that includes, for example, "Cum Dumpster." Clicking on "Cum Dumpster" yields videos with titles referring to "crack head sluts" and "homeless skanks" ("Strung Out Crack Slut," Pornhub; "Homeless Skank," Pornhub; "Crackhead Slut," Pornhub).

76 Pornhub, "cum dumpster" (search conducted 15 June 2023).

77 "Strung Out Crack Slut," Pornhub; "Homeless Skank," Pornhub; "Crackhead Slut," Pornhub.

78 "2 Stupid Sluts Getting Their Faces," Pornhub.

79 "Nothing but a Useless," Pornhub.

80 "Strung Out Crack Slut," Pornhub; "Homeless Skank," Pornhub; "Crackhead Slut," Pornhub.

81 Sarah Tosh, "Drugs, Crime, and Aggravated Felony Deportations: Moral

Panic Theory and the Legal Construction of the 'Criminal Alien,'" *Critical Criminology* 27, no. 2 (2019): 335; Cindy Brooks Dollar, "Criminalization and Drug 'Wars' or Medicalization and Health 'Epidemics': How Race, Class, and Neoliberal Politics Influence Drug Laws," *Critical Criminology* 27, no. 2 (2019): 307–8.

82 See note 75.

83 *Saskatchewan v Whatcott*, para. 41.

84 "Privacy Policy," Pornhub, last accessed 14 April 2022, https://www.porn hub.com/information/privacy.

85 *Saskatchewan v Whatcott*, para. 191.

86 *Canada (Human Rights) v Taylor*, [1990] 3 SCR 892 at para. 5.

87 *Saskatchewan v Whatcott*, para. 187.

88 Ibid., para. 74.

89 See, for example, Elizabeth Sheehy, *Sexual Assault in Canada: Law, Legal Practice and Women's Activism* (Ottawa: University of Ottawa Press, 2012); Janine Benedet, "Sexual Assault Cases at the Alberta Court of Appeal: The Roots of '*Ewanchuk*' and the Unfinished Revolution," *Alberta Law Review* 52, no. 1 (2014): 127.

90 "Crack Whore Fresh from Jail," Pornhub.

91 "Homeless Skank," Pornhub.

92 *Saskatchewan v Whatcott*, para. 76.

93 Bill C-36, 9 (see note 33).

94 Bill C-63, *An Act to amend the Criminal Code*, s. 34(3).

95 Tarleton Gillespie, "Platforms Are Not Intermediaries," *Georgetown Law Technology Review* 2 (2018): 210–11.

96 "Terms of Service," Pornhub, last accessed 28 December 2022, https://www. pornhub.com/information/terms.

97 Emily Laidlaw, "Creating an Online Harms Bill Is Tricky, but It Can Be Done Right," *Globe and Mail*, 25 October 2022, https://www.theglobeand mail.com/opinion/article-online-safety-harms-bill.

98 Safiya Umoja Noble, *Algorithms of Oppression: How Search Engines Rein-force Racism* (New York: NYU Press, 2018).

99 See, for example, Alex Colangelo and Alana Maurushat, "Exploring the Limits of Computer Code as a Protected Form of Expression: A Suggested Approach to Encryption, Computer Viruses, and Technological Protection Measures," *McGill Law Journal* 51, no. 1 (2006): 48 (arguing that computer code, for example, should be covered within the scope of section 2(b) and limits assessed under section 1); Jeffery Atik and Karl Manheim, "Social

Media Algorithms Are Not Protected Speech," https://thehill.com/opinion/congress-blog/technology/4035644-social-media-algorithms-are-not-protected-speech (arguing that algorithms should not be protected under free speech protections). I am grateful to Jane Bailey for drawing my attention to these sources and this debate.

100 *Irwin Toy Ltd v Quebec (Attorney General)*, [1989] 1 SCR 927, [1989] SCJ No. 36.

101 *RJR-MacDonald Inc v Canada (Attorney General)*, [1994] 1 SCR 311, [1994] SCJ No. 17.

102 See *R v Keegstra*, paras 104–106; *R v Butler; Little Sisters v Canada.*

103 For an explanation of why, and empirical evidence demonstrating that, placing legal limits on gender-based abuse online is unlikely to have a chilling effect on speech, see Jon Penney, "Can Cyber Harassment Laws Encourage Online Speech?," Berkman Klein Center for Internet and Society, 15 August 2017, https://medium.com/berkman-klein-center/can-cyber-harassment-laws-encourage-online-speech-4e1ae884bfba; see also Jon Penney, "Online Abuse, Chilling Effects, and Human Rights," in *Citizenship in a Connected Canada: A Policy and Research Agenda*, eds Elizabeth Dubois and Florian Martin-Bariteau (Ottawa: University of Ottawa Press, 2020), 207 (arguing that such regulation might, as an expressive matter, in fact have the opposite effect).

104 Renée DiResta, "Free Speech Is Not the Same as Free Reach," *Wired*, 30 August 2018, https://www.wired.com/story/free-speech-is-not-the-same-as-free-reach, cited in Cynthia Khoo, "Deplatforming Misogyny," LEAF, 2021, 204, https://www.leaf.ca/wp-content/uploads/2021/04/Full-Report-Deplatforming-Misogyny.pdf.

105 *Greater Vancouver Transportation Authority v Canadian Federation of Students*, [2009] 2 SCR 295, 2009 SCC 31.

106 Laidlaw, *Regulating Speech*, 204–5.

107 Simon Van Zuylen-Wood, "'Men Are Scum': Inside Facebook's War on Hate Speech," *Vanity Fair*, 26 February 2019, https://www.vanityfair.com/news/2019/02/men-are-scum-inside-facebook-war-on-hate-speech.

108 Danielle Keats Citron and Helen Norton, "Intermediaries and Hate Speech," *Boston University Law Review* 91 (2011): 1435.

109 Ibid., 1440.

110 "Hate Speech Policy," Pornhub, March 2023, https://help.pornhub.com/hc/en-us/articles/14512634908819-Hate-Speech-Policy.

111 Ibid.

112 Citron and Norton, "Intermediaries," 1456.

113 *Criminal Code*, s. 163.1. The exception involves synthetic media or deepfake porn. Currently, the distribution of deepfake pornography is not explicitly prohibited under criminal law in Canada. However, as Jane Bailey et al. argue, it could and should be prohibited by amending the *Criminal Code* prohibition on the non-consensual distribution of intimate images. They note that this could be achieved with a modest revision to section 162.1 to "include images that have been falsely created or modified," as has been done in other jurisdictions, and a recognition that a person has a reasonable expectation of privacy in sexual images of themselves created through artificial intelligence: Jane Bailey et al., "AI and Technology-Facilitated Violence and Abuse," in *Artificial Intelligence and the Law in Canada*, eds Florian Martin-Bariteau and Teresa Scassa (Toronto: LexisNexis Canada, 2021), 260. See also Suzie Dunn, "Identity Manipulation: Responding to Advances in Artificial Intelligence and Robotics" (unpublished paper delivered at We Robot, Ottawa, 4 April 2020); Danelle K. Citron, "Sexual Privacy," *Yale Law Journal* 128, no. 7 (2019): 1947–8.

114 See, for example, *Criminal Code*, s. 162.1, s. 163.1; *R v Spencer*, 2014 SCC 43.

115 Nicola Henry and Asher Flynn, "Image-Based Sexual Abuse: Online Distribution Channels and Illicit Communities of Support," *Violence Against Women* 25, no. 16 (2019): 1940.

116 See, for example, *R v Beattie* (2005), 75 OR (3d) 117, para. 23, [2005] OJ No. 1302 (CA), leave to appeal to SCC refused, [2005] SCCA No. 319 (regarding material that promotes sex with children as constituting child sexual abuse material ("child pornography")).

117 See, for example, *R v Spencer* (2014) SCC 43 ("knowingly making available" does not require a positive act – it is sufficient to provide the apparatus for distribution if the accused knows it will be used to make child sexual abuse material available). See, for example, *Criminal Code*, s. 22.2 (regarding liability for an organization in which one of its senior officers, with the intent to benefit the organization, is a party to the offence while acting within the scope of their authority or having the mental state required to be a party to the offence directs others to do the work specified in the offence).

118 Jane Bailey and Carissima Mathen, "Technology-Facilitated Violence Against Women and Girls: Assessing the Canadian Criminal Law Response," *Canadian Bar Review* 97, no. 3 (2019): 666.

119 Testimony of Stephen White, House of Commons, Standing Committee

on Access to Information, Privacy and Ethics, *Evidence*, 43-2, No. 21 (22 February 2021), 16.

120 *R v Libman*, [1985] 2 SCR 178, para. 74, 21 DLR (4th) 174. For a general explanation of the principle of qualified territorial jurisdiction in Canadian law, see Robert Currie and Joseph Rikhoff, *International and Transnational Criminal Law*, 3rd ed, 489 (Toronto: Irwin Law, 2020), 489. As the authors document, this "real and substantial connection test" has also been relied upon to apply the doctrine of qualified territorial jurisdiction regarding other Canadian statutes, such as the *Competition Act* and Canada's *Personal Information Protection and Electronic Documents Act* (PIPEDA).

121 "Ethical Capital Partners Undertaking Stakeholder Consultations," Ethical Capital Partners, 27 April 2023, https://www.ethicalcapitalpartners.com/news/ethical-capital-partners-undertaking-stakeholder-consultations. "Partnering with law enforcement in investigating and prosecuting online offenders is at the core of ECP's fundamental commitment to child protection and intimate image security" (ibid., para. 3).

122 PIPEDA Findings # 2024-001, "Investigation into Aylo (formerly Mind-Geek)'s Compliance with PIPEDA," 29 February 2024, para. 124, https://www.priv.gc.ca/en/opc-actions-and-decisions/investigations/investigations-into-businesses/2024/pipeda-2024-001.

123 I have examined some of the failings of the criminal justice system in this regard in earlier work. See, for example, Elaine Craig, *Putting Trials on Trial: Sexual Assault and the Failure of the Legal System* (Montreal: McGill-Queen's University Press, 2015).

124 *Intimate Images and Cyber-protection Act*, SNS 2017, c 7; *Intimate Images Protection Act*, RSPEI 1988, c I-9.1 s. 5.2(2); *Intimate Images Protection Act*, RSNL 2018, c I-22, s. 9(1)(c).

125 *Intimate Images and Cyber-protection Act*, SNS 2017, c 7; *Intimate Images Protection Act*, RSPEI 1988, c I-9.1 s. 5.2(2); *Intimate Images Protection Act*, RSNL 2018, c I-22, s. 9(1)(c).

126 Hilary Young and Emily Laidlaw, "Creating a Revenge Porn Tort for Canada," *Supreme Court Law Review* 96, no. 2 (2020): 147–8.

127 Ibid., 148, 159–60, 163; Khoo, "Deplatforming Misogyny," 122–55.

128 *Uniform Non-consensual Disclosure of Intimate Images Act*, s. 4(2)(d)–(e).

129 Ibid., 10.

130 Young and Laidlaw, "Creating a Revenge Porn Tort," 151.

131 Ibid., 150.

132 *Communications Decency Act*, 47 USC § 230 (1966).

133 Danielle K. Citron and Benjamin Wittes, "The Problem Isn't Just Backpage: Revising Section 230 Immunity," *Georgetown Law and Technology Review* 2 (2018) 2: 453–55.

134 Gillespie, *Custodians of the Internet*, 30.

135 There has been some concern over Canada's 2020 ratification of the Canada–United States–Mexico Agreement (USMCA), and in particular a provision of that agreement which stipulates that signatories will not adopt measures "that treat a supplier or user of an interactive computer service as an information content provider in determining liability" for that supplier (USMCA, 30 November 2018, Can TS 2020 No 5 art 19.17.2 [entered into force 1 July 2020]). However, as Cynthia Khoo observes, "[w]hile Article 19.17.2 of the USMCA imports principles similar to those of paragraph 230(c)(1), it does not necessarily import the judicial interpretations of those principles, which has resulted in the broad immunity provided in the U.S." Khoo, "Deplatforming Misogyny," 115, citing "Demystified: USMCA's Digital Trade Provisions on ISP Liability in Canada," Blakes, 14 November 2018, https://www.blakes.com/insights/bulletins/2018/demystified-usmcas-digital-trade-provisions-on-isp. See also Citron and Wittes, "The Problem Isn't Just Backpage," 459–62. Moreover, the USMCA is silent on imposing regulatory responsibilities on platforms regarding their own roles in causing these types of harms. In addition, to create immunity for platforms akin to the protections under section 230 of the *Communications Decency Act*, this provision of the treaty would need to be incorporated into domestic statutes. Khoo, "Deplatforming Misogyny," 115.

136 *Intimate Images Protection Act*, RSPEI 1988, c I-9.1, s. 5.3(1); *Intimate Images Protection Act*, SBC 2023 c 11, s. 12.

137 *Intimate Images Protection Act*, RSPEI 1988, c I-9.1 s. 5.3(1).

138 *Intimate Images Protection Act*, SBC 2023 c 11, s. 12.

139 EC, Directive 2000/31/EC of 8 June 2000 on Certain Legal Aspects of Information Society Services, in Particular Electronic Commerce, in the Internal Market, [2000] OJ, L 178/1 arts 12–15; Bill 161, *Act to establish a legal framework for information technology*, 2nd Sess, 36th Leg, Quebec, 2001, s 22 (assented to 21 June 2001) SQ 2001, c 32.

140 Khoo, "Deplatforming Misogyny," 120.

141 Young and Laidlaw, "Creating a Revenge Porn Tort," 151–3.

142 Ibid.; 183–4.

143 Ibid., 184.

144　"Pornhub Offers Free Pornhub Premium to Users Worldwide for 30 Days during COVID-19 Pandemic," Pornhub, 24 March 2020, https://www.pornhub.com/press/show?id=1951.

145　Hannah Price, "Coronavirus: 'Revenge Porn' Surge Hits Helpline," BBC News, 25 April 2020, www.bbc.com/news/stories-52413994.

146　Zara Ward, "Revenge Porn Helpline Report," 15, www.https://revengeporn helpline.org.uk/assets/documents/rph-report-2022.pdf?_=1681885542.

147　Andrea Slane and Ganaele Langlois, "Debunking the Myth of 'Not My Bad': Sexual Images, Consent, and Online Host Responsibilities in Canada," *Canadian Journal of Women and the Law* 30, no. 1 (2018): 73.

148　Samantha Cole and Emanuel Maiberg, "How Pornhub Enables Doxing and Harassment," *Vice*, 16 July 2019, https://www.vice.com/en/article/mb8zjn/pornhub-doxing-and-harassment-girls-do-porn-lawsuit.

149　CAS21-0614-Garcia, "Twenty Year Sentence in GirlsDoPorn Sex Trafficking Conspiracy" (press release) United States Department of Justice, 14 June 2021, https://www.justice.gov/usao-sdca/pr/twenty-year-sentence-girlsdo porn-sex-trafficking-conspiracy.

150　*Doe v Mindgeek USA Inc*, 558 F Supp (3d) 828 (Cal Dist Ct 2021), para. 111 (Statement of Claim) submitted by Brian M. Holm, https://www.document cloud.org/documents/20425190-mindgeekjanedoes1-40.

151　Ibid., para. 111.

152　"Pornhub Owner Settles with Girls Do Porn Victims over Videos," BBC News, 19 October 2021, https://www.bbc.com/news/technology-58917993.

153　Samantha Cole and Emanuel Maiberg, "Pornhub Doesn't Care," *Vice*, 6 February 2020, www.vice.com/en/article/9393zp/how-pornhub-moder ation-works-girls-do-porn.

154　Testimony of Serena Fleites, House of Commons, Standing Committee on Access to Information, Privacy and Ethics, *Evidence*, 43-2, No. 18 (1 February 2021), 1–2, 6–11; Testimony of John Clark, House of Commons, Standing Committee on Access to Information, Privacy and Ethics, *Evidence*, 43-2, No. 21 (22 February 2021), 4–5; Nicholas Kristof, "The Children of Pornhub," *New York Times*, 4 December 2020, www.nytimes.com/2020/12/04/opinion/sunday/pornhub-rape-trafficking.html.

155　Ethan Zuckerman, "The Internet's Original Sin: It's Not Too Late to Ditch the Ad-Based Business Model and Build a Better Web," *Atlantic*, 14 August 2014, https://www.theatlantic.com/technology/archive/2014/08/advertising-is-the-internets-original-sin/376041.

156　EC, Directive 2000/31/EC. This is similar to how liability applies to Internet intermediaries in the European Union.

157 Testimony of Lloyd Richardson, House of Commons, Standing Committee on Access to Information, Privacy and Ethics, *Evidence*, 43-2, No. 21 (22 February 2021), 6 (Lloyd Richardson, testifying that Pornhub responded more promptly when they received takedown requests from their organization than when they received requests from individual victims).

158 Michael Geist, "Government Departments Pressure Social Media Sites to Censor News Links, Mean Tweets" (blog), 13 April 2023, https://www.mi chaelgeist.ca/2023/04/government-departments-pressure-social-media-sites-to-censor-news-links-mean-tweets.

159 William Echikson and Olivia Knodt, "Germany's NetzDG: A Key Test for Combatting Online Hate," CEPS, 22 November 2018, 8–9, http://wp.ceps.eu/wp-content/uploads/2018/11/RR%20No2018-09_Germany's%20NetzDG.pdf.

160 "Solution Explorer," Government of British Columbia, accessed 3 February 2024, https://explore.civilresolutionbc.ca/ES_SummaryReport?id=a1ZM m000000YTQzMAO.

161 "Intimate Images Protection Service," Government of British Columbia, accessed 3 February 2024, https://www2.gov.bc.ca/gov/content/safety/public-safety/intimate-images/intimate-images-support.

CHAPTER EIGHT

1 Samantha Cole, *How Sex Changed the Internet and the Internet Changed Sex: An Unexpected History* (New York: Workman Publishing, 2022), 223

2 *Defining Sexual Health: Report of a Technical Consultation on Sexual Health*, World Health Organization, 2002, 5, cited in "Defining Sexual Health," World Health Organization, https://www.who.int/teams/sexual-and-repro ductive-health-and-research/key-areas-of-work/sexual-health/defining-sexual-health.

3 Elaine Craig, *Troubling Sex: Towards a Legal Theory of Sexual Integrity* (Vancouver: UBC Press, 2012).

4 *Defining Sexual Health*, World Health Organization, 5.

5 Alexandra Kirschbaum, "Pornography Is Almost as Present as Air and We Need to Talk about It," *Ottawa Citizen*, 3 April 2023, https://ottawacitizen. com/opinion/kirschbaum-porn-is-as-present-as-air-and-we-need-to-talk-about-it.

6 Dana Rotman and Jennifer Preece, "The 'WeTube' in YouTube: Creating an Online Community through Video Sharing," *International Journal of Web Based Communities* 6, no. 3 (2010): 325.

7 See, for example, Michael Geist, "Age Verification Requirements for Twitter

or Website Blocking for Reddit? My Appearance on Bill S-210 at the Senate Standing Committee on Legal and Constitutional Affairs" (blog), 10 February 2022, https://www.michaelgeist.ca/2022/02/age-verification-require ments-for-twitter-or-website-blocking-for-reddit-my-appearance-on-bill- s-210-at-the-senate-standing-committee-on-legal-and-constitutional- affairs; Michael Geist, "From Bad to Worse: Senate Committee Adds Age Verification Requirement for Online Undertakings to Bill C-11" (blog), 6 December 2022, https://www.michaelgeist.ca/2022/12/from-bad-to-worse- senate-committee-adds-age-verification-requirement-for-online-undertak ings-to-bill-c-11.

8   *Online Underage Users Detection: Can We Reconcile Efficiency, Convenience and Anonymity?*, Government of France, Pôle d'Expertise de la Régulation Numérique (PEREN), issue 4, 2022, 9.

9   The United Kingdom first attempted to impose age-verification require ments on foreign-based porn-streaming platforms in 2017 through the *Digital Economy Act*. This law would have created an age verification regu lator responsible for imposing requirements on commercial porn-stream ing platforms accessible in the United Kingdom in order to prevent access to their sites by users under the age of eighteen. The designated regulator was to be the British Board of Film Classification, the country's film cen sorship body. The Board would have had the authority to instruct Internet service providers to block platforms that did not comply.

10   Jim Waterson, "UK Online Pornography Age Block Triggers Privacy Fears," *Guardian*, 16 March 2019, https://www.theguardian.com/culture/2019/ mar/16/uk-online-porn-age-verification-launch.

11   Lux Alptraum, "Why the World's Biggest Porn Company Is Backing the UK's New Age Law," *Verge*, 23 February 2018, https://www.theverge.com/ 2018/2/23/17043978/uk-porn-age-verification-law-mindgeek.

12   *Online Safety Bill* [HL] (UK), 2021-2022 sess, Bill 87, s. 72(2).

113   Adi Robertson, "Louisiana Now Requires a Government ID to Access Porn hub," *Verge*, 3 January 2023, https://www.theverge.com/2023/1/3/23537226/ louisiana-pornhub-age-verification-law-government-id.

14   US, SB 287, *Online Pornography Viewing Age Requirements*, 2023, Gen Sess, Utah, 2023 (enacted).

15   Ayesha Rascoe and Saige Miller, "A New Utah Law Led PornHub to Ban Access to Its Site for Everyone in the State," NPR, 7 May 2023, https://www. npr.org/2023/05/07/1174631536/a-new-utah-law-led-pornhub-to-ban-access- to-its-site-for-everyone-in-the-state.

16 Ibid. See also Emma Roth, "Pornhub Goes Dark in Utah to Protest Age-Verification Law," *Verge*, 2 May 2023, https://www.theverge.com/2023/5/2/23707861/pornhub-utah-age-verification-law-protest.

17 Sam Metz, "Porn Industry Group Sues over Utah Age-Verification Law," PBS, 4 May 2023, https://www.pbs.org/newshour/politics/porn-industry-group-sues-over-utah-age-verification-law.

18 Robertson, "Louisiana Now Requires."

19 Bill S-210, *An Act to restrict young persons' online access to sexually explicit material*, 1st Sess, 44th Parl, 2023 (first reading 17 May 2023).

20 Geist, "Age Verification Requirements."

21 Ibid.

22 "But How Do They Know It Is a Child? Age Assurance in a Digital World?," 5Rights Foundation, October 2021, 4, https://5rightsfoundation.com/in-action/but-how-do-they-know-it-is-a-child-age-assurance-in-the-digital-world.html.

23 In December 2021, the chair of France's Audiovisual and Digital Communication Regulatory Authority (Arcom) ordered several porn sites to implement age verification mechanisms: Commission nationale de l'informatique et des libertés (CNIL), "Online Age Verification: Balancing Privacy and the Protection of Minors," CNIL, 22 September 2022, https://www.cnil.fr/en/online-age-verification-balancing-privacy-and-protection-minors. In March 2022, the Chair of Arcom sought a court order blocking five platforms that had refused to comply: Pornhub, xHamster, XNXX, TuKif, and XVideos. Mathieu Pollet, "French Regulator Calls on Court to Block Five Pornographic Websites," Euractiv, 8 March 2022, https://www.euractiv.com/section/internet-governance/news/french-regulator-calls-on-court-to-block-five-pornographic-websites.

24 Elisa Braun and Laura Kayali, "France to Introduce Controversial Age Verification System for Adult Websites," *Politico*, 9 July 2020, https://www.politico.eu/article/france-to-introduce-controversial-age-verification-system-for-adult-pornography-websites.

25 Julie Apostle, "Online Content in France: Challenge Raised to Block Online Porn Websites," Orrick, 12 September 2022, https://www.orrick.com/en/Insights/2022/09/Online-Content-in-France-Challenge-Raised-to-Block-Online-Porn-Websites.

26 Ibid.

27 Kristof Van Quathem, Alix Bertrand, and Nicholas Shepherd, "France Enacts New Law on Parental Controls," Global Policy Watch, 10 March 2022,

https://www.globalpolicywatch.com/2022/03/france-enacts-new-law-on-parental-controls.

28 Apostle, "Online Content in France." MindGeek has argued that this makes the law's impact on freedom of expression disproportional.

29 Commission Nationale de l'Informatique et des Libertés, "Online Age Verification."

30 Gabriel Geiger, "German Authorities Want to Implement DNS Blocks against Major Porn Sites," *Vice*, 26 October 2020, https://www.vice.com/en/article/bvx8v4/german-authorities-want-to-implement-dns-blocks-against-major-porn-sites; Arvid Peix, "KJM Approves New Internet Age Verification Method," IRIS Merlin, 2020, https://merlin.obs.coe.int/article/8761.

31 Geiger, "German Authorities"; Peix, "KJM."

32 "Why AgeID," AgeID, https://www.ageid.com/de/why-ageid.

33 Danielle Blunt and Zahra Stardust, "Automating Whorephobia: Sex, Technology and the Violence of Deplatforming: An Interview with Hacking//Hustling," *Porn Studies* 8, no. 4 (2021): 354.

34 Ibid., 354.

35 See, for example, Pandora Blake, "Age Verification for Online Porn: More Harm than Good?" *Porn Studies* 6, no. 2 (2019): 230.

36 Jim Killock, "The Government Is Acting Negligently on Privacy and Porn AV" (blog), Open Rights Group, 8 May 2018, https://www.openrightsgroup.org/blog/the-government-is-acting-negligently-on-privacy-and-porn-av.

37 Blake, "Age Verification," 230.

38 Zoe Kleinman, "Porn Check Critics Fear Data Breach," BBC News, 6 March 2018, https://www.bbc.com/news/technology-43292457.

39 Stephen Molldrem, "Tumblr's Decision to Deplatform Sex Will Harm Sexually Marginalized People," *Wussy*, 6 December 2018, https://www.wussymag.com/all/tumblrs-decision-to-deplatform-sex-will-harm-sexually-marginalized-people (this term was likely coined by Stephen Molldrem in 2018), cited in Katrin Tiidenberg, "Sex, Power and Platform Governance," *Porn Studies* 8, no. 4 (2021): 381.

40 Tiidenberg, "Sex, Power," 381.

41 Matt Burgess, "Twitter Has Started Blocking Porn in Germany," *Wired*, 15 February 2022, https://www.wired.co.uk/article/twitter-porn-block-germany-age-verification.

42 Blake, "Age Verification," 230.

43 Sex work in the digital era has the potential to bring significant, important benefits to sex workers in terms of autonomy and flexibility, reduced risk, and additional income: Heather Berg, "A Scene Is Just a Marketing Tool: Hustling in Porn's Gig Economy," in *Porn Work: Sex, Labor, and Late Capitalism*, ed. Heather Berg (Chapel Hill: University of North Carolina Press, 2021), 95. Angela Jones examines an additional benefit to content producers in the digital era in her book *Camming: Money, Power and Pleasure in the Sex Work Industry* (New York: New York University Press, 2020), 7: "the online environment fosters a space in which workers have a greater potential to experience various pleasures."

44 Blake, "Age Verification." Similar impacts on sex workers to the ones she predicts, such as a shift to street-based work or underground work, have been reported as a consequence of imprecise and ill-conceived amendments to section 230 of the *Communications Decency Act* under *Allow States and Victims to Fight Online Sex Trafficking Act* (FOSTA)/*Stop Enabling Sex Traffickers Act* (SESTA). See, for example, Carolyn Bronstein, "Deplatforming Sexual Speech in the Age of FOSTA/SESTA," *Porn Studies* 8, no. 4 (2021): 368; Danielle Blunt et al., "Deplatforming Sex: A Roundtable Conversation," *Porn Studies* 8, no. 4 (2021): 421, 428.

45 Susanna Paasonen, Kylie Jarrett, and Ben Light, #NSFW: *Sex, Humor, and the Risk in Social Media* (Cambridge, MA: MIT Press, 2019), 62, citing Emma Garland, "The Future of Porn Is Only Getting Worse," *Vice*, 15 August 2018, https://www.vice.com/en/article/zmk89y/the-future-of-porn-is-only-getting-worse.

46 Simone van der Hof, "Age Assurance and Age Appropriate Design: What Is Required?" (blog), London School of Economics, 17 November 2021, https://blogs.lse.ac.uk/parenting4digitalfuture/2021/11/17/age-assurance.

47 See, for example, Blake, "Age Verification," 229.

48 Neil Thurman and Fabian Obster, "The Regulation of Internet Pornography: What a Survey of Under-18s Tells Us about the Necessity for and Potential Efficacy of Emerging Legislative Approaches," *Policy and Internet* 13, no. 3 (2021): 424, 428.

49 John Dunn, "Want Porn? Prove Your Age (or Get a VPN)," Naked Security, 19 July 2017, https://nakedsecurity.sophos.com/2017/07/19/want-porn-prove-your-age-or-get-a-vpn.

50 Christopher Seward, "Best VPN to Avoid the UK's Porn Age Verification: Top 5," VPNCompare, 9 March 2019, https://www.vpncompare.co.uk/best-vpn-uk-porn-age-verification.

51 Tom Vincent, "How to Access and Watch Pornhub if It's Blocked in Your Country," dtechclub, https://dtechclub.com/en/how-to-watch-pornhub-if-blocked.

52 I am grateful to my colleague Suzie Dunn for bringing this point to my attention.

53 Matt Burgess, "Germany Is About to Block One of the World's Biggest Porn Sites," *Wired*, 14 July 2021, https://www.wired.co.uk/article/germany-porn-laws-age-checks (discussing an impending order of the German Commission for the Protection of Minors in the Media to block xHamster for refusing to comply with Germany's age-verification laws); "French Court to Rule on Plan to Block Porn Sites over Access for Minors," Reuters, 6 September 2022, https://www.reuters.com/world/europe/french-court-rule-plan-block-porn-sites-over-access-minors-2022-09-06 (Pornhub and xHamster both reportedly refused to comply with France's new age-verification laws).

54 Apostle, "Online Content in France."

55 "We Need to Talk about Pornography: Children, Parents and Age Verification," Internet Matters, 18, https://www.internetmatters.org/wp-content/uploads/2019/06/WeNeedToTalkAboutPornography-LowRes.pdf (one third of parents in this British government–supported survey reported that their children's first exposure was unintentional).

56 Christina Camilleri, Justin T. Perry, and Stephen Sammut, "Compulsive Internet Pornography Use and Mental Health: A Cross-Sectional Study in a Sample of University Students in the United States," *Frontiers in Psychology* 11 (2021): 7 (finding that approximately 45 per cent of males' first exposure occurred through personal curiosity, and for 33 per cent it was accidental exposure).

57 "Child Safety Online: Age Verification for Pornography," Department for Culture Media and Sport, 2016, 7, https://www.gov.uk/government/up loads/system/uploads/attachment_data/file/534965/20160705_AVConsulta tionResponseFINAL__2_.pdf; Darryl Mead, "The Risks Young People Face as Porn Consumers," *Addicta: Turkish Journal on Addictions* 3, no. 3 (2016): 389 (finding that by the time they approached eighteen, approximately 80 per cent of young men in nearly all samples in five European countries were active consumers). See, for example, Thurman and Obster, "Regulation of Internet Pornography," 429 (finding that a majority of sixteen- and seventeen-year-old men consume online porn regularly).

58 Geist, "Age Verification Requirements."

59 Thurman and Obster, "Regulation of Internet Pornography," 417.

60 Ibid., 417.

61 Ibid., 419.

62 Henry Talbot et al., "NZ Youth and Porn: Research Findings of a Survey on How and Why Young New Zealanders View Online Pornography," Office of Film and Literature Classification, 2018, 28, https://www.classification office.govt.nz/media/documents/NZ_Youth_and_Porn.pdf (66 per cent of participants reported porn websites as their source for online pornography).

63 Samantha Cole, *How Sex Changed the Internet and the Internet Changed Sex: An Unexpected History* (New York, Workman Publishing, 2022), 163.

64 Ibid.

65 Rob Cunningham and Deborah Wehrle, "A Note on the Average Age of Senators Since Confederation," *Canadian Parliamentary Review* 17, no. 4 (1994): 1, 2 (while the authors' data stops at 1993, absent modifications to the Senate such as a lower retirement age [it is seventy-five] or an elected Senate, and given the relative stability of the average age between 1983 and 1993, the authors predict that the average would be likely to remain about the same).

66 Elena Martellozzo et al., "A Quantitative and Qualitative Examination of the Impact of Online Pornography on the Values, Attitudes, Beliefs and Behaviours of Children and Young People," Middlesex University London, 2016, https://www.mdx.ac.uk/__data/assets/pdf_file/0021/223266/MDX-NSPCC-OCC-pornography-report.pdf.

67 Ibid., 60.

68 Saeed Abbasi and Kirti Parekh, "Personal VPN and Its Evasions: Risk Factors and How to Maintain Network Visibility," Unit 42, 16 August 2021, https://unit42.paloaltonetworks.com/person-vpn-network-visibility.

69 Blake, "Age Verification," 229 (arguing that this puts them in greater danger); Thurman and Obster, "Regulation of Internet Pornography," 428 (finding that 46 per cent of sixteen- and seventeen-year-olds in the United Kingdom had used a VPN or Tor browser).

70 See, for example, "How to Block Pornography on Your Child's Devices," Common Sense Media, 9 January 2023, https://www.commonsensemedia .org/articles/how-to-block-pornography-on-your-childs-devices.

71 *Online Underage Users Detection*, PEREN, 7 (see note 7).

72 Serkan Çankaya and Hatice Ferhan Odabaşı, "Parental Controls on Children's Computer and Internet Use," *Procedia Social and Behavioral*

Sciences 1, no. 1 (2009): 1108 (examining research indicating that 33 per cent of parents in homes with Internet access reported using filtering or blocking software on the computer their child used).

73 M.L. Ybarra et al., "Associations between Blocking, Monitoring, and Filtering Software on the Home Computer and Youth-Reported Unwanted Exposure to Sexual Material Online," *Child Abuse and Neglect* 33, no. 12 (2009): 867.

74 Paasonen, Jarrett, and Light, #*NSFW*, 2.

75 Peggy Orenstein, *Boys and Sex: Young Men on Hookups, Love, Porn, Consent, and Navigating the New Masculinity* (New York: HarperCollins, 2020), 3.

76 Ibid., 54.

77 Ibid.

78 Ibid., 221; Martellozzo et al., "Quantitative and Qualitative," 3, 60.

79 Joe Pinsker, "The Hidden Economics of Porn," *Atlantic*, 2016, www.the atlantic.com/business/archive/2016/04/pornography-industry-economics-tarrant/476580.

80 Peggy Orenstein, *Girls and Sex: Navigating the Complicated New Landscape* (New York: HarperCollins, 2016), 35.

81 Ibid., 37.

82 Ibid., 56.

83 Ibid., 37.

84 Martellozzo et al., "Quantitative and Qualitative," 62.

85 Megan S.C. Lim et al., "'Censorship Is Cancer': Young People's Support for Pornography-Related Initiatives," *Sex Education* 21, no. 6 (2021): 665.

86 Ibid., 665.

87 Ibid., 665.

88 Cassandra J.C. Wright et al., "Young People's Needs and Preferences for Health Resources Focused on Pornography and Sharing of Sexually Explicit Imagery," *Public Health Research and Practice* 31, no. 1 (2021): 2. Interview participants identified the need for more information and shame-free education to increase porn literacy.

89 Kate Dawson, "Educating Ireland: Promoting Porn Literacy among Parents and Children," *Porn Studies* 6, no. 2 (2019): 269.

90 Ibid., 90.

91 Shira Tarrant, "Pornography 101: Why College Kids Need Porn Literacy Training," AlterNet.org, 2011, 3, http://www.rolereboot.org/wp-content/themes/rolereboot/assets/ttp/pornography_101-_why_college_kids_need_porn_literacy_training.pdf.

92 Paul Byron et al., "Reading for Realness: Porn Literacies, Digital Media, and Young People," *Sexuality and Culture* 25, no. 3 (2021): 792–3.

93 Siobhán Healy-Cullen et al., "What Does It Mean to Be 'Porn Literate': Perspectives of Young People, Parents and Teachers in Aotearoa New Zealand," *Culture, Health and Sexuality* (2023), 3.

94 Ibid., 11.

95 Kate Dawson, "Establishing an Evidence Base for the Development of Porn Literacy Interventions for Adolescents," National University of Ireland, Galway, 2020, 32, https://aran.library.nuigalway.ie/bitstream/handle/ 10379/15826/Kate%20Dawson%20PhD%202020.pdf.

96 Niki Fritz and Bryant Paul, "From Orgasms to Spanking: A Content Analysis of the Agentic and Objectifying Sexual Scripts in Feminist, for Women, and Mainstream Pornography," *Sex Roles* 77, nos 9–10 (2017): 639 (finding that feminist porn was substantially less likely to include cum shots, genital focus, gaping, and aggression).

97 See, for example, Mark McCormack and Liam Wignall, "Enjoyment, Exploration and Education: Understanding the Consumption of Pornography among Young Men with Non-Exclusive Sexual Orientations," *Sociology* 51, no. 5 (2017): 975 (qualitative study on undergraduate-age students with non-exclusive sexual orientation, finding that porn consumption as a leisure activity in adolescence had educational benefits related to the development of sexual identities and sexual technique); Cassandra Hesse and Cory Pedersen, "Porn Sex versus Real Sex: How Sexually Explicit Material Shapes Our Understanding of Sexual Anatomy, Physiology, and Behaviour," *Sexuality and Culture* 21, no. 3 (2017): 765–7 (finding that consumption of sexually explicit material increased knowledge of anatomy, physiology, and sexual behavior among a sample of self-selected survey participants); Katerina Litsou et al., "Learning from Pornography: Results of a Mixed Methods Systematic Review," *Sex Education* 21, no. 2 (2021): 236, 248–9 (finding that porn use can offer education to young people, particularly young gay men, on the mechanics of sex).

98 Clarissa Smith, "Putting Porn Studies (Back) into Porn Literacy," *Synoptique* 9, no. 2 (2021): 175.

99 Paul Byron, "Porn Literacy and Young People's Digital Cultures," *Porn Studies* (2023), 5.

100 Kath Albury, "Porn and Sex Education, Porn as Sex Education," *Porn Studies* 1, nos 1–2 (2014): 178.

101 Ibid., 172.

102 Smith, "Putting Porn Studies," 175.

103 Ibid., 174–5.

104 Ibid., 175.

105 Paul Byron, "Reading for Realness: Porn Literacies, Digital Media, and Young People," *Sexuality and Culture* 25, no. 3 (2021): 792, 793; Dawson, "Establishing an Evidence Base," 32.

106 Byron, "Porn Literacy," 8.

107 Ibid., 6.

108 Dawson, "Establishing an Evidence Base," 270.

109 Ibid., 270.

110 Healy-Cullen et al., "What Does It Mean."

111 Byron, "Porn Literacy," 2.

112 Peter Alilunas et al., "Porn and/as Pedagogy, Sexual Representation in the Classroom: A Curated Roundtable Discussion," *Synoptique* 9, no. 2 (2021): 275.

113 Alexandra Kirschbaum, "Pornography Is Almost as Present as Air and We Need to Talk about It," *Ottawa Citizen*, 3 April 2023, https://ottawacitizen.com/opinion/kirschbaum-porn-is-as-present-as-air-and-we-need-to-talk-about-it.

114 ECP founding partner Derek Ogden states, "MindGeek has built a sophisticated, multi-layered Trust and Safety program combining leading-edge technology solutions with a team of moderators. Day in and day out, MindGeek's Trust and Safety, and engineering teams work collaboratively with law enforcement, advocacy groups and other stakeholders to prevent online abuse and to hold abusers to account … This culture of partnership and mutual trust is representative of MindGeek's ongoing commitment to personal privacy and public safety." Fady Mansour, ECP founding partner, asserts, "We hope that an open consultation process, whereby we report back to those we engaged, will serve to educate the public about MindGeek's absolute commitment to safe, responsible sex-positive free expression … We have said from the start that we are confident that MindGeek operates legally and responsibly, and the leadership team at MindGeek has our support." "Ethical Capital Partners Undertaking Stakeholder Consultations," Ethical Capital Partners, 27 April 2023, https://www.ethicalcapitalpartners.com/news/ethical-capital-partners-undertaking-stakeholder-consultations.

115 Amber Milne, "Porn Site's Free Service during Coronavirus Raises Sex Trafficking Fears," Reuters, 27 March 2020, https://www.reuters.com/article

/britain-women-trafficking/update-1-porn-sites-free-service-during-coronavirus-raises-sex-trafficking-fears-idUSL8N2BK415.

116 Elizabeth Nolan Brown, "Pornhub Isn't the Problem. That Won't Stop the Politicized Crusade against It," *Reason*, 16 December 2020, https://reason.com/2020/12/16/pornhub-isnt-the-problem-that-wont-stop-the-politicized-crusade-against-it.

117 Milne, "Porn Site's Free Service."

118 David Auerbach, "Vampire Porn: MindGeek Is a Cautionary Tale of Consolidating Production and Distribution in a Single, Monopolistic Owner," *Slate*, 23 October 2014, https://slate.com/technology/2014/10/mindgeek-porn-monopoly-its-dominance-is-a-cautionary-tale-for-other-industries.html.

119 Kal Raustiala and Christopher Sprigman, "The Second Digital Disruption: Streaming and the Dawn of Data-Driven Creativity," *New York University Law Review* 94, no. 6 (2019).

120 "Terms of Service," Pornhub, accessed 28 December 2022, https://www.pornhub.com/information/terms.

121 "Violent Content Policy," Pornhub, https://help.pornhub.com/hc/en-us/articles/4419863430291-Violent-Content-Policy; "Community Guidelines," Pornhub, accessed 31 May 2023, https://help.pornhub.com/hc/en-us/articles/4419900587155-Community-Guidelines; "Core Values," Pornhub, accessed 3 April 2023, https://help.pornhub.com/hc/en-us/articles/4419871944723-Core-Values.

122 Testimony of Feras Antoon, House of Commons, Standing Committee on Access to Information, Privacy and Ethics, *Evidence*, 43-2, No. 19 (5 February 2021), 3.

123 "Community Guidelines," Pornhub.

124 "Core Values," Pornhub.

125 "Non-consensual Content Policy," Pornhub, accessed 20 March 2023, https://help.pornhub.com/hc/en-us/articles/4419871787027-Non-Consensual-Content-Policy.

126 Ibid.

127 See comments of Fady Mansour, "Ethical Capital Partners Undertaking Stakeholder Consultations."

128 "Best Friend Fell Asleep" (video), Pornhub, accessed 19 June 2023 (82,000 views, 71 per cent approval rating).

129 "Teen Woke Up" (video), Pornhub, accessed 3 April 2023 (403,000 views, 87 per cent approval rating).

130 While Pornhub's Non-consensual Content Policy allows depictions of sex in which a person is asleep, provided they wake up within a "reasonable time," this description of sexual activity meets the legal definition of sexual assault under Canadian criminal law and thus the prohibition on depictions of any illegal activity in this policy and other Pornhub policies.

131 This advertisement, which encouraged users to "lock your door and fuck your step sister," discussed in chapter 1, was playing in front of incest-themed videos on Pornhub in the spring of 2023. It played in front of some videos that depicted the sexual assault of (step)sisters by their (step)brothers, such as the following: "Step Sister with Perfect Ass Woke Up When I Fucked Her" (video), Pornhub, accessed 3 April 2023 (804,000 views, 84 per cent approval rating).

132 Ibid.

133 See comments of Solomon Friedman, "Ethical Capital Partners Undertaking Stakeholder Consultations."

134 See comments of Fady Mansour, "Ethical Capital Partners Undertaking Stakeholder," (emphasis added).

135 "disgusting," Pornhub (search conducted 19 June 2023); "stupid," Pornhub (search conducted 19 June 2023); "dumb blonde," Pornhub (search conducted 19 June 2023).

136 "Throat from Stupid Ugly Cunt. She Almost Good at It Too" (video), Pornhub, accessed 20 November 2023 (11,500 views, 80 per cent approval rating).

137 "Stupid Blonde Fucks Her Sister's Boyfriend in Anal" (video), Pornhub, accessed 20 November 2023 (2,200,000 views, 90 per cent approval).

138 "Brainless Cunt Laughing and Waddling Naked for Live Webcam" (video), Pornhub, accessed 20 November 2023 (2,400 views, 100 per cent approval rating).

139 A search on Pornhub conducted on 20 November 2023 using the term "stupid cunt" produced videos with these titles, among others, on the first two pages of search results.

140 See, for example, Ari Ezra Waldman, "Disorderly Content," *Washington Law Review* 97, no. 4 (2022): 951 (analogizing to anti-vice enforcement).

141 Luke O'Neil, "Incent Is the Fastest Growing Trend in Porn. Wait, What?," *Esquire*, 28 February 2018, www.esquire.com/lifestyle/sex/a18194469/incest-porn-trend (interview with porn producer Bree Mills).

142 Neil Thurman and Fabian Obster, "The Regulation of Internet Pornography: What a Survey of Under-18s Tells Us about the Necessity for and Potential Efficacy of Emerging Legislative Approaches," *Policy and Internet* 13, no. 3 (2021): 419, 429.

143 See, for example, Paul J. Wright, Robert S. Tokunaga, and Ashley Kraus, "A Meta-Analysis of Pornography Consumption and Actual Acts of Sexual Aggression in General Population Studies," *Journal of Communications* 66 (2016): 183 (meta-analysis indicating that people who consume pornography more frequently are more likely to be sexually aggressive, particularly with respect to verbal aggression); Neil Malamuth, "Adding Fuel to the Fire? Does Exposure to Non-consenting Adult or to Child Pornography Increase Risk of Sexual Aggression?," *Aggression and Violent Behavior* 41 (2018): 74 (finding that it may add to sexual aggression for men who have a pre-disposition); Gert Martin Hald, Neil Malamuth, and Carlin Yuen, "Pornography and Attitudes Supporting Violence against Women: Revisiting the Relationship in Nonexperimental Studies," *Aggressive Behavior* 36, no. 1 (2010): 1 (meta-analysis finding a positive association between porn consumption and attitudes supporting violence against women); Gabe Hatch et al., "Does Pornography Consumption Lead to Intimate Partner Violence Perpetration? Little Evidence for Temporal Precedence," *Canadian Journal of Human Sexuality* 29, no. 3 (2020): 289 (finding that porn use does not predict intimate partner violence); Christopher J. Ferguson and Richard D. Hartley, "Pornography and Sexual Aggression: Can Meta-Analysis Find a Link?," *Trauma, Violence and Abuse* 23, no. 1 (2022): 278 (meta-analysis finding no evidence that non-violent porn consumption is associated with sexual aggression, and weak evidence that consumption of violent porn is correlated with aggression).

144 "Concluding Workshop Summary," Government of Canada, 2022, https://www.canada.ca/en/canadian-heritage/campaigns/harmful-online-content/concluding-summary.html.

145 Bill C-63, *Online Harms Act*, 1st sess, 44th Parl, 2024, s. 2.

146 "Concluding Workshop Summary," Government of Canada.

147 Ibid., 23–8.

148 Emily Laidlaw, *Regulating Speech in Cyberspace: Gatekeepers, Human Rights and Corporate Responsibility* (Cambridge, MA: Cambridge University Press, 2015), 147.

149 Bill C-63, *Online Harms Act*, s. 62(1)(h).

150 "Concluding Workshop Summary," Government of Canada.

151 EC, *Regulation (EU) 2022/2065 of the European Parliament and of the Council of 19 October 2022 on a Single Market for Digital Services and amending Directive 2000/31/EC (Digital Services Act)*, [2022] OJ, L 277/1 art. 35.

152 Ibid., art. 34.

153 "This hole has only one task" advertisement, Pornhub, playing at the beginning of the video "Dumb Girl Begs to Suck Your Dick and Get Fucked," Pornhub, accessed 27 June 2023 (8,500 views, 92 per cent approval rating).

154 "Fuck more bitches" advertisement, Pornhub, accessed 7 May 2023.

155 "Father in Law Tricks Stupid Bitch into Cheating Sex" (video), Pornhub, accessed 11 December 2023 (54,000 views, 81 per cent approval rating).

156 "College Student Takes out Finals Frustration on Hot Dumb Slut" (video), Pornhub, 11 December 2023 (59,200 views, 96 per cent approval rating).

157 Katrin Tiidenberg, "Sex, Power and Platform Governance," *Porn Studies* 8, no. 4 (2021): 389.

158 Ibid.

159 Waldman, "Disorderly Content," 909–11.

160 Ibid.

161 See, for example, Blunt and Stardust, "Automating Whorephobia," 354; Pandora Blake, "Age Verification," 230.

162 "Animal Welfare Policy," Pornhub, accessed 27 June 2023, https://help.pornhub.com/hc/en-us/articles/7906741373971-Animal-Welfare-Policy.

163 Ibid.

164 Ibid.

165 "Pussy Gets Soaked by Her First Toy" (video), Pornhub, accessed 27 June 2023 (36,900 views, 86 per cent approval rating).

166 "Playing with My Dogs, It's Not Sexual You Degenerates" (video), Pornhub, accessed 27 June 2023 (704,000 views, 74 per cent approval rating).

167 Ibid.

168 Ibid.

169 Gary Dimmock, "Jacob Rockburn Found Guilty on Two Counts of Sexual Assault," *Ottawa Citizen*, 17 February 2023, https://ottawacitizen.com/news/local-news/ottawa-court-ruling-makes-secret-sex-taping-sex-assault-in-ontario.

170 *R v Rockburn*, [2023] OJ No. 786.

171 Ibid., para. 236.

172 "Ottawa Case Sparks Debate: Is It Sexual Assault to Secretly Record Intimate Encounter?," *National Post*, 17 August 2023, https://nationalpost.com/news/canada/ottawa-is-it-sexual-assault-to-secretly-record-intimate-encounter.

173 Ibid.

174 Ibid.

175 "hidden," Pornhub (search conducted 17 August 2023).

176 "secret voyeur," "real amateur hidden," "spy," Pornhub (searches conducted 17 August 2023).

177 The surreptitious recording of sexual activity is a sexual offence pursuant to section 162 of the *Criminal Code*, RSC 1985 c C-46. These policies prohibit content with real or simulated depictions of illegal/non-consensual acts.

178 "MindGeek Becomes Aylo," Ethical Capital Partners, 17 August 2023, https://www.ethicalcapitalpartners.com/news/mindgeek-becomes-aylo.

179 Ibid.

180 Clarissa Smith and Feona Atwood, "Emotional Truths and Thrilling Side-shows," in *The Feminist Porn Book: The Politics of Producing Pleasure*, eds Tristan Taormino et al. (New York: Feminist Press at CUNY, 2013), 51.

Index